Planning Cities

Selected writings on principles and practice
by
Frederick H. Bair, Jr.
edited by
Virginia Curtis

American Society of Planning Officials
Chicago

For information address:
American Society of Planning Officials
1313 East Sixtieth Street
Chicago, Illinois 60637

Printed in the United States of America

Library of Congress Catalog Card No. 76-140949

SBN 0-910112-00-2

First Printing

to Dennis O'Harrow
1908-1967

Editor's foreword

One of Fred Bair's favorite exhortations is "Let's quit talking about it and start doing something *productive*." Over the years Fred *has* done many productive things—mayors, planning directors, planning staffs, and commissioners in cities all over the United States will attest to that. Over the years Fred has also done a lot of talking and writing about planning and related matters. For 17 years he was editor (and writer, proofreader, typist, and business manager) of *Florida Planning and Development*. He has given countless speeches, seminars, short courses, and diatribes to his fellow professionals, students, Chambers of Commerce, and anyone else willing to listen. All those articles, speeches, seminars, short courses, and diatribes were turned over to me for editing. At first I was very flattered; next I was very frustrated; then I was very tired; and now I am very relieved and extremely proud that we have come up with this book of his writings over the past several years.

It is a good book, I think, selective and representative of the things Fred has been thinking and writing about planning, what it should be, how it works, and how to do it in both large and small cities. He has been fairly consistent (stubborn, some would say) in what he has had to say. In 1960 Fred was pushing for techniques and ideas that are only now beginning to be talked about and accepted nationally. And in 1970 Fred is still writing and talking about things that some younger planners, academicians, and faddists have dismissed as simplistic. But to the vast majority of practicing planners—those out on the front lines *doing* planning every day and facing difficult problems—Fred Bair is an Olympian. He writes to them and for them, and what he has to say helps them in their work.

The book ranges from the abstract (principles and policies) to the concrete (how to draft a minor street plan), but all of it grows from experience on action fronts in planning, and it is meant to meet the needs of those who are where the action is—members of planning and zoning staffs and commissioners, members of boards of adjustment, elected and appointed public officials, and citizens interested in planning and related fields.

Most of the articles in this collection first appeared in *Florida Planning and Development* in the years 1960 to 1968. A few were originally published as ASPO Planning Advisory Service Reports. The rest have appeared (or been suppressed) in other publications, proceedings, etc., and are acknowledged where they appear in this book. I have attempted to fit together pieces which for the most part stood by themselves when first written. The book is intended for use as a planning reader and as a reference work on specific problems.

Fred continues to write, but we couldn't wait for him to finish writing everything he has to say about planning. We wanted to get on with *production.*

Virginia Curtis
August 1970

Contents

City planning principles

Planning ahead

Any planner worth his salt in the years ahead is going to have to be aware that in large measure he won't know what he is planning for. Conditioned along these lines, he may be increasingly useful. Blind or stubborn, he will spend much of his time fighting to preserve, defend, and embellish the mistakes of the past.

Shortly after 1900, Thomas Edison, a man with an alert and intelligent finger on the technical pulse of the nation, gave a reporter a forecast on what was coming in the years ahead. Although he was right about many things, he overlooked, underestimated, or misjudged many of the elements which were to mold the physical and economic form of the United States. He foresaw nuclear physics dimly, and was afraid of it—because railroads could transmute base metals into cheap gold and pay off their gold bonds, ruining thousands of investors. He neglected gasoline and diesel engines on wheels (the automobile, the truck, the tractor) and improvements in the generation and transmission of electricity. He foresaw a factory-type farm and a businessman farmer, but the tractors were powered by storage batteries.

He was wrong about many of the predictions he made, wrong about many of the principles involved, wrong about many of the things to which the principles would be applied, wrong about which inventions would be important, and he failed entirely to grasp the earthshaking significance of technical developments shaping up around him at the time. He was weak on what was out ahead, strong on tackling the jobs at hand.

The moral is not that Edison was shortsighted, but that long-range forecasting was a chancy business even in 1900.

Taken as a whole, Edison's predictions were far better than ours are likely to be now. In his time, technology was just breaking into a fast walk. It is now shifting into nuclear drive. In the past 10 years, we have seen breakthrough after breakthrough in fields Edison never dreamed of. Each multiplies potentials—potential problems and potential solutions.

From technological necessities and inventions and principles only now emerging will come new needs and new answers. Since we do not know which among our present set of inventions and innovations is likely to do what to the shape of cities, it is probable that we should not try to plan too firmly too far through the mounting complexities of the future. Before we go any great distance, we run into an impenetrable jungle of intertwined question marks.

Physical technology is only one facet. Social change accelerates as social mass grows, as the number of people moving to new environments increases, as mass communication intensifies, and as the educational level rises. Changes in the forms and functions of governments are so rapid that the wild-eyed radical of a generation ago would now be fairly comfortable on the far right. As Carr and Stermer said in *Willow Run,* "One who tries to predict specific events or even specific social conditions during a period of rapid and confusing social change has no means whatever except the violence of his language for carrying conviction to the minds of other people. There simply is no generally accepted framework or method for structuring the future in a situation of on-rushing social change."

This certainly does not mean that planning is going to run out of meaningful jobs. A great deal of planning is needed to catch up with where we are, and to move ahead on needs which are clearly foreseeable in the near distance or which, come what may, seem likely to endure—as for instance the need for open space in cities.

If we aren't dealing intelligently and energetically with the problems which are upon us now, or threaten like an impending avalanche, little fruitful purpose is served by diverting time and money to long-range prognoses which are bound to be so wide of the mark as to be useless and may even be harmful.

The planner who produces a working comprehensive plan for now and the short-range future has done a highly commendable job. Of course it will fade off at the edges five or six years ahead—and it should. As we mature in our knowledge and move into the future we foresee so imperfectly, we should be quick to adjust our plans to new attitudes and values, new techniques, and new wisdom. We must advance planning to the point where we find out faster when we are planning for the wrong thing. As it is, we have a tendency to hold to past solutions (which may or may not have been adequate for the problems of their time). Much of our planning applies the technological and economic and social patterns of yesterday to today's problems in the hope of building a better tomorrow. Many of our planning controls—zoning and subdivision regulation and tax structure—are designed on the same basis. Like law, a great deal of planning clings to the past, instead of looking to the future.

We can only be sure that the future toward which we build will be vastly different from the past and the present. Planning's job should be to make desirable transitions as efficient, economical, painless, and free from mistakes as possible—not to impede or delay needed change or ensure that revered but obsolete standards and principles are used in meeting new problems to which they are not applicable.

Planning must integrate with government (including politics) more than it has in the past. It must be far more effective as an intelligence function at the right hand of executives, elected officials, and candidates, keeping close track of what is going on and what seems to be ahead and appraising probable results of various courses of action and inaction. The growing importance of the intelligence function cannot be overstressed. In our times of accelerating change and increasing complexity, we must know what the score is *now* to plan effectively for today and tomorrow.

And there must be planning for more than mere physical development. The techniques of planning—fact-finding, analysis, weighing of alternatives, selection of goals—must be applied also to the evolution of suitable forms of government, suitable functions for government, and suitable areas for government. This job will require abilities beyond the present crop of urban planners. A merging effort with social and political scientists is long overdue. Weak as all three disciplines are in their present stage of development, they will achieve more and achieve it faster if they work together.

At this point, let us look at some errors of the past, and then look ahead to a few city-shaping elements which may be obvious when we look back on them in the years ahead, but which are now (so far as most of our planning is concerned) apparently unexpected.

Population prediction

It is currently popular to refer to U.S. population growth since World War II as an explosion. In fact, however, there have been only four decades since 1564 (when the Spaniards established the first settlement in our country) during which population failed to grow at a more rapid rate than from 1950 to 1960. We had an "explosion" only in terms of what our demographers had predicted on the basis of 1930-40 experience. The theory exploded, not the population.

In 1938, the National Resources Planning Board issued a report which stated as one of its conclusions: "The transition from an increasing to a stationary or decreasing population may on the whole be beneficial to the life of the Nation. The gradual decrease in the proportion of children raises problems of major national interest. We sound a warning against the hasty projection of past trends into the future without taking into account new conditions."

Taking anticipated new conditions into account, the report states an optimistic view: "Even on the minimum assumption described above, the population of the United States in 1980 would be equal to that of today."

About the same time, Stuart Chase wrote a worried article about the empty schools and unemployed teachers to be expected in the late forties.

Came then the war, a revolution in the economy, and a flood of births. But the conditioning of the thirties continued to outweigh current facts at the Bureau of the Census, which in 1947 (when we were outrunning the diaper supply) issued new population estimates. The highest estimates in the series indicated that in 1975 it was possible, but highly unlikely, that we would reach a figure of 185 million. (This total was passed early in 1962.)

"The outlook after 1950 is for a continuation of the long-term decline in population growth, both in absolute numbers and rate," says *Forecasts of the Population of the United States, 1945-1975*. "Moreover there is a strong possibility that within a few decades the population will reach its maximum size and will begin to decrease unless heavy immigration is resumed."

The report treats implications of diminishing population growth in considerable detail. "The foregoing effects of demographic changes on national life are fairly certain and simple. . . ." It stresses quality of population as opposed to mere numbers, and points out that although the U.S. had already passed the economic optimum population, even the larger population expected in 1975 (162 million) might be expected to have a higher level of living than in 1947. Although the study does not advocate a large increase in numbers, it suggests that such a goal could be attained: "While there is no immediate prospect that the United States will adopt a national program designed to maintain or increase the birth rate, and hence to affect the future growth of the population, it should be remembered that such programs are already in effect in Canada and several European countries."

Bear in mind that this report was prepared when the handwriting was bold and clear on the wall. Private enterprise, through unremitting efforts of our returning heroes, maintained and increased the birth rate without federal intervention.

The significant fact is that our most eminent demographers, distracted by squalls of mounting numbers of grandchildren, continued too long to revere the mistake that had been made in the thirties.

Are we doing better now? Not much. We do not know how to estimate current population with reasonable accuracy (witness frequent embarrassment when census counts become available for comparison with estimates). And we have not demonstrated ability to predict future population with reasonable accuracy, even for relatively short periods or for large areas.

On local forecasts, more difficult than national, regional, or state prognostications, accuracy is generally very bad, particularly when the time period is extended. A rough analysis of predictions by a random selection of estimators (many of them highly qualified) indicates an average error far above 50 per cent in 20 years in amount of change predicted, without much choice in direction of error. Some of the estimates are high, some are low. The ones closest to actual performance were based either on no ascertainable formal method or on methods applied in the same study to other areas which turned out wide of the mark.

Elements in population forecasts

Deaths. Of the three principal elements in population forecasts—births, deaths, and migration—we have been reasonably competent only in handling deaths. In areas where population mobility is minor, or of a nature that does not upset age distribution, we can predict with reasonable certainty how many deaths there are likely to be from natural causes and accidents—provided, of course, that disaster does not upset the computations.

Births. On births, we have certainly not distinguished ourselves on accuracy of predictions, even at the national level.

Demographers usually fail to give appropriate weight to the effects of social, economic, and political stimulations and inhibitions on the birth rate. It is not enough to know how many women of childbearing age will be in the population. The crucial question is: How many children will be born? Neither demographers nor any other specialists are in a very good position to say. The equation has too many unknowns for even approximate solution.

Technological advances in contraceptives make social attitudes and values a prime determinant in number of births in this country.

During the mild recession in 1958, the marriage *rate* dropped to the lowest point since 1932, when there was a real depression. It picked up again rapidly as the economy moved forward in 1959. Does this mean that the attitude toward marriage and childbearing is increasingly sensitive to economic conditions? If so, we must temper our estimates on births in the years ahead by estimates as to the number and severity of economic slumps. How many will there be? How long will they last?

Longer education for growing proportions of the young population seems inevitable. Job opportunities for the unskilled and poorly educated are diminishing. Social attitudes favor increased education. Will added time in school raise the median age for marriage? Will raising the median age decrease births? Will a rise in the educational level encourage larger or smaller families?

In the face of prolonged international uncertainty—will young parents decide to have more or fewer children?

There is a very real explosion of world population and growing strain on world resources. If present trends continue, widespread catastrophe is only a couple of generations away. Campaigns for limitation of population growth are mounting. To what extent, and how soon, are they likely to be effective in the U.S.? An educated population should not have to begin to starve before it sees the point, and an enlightened government must do what it can to put on the brakes.

All of these things, and more, influence individual decisions which determine the number of births. We can compute how many children a population with given age-sex distribution could be expected to have on the basis of past experience and current trends, but this is a futile exercise. The one thing that past experience should have taught us is that in the future, the same factors, in the same balance, will not be present to affect birth rates in the same way.

Migration. Natural increase, the balance of births over deaths, is obviously not easy to predict with accuracy even if the population involved stays in the area for which predictions are being made. To complicate matters, population does not stay in the same place. At the state level, a recent Bureau of the Census report, *Preliminary Estimates of the Components of Population Change, by States: 1950 to 1960,* indicates: "Between 1950 and 1960, all States had an excess of births over deaths, but many States (27) and the District of Columbia lost population through net out-migration. . . . There was relatively little variation from State to State in decennial rate of natural increase. . . . The range of net migration was much greater—from a net out-migration of 22.7% of 1950 population for Arkansas to a net in-migration of 58.3% for Florida."

When the area involved drops to the metropolitan level, the range in the 1950's is much greater, from 266 per cent migration gain to 18 per cent migration loss among the 211 metropolitan areas reported by the Bureau. The migration pattern in many of these metropolitan areas changed radically from the forties to the fifties. In some cases migration gains in the fifties more than doubled those in the forties, in others the gains were halved, and in a number of instances migration gains in the forties changed to migration losses in the fifties and vice versa.

Below the metropolitan level, the range in migration shifts increases again, and the inconsistency in pattern from decade to decade becomes even more pronounced.

Unless the causes of migration into and out of areas are clearly understood (including the effect or lack of effect of government efforts to shift the "natural" balance of economic opportunity), it is certainly unlikely that we can produce meaningful forecasts even if we improve our techniques for predicting natural increase.

What we can do, and must do to the extent that knowledge about population is important in short-range planning, is to improve our techniques for keeping abreast of the current situation. If we know what happened in our cities last year and this year, and where it happened and why it happened, we will know a great deal more about what we should be doing about present and short-range future problems. Until we can deal more effectively with these matters, perhaps we do not need to be unduly alarmed about our inability to predict into the long-range future with greater precision.

Then there is the question of planning objectives. To what extent may it be assumed that long-range goals set under present conditions will be appropriate to future physical technology operating in a changed set of social attitudes? Again, an examination of past performance is instructive.

Planning objectives we might have had

Had there been organized planning in 1905, what kind of cities would we have planned for? Looking ahead, we would have seen rapid population growth, with a substantial part of it on farms. From 1890 to 1900, five persons were added to the rural population for each eight added to urban areas, and in that era more than a third of the labor force was in agriculture.

For cities, we would have projected high population densities with minimum walking distances to work and to shopping facilities. This would have meant a close intermingling of residences, industries, and stores in the core city. The trolley lines would have foreshadowed shoestring development out into the country. The automobile would have been considered a rich man's toy which frightened horses and was unlikely to amount to anything—entirely too complicated and expensive ever to be common.

As lovers of beauty in theory, we would have planned showpiece boulevards and parks—well away from the most densely populated areas. These would have been for decorative rather than recreational purposes. In those days, play was considered so frivolous as to be well-nigh sinful, and everybody (except the rich) was expected to be constructively occupied about 72 hours a week. It had not been discovered that the pedestrian powers of children were limited to a quarter of a mile, nor that schools required substantial acreage.

On the basis of our knowledge, attitudes, and values in 1905, it is fairly obvious that we were poorly equipped to plan for what was ahead of us. If a 20-year master plan had been developed in 1905 and "appropriately implemented"—and if we had not been alert to the fast-breaking need for radical change—we would probably have developed a worse mess than actually came about without planning.

In 1935, our planning objectives would have been conditioned by the assurance that we were planning ahead for a mature economy in which population was approaching its peak. We would have given due consideration to a high proportion of old people, a lower proportion of children. Many of our cities were in the process of replacing obsolete installations or were getting ready to provide certain improvements for the first time. As planners, we would have been concerned about building to appropriate scale—avoiding overextension of municipal facilities and utilities even though WPA and other federal funds might tempt us.

In 1935, we were becoming aware of the error of our past ways. Jamming people into cities produced unhealthy concentrations—the logical outgrowth of what we would have planned for in 1905. Newly awakened social conscience introduced new facets into planning. There was a striving to get people out into the sunny suburbs and beyond to greenbelt towns, out to subsistence farms where they could piece out small incomes. There was a feeling that new lots should be at least large enough to permit kitchen gardens (which may in part account for the magical 6,000 square feet as a minimum lot size).

During that same period, consternation reigned because we had permitted commercial and industrial and residential uses to mix (a solution which was both practical and accepted in earlier times). Zoning devoted itself to protecting residential areas from new commercial and industrial intrusions, but we did not have courage enough to keep new residences out of commercial and industrial districts.

Most of the mistakes we would have planned for in 1935 happened. We laid the ideological foundation for urban sprawl and we got urban sprawl. We developed fixations concerning large lots which have added immeasurably to the costs of providing urban facilities and services and augmented the spread. Certainly we did not overbuild urban facilities and utilities, did not provide too many schools or train too many school teachers, did not lay out highways on too expansive a scale, did not go overboard on providing parks or parking space.

In these examples, we see a great deal of evidence against planning too rigidly too far ahead. And we see—or should see—that we need to be far more alert to emerging change and to the need for making corresponding changes in our plans. In the years ahead, the changes are coming faster, and are likely to have a far more massive impact.

The future will not be a straight-line projection of the past. It will follow interesting and unexpected curves. Planners are unlikely to get ahead of it. The least they can do is to turn as closely behind it as possible. Otherwise they will be carried into the ditch by their own momentum—and being planners, will call for the world to follow.

Our past mistakes did little damage, fortunately, since they were made while planning was having little effect on cities. In balance, planning has probably done more good than harm, but there is nothing in the scale or quality of the results to encourage complacency.

In the future, planning may be more effective, which is excellent reason for being more careful how we go about it. By "careful" I do not mean conservative or timid or unimaginative. I mean that within limitations which we should recognize (and have not, generally) we should examine a broader range of objectives and means for reaching them, and should be more alert to changes affecting both objectives and means.

One of our principal mistakes in the past has been that we have been insensitive to potential effects of technology developing around us both in terms of what it is doing and in terms of what it makes possible. Looking to the future, let us consider elements already here or on the way which might well change the shape and physical, social, and economic organization of cities.

Technology which may shape things to come

(In this section, which originally appeared in 1962, the author wrote at some length on possible future technologies. Included were discussions of windowless buildings, increased urban sprawl, modular housing, mass transportation, and automation in manufacturing. While most of the author's speculations and predictions have come to pass, some of the discussion is now out of date. The following includes those parts of the original article that are still current.—Ed.)

In spite of generous use of jargon and numerology as a substitute for ideas, there has been some advance in social and economic technology, although our ability to work with our natural environment far outstrips our ability to work with our fellows.

In economics, we are learning to measure and understand and control somewhat better than in the past. In law, we are slowly improving old tools and devising new ones. In governmental finance, the obsolescence, inadequacies, and inequities of our revenue collection and distribution methods become painfully apparent. Failure to produce or allocate governmental income in the right amounts at the right levels has strong and damaging side effects on the character and quality of urban development. This is forcing some reconsideration.

In the field of taxation, responsible voices are raised against forms of real estate taxes which encourage decay and penalize sound development, which result in misuse of planning controls to inhibit good low-cost housing, and which otherwise contradict common sense.

Legal advances, with accessory administrative improvements, are coming slowly: better public control of land use and timing of development; better devices for acquiring land for public purposes (with excess condemnation powers to protect public interest in public improvements); and improved means for clearance and redevelopment of residential, commercial, and industrial slums.

There must be better ways to assure that land developers are neither subsidized by the public or unduly penalized. Present law and administration errs in both directions on occasion. Certainly it is not good sense to force developers to adopt obsolescent patterns of development simply because planners don't know what they are after or what they should be after.

On zoning, reform is long overdue. Developed in times even more primitive than these, New York City zoning was a magnificent first step. After that first step, zoning sat down among its withering laurels. Thousands of cities produced handmade facsimiles of the New York ordinance, discovered its shortcomings—and did nothing about them.

A model state zoning enabling act developed by the U.S. Department of Commerce in the mid-twenties drew heavily on the New York prototype, was adopted verbatim (including some very obscure language) by most states, and still stands as the foundation for zoning in many cities. Generally speaking, zoning is entirely too close to where it started.

Zoning was one answer to the problem of frictions between land uses. As a crude approach, segregation of uses with incompatible characteristics into different districts was better than nothing. Perhaps at the time it was the only practical solution. Now we should be able to do better. As an obvious alternative to the isolation ward approach, we might try curing the disease. Where we can remedy the elements which cause incompatibility, the walls can come down.

We have taken some steps in this direction with performance standards for industry. We should go on to develop performance standards for commercial and residential uses. What is a yard? What do we expect it to do? If we know, we can say that if the things a yard is expected to do are done otherwise, the yard is not required, and if the things a yard is expected to do are not done otherwise, the yard must be shaped and designed to do them.

Why is an industrial plant or a store offensive in a residential area? If we know, and can control the offensive characteristics, there should be no objection to permitting plants and stores in residential areas subject to such controls.

Given sound taxation policies, zoning or land-use control with the same general objectives should be closely tied to taxation. The privilege to use for more profitable purposes should have a price tag. This would cut down substantially on overzoning for commerce and industry to create speculative opportunity. It would also be helpful in timing land development of all kinds.

The board of adjustment, required to be a highly qualified body in the New York prototype, has generally failed to apply the "discretion of experts" when it is not made up of experts, as is usually the case. Entirely too often, existing boards are bodies of amateur arbiters dispensing favors according to political pressure, compassion, or the amount of noise made by those applying for "relief." Quite generally such boards operate with only the vaguest knowledge of, and less regard for, the limitations on their powers and the procedural requirements governing their exercise.

Whether there is general reform in zoning or not, the board of adjustment hole should be plugged. In operation or proposed are several remedial moves: trained and paid zoning examiners; paid and qualified boards set up on a statewide or regional basis; and special courts.

This hasty discussion of what may lie ahead in physical and social technology suggests a number of things. The repetition of old planning incantations is even less likely to produce miracles in the future than in the past. The range of potential means and ends is increasing. The vast diversity of things which may happen, and ways in which they may happen is both a threat and a promise.

Even individually, the elements discussed point in many directions. Collectively, they do not balance out to any neat averaging of forces moving cities one way or another. The small sample package assembled here may not include some, or any, of the major determinants which will in fact shape the future urban scene, but should serve to demonstrate the explosive potentials if all the real elements are thrown together.

Harnessed to clear objectives and driven with a steady hand, there are tremendous powers for human benefit. Left free to pursue their own courses, exploited for maximum private gain regardless of public impact, or handled by public agencies on a hit-or-miss basis, the forces released by technology will boil and fume to monstrous urban mess.

I emphasize a message which should be clear without emphasis. Increasingly, in the years ahead, the challenge to planning will be "for what" rather than "how." The wise selection of major goals is of primary importance. Both potential goals and means for reaching them multiply apace, but without selecting ends, the application of means is aimless.

Have we come full circle at this point? I began by saying that in large measure the planner in the years ahead will not know what he is planning for. I am now saying that the effectiveness of planning will depend on wise selection of major goals. Both of these statements are true, and the contradiction states the basic problem facing planners. Stating the problem helps. Is there a solution? Does planning have a chance to survive, or should planners seek other employment?

I think planning will survive and prosper, but it may have to change some of its ways. First, it will have to sort out what it can and cannot do, and second it will have to go about its job a little differently.

First of all, we should abandon the detailed Master Plan for the Year 2000 (or for eternity) in favor of something useful. There remain a few permanent general objectives which planning should defend. For example, cities must have land, water, and air.

On air, the problem is pollution, and one of the eternal objectives of planning should be to hold air pollution to a minimum.

On water, the problem is quantity and quality. How much water will be needed? Mark this down privately as unknown, prepare plausible projections, multiply by a fat safety factor, and then operate consistently to conserve and protect plenty of watershed and plenty of water supply, and to prevent or correct pollution of surface water and water in the ground.

On land, the problem in long-range terms can probably be stated only in such general language as "suitable division between public and private lands." The purpose is to provide an ample and convenient framework for public and private uses without knowing in detail what those uses will be. It will be hard for planners to stop at this—we will want to compute population densities and traffic flow and areas for residential, commercial, and industrial uses, and so on. No. Not now. This is one of the really long-range things. We are groping here for a framework within which many kinds and varieties of public and private uses, balanced out in detailed short-range plans, can shift and change and mix and separate through the centuries. And we should start with public land.

On this, we should move consistently toward an extensive and, where possible, continuous network of public land adapted to multiple purposes—open space, recreation, protection of watersheds and water supply, parks, schools, public and quasi-public buildings, transportation in whatever form it may take, and things as yet unknown.[1] The public land net is the permanent objective, the historic goal. It can be achieved by pursuit of a series of short-range ends (which in relation to it become means). As present and future short-range public requirements unfold in a succession of plans adapted to their particular time, lands contributing to the net should be acquired and held. Basic policy should add land to the net by every possible device.

Except for things like these, the blindfolded broad jump into everything should cease. Come back out of the millenium, and let's go to work.

Where does planning belong in government in the years ahead? There has been an inclination on the part of some planners to believe that there are four divisions of government: planning, legislative, executive, and judicial. The planning branch defines what is good for everybody. The legislative body passes laws to make these things possible and to keep anybody from doing anything which is bad for him or anybody. The executive body does all the routine work, and the judicial body decides that whatever the planners want done is legal. There is a stark simplicity about this which is very attractive.

But in the kind of government environment in which we find ourselves, and with the problems we face, planning is going to have to become a workhorse rather than Queen of the May. Planning should be the intelligence arm of the executive body, a function conducted with a trained staff reporting to the executive. It should keep a constant finger on the urban pulse, collecting, analyzing, and reporting currently vital information about what is happening to the city and its parts. It should keep abreast of planning technology—the way other cities are meeting their problems.

1. See "The Open Space Net," p. 161.

The planning department should be responsible for the preparation and maintenance of the comprehensive plan. The elements of this plan should each be time-scaled in accordance with usable foresight.

I do not see the comprehensive plan as a beautifully printed compendium, with 47 colored illustrations, a title including the word "Tomorrow," and a letter signed by the mayor, including the phrase "This is your plan." Public relations is important, of course, and there should be a great deal of public reporting, but I sometimes feel that we spend too much time preparing professional-looking publicity releases and splendid exhibits and not enough time on more basic parts of our jobs. If planning is well done and consistently done, it will be news, and word of it will get around in the papers and on TV. This kind of reporting, dripping constantly, wears away more stones.

I see the comprehensive plan as a series of elements always in the process of being fitted together, and usually being changed as new needs become apparent or new information becomes available or as the city changes its objectives. In its broader outlines, the plan is a statement that this is what we are trying to do, this is why we are trying to do it, and this is how we propose to do it. Against this statement of policies, measures, and objectives, which should be adopted in principle by the legislative body, the executive branch (including the planning department) should measure and fit and schedule programs of the line agencies of the city, and should exercise controls approved by the legislative body to ensure that private actions do not upset the applecart.

This is not to say that plans should be changed on the basis of whimsey. Shorn of extra language, a statement of the National Resources Board in 1934 expresses my feelings well: "Stubborn adherence to an outworn plan . . . is a mark of stupidity. Prudence dictates that reasonable stability should not be endangered by capricious or arbitrary shift of plans . . . but insists that policies must be promptly modified as emerging trends and new situations necessitate recasting."

The challenge ahead of us (and in fact behind us) is twofold: We must learn to be alert to the implications of the unexpected obvious before it happens, or when it happens, or at worst not too long after it happens. And we must learn to fit applied logic (whether it be called planning or by some other name) into the workings of government, so that governments—and the people to whom governments belong—make the most of change instead of being overwhelmed by it.

City planning: *what it should be and do*

City planning is the systematic and continuing application of organized knowledge and foresight in pursuit of clearly defined and properly related urban development objectives. Physical form and function, the most obvious manifestations of city planning, are not the only elements of planning concern. The physical city is both a cause and effect of the social and economic city; and social and economic considerations are given increasing weight in urban planning.

The kind of planning discussed here is a technique applied through local government to guide public and private actions for the common good. Because of this relationship to government, the effectiveness of planning depends not only on the quality of the planning but also on the quality of the government through which planning is applied. The kind of planning and the way planning is done should vary according to the kind of local government the planning is to serve.

The kind of planning should fit the kind of government

At the lower end of the scale, where local government is in its most primitive state, even the best planning is likely to be futile, and it might be well to concentrate effort on improving government rather than on producing plans which existing government cannot use intelligently.

In the intermediate range, planning adapted to government capability can be very helpful, but planning with techniques for maintenance which are too complex or too expensive, with objectives which are too sophisticated, with implementation which is beyond ability to administer, may lead to disenchantment with all planning.

At the upper range of governmental size and quality, upper-range forms of planning are not only appropriate but essential. There cannot be top-flight local governments without top-flight planning, and such governments equip themselves to maintain, use, and administer such planning.

In short, the kind of planning should be adapted to the kind of government. It should produce improved governmental effectiveness and improved governmental structure and organization.

Development objectives and policies

The first step in preparing a plan *should not* be immersion in basic studies, but careful preparation of a statement of major development objectives and policies. A great deal of planning begins as a complex organization of detailed information without much thought as to what the information is to be used for. This accounts for many of the thick planning documents with thin conclusions which were often obvious before the data was compiled and analyzed at great expense.

Decisions concerning major objectives go beyond determination to proceed with the catalog of basic studies, land-use plans, plans for public functions and facilities, circulation plans, and implementing devices. This is not a matter of deciding how we will plan, or what details will be included in the plan, but what we are planning for.

We are planning to correct the accumulated errors of the past, to preserve and enhance what is good about the present, and to pave the way for smooth transition to the future. We begin with the realization that our knowledge of the future is increasingly uncertain as the range increases: We can predict with more accuracy for five years than for 10, for 10, than for 20. Even at a range as short as 20 years, most of our projections turn out so wide of the mark as to be of doubtful usefulness for detailed planning purposes.

We should clearly begin our planning from the present and work forward, rather than trying to predict what the city should be like in 20 years and work backward from that. This has the advantage that planning can start by devoting at least part of its attention to problems of the "any fool can plainly see" variety.

Future town forms: *a matter of choice*

Future town forms will be what we make them, by action or by inaction. Physical technology broadens the range of goals to choose from. Social technology strengthens and multiplies means for reaching goals. Rising economic levels make it possible to pay the bills.

Concern over the growing gap between physical and social sciences and arts obscures the rapidity of social advances. For example, we communicate faster with a higher proportion of the population than ever before. We educate, condition, propagandize, advertise more effectively, preserving or changing attitudes and values. This could be important in making planning work.

To take another example, government, responding to the growing complexity and interdependence of our time, takes forms far more sophisticated than those of a couple of generations ago and performs functions which would amaze our grandfathers (sometimes performing them in ways which would have induced grandfatherly apoplexy). Health, education, welfare, commerce and industry, transportation, communication, finance, housing, agriculture, urban affairs, working conditions, income, recreation, the kind, quantity, and price of the food we eat and the drugs we take, and so on and on are controlled by governmental legislation, judicial interpretation, administrative mandate, taxation, the giving or withholding of grants and loans, and a wide variety of other gentle or ungentle persuasions.

In both physical and social fields, we produce tools and techniques faster than we learn to use them wisely. It has always been so. Man burned his hand before he learned to roast other forms of meat, and kings and chieftains governed selfishly before they discovered that survival required a broader view (a lesson learned first in terms of personal survival, and extended later to include survival of the tribe).

Government has lately bestowed increasing powers on planners. With power comes responsibility to use power wisely for the benefit of all the governed. And because of the nature and effect of planning, we must use these powers not alone for our time, but for time to come. Choosing the right goals for neighborhood form, for town form, for the metropolitan and megalopolitan form which grows from neighborhoods and towns and cities, is an appalling responsibility, particularly when we consider the magnitude of urban growth just now beginning.

We are putting the brakes on population growth, but not in time to make much change in the outlook for 75 million more urban people between 1960 and 1980. Suppose we hold growth down to another 75 million between 1980 and 2000. That makes 150 million newcomers well within the remaining lifetime of many of us.

For scale, we would need 3,000 new cities of 50,000 each to house that many new people. We now have about 350 cities in the U.S. with 50,000 or more. Or we could put them in 150 new cities of a million each. We now have only half a dozen with populations over one million.

That's for scale, but that isn't the way growth will come. The vast majority of the added population will go to existing urban concentrations, not new ones. To be realistic and practical, we must discuss both. What form should new neighborhoods and towns take, particularly in metropolitan areas? And how can existing towns, under tremendous growth stresses, achieve some right directions with current development policy? Are we, as pilots, using our powers and skills to drive our ships forward with matchless swiftness and efficiency onto the rocks?

Planning for or against the future

Consider three parables and what they teach:

In Virginia, in 1610, the Powhatan Planning Commission is concerned about threats to the public welfare including disease, extermination, and graver disorders including land speculation. The commission drafts policies in accordance with a comprehensive plan. Major emphasis is on preservation of open space and protection of the character of existing neighborhoods. This excellent statement is adopted by the

Algonquin Regional Planning Council as a model for emulation throughout its jurisdiction. Jamestown is eliminated in a slum clearance program, and when the Pilgrims arrive they are denied building permits. Where are we now?

A couple of centuries later, the North Manhattan Planning Board views with alarm the disrupting influence of urbanization spreading from New York City, rapidly becoming a mess as its population soars to the unwieldy total of 100,000. Zoning is adopted permitting only agricultural uses from Harlem north, with minimum farm size set at 160 acres. Where now is New York City?

These things couldn't have happened, partly because social technology hadn't as yet produced the controls. The controls are here now. The third parable reflects what *is* happening in many towns in the metropolitan areas where our future growth must come.

Suburbia Village Planning Commissions adopt policy expressed in various language, but with the uniform intent of assuring that the only newcomers to be welcomed will be like persons already there, housed in single-family detached residences like those already there on large lots in subdivisions like the ones already there. No apartments. No town houses. No mobile homes. No housing which doesn't look like present housing, or is likely to appeal to renters, or costs less. No increase in density.

At meetings, there is applause for staff reports on the advantage of planning, particularly as applied to new neighborhoods and new towns. Turning to unfinished zoning business, commissions reject proposed amendments permitting planned unit development, indicating that less extreme forms might be given favorable consideration. Changes required? Well, existing low densities must not be exceeded and perhaps should be lowered. Street and lot patterns must conform to existing zoning and subdivision regulations. Housing must be exclusively single-family, with yards to match. And of course, troublesome common open space must be eliminated. With these minor changes, planned unit development might be acceptable.

Such actions by Suburbia Villages ringing our metropolitan centers may set the future form of both the towns and the metropolis. Is the pattern good, in the long run, for Suburbia Village? For metropolis? Where does the great mass of newcomers go? Where do all the people go who need forms of housing other than single-family detached at some stages of their lives?

If our new controls are used to defend the past against the future, to hold the line for lesser publics against the needs of the greater, planning may well do more harm than good.

The town planner (layman or professional) must of course look at the town as it is. If he is true to his calling, he cannot stop at this. He must look backward, to see how it got that way. He must look around him, to see what the greater public interest demands of his town. He must look ahead, to see what his town is likely to become and what it should become. After he has done these things, if he is a wise planner, he will be guided in what he proposes by a simple rule: *No town is an island, no time is forever.*

The job is to guide change to fit need, not to stop change. The change should be staged and ordered to be as painless as possible, but if general public needs demand change, the planner who blocks change betrays his trust.

Who are we planning for?

Before making broad sweeps with pastel crayons, there are some questions to answer. Who are we planning for? Keeping it simple and short-range, we are planning for our retirees, our middle-aged generation, our children, and their children. This carries us to the year 2000. What does it mean in numbers in age groups and in housing demand?

In 2000, the retirement crop will have doubled to about 37 million, assuming retirement then at age 60. A third of these (12 million) will be 75 or over, again doubling present numbers. Most of the older retirees would be glad to find suitable apartments, or small houses, or congenial retirement homes, and few will want or be able to maintain the larger residences in which they raised their families. If possible, they would like to stay in their own communities within the circle of old friends.

Stay-at-homes in the newly retired crowd will want to stay at home. A lot of the more venturesome or less labor-loving would like to get in smaller quarters, including apartments and mobile homes. Most of the younger retired would also prefer to remain in their communities if they can find the right living facilities. If they stay, they are a rich source for public duties, a powerful force for stability.

The next group, from 30 to retirement age (best prospects for conventional single-family housing) will rise by only half, going up from 75 million now to around 110 million in 2000. These are the relatively settled bread-winners with school aged children.

In the 20-30 age group are the new family-formers with starry eyes, pre-school children, high mobility, and relatively low incomes. Now there are 24 million of them. In 35 years, their number will about double, rising to over 45 million by 2000. For this group, rented small houses, apartments, or mobile homes make a good start.

As to our children's children, the group under 20 in 2000, barring unexpected developments in population control, will number about 100 million, just under three times the 37 million on hand now. This will come as little comfort to those who have been school board members recently, and neither will the word that educational costs are rising rapidly and should continue to rise, or that children are remaining in school longer, a trend which should also continue. To this, too, we are adjusting, particularly in the manner in which we spread the load for school support to county, state, and federal levels.

That's who we are planning for between the present and the year 2000—ourselves and enough newcomers to equal total U.S. population in 1950. Now we have some policy choices to make.

Policy choices

Do we want communities or compartments? In the long run, segregation by housing types creates compartments rather than communities, and one-class housing may mean premature obsolescence and decay. These things are likely to happen to single-family detached Suburbia Villages as time passes:

Retirees, treasurers of tradition, move elsewhere for lack of housing suited to their needs. As children reach adulthood, their loyalties and friendships may incline them to stay, but they too must find housing elsewhere to fit their needs and pocketbooks. Having formed new friendships, they are unlikely to return to take over family-raising homes left vacant as retirees move out.

Since Suburbia Village has driven away replacements who might have come from within its own borders, it must attract outsiders. But in most cases, the old Suburbia Village does not attract the same kind of people who settled in when it was new. The new crowd moves to the latest developments to keep up with the current crop of Joneses.

Suburbia Village must settle for what it can get, which usually means a filtering down of housing.

Of Suburbia Villages started in the last three or four generations, few retain position as prestige communities. Most have deteriorated in appearance and spirit. Some have disappeared already under the slum clearance bulldozer. Out ahead, pressures piling up are likely to turn the cycles more rapidly unless communities are built to stay communities.

To help keep communities from becoming deteriorating housing compartments, we should provide a range of housing encouraging community continuity. This does not mean a conglomerate jumble of single-family detached residences, apartments, and mobile home parks. It does mean careful planning and intelligent development control.

Higher density or more sprawl? We will have higher densities within present metropolitan borders, and the borders will spread out. The question is how much of each, and how to avoid the liabilities of each.

Urban sprawl is getting a bad name. It increases travel time and raises costs of public and private facilities and services. Temporary advantages of fringe dwellers next to open country disappear as waves of development move beyond them. Since controls do not move as fast as urban fringes, we appear to have built hundreds of square miles of single-family detached slums.

High density has had a bad name for a long time, and is equated in many minds with teeming tenements, sordid apartments, blight, crime, disease, high governmental costs, and all the rest of it. Lately it is also equated with footloose renters with no feeling of responsibility to the area in which they live, strange people who do not want to take on 40-year mortgages on homes built to last 30 years (with extensive maintenance).

If we learn to use land efficiently, we can extend our urban areas at far less cost than has been typical recently, and can avoid some of the disappointments which have come to fringe dwellers in the past. If we control high-density developments wisely, we can gain rather than lose amenities, particularly in urban open space which is not just a patchwork of fragmented small yards, but is big enough to have real meaning, landscaped enough to provide functional green area.

In choosing policy, most people with a real concern about what lies ahead will vote for communities rather than compartments, higher density if it can be achieved without loss of amenities, containment of urban sprawl by more efficient use of fringe lands, and minimized private and public costs in providing necessary services and maintaining necessary facilities.

If that is what we vote for, and if we are agreed that population will be coming along in total numbers and age group proportions about as indicated, we have both outlined the size of the job in the years ahead (for us) and set some standards on how it is to be done. A few tentative brush strokes are now in order.

Design specifications

Planned developments are a good source of ideas about desirable town forms for the future. Already there are some details from planned developments which can be used to make improvements as our existing neighborhoods and cities fill out and are rebuilt.

The planned development approach has revolutionary advantages over conventional lot-by-lot development. Perhaps we should make the most of them by requiring that any sizable open tract suitable for development should be developed *only* as a planned unit, rather than subdivided into conventional lots for sale.

Unified development, with approved detailed plans and construction schedules, distinguishes the planned unit approach from present general practice under which land is subdivided and required improvements installed before lots are sold. After the lot is sold, some kind of a house will be built, perhaps. Since we do not know how its interior functional areas will be related by windows to houses on either side, our regulations are clumsy and wasteful. We establish lot width and area and yard requirements and limitations on height to keep the worst from happening and the worst doesn't happen.

The best doesn't happen either. In rows of look-alike houses, living room picture windows frame principal vistas composed of identical front yards, sidewalks, streets, passing traffic, and parked cars. Front yards are extensive but limited in function. Side yards are so divided as to give minimal insulation and increase street and utility runs. If there is any parklike open space, public or private, it is likely to be blocks away across many streets. The rear yard is the only private and quiet area on the lot suited for multipurpose use, and about the only vestige of the country atmosphere people moved to the suburbs to find. We can do better than that—much better. Good planned developments prove it.

Future neighborhood and town forms possible through good planned unit development have streets which serve rather than dominate. Land area in streets is kept to a minimum, with loops or cul de sacs holding down traffic in low-density areas. The dominant design feature is the parklike common open space system, continuous through superblocks and threaded with walkways (well away from streets) leading to schools and other principal destinations.

Detached single-family residences and town houses are oriented toward the interior parks and away from streets, grouped in clusters on lots smaller than has been customary, but with increased utility and a feeling of greater space rather than less. Careful design and siting of individual residences makes excessive side and front yards unnecessary.

Medium- to high-density facilities are separated from low-density by the parks, and have direct but controlled access to collector and arterial streets without pouring traffic through low-density neighborhoods. Extensive parking areas are screened to avoid the sea-of-cars appearance. Shopping facilities, where provided, are integrated conveniently and painlessly into the overall scheme.

The result is a great deal more amenity than is common in usual subdivisions, considerably higher density, a designed mixture of housing types and major economies in land, improvement, service, and maintenance costs per unit.

If we can have that kind of development, we should certainly take what steps we can to promote it.

Improvements in older areas

Some devices used in planned developments can be adapted for use in partially built-up sections and in rebuilding older areas. In zoning for individual residential lots, we can shift from present crude flat specifications to performance-related standards giving equal or better protection of public interest, but allowing improved land use and more flexible residential design.

On individual lots, required visibility triangles protecting traffic safety, and view, might replace usual front yard requirements. Instead of side and rear yard minimums (with rear yards hopelessly confused by usual permission of accessory buildings but not portions of principal structures) we could move to limitations assuring safety and access, requiring portions of buildings to be separated as necessary for safety and access—and that's all. (Whether the building is main or accessory makes no difference.) One promising possibility is recorded agreements between adjoining lot owners, with enforcement running to local government as an alternate to meeting general yard requirements, allowing adjoining owners to adjust relation between portions of buildings on their lots without rigid limitations based on location of lot lines.

As to privacy and relation of interior function to open space on the lot, we can do much better than at present. From housing codes we have indications as to amount of glassed area required in relation to floor area in rooms used for specific purposes. Using the approach of some planned development regulations, we might say that where 75 per cent or more of required glassed area of a living room or bedroom is involved, one set of dimensional minimums apply to related open space; where less than 25 per cent of such required living room or bedroom glassed area or windows for kitchens, baths, or other interior space are involved, a second set of related open space minimums apply; and where no glassed area is involved the only requirements are for building separation for safety or access.

These approaches leave much more of the lot available for buildings than at present, allowing more flexible design, but creating the danger that too much of the lot may be covered. Here again the regulatory approach is related to performance, with a figure set on maximum lot coverage by buildings or with floor area ratio established. When the site designer has met other open space requirements, land left over as a result of maximum building coverage limitations must be used for courts, patios, and the like, but it can be used flexibly.

Height regulations are primarily to assure adequate light and air. Make them do it by leaning suitable light planes inward over the lot from above its boundaries or buildable area limits, with lower portions toward the center of the lot. This is better than the usual flat limit applying anywhere over the buildable area, and often too high at its edges.

On streets in existing subdivisions we can make some improvements. Traffic diverters at strategic intersections allow local drivers to get home, but make routes unattractive to short-cutting outsiders. We can not do much about excessive street lengths which waste land and raise maintenance costs, but we might reduce excessive right-of-way widths on minor streets by giving strips to adjoining owners. In the course of building or rebuilding, the added area available in the lots would allow more flexibility in structural location and increase potentials for more useful arrangements of open space on the lot.

Toward the public land net as a key element

Moving from details to the total urban scene, what steps can we take toward gradual betterment, particularly in suburban sectors? We can practice more assiduously what we have been preaching—that planning is an instrument for coordinated and efficient development.

Out ahead, we take many public and quasi-public actions involving major land acquisition: building interstate highways, major expressways, and other large-scale automotive arteries; providing mass transportation; extending trunk sewer, water, gas, and electrical systems; building new schools, colleges, universities, public administration and public service buildings; adding new parks and recreation areas; building new churches; adding new cemeteries.

We have tended to plan for these things separately. Perhaps we should begin to plan for them together, wherever "togetherness" can be made appropriate. The new (and much needed) coordinating planning concept proposed is the public land net.[1] If we make a continuing effort to relate public and quasi-public actions to building the public land net, in the years ahead we can multiply benefits (and particularly amenities), reduce costs, minimize the effects of errors in foresight, and provide for both present and future needs.

Summary and conclusion

To sharpen focus and tie things more closely together, these main points are emphasized:

1. To a degree never before possible, we have the power to shape future urban form and to influence the wishes of men as to what they want cities to be. Persuasion may be necessary for those who are reluctant to leave the past.

2. With these powers comes responsibility to act wisely and in the general public interest. The general public interest is broader than our towns or our time.

3. Ahead of us is massive urban growth which cannot be ignored

1. For further discussion of the public land net, see "The Open Space Net," p. 161.

and a change in the age structure of population which demands a shift in housing mix. Between 1960 and 1980 we will add as many people as there were in the country 15 years ago, but the balance between age groups in this population will not be what it is now. Retirees will double. The number between 30 and retirement age will increase by only half. The family-forming 20-30 age group will double. The children will triple. There is evident need for proportionately more apartments, town houses, and mobile homes in the new housing supply.

4. Adding more housing of this kind in our towns seems likely to strengthen them as long-lived communities, to protect them from becoming deteriorating housing compartments. The increased density makes possible limitation of excessive urban sprawl, which is the inevitable alternative if present suburban densities are maintained and set the standards for new suburbs farther out.

5. Planned unit developments, with higher densities, improved housing mix, and increased amenities are a major advance over the current urban pattern, where they can be required or encouraged. They should be.

6. Within existing suburbs and new ones not built on planned development principles, we can at least encourage slow improvement. We can amend our crude zoning ordinances to permit greater freedom in the use of lots to permit departure from building forms which set a rectangle crossways within a rectangle, to allow more effective use of the now-fragmented open space around buildings, to set more sensitive and functional height limitations. We can relieve some of the discomforts and hazards of through traffic in residential neighborhoods.

7. At larger scale, the open space net has great promise as a planning and development tool, with patient and persistent application offering numerous and substantial rewards.

8. Predominantly residential areas within the meshes of the net are helped by its effects to evolve into more pleasant, convenient, and intelligent patterns.

We have the power to shape the future of urban America. We have the responsibility to use it unselfishly and wisely. The rewards for success are great, the penalty for failure incalculable. We must not fail our own time, or time to come.

Obstacles in planning: *summary and conclusions*

1. If you are going to plan, plan well and plan for action. If you aren't going to plan well and plan for action, don't mess with it.

2. Planning works best in a reasonably mature government, in which the elected representatives set policy and pass laws, leaving administration and enforcement to a qualified executive, with a qualified planner under him, working closely with him, and directly responsible to him.

3. In the present state of planning, a planning commission is usually essential. Pick commission members as carefully as you do your executive and your planner. They should be people with an ability to take a broad and intelligent view of the general public interest, and people whose opinions will be respected. Don't use the planning commission as a political dumping ground, or pack it with people having business interests which may affect their views as to what promotes the common good. Don't involve the planning commission in routine administrative operations. Save their time for formulating advice on public policy.

4. Make your plan general enough so that no important parts of the jigsaw puzzle are left out. Get the facts before you draw conclusions. Once you get a working plan, keep it current as you learn new facts.

5. Members of the governing body should understand a plan before approving it. Rubber-stamp approval won't make the plan work.

The full article on "Obstacles in Planning" appeared in *Florida Planning and Development,* January 1967.

6. Once understood and approved, the plan should trigger action. Matters involving expenditure of public money should be analyzed in terms of amount and timing (the capital improvement program) and should work their way into the budget. Matters involving legislative or other regulatory measures should be reflected rapidly in new or amended zoning, subdivision controls, and so forth.

7. When you have a sound plan and good zoning, subdivision regulations, capital improvement programs, and so on, don't move from them unless there is convincing public reason for doing so, backed by the planning commission and planning staff. If there is solid reason for change, then change. But don't be pushed around by special-interest pleading to the point where you injure the public interest to grant an individual favor. Always be ready to improve and strengthen the plan and the controls which go with it. Never be ready to weaken it.

If you do these things, there will still be enough obstacles to planned action to exercise governmental mind and muscle, but none of the obstacles will be insurmountable.

Planning archaeology: *a new science rises*

Planning archaeology is the coming thing. It should now be a required basic study in the professional planning curriculum. No serious observer of the Science and Art can remain unaware that some current policies of massive impact are derived from researches in planning ruins and midden heaps rather than from the forefront of planning thought.

As an example, new federal aid policies for highways are apparently based on Dead Sea scrolls from an almost forgotten planning era. Resurrecting financial streams pump into mummified veins of the Master Plan for Ultimate (20 Year) Development. It stirs and rises from the dust, dropping its withered lilies, to scatter federal bounty to worshipping staff planners and consultants alike. Nonworshippers are not to have any.

Traffic specialists, discovering the hazards of planning for traffic alone, propose to join with planning-type planners in making planning more comprehensive. This is an excellent if belated move. But the manner of planning now proposed by the Bureau of Public Roads—and the proposal is persuasively supported by offers to withhold federal-aid highway funds unless we do it their way—is something from the neolithic layers. (What else is down there? It behooves planners to find out.)

Parchments of an ancient planning priesthood apparently guide the Bureau. The old ritual called for prophetic structuring of a 20-year future as a primary step. This shaped the plan which followed. Then everyone was supposed to follow the plan—but few did. Perhaps this was just as well. In most cases, what happened in 20 years varied widely from the visions of the prophets. Planners in general learned this, and most of them now grope their way cautiously from the present into the relatively near future, aware that even this may be full of surprises.

Traffic engineers have demonstrated that long-range projections on traffic are no less wildly erroneous if made by complex and costly methods than if made by simpler means. Planners long ago made similar demonstrations on population, land use, employment, and a number of other items. They even proved that they too could be wrong about traffic, although in general they weren't as scientific about it as the traffic specialists.

Early planners, proceeding according to the old rituals, led small bands of mistaken assumptions through primitive calculators and across a wilderness of graph paper to erroneous conclusions. Under the New Order, based firmly on the old and ignoring the wisdom which should have accumulated in the years between, the Rite for Beginning Planning takes the same basic form, but is to be richer, fuller, more complex, and a great deal more expensive. The process proposed, judging from ceremonies initiated by those of the devout who have received the Word, involves an awesome parade of unknowns flashing in electronically transmuted splendor through computers miraculously quick to handle facts. This does not make facts out of unknowns. The conclusions reached, in addition to being further afield because of the multiplied number and range of dubious assumptions, will be a great deal more costly than any heretofore derived.

But isn't the technology marvelous?

Before you can get program approval for federal-aid highway projects after July 1, 1965, evidence is mounting that it will be necessary to set up a "continuing, comprehensive transportation planning process" involving as an early step detailing for small areas (divisions of census tracts) a 20-year forecast as to employment opportunities, population, per capita incomes, consumption of goods and services, car ownership, land-use patterns, and a number of other items. Summarizing from an actual proposal, in making forecasts, industrial location decisions will be considered including costs of production, characteristics of the labor force, natural resources, and the fiscal and financial policies of governments (including tax structure). "Analyses of data and forecasts will take account of the effect on the local economy of variations (recent or otherwise) in the national economy; the effect of economic fluctuations on different industries, and the probable effect of technological developments on local industries over time."

"Regardless of the method used to make future estimates, the results obtained will be tested for reasonableness and consistency. A population forecast will be prepared based on the employment forecast and this will be compared with the independent population forecast based on demographic techniques."

This sounds logical, but perhaps it won't be a bad idea to test it by a trial run, a laboratory exercise. Take half of 1 per cent of funds now earmarked for this kind of detailed forecasts. Pick a couple of cities. It is now 1944, and the only difference between now and then is that you have the computer. Aside from that, you have your cities as they were then and the foreknowledge you had then. Do what you are proposing to do now. Go!

Now check your 20-year forecasts for the cities and their subareas against what really happened by 1964. How did you come out generally? By major areas? By subareas? How did you come out on the 320 acres which was Jones Dairy? How many families did you say would be in there, what did you say would be their skills, education, employment patterns, per capita incomes, car ownership? What would be their origin and destination patterns?

Which industries did you anticipate, what skills did they require, what resources, what transportation facilities? How much mass transportation did you grind into your estimates? When did you have World War II ending, and who won? Did the war industries convert or were they abandoned? Were tourists to be big or small in the picture, and did they come by car, rail, or plane? Where did you locate your new airports? How much *through* vehicular traffic—passenger and freight—did you anticipate? Did you figure on piggy-back?

Did you allow for the pickup in technological tempo which still continues? Did you anticipate correctly the effects of continuing international uncertainty, foreign trade and foreign aid, the effect of tariff changes, Japanese electronics, the VW and its friends, federal policies on housing, the radical shift in population trends?

On this latter point, what were your honest predictions (made with computers and with the best expert guidance on assumptions available in 1944) as to 1964 population of your cities? This is certainly a key point. If you didn't come reasonably close on this estimate, you probably were far off on the number of cars and their origins and destinations.

Now do you really believe that it will pay to put the projected amount of time, money, and manpower into making the kind of detailed estimates which are apparently a mandatory part of the "continuing, comprehensive transportation planning process"? Should we be *required* to go through all this, funds or no, computers or no, as a precedent to receiving approval of new federal-aid highway projects? Who dug this out of the dump, and why?

What it all boils down to is this. Maybe, if we will use our heads, planning archaeology can teach us some lessons we aren't learning from it. Certainly we should find out how to use it better if we are going to use it at all. If we will study it thoroughly, we can find out not only what the ancient rituals were, but whether they worked.

Planning, the people, and the strength of nations

Planning, the oldest of the arts of mankind, distinguishes him from the other animals. In the relatively brief period during which man has been able to keep records, there is considerable evidence that those civilizations have advanced most rapidly in which planning has been most effective as a guide to action.

It is also notable that the empires which fell apart most rapidly were those in which the power to plan (to decide what to do) was concentrated in the hands of the few. In such regimes, discipline was the chief virtue demanded of the people, and the ability of the common man to think and act for himself or for his group atrophied. When the imperial line lost the qualities of kingship or the ruling group fell out among themselves, chaos followed for the nation.

In our time, and in our civilization, we are trying a hopeful experiment. It may work, or it may not, depending on whether we can agree on what it is we are trying to do, and on our stubborn persistence in the pursuit of our real objective—the survival of a new form of society.

For the first time in history, we are putting the common welfare above the welfare and aggrandizement of any group or class, and we are trying to encourage all the people to think and act to promote and protect the common welfare. This is something new, and it shows promise.

War is one test of the real strength of nations, and the last few major wars have been won by nations in which decision-making is spread out. Dispersal may be the key to survival of something more than cities.

If this pattern of military victories is more than a mere statistical coincidence, it may be indicative of an important social gain. Have we found a means by which the vitality of a culture can be extended, a key, even, to a kind of human progress which does not come in cycles of advance and slow or revolutionary decline, advance beyond the first and then again catastrophe?

We think so. We are gambling heavily on it. We are educating a larger and larger proportion of our people and teaching them more and more. Labor has become one of the interests, and not a "tool of the interests." Few of our major corporations are now "family" corporations. Over the long pull, the quality of our government—federal, state, county, and local—is improving because an increasing segment of the populace is taking an informed part in governmental affairs.

For the most part, these things are happening slowly—sometimes almost imperceptibly. But they are happening. If our goal is a constructive decision-making process in which everybody plays a part, we have a long way to go, but we are headed in that direction if the history of the last 200 years means anything.

Assuming that enduring and superior strength grows from the kind of political and economic and social order which is slowly emerging in the United States and some of our sister nations, we need not fear that the Communists will engulf us. The thing which we *should* fear is that we will lose what we have gained, and become like the Communists and the builders of all broken and vanished empires which preceded theirs—the long and tragic parade of transient power in the hands of a few, or of one man, dominions marked by the name of a man rather than of a people—Stalin, Hitler, Mussolini, Napoleon, Charlemagne, Caesar, Alexander.

The strength of our democracy lies in the sharing of knowledge and in the sharing of decisions as to how to use it. This is a hard way and a slow way to progress, but it shows promise of being a sure way to progress which endures. If in our haste we make the acquisition and use of knowledge the exclusive province of the few, or enthrone the expert as king, we lose ground which has been hard-won, and gain only transient and illusory security. In the long run, if we do not advance together, we are likely to find that we have not advanced at all.

Prologue to the future

Experience is a great teacher for those to whom it happens, but it isn't easy to transmit. Every generation must learn too much for itself, because the fathers are too busy experiencing to teach and the children are too busy experiencing to listen. Improved techniques for communication in our time aggravate the problem by drowning too few ideas in too much audio-visual clamor.

As a nation, we demand disasters. If we don't have any, we invent them; if they are too small, we enlarge them. The world is always going more and more to hell in bigger and bigger handbaskets. Looking backward, it seems to me that in all honesty some things have been worse than they are now. This kind of perspective spoils the fun. It means that for the moment we may be working with inferior disasters. We make up for this by attacking them with greater frenzy and greater expenditures of manpower and money, although it isn't clear that our effectiveness improves correspondingly—in doing more, we may actually be accomplishing less. Anyway, this activity makes it possible to increase both taxes and the national debt, and keeps Washington busy.

How does all this relate to the future environment of democracy? Well, considering whence we have come since 1917, 1933, or even

This article originally was prepared as introductory comments for a session at the American Institute of Planners' Fiftieth Anniversary Conference, "The Future Environment of Democracy," October 1967.

1943, and whither we appear to be going in the 50 years ahead, we are sure that there will be a future environment. As to whether democracy survives and evolves to a more constructive form, there is less assurance. The increasing tendency toward what can only be described as enervating self-abuse is not hopeful.

It's easy to prescribe—we need more reason and less rioting, fewer grandiose programs and better performance, less buck-passing and more self-reliance, more productive work and less filling out of application forms. Can we swallow these prescriptions—or do we want to—in these permissive, undisciplined times? History gives both warning and a formula for hope.

The threats can be variously stated. The fat are eaten by the lean. Bread and circuses do not add to national longevity. It may be that history will not repeat itself, and that the new form of consumption-oriented economy assures national immortality even though the rich and broadening availability of goods and comforts produces a nation too much characterized by fat bodies, flabby minds, and outstretched palms.

The formula for hope which comes to us from history is not a promise but a challenge. If we really try, and don't get stampeded by Russia, the AFL-CIO, the Republicans, the space race, the Democrats, lawyers, Communists, the feds, WASPS, people who live in apartments, Negroes, planners, Jews, Red China, or other vocal or nonvocal minorities, we may be able to achieve mature and well-balanced government which serves rather than dominates—a "government of the people, by the people, and for the people"—all of them.

Let us now get on with it, with dedication, zeal, humility, and a great deal less selfishness. At the moment we aren't doing very well. Maybe we can do better.

Democracy is threatening the American way of life

During international crises, elections, public hearings, and other times when orators soar on star-spangled wings to stratospheres of eloquence, there rings a refrain which makes it clear that the elevation is too much for the oxygen supply: "We must strengthen and defend democracy and the American Way of Life." But the speaker, as appears from the context, usually considers the "American Way of Life" to be founded and centered on free enterprise in a capitalistic economy.

Evidence mounts that as democracy is strengthened, capitalism is loaded with impediments and free enterprise is decreasingly free. The orator who urges strengthening democracy *and* capitalism in the face of what democracy has done and is doing to capitalism should make up his mind to promote one or the other.

At this point, let's be sure that we are talking the same language, and try to free ourselves from emotional entanglements. Capitalism, to quote Webster, is "the established economic system of most modern civilized countries in which the ownership of land and natural wealth, the production, distribution and exchange of goods, the employment and reward of human labor, and the extension, organization and operation of the system itself are entrusted to, and effected by, private enterprise and control under competitive conditions."

Socialism, again quoting Webster, "is based on collective or governmental ownership and democratic management of the essential means for production and distribution of goods." Socialism "aims to replace competition by cooperation and profit seeking by social service, and to distribute income and social opportunity more equitably than they are now believed to be distributed. . . . Moderate or democratic socialists believe in a slow, evolutionary transformation of capitalist into socialist society, while radical or revolutionary socialists believe in class war and the overthrow of capitalism by political uprising or a general strike."

The United States is a free democratic republic, a representative democracy in which power, ultimately in the hands of the electorate, is exercised by elected representatives responsible to those who elect them.

In the United States, we have moved a long way from pure capitalism. "The extension, organization and operation of the system" is decreasingly "entrusted to, and effected by, private enterprise and control under competitive conditions." Private employment and reward of labor is strongly influenced and in some ways directly controlled by government, and government itself hires one-sixth of all those now employed. Government owns vast amounts of land and natural resources. Government produces, distributes, and exchanges many kinds of goods, generates, transmits, and sells electricity, provides water and sewers, and engages in a wide variety of operations which could quite readily be handled by private enterprise.

There is no firm rule about division of operations between private enterprise and government. In one city, the power system is owned and operated by local government, in the next by much-controlled private "public" utilities, and around the outskirts of both REA may provide power. One governmental body may do its own printing, the next may contract to have printing done. Here, mass transportation is handled by private enterprise, there directly by local government, and in a third place by an authority set up democratically at least in part to remove operation from political (democratic?) interference.

But while we do not have pure capitalism, we are yet a long way from pure socialism, although we are moving toward some of its objectives. In many areas, competition is being displaced, if not by cooperation, at least by regulation which greatly reduces the effect of competition in guiding decisions by private enterprise. We have not gone so far as wholesale governmental ownership of the means for production. Rather we have superimposed democratic management (called for by socialism) on private ownership, and on the distribution of privately produced goods. This democratic management is often indirect, but it is generally effective. It stimulates or slows private operation, or guides private operation in directions which the free enterprise system would not select.

Here are random examples of things which might be different if free enterprise operated freely and competitively, with neither hindrance nor assistance from government: Present housing production would be much lower. There would be fewer balconies on apartments. Hotels in New York City would be run more as hotels and less as tax shelters. Residential lots would be narrower. There would be more mixing of residential, commercial, and industrial land uses. There would be less home "ownership" and more rental property. There would be fewer airports, a smaller railroad network, less trucking, less shipping by waterways. Buildings would be built differently. The entire complexion of agricultural production would be different.

The list is endless. In almost any facet of our economy, and in many phases of our social lives, democratic management of private operation results in doing things or not doing things which would be done differently or remain undone if the "extension, organization and operation of the system itself" were entirely "entrusted to, and effected by, private enterprise and control under competitive conditions."

Depending on the viewpoints and personal interests of observers, some of the results of this kind of democratic management are excellent, some mediocre, some weird and inexcusable. If there were general agreement among the voters as to which are good and which are bad, there would be rapid changes. Where things get bad enough to create general agreement there are changes, but in a democracy with a wide variety of interest groups and voter motivations, general agreement is not always easy to come by.

Without the consent of the governed, the move away from uninhibited capitalism toward many of the objectives of socialism in this country would have been impossible. If our democracy did not demand all of the changes, at least it allowed them. The move toward increased direct governmental performance of what might otherwise be private enterprise functions, decreased disparity in incomes through government controls, more general access to a wider range of social opportunities—all these are among the objectives of socialism, and all have been actively or passively endorsed by our democracy. Our democratic society has produced a "slow, evolutionary transformation" of capitalism into something which has many of the overtones of a socialistic society—but which has not yet gone all the way.

Thus when the orator calls for strengthening democracy and the

American Way of Life, if by the latter he means the free enterprise system he may be praying for both rain and a dry spell.

Among vital questions affecting the future are these: In what has been, and holds much promise of continuing to be, increasingly rich and complex social and economic society, can the great mass of voters be adequately informed about the issues or personalities involved in their choices? Can honest fact-finding and communication make democratic choice something more than a selection between platforms framed to attract voters from both sides of the fence and leave political selectees uncommitted? Will the richness of the economy indefinitely support trial and error with trials frequently ill-advised or unnecessary and errors corrected only when they attain first magnitude?

Democratic management has found means to curb abuses which developed under an uncontrolled free enterprise system. Can means now be found to curb the abuses discernible in democratic management?

The ground has shifted, the rules have changed, but the battle remains the same. Democratic management has been imposed by the voters on the private enterprise system to correct what the people considered to be overreaching greed and concentrations of power dangerous to the common good. Now the question is whether the people can control their own greed and use their own power wisely.

As voters, we have many lessons to learn. Some of them are tremendously involved and complex, but the first is simple, even if it is hard: *No government can long survive in which everyone receives more than he earns or gets more than he pays for.*

City planners: *what they should be and do*

One very real handicap to planning is that we don't know how to do it very well. We'll be all right if we know that we don't know all we think we know about it. It has been wisely said that the planning profession is about where medicine was at the turn of the century. There is one difference. At the turn of the century, big government wasn't institutionalizing mistakes by requiring them to be multiplied as a condition for grants. I am told that in the past few years, the federal government has spent over $20 million on local zoning. Now there is a project for $300,000 to find out what's wrong with local zoning and how it can be improved, but it comes a little late.

This isn't to say that planning is useless, even though it is in a primitive state like medicine in 1900.

I'm not nearly as worried about improvements needed in planning as I am about some other things. Planning which comes up to the best of current planning standards is a great deal better than no planning at all.

What planning is, and what planners do

Before going further, it might be well to indicate what I think we are talking about, what planning is, what it is for, how it works. Maybe we can do this without the use of words like "comprehensive," "coordinated," or "the major elements in the physical, social, and economic environment."

Most people go along in principle with the adage: "Look before you leap." Some would agree that it pays to look two or three moves ahead, particularly when you are playing a chess game as complex and expensive as city and county development in our time. The planner is a professional looker, the best we have been able to develop, and his job is to advise as to what is likely to happen as the result of various possible leaps.

The planner's job is to keep informed as to what is likely to be out ahead, what's catching up from behind, what's coming in from all sides, to appraise present and future perils and potentials, and to suggest measures which will promote the common good. He is working with development, with evolution, with change. This means he has to keep moving.

If the planner is an able man, trained and experienced in performance of his function, he keeps a constant eye on the unrolling horizons and what lies above and below them, he scouts, he watches for signs, he weighs, he interprets, he thinks, and having done these things he reports on the need for action and the advantages and disadvantages of various courses. Having reported, he moves out again to watch for new dangers and new opportunities, and then reports again as to need for alteration in plans in the light of new knowledge.

The planner, his obligations, and his bosses

Now let's discuss the public planner, his obligations, and his bosses. On entry into the medical profession, the Hippocratic Oath is administered. It wouldn't be a bad idea to have a similar code for planners. One of the binding obligations would be this, paraphrasing a section of the Hippocratic Oath: "I will inform myself before advising, and my advice shall be, according to my knowledge, ability, and judgment, for the benefit of the general public, and not for their hurt or to do them any wrong, or to give any man advantage which is harmful to the general public interest."

Whether such an obligation is taken formally or not, it makes good sense in terms of what the public planner should be employed to do. The first responsibility of the public planner is to the public, present and future, and to the greater public above any lesser public. If he is ordered or asked to give his stamp of approval to a course of action, or to design a course of action which serves other ends, he should exercise such missionary abilities as he may have to bring the wanderers into the fold, and if he fails in this he should move on to another job. The public planner's top boss is the general public.

What I have said doesn't mean that the planner should be a butt-headed and uncompromising character. He should be very flexible indeed, and alert to the need for a great many compromises—if they are for the right reasons. Of course, there are times when he should not compromise and should not be asked to compromise.

As a simple example of this, a planning director and his staff report unfavorably on a spot zoning application. Their argument is well reasoned and thoroughly grounded in fact and policy. The planning commission reverses the recommendation for reasons best unexplored and instructs the planning director to prepare a report endorsing the change to city council, buttressed with appropriate vague planningese. At this point, the range of choices open to a planning director who has taken the Hippocratic Oath for Planners does not include doing as he is told. He can engage in friendly persuasion. If he has another job lined up, he can even engage in unfriendly persuasion, suggesting where the planning commission might go. But he should never sell the public down the river, and he should never be asked to do so.

The general public, as we have said, is the planner's top boss. And if he is an honest planner, the generality of the public served may create problems for him. To a far greater extent than most public officials, he must be aware of the part of the general public which lies outside his particular political limits, beyond the city line or the county line. To the best of his ability, every local planner should be also a regional planner. Planning ethics and necessity go hand in hand here. If planners with highly localized viewpoints continue building Chinese walls around their communities, the communities are very likely to find that their planning is being done for them by a supergovernment, and that their power of local control has been removed. It can happen here. It is happening.

So the planner's public is broad in its generality. It is also deep. There is a lesson to be learned from a Nigerian chief who said "My people are a family in which some are dead, a few are here, and many are coming." The job of the honest planner is to plan for those who are coming, and not merely for the few who are here.

The many who are coming should be served economically and well when they arrive, and they should be entitled to health, safety, comfort, and convenience. It therefore seems to me to follow that we should be planning for the highest population densities which can reasonably be achieved without loss of an acceptable level of amenities. In housing, we should provide a range and variety appropriate to the age and income groups to be expected. Nothing about that sounds very revolutionary—unless you happen to check it against what much of our present planning and accessory regulation is doing.

One of the obstacles to success of planning (*local* planning, at any rate) is that it often serves too narrow a public in terms of both area and time. Thus it is common to find planning and its supporting regulations used to protect the present against the future, rather than to make way for it; to frame permanent future development patterns to fit a transitory taxation crazyquilt; to make housing and the servicing of housing as expensive as possible; to assure monotonous and wasteful uniformity in development; and to protect against difference.

A great deal of our planning is in accord with comprehensive zoning which has the wrong objectives.

To state the planner's problem (and an obstacle to successful planning) in another way, let's be democratic about it and go into as yet limited suburbia with a poll. "How large should lots and yards be? How expensive should houses be? What types of houses should be allowed?" Here are the answers. On lots and yards, 86.2 per cent vote for the same size as at present or somewhat larger. On housing costs, 89.3 per cent indicate that present levels or higher would be optimum. On types of housing, 88.4 per cent indicate only single-family detached. Several respondents note concern about townhouses and apartments, and particularly high-rise.

There is the suburban planner's mandate from the people who pay him to do long-range planning and to propose regulations and development policies. If he has any depth of historic perspective, he recognizes the dangers. If a poll had been taken in the same area a generation or two ago, the vote would have been overwhelming that everybody should live on a farm. Going back further, a plebiscite would have indicated that everybody should be Cucamonga Indians. In each case, the public concerned wasn't really giving much thought to the public that was coming, or assumed that in the normal order of things it would be identical in resources, tastes, and character to the public already there.

The planner, if he is a good one, knows that the rate of change is more rapid than ever before and is accelerating. He knows a number of things that should be done to make way for the future, but he has his mandate to protect the present against it, rather than to prepare for it intelligently. So there is the short-legged planner astride the high fence—which makes it more than a mere obstacle.

Serving the general public, the planner's supreme boss, isn't easy because the part of the general public which happens to be on the scene isn't much interested in what happens to the larger part of the general public which isn't there yet. *One of the defects of democracy is that the unborn can't vote.* The planner must plead their cause for them, and it isn't easy.

This brings us to the matter of the planner's other bosses. (The first, as we have seen, is the general public.) The second is the governing body, the elected representatives of the people. The third is the executive head of the government, the city or county manager or chief administrator. Then comes the planning commission, in most jurisdictions. And then there is the consideration that, to some extent at least, the good planner is his own boss.

This makes things a little complicated for the planner, particularly since the chain of command is frequently not clearly established. He knows that he is to work with the planning commission, and usually it is made clear that he is to work somehow under the chief executive, but he also finds quite often that he is called upon directly by the governing body. In a great many instances, it would be helpful to all concerned if the lines of authority were more firmly delineated.

The governing body is elected, and is supposed to be politically responsive. Like the planner, the governing body is presumed first and foremost to be serving the general public. Its proper function is to determine the best public policy and to establish it in the form of regulations, laws, budgets, and so on. As local government has evolved in this country, the legislative body is not supposed to be the executive arm or the judicial arm. In small cities and counties where the needs of government are relatively simple and the resources of government small, there still linger commission forms of government in which legislative and executive functions are combined, but the trend has been toward separation of function.

With separation of function, there has developed a move toward the use of trained specialists in the executive and administrative branch. City and county managers are increasingly persons who have been trained in this field and have served as interns after graduation. Planners should certainly be trained, experienced, and proven before they are placed in positions of responsibility. It would be difficult indeed to find valid reasons for not hiring a professional to do a professional job, either as city manager or as planner, if the primary objective is to secure efficient and economical public service. If the executive is a qualified executive and the planner is a qualified planner, and if the legislative body sets sound policy and leaves it to the executive and the planner to do their respective jobs, one of the principal obstacles to successful planned action has been removed.

Now what about the planning commission, the planner's fourth set of bosses? One thing planning commissions should not be expected to do—or at least should not be expected to do any longer than it takes to get a competent professional staff—is to render amateur judgments on relatively complex technical matters. Policy, yes. Determinations as to whether drainage for a 40-acre subdivision is adequate, no. If regulations are well-drawn, and if the planning staff has necessary technical ability or knows where to go to find out if it doesn't, the less the planning commission gets into details the better. One obvious obstacle to planning action in many cities and counties is the tendency to make big ones out of little ones to the point where we can't find time to deal properly with really large issues.

Who belongs on planning commissions?

The planning commission, like the planner, has a primary responsibility to promote and protect the general public interest. The first qualification for a planning board member should be that he will take a reasonably broad view of what the general public interest is, and will support intelligent action to promote and protect it.

I have seen efforts to assure appropriate representation by requiring that planning board members be representatives of specific interest groups—the apartment owners' association, the realtors, the merchants' association, the builders' council, land developers, and so on. This usually doesn't work out well, because their interests do not add up the general public interest. It has been said by unkind critics of this approach that wolves are being used to guard the sheep.

If planning is to move ahead and get things done, the planning board should be made up of people who are able to perceive the line at which public controls are essential and be ready to hold that line, but they should also be alert to the danger of regulation for regulation's sake.

If the governing body is willing to heed the advice of those it has employed and appointed to give advice, and if there is clear-cut governmental organization, with the governing body setting policy and adopting laws and the administrative arm carrying out policy and enforcing laws without political pressures for favoritism for individuals or groups, planned action will find fewer obstacles in its path.

"Planners should have to run for office . . ."

Someone recently sang the old refrain: "Planners should have to run for office." If not, why not? Here's why not:

The planner's job is not to run for office, or even to stay in an appointed office if straw-vote popularity polls are to influence his thinking. The planner's job is to a very considerable extent to give those who do run for office defense against the consequences of untrammelled democracy. Monuments to clamor may ensure reelection for an individual office-holder but wreck the city and the economy. Bread and circuses are popular, but make an insecure foundation for a lasting culture.

The prime function of the planner is to apply calm and disciplined reasoning in appraising probable results of courses of action or inaction. If this job is well done, an able political leader can turn it to good account, influencing the public so that wise actions become popular and unwise actions lose public support. If the job is poorly done, the political leaders and the public will be better off to ignore it.

But if the job is done well and unskilled politicians willfully ignore it to take "popular" actions leading to certain public disaster, they are in a poor position to insist that planners should join them, abandoning reason for popularity. What virtue has a democracy in which the voters are unenlightened and their elected leaders follow them?

There is, in our time, unlimited demand for carefully reasoned public policy of the kind which planning promotes, and for statesmen who are leaders rather than followers. The planner must be politically aware, but the public can ill afford to have planners who are primarily politicians. On the other hand, most politicians have neither temperament nor time to be planners.

When the planner runs for office, he has to that extent ceased to be a planner.

Defining planning and other more important things

When professional planners meet formally, it is customary to establish another committee to define planning. Countless committees of this kind have been formed. Many have reported. A few have reported results. The results are never satisfactory to everybody and seldom satisfactory to anybody (except in the case of committees of one).

Urban planning remains undefined in language having broad acceptance or real meaning. Planners do not universally insist that language must have real meaning, but even the most ornamental accumulations of vague verbiage have failed to produce consensus among them, nor is there prospect of agreement in the near future.

Some say the planning world is flat—that those who venture too far from its charted ways will be engulfed by statistical maelstroms, lured to disaster by ideological sirens, shrivel and die as foundation or federal nourishment is exhausted, fall off the edges into Hell, or become city managers. Others assert that the planning world is round, encompassing everything, and that the inclusive sphere is the true symbol of planning perfection.

In this medieval stage of planning, no man and certainly no committee is likely to come up with a meaningful definition of the field. Urban planning is a method to appraise, anticipate, and direct human behavior in the development of urban areas. This "definition," so loose as to be virtually meaningless, may yet (for its time) be tighter than it should be. Seeking a more precise definition from present planners is like asking the present astronauts to produce an atlas of Venus.

Current definitions of planning are, as the courts might say, void for vagueness. They are also vague for voidness, as any attempt to circumscribe vast areas of ignorance with language is bound to be.

At this point in the evolution of planning (if indeed it is evolving as a separate discipline rather than merging indistinguishably into the urban managerial process) it is far more important to know how to make what planning we have work, and to improve it, than to define it.

Little is known about planning as a working part of our form of government, and much of what is assumed to be known is open to question. Among many widely held assumptions needing reexamination are these:

Good planning results in sound development. Impartial examination of the evidence does not bear this out. The vast majority of urban areas having comprehensive plans (good, bad, or indifferent) are evolving in a manner which has little recognizable relation to the specifications and timing suggested by the plans. If plans are to be ignored, or carried out only in part (with other development aborting the effectiveness of the parts of the plan which were followed), the quality of the plan makes little difference.

Planning, in and of itself, results in nothing but planning. If action does not follow the planning, the effort is wasted. This is obvious, but the obvious is often overlooked by those who find it inconvenient. It is certainly overlooked by a great many cities which buy plans on the assumption that they will carry themselves out, and by a great many planners who sell plans to cities with foreknowledge that there is little chance that the cities will use them.

Planning results in able government. This assumption must be very widely held, and in high places. Else why the outpouring of federal funds to subsidize the kind of planning least likely to succeed (the master plan package with mumbles about stopping back some time if questions come up)?

Such plans, technical documents of considerable complexity, are being urged on cities which have done nothing to meet long-standing and obvious needs with obvious solutions. Such plans are being urged on cities whose elected and appointed officials would rate low on the most charitable literacy or reading comprehension tests. Such plans are being urged on officials who have been elected and reelected on promises to do as little as possible and to keep local taxes and utility charges at submarginal levels, and who are planning to run again (and will run successfully) on the same platform. In short, such plans are being urged on cities which are in very poor shape to use them. It must follow that someone, somewhere, believes that plans will *produce* the kind of government needed to carry them out.

Successful action programs based on planning require good government, but the planning does not create good government. If planning is part of the regular administrative process in a city with a competent manager whose judgment is trusted by a competent governing body, its chances for success are excellent. As planning is placed in less and less favorable governmental environment, its chances for success, or even survival, diminish.

There comes a point where it is obviously wasteful to sow planning unless the soil of local government is first improved and enriched. The basic problem in such circumstances is not absence of planning, but absence of suitable government. Nor are promissory notes in the form of Programs for Community Improvement sound evidence of anything but a desire to latch on to federal money.

Planning can't start too soon. This is another fallacy, if the objective of planning is an intelligent and continuing action program. As pointed out previously, there is little point in starting planning before local government is ready to use planning. Planning "adopted" on schedule to qualify for federal loans and grants may not only be ignored after adoption, but may condition the city against future planning.

Planning saves money. This assumption, trumpeted loudly and often, is misleading under a number of circumstances. Planning not used does not save money, but wastes it. The money invested in unused planning is certainly not saved, and quite frequently would have done the city a lot more good if invested in better local government—say trained city managers in cities which don't have one.

In cities which have been subsisting at submarginal levels of facilities and services and taxes and charges, there is frequently disillusionment with planning which has been guaranteed to save money when it turns out instead that carrying out the plans requires substantial expenditures—particularly when some of the money will have to be raised through increased local taxes or service charges.

Planning rarely reduces city expenditures to a level below pre-planning periods. It provides a guide for amount and timing of spending necessary to bring the city up to some sort of standards for the present and to prepare it for as much as can be foreseen of the future. It does not tell cities which have been spending practically nothing how to spend less, and cities which expect it to do so (as many apparently are led to believe it will) are hardly likely to use the plans or to develop a fondness for planning.

The need for finding out

If the observations above strike a responsive chord, it may be time to do something about it.

There is no allegation here that planning is no damned good. The point is that the results are not as good as they should be. Something is obviously wrong with the way we are going about planning, and it is past time for an agonizing reappraisal of federal, state, and local programs—particularly of federal programs, since they are stamping and molding local planning into a form which at best is no more successful than most of what went before and at worst is not as good.

We think that planning is being applied wholesale, as a patent medicine guaranteed to cure the urban patient of every conceivable disease at every stage of its development, with no diagnosis except that of course everybody needs planning, and with strong inference that planning is all they need.

We think considerably more attention should be given to diagnosis and prognosis, to determining whether cities are ready for planning or need something else first, to deciding what kind of planning is indicated and how and when it should be applied, and to finding out how best to ensure that urban areas with their multitudinous chronic ailments receive continuing treatment as they need it. In many cases, the treatment indicated might even be something other than a strong dose of planning.

It is not necessary for planning to stand still while it is being appraised—it is unquestionably doing a lot of good in some areas. But we do feel that it is past time to be finding out how it could be doing better in more areas.

Virgin territory

There is a fertile and unexploited field in a real study of the successes and failures of planning. So far as we know, no major and continuing investigation is under way to find out what kind of plans, in what kind of situations, are followed by action consistent with the plans. Conversely, what kind of plans, in what kind of situations, prove to be wasted efforts, achieve relatively limited results, or trigger reactions which damage both planning and the city involved. And in all cases, why?

It is suggested that in making this analysis, planners should stand aside. We are a prejudiced special interest group, quite possibly too limited in the scope of our experience and training to be competent to render an informed and unbiased opinion. This is a job for other kinds of experts, if they can be found, probably specialists in public administration, public law, political science, social behavior and social psychology, urban sociology, propaganda (by some other name, of course—information communications, public relations, or something palatable), and others competent to judge why planning so often falls short of guiding action as intended and why, in its relatively rare moments of success, it does its job so well.

It follows, of course, that when the comprehensive plan for comprehensive planning comes in, planners should be guided by it. If planners find that they cannot or will not be so guided, that the experts did not understand their problems, how they work, what they are trying to do with the means at their disposal, and why they hold sacred the things which they hold sacred, they will at least have a clue as to why cities sometimes cannot or will not be guided by the plans of the planners.

It seems likely that as the result of such an operation, planners, like cities, will find that they would profit more from continuing technical assistance than from a one-shot report. Certainly planners would find that their "comprehensive" planning is far from being comprehensive enough, that in their emphasis on plans for physical development they have failed to take many steps, to learn from many disciplines, which would increase the chances of successful action based on the planning, and would improve the validity of the planning itself.

We believe that an impartial appraisal would indicate that planning is poorly designed for its purpose—guiding action by nonplanners—because it is designed for the wrong purpose—preparation of a comprehensive plan for physical development which makes sense to the planner. To planners, the plan is too much an end, too little a means.

The only true measure of the success of planning is the amount and kind of action it induces, guides, or prevents. If this is accepted as the scale in which planning must be weighed, planning will broaden its horizons, its reach, and its effectiveness, and at the same time discover that it is not at the center of the universe. It will then be time to worry about defining planning. We will know enough to prepare a definition which means something.

The naked and dangerous men

A comfortable and well-worn set of ideas is more fiercely defended than any other possession of man—and for good reason. Ideas are hard to come by, and take a substantial part of a lifetime to match up in properly insulated contradictions. Most men would rather accept a prefabricated set than to try to turn out one of their own.

Once accepted with docility as a mass-produced gift from society, or in rarer cases painfully put together by the individual, any major alterations are difficult and suggestions for change meet vigorous opposition.

Teaching in youth, and less formal but no less effective methods for inducing imitation in later years, lead most men into groups in each of which the members wear common uniforms of thought and use common cliches for watchwords. There are many of these groups, differing between themselves in greater or smaller degree, but within themselves alike in that the members have closely parallel notions as to what makes their own universe tick and how to make certain improving adjustments if they had a mind to, and if the world were not so full of heel-dragging muddleheads. The unfailing token of membership is willingness to follow, and the nominal leaders are chosen because they will preserve, protect, and promote the accepted set of fixed ideas with strong and unyielding consistency, and without questioning.

Left alone, these clans are willing to leave alone, to drift in a

This article originally appeared in *Bair Facts,* published by Chandler-Davis Publishing Co., West Trenton, N.J. (1960). Reprinted by permission.

pleasant atmosphere of mutual admiration, petrifying their prejudices and hardening their armor of conformity. But in drifting, or because of it, such groups occasionally meet head on. There are only two alternatives, to fight or to think. The battle begins without perceptible pause. There is carefully rehearsed posturing in formal conflict. There is ritual shedding of synthetic blood. The hardened armor holds against the hardened armor. Then, at the sacred cocktail hour, both sides retire in good order, chanting hymns of victory.

Yet there are men, a diminishing few, who will not be molded and who will not follow blindly. They go their lonely and uncomfortable ways in mental nakedness, unprotected and unhampered by the conformity with which their years should have clothed them, poking and prying and shaking the established order into new forms. They practice thinking rather than acceptance. They arm themselves with keen and penetrating queries, and when they attack the carnage is fearful.

If preservation of what is, or in some cases revival of what was, is a desirable objective, these thinking nonconformists must be strait-jacketed into harmlessness. If rapid and orderly improvement based on application of intelligence is the major goal, their ranks should be swelled.

There was a time when most planners were among the naked and dangerous men. Now there is evidence that large numbers are forming into societies for uncritical repetition of tradition-endorsed incantations, performance of fixed and formal rituals, and increasingly frequent orgies of pursuing the same exhausted ideas around in circles.

Planning the gross society

They were always having grand tournaments there at Camelot, and very stirring and picturesque and ridiculous human bullfights they were, too, but just a little wearisome to the practical mind.

Mark Twain, *A Connecticut Yankee in King Arthur's Court.*

On January 22-25 there came together in Washington, D.C., in order to frame a more perfect union of policies on federal action concerning metropolitan problems, some 150 of the nation's top professional planners. This was too many.[1]

Urban America's problems get bigger and more complicated. The federal government is setting out on massive campaigns to do something about all of them. It has a lot of help, thinking up things to do, from local governments which haven't found it politically expedient to act closer to home, and see an easy way to get off the hook. The circuitous workings of the present form of our democracy require passing the buck as far as possible, with discounts chipped off along the way and directives added on to make up the weight. Federal programs are the ultimate expression of this principle.

This article first appeared in *Landscape Architecture Quarterly,* July 1965. Reprinted by permission.

1. Entitled "Government Relations and Planning Policy," the conference was under the auspices of the American Institute of Planners.

To make sure that everything is covered, there are often several programs in several agencies (or even in the same agency) for doing about the same thing, but in different ways and with different proportions and forms of federal contributions and different local requirements and restrictions. Free enterprise has taught democratic federal government the virtues of competition, giving local governments multiplying opportunities for comparison shopping.

One way of looking at all this is: "We can use a lot of action fast, even if we make some mistakes. Maybe it's time to make mistakes of action instead of continuing the mistakes of inaction. If we can't afford mistakes, who can?"

What brought the planners together (physically) was that federal government seems to be going on without them. Obviously the Great Society must be a Planned Society. Planners accepted this conclusion with enthusiasm, assuming that they would be the master craftsmen. Overlooked was the possibility that the Great Society might become impatient with the profound debates which preface even simple decisions of professional planners, make off with the tools, and start building on a do-it-yourself basis. Greatness can become grossness.

Dr. Robert Weaver stated the problem in most unprofessional terms: "If planners are to perform a role, they will have to perform. We need a type of planning which is more than an art-for-art's-sake process. What matters is what happens. We have moved from being against sin (the absence of planning). We have not come to support of Motherhood (production)."

Other federal officials urged with one voice that myriad municipal, county, special-district, and special-authority programs in metropolitan areas (plus those in the rural fringes of metropolitan areas) should be bundled together under a coordinating central agency representing all metropolis, instead of running off in all directions to do everything, including undoing each other. Metropolis should have clear, coordinated policy, and an administrative structure to carry it out.

In response, local planners urged with one voice that the 43 programs in 13 federal departments and agencies which are engaged in helping metropolitan areas (plus others in other departments and agencies engaged in helping rural development) should be bundled together under a coordinating central agency representing federal government as a whole, instead of running off in all directions to do everything, including undoing each other. The nation should have clear, coordinated policy, and an administrative structure to carry it out.

Each group expressed willingness to advise the other as to what it should do.

Ten proposed position statements, averaging 15 pages in length and usually beginning about page five, came in for discussion in this three-day intensive effort. Most of them contained provocative ideas, and one or two were so written that it was relatively easy to find out what the ideas were.

The theme which semi-emerged from several of the papers is that confused but active federal government, lacking any clear policy, should tell weak and inactive state governments without any clear policy what they must do to serve unidentified national interest, including becoming active. Weak and inactive state governments without clear policy and without much interest in urban affairs are to leap into action, prodded by the federal goad, and tell regional quasi-governments which may or may not exist what they should do to serve unidentified state and national interests. Regional interests, learning what the "consensus" is, must then pass the word to county and municipal governments. Municipal governments are to "sublimate" most of their planning functions to county or higher levels and concern themselves, at least temporarily, with what the cynical will call pansy-planting, secure in the knowledge that they have been promoted to the top of the pyramid. Later, if state or federal interest in an aesthetically pleasing urban landscape becomes greater than local, local planning might be promoted off the top of the pyramid entirely.

Weak as municipal planning efforts have been, in sum they have accomplished a few things. The planning-from-the-top-down pitch got a good try in the thirties and fizzled out. The current availability of computers doesn't change the picture. True, we have a federal form of government. But it is also a democratic form of government, and as long as it remains so, authoritarian dictation from the upper levels will often be greeted with Bronx cheers.

There may be a more practical approach. Suppose we forget about preservation and improvement of American federalism in its present form, and leave artificial insemination of state governments to another time. Instead, perhaps we could start by recognizing that planning *purposes* are continuing compromises between national, regional, state, subregional, metropolitan, county, municipal, and submunicipal interests. We would like to see those compromises reached in a reasoned manner and in the democratic tradition. It may not be possible to have both reason and democracy, but we can try, as we have been trying. It would be helpful if we could avoid having local planning methods, objectives, or scope determined by a remote and confused federal bureaucracy, using friendly persuasion involving agreements to return part of our money if we will do it their way.

Continuing this minority view, having arrived at our compromises, we might do better to proceed to act by *whatever* means seem indicated, starting from the bottom and working up. If metropolitan governments best suit metropolitan purposes, establish them, whether they irritate county and municipal office-holders or not. This country did not become what it is by adherence to traditional governmental forms, but by departure from them.

Improving community planning: *some suggestions to the Chamber of Commerce*

In sharing with you my limited knowledge and boundless ignorance, I probably won't do you as much harm as someone with all the answers. I am deeply concerned about the number of planners who think they have them—and are eager to write their convictions into mandatory requirements in connection with federal aid.

Federal aid in planning matters (and in actions growing out of planning) is increasingly dominant on the local scene. It is a device for getting part of your money back if you will (1) put up as local share what it would have cost to do the job for yourself in the first place and (2) do it the federal way. In local planning, the federal contribution helps cover the inflated planning costs resulting because there is federal aid.

Why is there increasing federal dominance of local planning and other local affairs? There is an easy (and erroneous) answer: It comes from a "do-gooder" bureaucracy with empire-building socialist tendencies, pushed by executives motivated more by political expediency than national interest, and backed by a legislative branch with enough members aiding the drift to the left so that the rest are powerless to stop it. This rousing indictment has just enough half-truths to convince the unthinking.

Before endorsing this easy answer, meditate on this question: "Who passed the buck?"

If we meditate long enough and honestly enough, a still small voice may say to us, "We did." And in our hearts, we'll know that's right.

Federal programs in urban affairs have not luxuriated as a result of Communist conspiracy, nor through unaided efforts of a bunch of empire-building federal welfare workers. Federal aid has grown primarily in response to calls for help from local governments—city, county, and state—and from the great nongovernments of metropolitan areas. These are the governments (and nongovernments) closest to us, "our" governments. Why do they run to Washington with their problems? Again meditation, and again the small voice, "Because we chased them that way."

Some will say, "No! That's not true! We didn't do anything." And, again, that's right. That's what chased them to Washington—we didn't do anything. In some cases we did worse than nothing.

Mounting population (total, child, and automobile) creates mounting *local* demands for governmental facilities and services. Mounting abuses in the way we use urban land lead to mounting *local* demands for land-use regulation—zoning and all the rest of it. Mounting local blight and health hazards lead to *local* demands that something be done about it. What have we done *locally* to meet the crisis?

Have we made major and continuing efforts to improve local government? Have we done what we should to assure continuing, sound, practical planning to appraise present and future problems, and to weave the best solutions into a program for action which provides maximum satisfaction of public needs at minimum expenditure of tax dollars? Have we done what we should to overhaul our miserably obsolescent and inequitable systems for deriving local revenues needed to meet local needs?

On the whole, we have not. We have let things drift, each defending his own interests, few concerned about the general interest. When crisis reaches critical mass, we blow what money is available in haphazard crash solutions, some of which cause more trouble than they cure. We rush to the ramparts to vote against bond issues and to hold the line against increases in local taxes.

We pit local government which is often undermanned, underequipped, underpaid, and undertrained in a struggle against complex and increasing problems. We have set local government astride a fence which keeps rising and told it to make itself as comfortable as possible. Need for action increases faster than local revenues. We have spent or pledged all the local funds which could be scraped together, and have done it in ways which are often foolish from a fiscal angle and misguided in purpose. We have resolutely declared that we can't raise more money locally—or won't, which is usually closer to the truth.

So (in a spirit of political escapism) the city goes to the county for help, and soon the county finds itself in the same shape. Cities and counties join forces and go to the state (taking with them the metropolitan areas). The state joins the parade. Where next? You know where next.

Locally, we "can't afford" good government, we "can't afford" good planning, we "can't afford" to pay for schools and water and sewers and highways and public buildings and open space and slum clearance and other improvements, facilities, and services which the public demands. So *we* pass the buck. Nobody wrestles us for it.

In passing the buck, we give up local control. From here on out, if we fill out all the forms on schedule, do as we are told, and mark all documents to show that they are financially aided through a federal grant, we get enough of our money back from the feds to do some of the things we "couldn't afford" to do with our money if we had to raise it at home. Administrative overhead, red tape, and odd-ball requirements make these things far more expensive than if we had done them without sending our dollars on the Grand Tour. But now, somehow, we *can* afford them. We won! And now we dislike the results of our victory.

If people don't earn the kind of government they want, they are very likely to get the kind of government they deserve.

How do we recover local control? The answers are clear and painful. We must take local initiative, recognize local responsibility for meeting a broader range of local needs, and be willing to pay more of the local bill with dollars which have not been eroded away by excessive travel.

What has this to do with improving community planning? A great deal. Unless there is mature and able local government and sound local financing, local planning isn't likely to accomplish much beyond producing artistic reports. We aren't after improved local planning as a decorative art. We are after a kind of planning which not only indicates what action *should* be taken but which fits into the administrative and legislative structure of government in such a way that the action *is* taken.

Here are some specific recommendations:

1. Build better local government. Get people to run for office who will represent the public interest rather than their own, and represent it ably and well. See that they get elected. Work with them after they are elected.

As to staff, push for trained, intelligent administrators, pay them well, and provide them with the help, equipment, and money needed to do their jobs. And work with them after they are appointed.

In both cases, keep abreast of what is going on, help when help is needed, and don't demand personal favors. If local government grants you favors, it is very likely to grant favors against you to somebody else. Demand equitable treatment. Don't demand preferred treatment.

2. Build local fiscal responsibility. Your local government should have, in clear form, a statement as to how much present and near-future income is from local sources, how much from nonlocal sources, by category. It should have a report on how local revenues are raised and prospects for the future. It should have a report on existing commitments against present and future income, by kind. It should have a budget which means something this year, and tentative budgets for several years ahead. As part of that budget, there should be capital improvements budgeting, by item, for at least five years ahead.

This is fiscal planning. It is of at least parallel importance with physical planning, but normally it does not receive as much attention. We plan for physical development but we don't plan how to pay for it, which is one of the reasons for the march on Washington.

In many localities, it will be found that finance is on a haphazard, catch-as-catch-can basis, that revenue production is a crazy quilt of inequitable expedient piled on expedient, with sources for extraction selected on the basis of political defenselessness. Fiscal reform should seek order and equity.

3. As to physical planning, bring it home. Planning for your community should be a continuing activity of a competent staff employed by your community. There may be times when consultants will be helpful in getting the planning apparatus set up and started in the right direction, or in doing specialized jobs for which your staff is not particularly well qualified, but you should set up and support a good local staff, and when consultants are called in you should be sure that they work closely with the local staff.

Don't expect a plan prepared by a consultant to do you much good unless your local staff has played an important part in making it, your local government has been exposed to it in digestible chunks, and it is understood and accepted as something to keep current and working. In many cities, the principal function of expensive plans is to protect from dampness the old tax records piled on top of them.

4. Federal aid for planning. If federal programs fit your need and your pace well, take advantage of them, but be sure that they don't take advantage of you. Read the fine print in the contract. If you find (as is entirely possible) that in order to get federal funds for (a) you are required to commit yourself to (b) through (z) and it is not timely to proceed on (b) through (z), forget it. If you find that the red tape will run up your costs to the point where the net gain is negligible, forget it. Above all, don't get in a position where continuation of local planning depends to a major degree on federal aid.

One other note on this score. If federal requirements don't make sense, and you can prove it, argue about it. My limited experience with the feds leads me to believe that they will listen to reason, if the reasoning is sound. Very often, they are just as bewildered as the rest of us. And although it sometimes doesn't appear that way, the federal government is just as much our government as local government, and we should be just as much concerned about improving it.

5. Start from now and work forward. You will get arguments on this. Many professional planners (staff or consultant) feel that the thing to do is to prepare a plan for 20 years out in the future and work back from it. This gives them a couple of years to figure out what things will be like in 1985 before coming to grips with more pressing problems.

I am not saying that it isn't important to look at the long-range future in planning. What I am saying is that we can't predict in detail with any usable degree of precision, and that many spectacularly expensive efforts in this direction have proved to be a form of busy-work. Avoid analysis ad absurdum, particularly where the end result is bound to be cockeyed.

One objective in starting from now and working forward is development of community muscle and community morale. If there are things which plainly need doing, try doing them—the simplest ones first. If they can be done while the comprehensive plan is being developed to detail and relate less obvious needs, it will be easier to move in on more complex operations. Until we can move ahead on the simpler things which obviously need doing, of what use is a comprehensive plan listing other things to do?

6. About pigs and planning. Community planning should not mean to you a device for shouldering everyone else aside to get what you want—forcing a high-rise apartment to locate where it doesn't belong because you don't want it near your house or forcing development which gives you maximum speculative advantage (but doesn't belong there) into someone else's neighborhood.

Nor should "community" planning in these times of massive population growth be a means for building a wall at accidental city lines for the purpose of containing uses with maximum tax or other advantages, and dumping problems on the neighbors outside. Our cities grow together into megalopolitan clusters. Unless you are willing to look at the *whole* community—not merely the narrow boundaries of your city—someone else will, and you may not like it.

In conclusion, I make this plea. You are community leaders. As leaders, lead! You run your own businesses. You plan for your own businesses. If your community (the whole community, not merely your city) is important to you, give it your leadership, your knowledge of sound administrative and fiscal practice, your knowledge of planning. So conduct yourselves that when your community needs help, it turns to you instead of to Washington, and when it does turn to you, strengthen it so that it will be more self-reliant in the future.

More than two thousand years ago, Pericles said in one paragraph more than I have said in 20 minutes, and his words make an excellent closing statement: "Athens expects every citizen to take an interest in public affairs. We do believe in knowledge as a guide to action: we have the power of thinking before we act, and of acting too. I would have you fix your eyes upon Athens day by day, contemplate her potentiality, not merely what she is but what she has the power to be. Reflect that her glory has been built up by men who know their duty and had the courage to do it. Make them your examples and learn from them."

Hold up on all that planning jazz

> The reason that I am writing you is that ——— does not have a planning department and the present mayor and, in fact, most of the business leaders are against the city spending money for a full-time planner. The city several years ago did have a planner who was here two years at a salary of less than $10,000 and when he was offered a higher paying position he took it. So the feeling is that if we acquire another planner the same thing could happen and we are only wasting our money.
>
> I have been trying to campaign for a city planner, and I am writing you in an effort to secure information which I might present which would aid me in selling a need for a city planner. . . . Unless there is a city planner who will see that plans are carried out, then the whole idea of planning is put on the shelf as you so well stated about the master plan to protect old tax records from dampness.

The City of ——— has 65,000 people, marked down from 110,000 when it was capital of a type of industry which became footloose. In addition to having no planner, it has no city manager, and all the earmarks of struggling with a jealously-guarded small-town form of government long after it has outgrown it (including an extraordinarily high number of municipal employees for its size).

In such a situation, the best advice we can give is to hold up on all that planning jazz. Take the money, add some more to it, hire the best city manager you can find, and see to it that he is allowed to manage. Push for better, more efficient local government, improved tax records and revenue production systems, a more careful analysis of where money comes from and where it goes. Insist on sound annual budgeting and capital improvement budgeting for several years ahead. As you make progress toward these objectives, you will get planning, and you will get it in its proper place, as part of general and continuing operation of good government, in an administrative environment where it can work efficiently. It may or may not be *called* planning, but this doesn't make any difference.

The alternative course is like forcing a highly automated shoe machine on a bunch of unprepared handicraft cobblers. Forcible injection of a lonesome and unwanted staff planner into a hostile and inept local government, with instructions to make plans and see that they are carried out, will once again demonstrate to the locals that planning is no damned good.

Planners, from locals right on up to the feds, generally have yet to learn that planning is just a little piece of good government. It won't make good government, and it won't work without good government. Neither a 701 package plan nor a planner in the house is likely to amount to much unless local government has reached the stage where planning is accepted, welcomed, and a routine part of team play.

Who needs research?

At the outset, I suppose we are in agreement that the prime function of a university is to educate. To the extent that education and its related activities can serve communities facing increasingly complex governmental problems, a secondary function, particularly for a tax-supported university, is to provide such service, so long as it does not detract from the primary purpose. In our time, education at the community level is one of the crying needs, so that service and education are complementary rather than conflicting functions.

Evolution and improvement of new techniques for coping with governmental problems far outstrips willingness to use them. The provocative topic assigned might infer that I am anti-research. This is not the case. My position is that we have become so research-oriented that we are neglecting application of what we know and what we are learning. It is time to establish better balance between research and action, and there is no better place to do it than in an institution proposing to establish a new community service program, and which is open minded about what it should be.

In the competitive marketplace, there is a moving balance between pure research, research applied to product creation and improvement, and sales. It is true that in an economy of abundance, advertising can promote, at least briefly, sales of products which are defective or

This paper was originally presented at an education conference at the University of South Florida, March 1967.

relatively worthless, but in the long run, given reasonable advertising support, we can assume for the sake of this argument that the best product at the best price will be the best compromise for both the producer and the consumer.

In the government marketplace, the situation is otherwise. As institutions of higher learning tend to depend increasingly on grants and direct payments for requested services, and proportionately less on assured revenue, endowment, and tuition sources, research and professional service tends to become oriented toward what there are grants-in-aid of, or direct payments for. This establishes an attitudinal pattern on the part of university staffs which may lead in the direction of more of the same.

Some years ago, communities could ask for advice from a university and get it—a statement as to what seemed to be the best way to attack a problem, based on the accumulated knowledge of what was known about it. If field work was required, there might be a charge for expenses.

Given the same situation now, rumors have spread that the answer might run along these lines: "The problem itself is complicated and difficult, but it cannot be considered in isolation. It must be viewed in the context of community governmental structure and resources and the regional physico-socioeconomic framework. Parameters* of research, involving that which can be computerized and other, appear in the attached outline. If financial support as suggested in the outline is forthcoming, (a) the staff will work on the problem, or (b) the professor answering the letter will take on the assignment as a quasi-independent consultant. If the city is interested, we can suggest federal, foundation, and other sources of support which might be explored (some of which will require as a condition local action which has nothing to do with the problem at hand, but probably should be taken anyway). If financial arrangements can be consummated" (a term which I hesitate to use, but which seems richly appropriate) "help is on the way. If not, staff commitments and budget limitations are such that we regret to inform you that we cannot provide assistance at this time."

At this point, local government often says to hell with it and

*Parameter is a term which sounds more scholarly than perimeter and is therefore misused to mean the same thing by professionals indicating to laymen how complicated everything is. In mathematics, the term means an arbitrary constant characterizing by each of its particular values some particular member of a system of expressions, curves, surfaces, functions, etc., or it can mean some other things, none of which are likely to do us much good here.

bumbles on as best it can. Or it may take the bait. The bait is usually worth taking only if the work is well and economically done and if local government is well and competently staffed and has an able legislative body selflessly dedicated to broad public interest and supported by a citizenry willing to take the long view. It is probably safe to say that something less than a majority of current situations meet these tests.

Consider the following not-altogether-apocryphal anecdote. A small city had a drainage problem in its downtown area. It did not wish to spend $100,000 of local money to cure it. If the main highway through town could be divided into a one-way pair, the State Highway Department would divert the water through highway-related storm drainage, flooding the Negro area instead of downtown. This was the main advantage indicated by proponents, but there were others. Heavy traffic would run six blocks out of its normal course to go through a residential section within 800 feet of downtown, benefitting the downtown merchants. The new frontage would for the most part be zoned commercial, benefitting the ex-mayor (who owned a tract adjacent to the proposed route and was one of the strongest supporters), increasing the tax base, balancing commercial development already decaying along the existing route, and making it possible for occupants of residences to sell out at inflated prices when their property became insufferable to live in.

But there were disadvantages, too. It would be necessary to buy right-of-way for access to the route (which could otherwise be widened along existing streets by cutting back front yards). Here the advantages of a federal program became attractive. To get the necessary federal aid, it was necessary to prepare and proceed on a Workable Program, involving planning, zoning, subdivision regulation, codes, code enforcement, establishment of an advisory planning commission, and establishment of a committee to advise the planning commission and insure citizen participation. Done.

For a year, there was intensive action on planning and the preparation of codes. The planning was designed for continuity—for the first time there were good city maps, related to aerial photography at the same scale. There were land-use maps and maps on property values and condition of property, neighborhood analyses, a major street plan, a land-use plan, a CBD plan, a utilities plan, a park and recreation plan—the works. A new zoning ordinance was drafted and passed, with alterations to suit the requirements of the ex-mayor whose property adjacent to the proposed branch of the new highway had been indicated as residential rather than commercial, since it was across the street from the school. The alteration was done by the planning commission rather than the professional advisor. The ex-mayor was on the planning commission, and felt entitled to some recognition for his services. He voted for the change, which made it unanimous.

Subdivision regulations were also drafted and passed, with no substantial changes because no one on the planning commission or the city council had any land they wanted to subdivide.

In their eagerness to qualify for federal funds for right-of-way acquisition to enable the state to mislocate the highway to divert the storm water from downtown to the Negro area and benefit the ex-mayor and the merchants by bringing in traffic to produce trade, city council had agreed to adopt a housing code by a certain date as part of the Workable Program. This blew it.

One of the council members was a substantial owner of property for the housing of the deprived, and doing well by adding to their deprivation. (Afterward he left town, assisted by the sale of his home at a handsome profit to an industry which appreciated his assistance in fighting annexation, but this was too late.) The city attorney was also benefitting extensively from family holdings of property in the less-exclusive sector of the city. The editor of the local paper, while not a slum owner, was of that persuasion which would welcome addition of John Birch headquarters to the local scene except for a suspicion that that organization was riddled with Communists.

When the housing code, a watered-down version of a simplified draft of a model code for small cities, was proposed for passage, the full front page of the local weekly departed widely from the practice of separating editorial opinion from news and made it apparent that the rankest form of socialism impended, threatening the comfort of ancient and lovable widows who would be thrown out of their lifetime homes because they couldn't afford the onerous improvements demanded in a monstrous theoretical fabrication of an obvious pinko. The city attorney found the proposed housing code legally reprehensible.

City council, influenced by the newspaper spread and led by the member most qualified to judge the influence of the proposed code on the part of the public interest he championed, voted a vigorous no in spite of support from the Garden Club and the League of Women Voters.

That's been several years ago, and that was the end of planning or any other formal continuing efforts for improvement. When last seen, the maps, studies, and plans were in a closet in the fire department.

The county put up the money to buy right-of-way. Nobody did anything about relocating the people in the houses involved, but maybe it wasn't necessary. The state highway department refused to put the road there anyway. As for the downtown drainage problem, there was a compromise solution. Now the stores are flooded only half as often. Nobody seems at all interested in reviving planning; it upsets too many applecarts. About the only thing remaining from the effort is the zoning ordinance, which thrives on variances which aren't quite what the state legislation envisioned, spot changes, and other curious adaptations to the local situation.

What I have said is an effort to set a realistic background for discussion of a program with a potential for maximum utility the way things are. There is a question as to whether democracy at any level, and particularly at the local level, is ready for the managerial revolution. There is also some question as to whether the managerial revolution is altogether ready for government, but certainly we know *how* to improve on our present performance. The basic problem, for now, is getting more of the improvements accepted.

Most of our communities are not prepared in their legislative bodies, their administrative staffing, or their citizenry to take advantage of what can be done to solve existing problems and reduce those which are emerging. (Certainly few are ready to take, digest, and profit from the highly formalized prescriptions which come with federal aid programs.) Two needs are clearly undersupplied:

One is education—of elected officials, of administrators, and of citizenry. This includes education of students within the university—who will inevitably be citizenry, and may become administrators and elected officials—as well as persons who have left the halls of learning. (In the long run, it will be the education of the students which will have the greatest effect. In the short haul, we must do what we can.)

For nonstudents, emphasis should be on short courses. Most short courses could be held at a university, allowing for more extensive use of exhibits than would be the case where the courses were held in the field. One innovation which might be helpful would be issuance of study materials and assignments well before the short course meeting to maximize discussion rather than presentation during the sessions. A failing of many short courses is that the instructors tell what they want to tell, but the students don't have a chance to find out many of the things they want to know.

As a related function, it would be most helpful to have correspondence courses in fields where more intensive preparation or retraining is necessary. Correspondence training would be easy to supplement by visits to the institution and by visits from instructors to locations where they could make on-the-job observations and suggestions.

As to preparation of students for useful careers, one of the great gaps in the labor supply for urban government, and particularly for the small cities which are numerically in the majority among urban governments, is the generalist. In the nature of things, the kind of generalist I am talking about should probably be primarily oriented toward administration, but his training should not be merely as a city manager. He should know enough about city planning to do some of it, to appraise planning needs, to get planning done by the under-used device of volunteer efforts, to contract wisely for planning services, and to assure that planning is continuous. He should know enough about economic development to provide guidance and leadership in this field, and to fight off ill-advised proposals. He should know enough about practical politics so that he can improve them by boring from within, so that he doesn't get fired for the wrong reasons, and so that if he does get fired for the wrong reasons, he can pull down the pillars of the temple, if the situation warrants it, and take a few Philistines with him.

In essence, we are talking about managers for small cities who can do far more than manage—managers who can provide broad leadership. The small city can't afford a manager *and* a planning director *and* an economic development specialist, much as it needs the services of all three. But it can make the manager's job financially attractive if the manager is all three.

Production of such generalists would require building a university staff and curriculum in municipal administration, planning, and economic development. Initially, this staff could be small. Later, as experience indicates areas of need, staff could be increased to the point where there might be full-scale intensive training of local government administrators, urban planners, and economic development specialists. In such an academic environment, the generalists would take introductory courses in several fields, the specialists would go on to advanced courses.

This kind of education is one of the two needs indicated. The other is something which might be called an urban extension service, similar to the agricultural extension operation in many ways. If you want to quibble, this too could be called an educational function, but it is a different type. This division would be responsible for providing information and leadership for off-campus work in cities and counties, and for establishing and maintaining a rapid question and answer service. In the nature of things, staff would overlap and might almost entirely duplicate that for academic training, and the work would reinforce and benefit from the academic resources. The generalists mentioned earlier can hardly be expected to be as proficient in each of the fields involved as specialists in any of them, but back at the alma mater there is specialized information and advice for generalists who get beyond their depth. For the community just awakening (or needing to be awakened) to the need for improvement in government, there is promotional service geared to its level of evolution. For cities and counties where do-it-yourself volunteer activities can be encouraged, guidance is at hand.

(The do-it-yourself approach is much neglected of late, but we are coming back to it in our foreign aid programs and may learn from that in our domestic programs. The high school civics class or the Junior League, given guidance, can do about 80 per cent of the local research and map-coloring required for planning as well as a full member of AIP, at considerably less expense, and with considerably more local impact. This form of local participation is different from setting up mandatory committees composed of citizens who aren't sure what they are supposed to do and exposing them briefly to a plan constructed somewhere else.)

In a good many cases, the academic program and the service program would dovetail by using students in field work under careful supervision on projects on which this intermediate-level expertise is needed, and the experience would benefit the students.

The combination of the urban extension program for stimulating and assisting improvement in local government, resident leadership from trained generalists, and the back-up and reference service available from the combined operation, should go far to assist in solution of local problems *beginning from where they are,* and applying what we know now. From this, research needs will appear in profusion, we will know who needs it, and it will be used as it comes off the assembly line rather than shelved for possible application somewhere, sometime.

As a closing practical note, it should be easier to "sell" research with demonstrated imminent need and purpose and broad immediate application than much of that which is now being supported by federal, foundation, and other funds. But the research would evolve from requirements of the action program rather than dominating academic activity as an end in itself.

". . . and a little child shall lead them"

This is all I can do for a little boy I never saw, and now will never see. The day before he had a wonderful party. He blew out both candles at once, and laughed, and was so joyful about his toys and so full of life that his four older sisters and his mother and father and his grandma and grandpa together couldn't have kept him still a minute if they had wanted to.

He's still now.

At first, from the broken voice over the phone, we didn't know just how it had happened, but we did know what had happened, because it has happened too often before: "A car . . . he was *such* a sweet little boy . . . and when Betty came back from the hospital, she held out empty arms . . . he had so much fun at his party yesterday . . . a broken back and a broken leg and his brain—the doctor said it was just as well . . . services Wednesday morning, but you'd better not try to come, it's so far . . . he had such fun . . . no, thanks, there's nothing you can do."

There's nothing we *can* do—now—for Buzz Bryan, who was two years old. He ran out between parked cars, and the driver couldn't stop in time. But the driver was just incidental.

We killed this child. We killed him by our failures, and he died for our sins—for the things we have done which we ought not to have done, and for the things we should have done, but did not do.

This article originally appeared in *Bair Facts,* published by Chandler-Davis Publishing Co., West Trenton, N.J. (1960). Reprinted by permission.

This little boy did not need to be smashed by an automobile, and we can, *if we will,* keep other children from dying the same way. As humans, we should. As citizens, we should. As parents, or grandparents or aunts or uncles, we should. (And those of us who call ourselves planners certainly should.) " . . . a comprehensive plan designed to promote and protect the public health, safety, comfort, convenience and general welfare."

This is not merely a plea for more "Drive Safely and Protect our Children" signs, or for lower speed limits, or for more traffic cops. Nor is it a meaningless statement that children should not be allowed on the streets. We must plan and act to keep children and automobile traffic separated, and we must work at it as though the lives of our own children depended on it. *Some of them do!*

We can design minor streets in subdivisions and residential areas to discourage through traffic, and to hold down driving speeds. We can separate major streets from residential developments in our planning of new cities or reworking of old, and we can provide buffer strips or other insulating devices where such thoroughfares skirt residential areas.

We can discourage residences in commercial and industrial districts.

If there are to be sidewalks in residential areas, and particularly in new subdivisions, we can run them down back lot lines rather than at the curb. Only half as much sidewalk is required, and crossings are in the middle of the block, where there are only two ways to look for traffic. A mid-block sidewalk provides the paved play area which children on wheels will seek somewhere, and it puts this center of attraction where mothers can watch it from the windows of kitchens and utility rooms.

We can provide back-yard play areas and block-scale playlots (and if they are combined with mid-block sidewalks they will be easy to oversee and irresistible to children).

We can provide playgrounds and playfields away from the streets, preferably tied in with schools and parks to make supervision and management easier and more effective.

We can make all planned play areas, from those in back yards to the great playfields in parks, so much fun that kids would rather play there than anyplace else.

We can require off-street parking in residential districts, and we can prohibit parking at the curb. "The child darted out from behind a parked car, and the driver. . . . " How many times will it happen?

"No structure, wall, planting, or other impediment to visibility between the heights of two feet and ten feet shall be erected, planted, maintained or allowed to grow at any intersection of streets, or of streets and driveways, within a triangular area described as follows: . . . "

We can lay out streets and locate schools so that school-bound automobiles are concentrated on major traffic-ways. Streets designed as minor streets should not be laid out in such a way as to encourage their use as important automobile routes to schools. But minor streets and walkways, in combination, should form a short, convenient, and attractive way of access for children, afoot or on bicycles. The long and short of it is that automobiles headed for school should go *around* residential areas, and children headed for school on foot or on bicycles should go *through* residential areas.

These things, and dozens of other common-sense things, we can do if we will. This kind of planning is a matter of life or death.

Buzz, that's about all your Uncle Fred can do, now, and it's too little, and it's too late, and one "No Parking" sign would have done a lot more good. This doesn't help you, but it might help some other child. I'll think of you whenever I work with the people called planners, and with all the other people trying to make their cities better and safer. Telling them about you may help them the way it will help me. Maybe you've taught us all something even though you were only two years old.

Your picture on the Christmas card was lovely. I wish I could have known you. I wish I had seen your face when you blew out the two candles. Most of all, I wish we hadn't failed you, so that you'll never blow out three.

We'll try to do better, Buzz.

Chapter 2

Planning and the general welfare

Comprehensive planning, zoning, and the welfare of metropolis

"I am not enhanced by the abracadabra phrase, 'in accordance with a comprehensive plan,' " says a letter from eminent planning-law specialist Richard R. Babcock. "What is your definition of comprehensive plan? Please don't end with a reference to 'desires and goals of the community.' Is it sufficient that the plan accurately reflect these 'desires and goals' if they are self-centered, and bear no relationship to interests of other communities in the metropolitan area?

"Is a 'plan' still valid in a democratic society if, in fact, it is intended primarily to build a Chinese wall around the community to avoid or mitigate any unfortunate consequence of the exploding metropolis? Can a community reasonably state in a comprehensive plan that it would totally exclude all trailer parks; totally exclude all 10,000 square foot lots, even with sewer and water; and totally exclude all nursing homes and summer camps for retarded children?"

Zoning, supposed to be in accordance with comprehensive plans, is attempting with some success in some areas to do all the things Babcock mentions and more. It is time to firm up thinking so that proposals can be matched against solid policy and judged as to whether they are right, wrong, or ridiculous. At present there is uncertainty among planners and in the courts. Plans show it. Judicial decisions show it.

To streamline discussion, begin with the assumption that a comprehensive plan, and the zoning ordinance presumably adopted in accordance with it, is intended to promote the general welfare. In what follows, the term "general welfare" is intended to include without specific restatement: health; safety; morals; provision of light and air; "facilitation of adequate provision" of transportation, water, sewerage, schools, parks, open space, etc.; public comfort and convenience; urban amenities; urban aesthetics; appropriate urban design; and all the decorative language commonly added to convince courts which now seldom need convincing that the general welfare is very broad indeed.

How do we understand the words "comprehensive planning for the general welfare"? This is a keystone phrase. What should these words come to mean in a period of rapid change in which more and more of the national population lives in metropolitan areas? There is substantial evidence that we don't fully understand the phrase now and aren't sure what it should mean in the future.

The word "comprehensive" is presumptuously excessive in degree, although somewhat less arrogant than the term "Master" which it has come to replace. By no stretch of the imagination can present or probable future planning be considered comprehensive in terms of subject matter, and even metropolitan planning is now rarely even approximately comprehensive in terms of the area for which plans should be made if essential expansion and inter-urban relationships are to be considered. The prospect of megalopolis shrinks current planning efforts even further.

Planners have been unable to agree upon a definition of the words "comprehensive plan," or indeed of the term "planning."

For the moment, it is necessary to let "comprehensive plan" stand uncertainly as representing an organized effort to dovetail public and private actions in fields we can't as yet completely number or identify in order to reach a variety of objectives, many of which have not as yet been clearly defined, but all of which will serve the general welfare. The physical area to be covered by such a plan varies with local circumstances, including inclination of the planners involved, financing, and legislation.

"General welfare" is also an unbounded phrase, becoming more so as the area being planned increases and the concept of welfare enlarges. "General" in relation to what? Standard zoning enabling legislation says "the general welfare *of the community*." Properly understood, this is a good guide.

In *Berman v. Parker,* the U.S. Supreme Court said: "The concept of public welfare is broad and inclusive." A series of legal decisions in the past two decades indicate that it is becoming more so all the time, without indicating where it is likely to stop. Thus "general welfare," like "comprehensive planning," is an open-ended phrase.

Comes now a point which may be crucial, the definition of the community. The concept of community is also broad and inclusive, and has been so much longer than the concept of public welfare.

Applicable dictionary definitions of "community" run as follows: "(1) A body of people having common organization or interests, or living in the same place under the same laws and regulations . . . (2) Society at large; a commonwealth or state; a body politic; the public, or people in general;—used with the definite article: as, the interests of the community; restrictedly, the people of a particular place or region."

Thus the community, as it unfolds from small to large, is the family, the block, the neighborhood, the district, the city without its suburbs, the city with its suburbs, the county, the metropolitan area, the state, the region, the nation.

"General" welfare, as defined by and applied to each of these communities individually, does not add up to general welfare for the larger group. Thus the family which wants to add a grocery and filling station on its lot in a residential area may have as its objective putting the property to its "highest and best" use in terms of income, but runs afoul of deed restrictions covering the block and zoning covering the municipality.

The city may attempt to apply persuasion through zoning restrictions limiting location of state or federal installations within its boundaries, but federal or state governments may ignore such limitations with impunity. The state may declare that public welfare demands segregation of the races in the schools, but federal policy supersedes.

Conflicts between lesser interests and greater are in substantial measure responsible for government, for law, for planning and zoning. In a democracy, majority rules. If minority rules, democracy fails. The more general welfare takes precedence over the less general welfare.

Whatever else it may be, planning at its best is a reasoned compromise resulting in maximum benefits for the broadest community directly involved, with no more restraint on the freedoms of individuals and smaller communities than is necessary to achieve general purposes.

Metropolis happens

In an ordered hierarchy of communities, each with formal status and organization, the "generality" of the welfare to be considered increases with each step upward to a larger population and outward to a larger area. There is a form of government to match—except, thus far, for metropolis.

Metropolis happens. Metropolis-in-fact precedes metropolis in institutional form. There were cities and suburbs and space between, and then there was no space between. When metropolis occurs (when conurbation takes place, when on a sudden tomorrow there is realization that the magic "criteria of metropolitan character" of the Bureau of the Census have been met, or by whatever rule the birth of a metropolis is judged) then and at that point a new and very real general welfare has been created. It has no government of its own, but it is there, demanding government which represents more than the sum of its parts.

As something new has been added, so also has something been taken away. When the greater community is formed, the lesser communities which join together to create it lose their right to complete self-determination on matters which affect the welfare of the whole. This is not yet a rule of law, but it is clearly a rule of order for which legal expression is needed.

The alternative to legal recognition of metropolis-in-fact and creation of formal institutions adapted to its needs is that metropolis becomes and remains an amorphous conglomerate of proliferating municipal lumps in assorted sizes interlarded with unincorporated areas in various stages of decomposition, and the whole mess ferments destructively toward disorder and massive waste. Some students of government predict that we will put up with this. It is unthinkable that we should put up with it indefinitely.

There are moves both toward and away from solution. Annexations by cities in the metropolitan area are generally to the good, providing fewer and larger units with which to work. Formation of new municipalities to escape annexation is damaging because of needless increase in number of governmental units and because motives behind new incorporation are usually adverse to general public interest.

In other moves toward partial solutions, there have been a few consolidations of cities. There is some organized voluntary cooperation of most or all of the political units in a few metropolitan areas (tending to break down at points where effectiveness is most important if local advantage is threatened).

In some states, extraterritorial jurisdiction helps limit fringe problems. State zoning into broad categories is in effect in Hawaii, and should limit urban sprawl. In California, state enforcement of housing codes as a backstop for local nonenforcement or failure to enact codes should reduce slums in and out of cities.

The effect of federal influence should not be overlooked. "Do it according to these methods and standards or you don't get the money" is a powerful inducement on subdivision, housing, highways, urban renewal, public works, open space, and other fields in which federal programs are active. On planning in general, federal encouragement for enlargement of subject matter and for enlargement of area to metropolitan and regional scope has had a salutary effect.

Thus things are not standing still. But they could move ahead far more rapidly and far more intelligently. Metropolitan problems are growing faster than metropolitan solutions.

Things which are needed

In any metropolis (and in places which are growing toward metropolitan status) the following things are needed. They intertwine in a manner which makes establishment of priority difficult, and each of them involves issues as yet unresolved (some of which are discussed later):

1. A general plan for development of metropolis, and general zoning related to it. Borrowing from established zoning language, local plans and local zoning should be required to be in accordance with the general plan. Borrowing from Hawaii, the plan and the zoning should be general, leaving details to local units of government. Borrowing from California, if the local units fail to perform, or fail to perform effectively, higher government should step in and do the job. The general plan and general zoning, as expressions of the broader general welfare, should prevail in conflicts with local proposals representing smaller publics. The majority should rule.

2. Legal recognition of the existence of the broad general welfare of metropolis-in-fact as soon as there is reasonable evidence as to the nature of the broad general welfare. On common sense matters, it should not be necessary to wait for the adoption of a comprehensive plan. A city which proposes to encourage industrial smokestacks up-wind from the best residential area of a neighboring municipality should be stopped, whether a general plan for metropolis has been prepared or not.

3. Annexation and consolidation should be encouraged, to reduce the number of governmental units and the amount of area outside governments designed to deal with urban affairs. It would help if independent authorities, districts, and boards could also be consolidated where there is logical reason for doing so. Legislative action in this field might well include simplification of methods for annexation and consolidation.

4. Prevention of new escapist municipalities. In metropolitan areas (and elsewhere, for that matter) it should not remain possible to escape responsibility to the larger public, to escape controls needed in the larger public interest, or to escape taxation by what might be called incorporation for avoidance. Again legislative action is indicated, this time to tighten requirements for the creation of new municipalities, particularly in metropolitan areas.

5. Provision for abolition of some governmental units. Some escapist municipalities already formed might well be required either to consolidate with some other cities or to revert to unincorporated status. The same choice might well be given to existing cities too small to have any chance of functioning effectively, whether they were set up for avoidance reasons or not. And a careful look might be taken at abolition or consolidation of obsolete or ineffective special districts, authorities, and the like.

Unless some such action is made possible, a number of past mistakes will be ineradicably imbedded in the structure of metropolis.

6. Pooling tax revenues. Under existing taxation systems long due for revision, metropolis or not, too much local planning and governmental policy is dominated by whether this or that kind of development will be most profitable or most expensive in terms of net income.

The optimum city, on this basis, would be composed of high-value industrial plants adjacent to major highways provided by other governmental levels, high-rise apartments providing their own open space and barring children, successful regional shopping centers, and an eternally youthful and valuable CBD. Single-family dwellings assessed for tax purposes at $50,000 and up would be allowable if they paid directly for construction and maintenance of streets and utilities extended to them and if they were inhabited by childless families. Under exceptional circumstances, two children per block might be permitted if sent to private schools.

The workers would live somewhere else. The children would live somewhere else. The public schools, parks, and playgrounds would be somewhere else. Lower-cost housing would be somewhere else. All commercial, industrial, and service facilities except those paying high taxes and requiring low municipal expenditures would be somewhere else. Anything not profitable tax-wise would be somewhere else.

Present tax methods are largely responsible for the somewhere-else complex among planners and policy-makers. But there isn't enough somewhere-else to go around in metropolitan areas, and what there is of it is poorly located. So a way around present tax methods must be found, in order that land uses in metropolis can be located where and on the scale needed for effective functioning, rather than being pushed or pulled around because of tax appeal or lack of it.

There is some hope in arrangements for pooling at least part of the tax take and evening things out.

7. Metropolitan government. Some form or forms of metropolitan government must be developed to do things which must be done or can best be done at the metropolitan level, and to represent the broader community welfare in conflicts with the welfares of lesser communities.

Special issues and tentative policies

In listing needs in summary form above, running down inviting bypaths was avoided for the sake of brevity. Here are two:

How should the general plan and general zoning be prepared? How should developed areas, partly-developed areas, areas in transition, wrongly-developed areas, and undeveloped areas be handled? Incorporated and unincorporated areas?

The land-use plan, and the zoning which grows out of it should start with the present and work toward improvements. As with planning for any urbanized area, it will be discovered that there is too much of this and too little of that and that many things are firmly rooted in the wrong places, but that quite a substantial amount of what has happened is about as it should be. Planning for metropolis will have to build on such foundation as is firmly in place and to design around many of its defects. But planning will also have to distinguish between real foundation and wishful thinking.

When policy decisions about future development firm into zoning, there will be lamentation. This is nothing new, except that the lamentation will be municipal as well as individual.

Take the example of industrial location. Some industrial areas will be well located, reasonably well built up, and room could be made available for expansion. Some new and well-placed industrial area could be promoted by planning and zoning. There is little likelihood of major opposition in providing in the plan and the zoning for expansion of well-located areas or for creation of new ones.

Some industrial areas will be poorly located. Whether wholly or partially built up, these should be contained and limited by the plan and the zoning. Expansion of the area would be prohibited, but continuation of existing industrial operations and filling in or replacement by new ones would be allowed in the present area. This would be an elaboration of nonconforming use techniques to include what might be called nonconforming industrial districts. It is unlikely that amortization provisions could be made to apply to a poorly located district in which there is substantial development, and a policy of containment is probably about as far as metropolitan zoning could go.

But now come the really difficult cases. In the urbanizing area around a central city lie 10 yet-rural communities clearly in the path of metropolitan growth. Each of them contains around 20 square miles, each has a population of from 10,000-20,000, each has a zoning ordinance, and each has set aside five square miles of indifferently located land for industry, because it needs the taxes. There is little or no industrial development as yet. What should be done?

Here the *planning* solution is clear. The land is well located for residential development which is needed. It is not particularly well located for industry, and certainly nothing like 50 square miles of it could conceivably be used for industry. Metropolitan planning and zoning should obviously earmark most or all of it for residential development. If it does, the political explosion is likely to maim metropolitan planning and zoning.

Which is why the point was made earlier that *if metropolitan development is to proceed in an orderly manner, something should be done about the tax situation.*

The same kind of circumstances and reasoning leads inevitably to the same conclusions with respect to actual commercial development as compared with commercial areas set aside in local zoning ordinances. So long as local commerce and industry provide a major share of tax income, there will be competition for local commerce and industry regardless of the damage to the general metropolitan welfare.

In reverse, unless there is metropolis-wide collection and redistribution of some tax monies, land uses which in themselves create larger public expenditures than public income will find few places to go, regardless of how essential they may be to metropolis.

How can courts be induced to recognize the general welfare of metropolis being born, or metropolis-in-fact before metropolis is institutionalized? This will require preparation and presentation of solid evidence that there is such a thing as the broader general welfare, and that it can be injured by unbridled exercise of permissions or prohibitions of smaller publics pursuing ends which are to their own immediate advantage. Justice may be depicted as blind, but the courts are not—if they are given something to see. There is some hope already.

A dissenting opinion by Justice Hall, of the Supreme Court of New Jersey, contains judicial reasoning which should become the basis of majority views in the future. *With proper presentation of cases,* views like his will not be in the minority long. In *Vickers v. Township Committee of Gloucester Township,* the New Jersey Supreme Court upheld the right of the town to bar mobile home parks. The township contains 23 square miles, has a population of about 17,500, and is in the path of metropolitan growth. A large area is zoned industrial, but the zoning permits residences in the industrial area and at the time of application for a permit also allowed "trailer camps." When the permit was applied for, it was refused, and thereafter the town hastily amended the zoning ordinance to prohibit mobile home parks entirely.

Luminous excerpts from Justice Hall's opinion follow:

> The majority decides that this particular municipality may constitutionally say, through exercise of the zoning power, that its residents may not live in . . . mobile homes. I am convinced that such a conclusion in this case is manifestly wrong. Of even greater concern is the judicial process by which it is reached and the breadth of the rationale. The import of the holding gives almost boundless freedom to developing municipalities to erect exclusionary walls on their boundaries, according to local whim or selfish desire, and to use the zoning power for aims beyond its legitimate purposes. Prohibition of mobile home parks, although an important issue in itself, becomes in this larger aspect somewhat a symbol.
>
> The case, both in its physical setting and in the issues raised is typical of land use controversies now current in so many New

Jersey municipalities on the outer ring of built up urban and suburban areas. These are municipalities with relatively few people and a lot of open space, but in the throes of . . . migration from the already densely settled central cores. They are not small, homogeneous communities with permanent character already established, like the settled suburbs surrounding the cities in which planning and zoning may properly be geared to things as they are and as they will pretty much continue to be.

On the contrary, these areas are sprawling heterogeneous governmental units, mostly townships, each really amounting to a region of considerable size in itself. Present rural, semi-rural, or mixed nature is about to change substantially, and they are soon to become melded into the whole metropolitan area.

Their political boundaries are artificial and hence of little significance beyond defining one unit of local government. Their existing conglomeration of land uses is sectionally distributed—large or small agriculture, residences in separated communities . . . or in the open country, business establishments in the populated sectors and along through highways, and perhaps a spot or two of industry much sought after to aid municipal tax revenues.

Many differing land uses, both present and future, are and can be made comfortably compatible by reason of the distances involved and the varying characteristics of geographical sections. Present municipal services are not more extensive than necessary to serve a population scattered over a large territory. Increased facilities, especially schools, required to accommodate a sudden population growth of large proportions must be provided almost solely at local expense, which in New Jersey means from additional taxation on real estate within the municipal boundaries. And it is elementary knowledge that small homes with children to be educated in local schools cannot pay their own way tax-wise.

Such municipalities, above all others, vitally need and may legally exercise comprehensive planning and implementing zoning techniques to avoid present haphazard development which can only bring future grief. They are entitled to aim thereby for a sound and balanced area, with varying uses confined to specific districts and appropriately regulated. They may even limit the pace of growth to coincide with the availability of the necessary additional facilities and services so as to minimize growing pains. . . . They need not allow every land use wherever someone wants to put it or the property is suitable, and in accordance with a comprehensive plan may reasonably restrict districts to a particular future use even though another use would be equally suitable.

They would be well advised to plan with adjoining communities, especially for joint public services and facilities. Intercommunity planning is also best able to accommodate those categories of uses that ought not to be excluded everywhere, but which may be more desirably located in one municipality rather than another. Unfortunately, our statutory provisions for voluntary regional planning boards . . . have been little used.

And this gets to the nub of what this, and similar cases, are really all about, i.e., the outer limit of the zoning power to be enjoyed by these municipalities. . . . What action is not legitimately encompassed by that power and what is the proper role of courts in reviewing its exercise?

The inquiry involves important fundamentals. In the broad sense the considerations are well posed in Williams', "Planning Law and Democratic Living," 20 *Law and Contemporary Problems* 317 (1955):

"The main premises of American constitutional law represent a codification and institutionalization of the primary values of a democratic society—equality of opportunity and equality of treatment, freedom of thought and considerable freedom of action, and fairness. Under the American system, a more or less independent mechanism of judicial review is established to provide an independent check on whether specific governmental decisions conform to these standards. *While controversy has often raged about judicial action in other areas, it has always been recognized that it is an essential part of the judicial function to watch over the parochial and exclusionist attitudes and policies of local governments, and to see to it that these do not run counter to national policy and the general welfare.* [Emphasis supplied.]

"Constitutional law should be required to shed light upon thinking about local planning, by requiring those concerned to do what they should be doing anyway—to work out the relationship between planning the future environment and the great issues connected with human freedom and opportunity.

" . . . No major problem in planning law can be really understood except by an analysis thereof of relation to the whole background of the changing physical, economic and social environment. . . .

"The leaders of liberal-democratic thought are all too often so confused with abstractions (health, safety, morals and welfare, character of the neighborhood, etc.), so full of respect for local autonomy, and so fearful of judicial review generally, as to be unable to understand the implications of what is going on. It has not been generally realized that in many instances the problems arising in this field of constitutional law are closely akin to those involved in civil liberties law, and call for similar attitudes toward the exercise of governmental power."

The purpose "to promote the general welfare" does not stand alone in the statute. Its meaning and scope must have some relation to the other specified standards and the whole authorized scheme. Certainly "general welfare" does not automatically mean whatever the municipality says it does, regardless of who is hurt and how much.

And no matter how broadly the concept is viewed, it cannot authorize a municipality to erect a completely isolationist wall on its boundaries. This was early recognized in the foundation case of *Euclid v. Ambler Realty Company* . . . where the court was careful to say: "It is not meant by this, however, to exclude the possibility of cases where the general public interest would so far outweigh the interest of the municipality that the municipality would not be allowed to stand in the way."

Two of our own landmark decisions (one wonders what has lately happened to them) made it very plain, even though our zoning scheme is legislatively keyed to municipal lines, that validity of local use prohibitions is to be judged, among other things, by availability of other appropriate locations . . . and that one town's boundary should give due recognition to conditions across its boundaries. . . .

Though the Cresskill cases dealt with built-up suburbs, their underlying philosophy is equally applicable to developing municipalities in a vast metropolitan complex.

The Cresskill cases *stand for the proposition that "general welfare" transcends the artificial limits of political subdivisions and cannot embrace merely narrow local desires.* [Emphasis supplied.]

I have at least equal difficulty with the breadth of another major aspect of the majority's thesis—that the local power to zone is especially *carte blanche* when the municipality is a relatively virgin one, and in the path of metropolitan expansion. The specter of future blight and a present inward vision of what the municipality hopes or dreams of someday becoming or remaining seem enough to sanction almost any restriction, however drastic or provincial. . . .

Townships like Gloucester, with their vast areas of vacant land, have plenty of room in which to accommodate the variety of land uses people of all income levels and individual desires may want to enjoy. Sound planning and zoning regulation by appropriate districts can easily make such uses compatible while avoiding detrimental impact on each other. . . .

In my opinion legitimate use of the zoning power by such municipalities does not encompass the right to erect barricades on their boundaries through exclusion or too tight restriction of uses where the real purpose is to prevent feared disruption of a so-called chosen way of life. Nor does it encompass provisions designed to let in as new residents only certain kinds of people, or those who can afford to live in favored kinds of housing, or to keep down tax bills of present property owners.

[A footnote here states: "That this kind of motivation was not entirely absent in the barring of mobile homes from Gloucester Township is indicated by the statement at oral argument of the township's counsel, during the course of discussion of the local reasons for the action, that people who lived in trailers were a shifting population without roots and did not make good citizens. Aside from the fact that such characterizations are today without true foundation, the statement is an example of frequently-found resentment and distrust by present residents of newcomers, including renters, who vote on school budgets and the election of local officials with the power over municipal appropriations, but who do not pay real estate taxes directly or in sufficient amount to cover the cost of local services rendered to them."]

When one of the above is the true situation, deeper considerations intrinsic in a free society gain the ascendency and courts must not be hesitant to strike down purely selfish and undemocratic enactments. . . . It seems contradictory to sustain so readily legislative policy at the state level forbidding various kinds of discrimination in housing . . . and permitting the use of eminent domain and public funds to remove slums and provide decent living

> accommodations . . . and at the same time bless selfish zoning regulations which tend to have the effect of precluding people who now live in congested and undesirable city areas from obtaining housing within their means in open, attractive and healthy communities.
>
> *Lionshead Lake, Inc. v. Township of Wayne* and *Fischer v. Township of Bedminster* rationalize such exclusionary results, as does the majority here, by reference to the statutory zoning purposes . . . of "conserving the value of property" and "encouraging the most appropriate use of land" and in the name of preservation of the character of the community or neighborhood. I submit these factors are perverted from their intended application when used to justify Chinese walls on the borders of roomy developing municipalities for the actual purpose of keeping out all but the "right kind" of people or those who will live in a certain kind and cost of dwelling. . . .

Here, surely, is evidence that the courts are on a track which has considerable promise, even though the views expressed appear for the moment in minority opinions.

Suburbia versus everybody else

We have heard about administrative and legal approaches to planning the future residential environment, sociological implications of residential planning, and design, financing, and construction of the future residential environment. Something is left over, a note about what you may expect when you try to put this knowledge to use in suburbia, the broadest arena for housing.

It is only fair to warn you that there will be vigorous and often vicious opposition to anything proposed for the suburban residential environment which involves any kind of housing but single-family detached residences on large lots in conventional subdivisions. Can-of-worms subdivisions are now reasonably safe in most areas, but beyond that be on your guard. Even the cluster of single-family homes is suspect—who knows what dangers lurk in common open space?

Proposals for town houses indicate incipient socialism. Planned developments for mixtures of housing types including garden apartments are evidence of leanings toward Moscow. Mention high-rises in planned developments and you are clearly taking from Mao Tse Tung and sending packages to North Viet Nam.

The essence of what I'm going to say is this: If you are going to join the struggle for improving the residential environment in suburbia, technical preparation is not enough. Prepare yourself also for political

This article is a composite of a paper presented at the Tenth Annual Planning Conference, Organization of Cornell Planners, Cornell University, March 1967, and "Planned Development in Suburbia," as published in *Soil, Water and Suburbia,* proceedings of a joint USDA-HUD conference, June 1967.

warfare, because you will be up to your ears in it and some of it will be dirty. And beyond that, get some feeling for emerging trends in law. It is increasingly clear that major chances for making the most of opportunities for progress in the residential field will probably come only as a result of successful legal attack on current suburban planning and zoning practices designed to protect the present against the future.

We are perched on an emerging sandbar of knowledge in a limitless sea of ignorance. We don't know much about urban man, his classes and subclasses, as he is or as he will be, and we don't know much about cities, their classes and subclasses, areas and subareas, as they are, as they will be, or as they should be.

We have technical and economic ability to build cities in an ever-widening range of forms. Our problem as planners is twofold: First, as professionals we aren't sure how to use this ability. Second, even if we were sure, our democratic forms of government, particularly in their fragmented state at local levels, pose major problems in application of even the best-grounded planning concepts.

We are, or should be, humble about our uncertainties, and we should labor diligently to enlarge our sandbar. We are dedicated to the principle of comprehensiveness in planning, to planning which includes not only physical but socioeconomic elements, to planning which begins with the individual and ranges outward to the family and its dwelling unit, the block, the neighborhood, the community, the metropolitan area, the region, the nation, and the community of nations, to planning for present populations and populations which will follow. We have had a few technical successes (which must be considered limited in the context of what remains to be done). We know how to handle some problems demonstrably better than they have been handled in the past, although we must admit that there are few fields in which solutions could not be improved.

On the other hand, there have been occasional failures of applied planning (or failures of occasionally applied planning) which have not narrowed the public's credibility gap. These should serve as laboratory experiments from which we can learn (although we have made little organized effort as yet to analyze planning failures, preferring to proceed on a sort of mystic faith and ignoring past results). We have in our own ranks divisions of highly expert opinion pointing in opposite directions. So long as such divergence is honest, it must be considered healthy, considering the current evolutionary stage of planning. But much of the divergence is dishonest, an attempt to keep planning from evolving.

Adding to obstacles inherent in the less-than-mature state of the art, there are the difficulties inherent in democracy localized to the point where the smallest unit of general government has high powers of self-determination. In his famous speech on the Four Freedoms, Roosevelt indicated as objectives freedom from want and from fear, and freedom of expression and worship. There is a fifth freedom which exists not as an objective of our society, but as a necessary concomitant of democracy which diminishes its potentials.

Freedom to ignore

The freedom to ignore may be divided into several subcategories, all of which create problems for planners at all levels, but which are particularly hard to deal with in the smallest units of general government. Some affect only the unit and its current population, and some have effects reaching to the region and beyond, and to the next generations and beyond.

Three troublesome subdivisions of the freedom to ignore are these:

1. Freedom to ignore those outside our community.
2. Freedom to ignore the unborn.
3. Freedom to ignore the lessons of experience concerning probable consequences. To the planning practitioner, public or private, this freedom may be painfully personalized as freedom to ignore the advice of experts.

On ignoring the advice of experts, it cannot be said honestly that retribution is swift, that those who transgress get a rapid comeuppance, that those who discard the advice of true experts and follow quacks soon discover the error of their ways.

Ours is an opulent society in a stage of social and economic evolution which *for the present* has ample room for mistakes, waste, and inefficiency, and for destruction of amenities. As planners with concern for generations to come as well as present populations, for the region and the nation as well as suburban Warners Corners, we plan for efficiency, economy, and amenity on a broad and long-range scale. Our advice is often ignored because it doesn't fit what the people of Warners Corners want on a narrow, short-range scale.

In general, in our time, the power structure of the suburban community is firmly defending the status quo. They like it, and they like their group. The single-family detached residence on the large, very large, or extremely large lot is the ideal, and nobody should live in their community in anything else. In fact, nobody who is anybody should live anywhere in anything else, and since they don't want anybody who is nobody living in their community, the nobodies can go live somewhere where they won't make any difference—to the somebodies, at any rate. If this leads to urban sprawl, major transportation problems, inefficiency, wasteful land use, elimination of possibilities of meaningful open space in the suburban environment in favor of small private preserves fragmented into yards of dubious utility, that doesn't bother the Warners Corners power structure. What they are doing is to plan for protection against difference, which is not the kind of planning we need for the kind of residential environment we should have if we want to be numbered among the good guys in the planning profession.

Unfortunately, if you happen to be working for Warners Corners as a staff member or consultant, you may find yourself in a position where you either give the advice the power structure wants, finding cogent reasons why the status quo is the best of all possible worlds (which means you have sold out as a planner and become a quack) or you give the advice you should give (which keeps you on the side of the good guys but is ignored and is likely to lead to abrupt unemployment).

There is a middle course which is slow, but offers some chance for both progress in the direction in which we should go and survival in the local labor market. This involves friendly persuasion as an initial step, aiding and abetting unfriendly persuasion if necessary.

Friendly persuasion, if it is to be successful, should be based on reason, but should take into account that suburban man particularly is a nonlogical animal. Thus the reasons emphasized should be those which appeal to the in-group. "Unless you allow planned development, your taxes will rise. Governmental costs for planned developments are lower. In planned developments, the number of children per household is smaller than in single-family large-lot residential areas because some of the units are townhouses and apartments. The per capita income of occupants of planned residential developments already existing in similar suburbs in this area is higher than the per capita income of occupants of single-family detached residents. Surveys in this general area indicate that 95.62 per cent of occupants of planned residential developments are white Anglo-Saxon protestants and the remainder are acceptable Jews. Voting records show that 74.53 per cent are Republicans" (or Democrats, if this is what is needed—highly unlikely).

The next series of arguments must be approached tactfully, because it indicates that *all* housing in planned developments may not be terribly expensive. It is a well-known fact that one of the principal objectives of suburban planning and related regulations is to make housing as expensive as possible. For any departure from this principle, the foundation must be laid very carefully, as indicated above. It must be made clear that only the well-to-do poor will be accommodated. It must be emphasized that there is a better than average chance that they will come from *within* the community.

"Without the variety of housing facilities usually available in planned developments, the healthy longevity of the community is threatened, and the conservative body of tradition which makes for our kind of community spirit may not develop. When our children mature and form their own families, they need forms of housing which fit their needs and their pocketbooks. If we don't provide it, they will leave the area and we lose all that we could gain by keeping them with us, building on their identification with our community. At the other end of the age scale, our retirees often prefer to move to less burdensome quarters than the large homes in which they have raised their families. Unless forms of housing suited to their needs (the same forms which appeal to the young family-formers) are available in our community, they move elsewhere and we lose their guardianship and wisdom. Moreover, unless we have managed to keep the young with us to move from townhouses and apartments into single-family detached housing as their families and incomes grow, the housing vacated by the Senior Citizens (always capitalized to indicate unctuous reverence) will be sold to Outsiders (also capitalized—to indicate loathing).

"Unless we arrange for this community continuation (avoid the term renewal) from within, keeping traditions high so that any admixture from outside is of the proper quality, the outlook is dark. When we moved in, Warners Corners was a new and attractive community with the kind of prestige appealing to executives. The coming executive generation will move to communities similarly new and attractive unless we maintain our selective and discriminating atmosphere by building on our established traditions. Thus we are threatened by what Washington Planners (capitalized) approvingly call 'filter-down' or 'trickle-down' (or something-down) of high quality housing, with all this means in loss of values when we want to sell our residences."

That's the essence of it. Friendly persuasion involves fright, blackmail, and appeals to cupidity, coated with plenty of conservative icing about community character and tradition (which can be interpreted as keeping the best for us, and to hell with anybody else). The arguments above include some which are valid and some which are not, but carefully avoid esoteric theoretical consideration of the needs of the metropolitan area as a whole or concern with the future of anyone except those in the closed circle and their immediate descendants.

This is the kind of stuff the suburban in-group may listen to—but the chances are they won't. Certainly they don't seem inclined to listen to anything less self-related or more abstract. But since this is the kind of local democracy which governs, that's the kind of sales pitch which offers the greatest promise of getting the vote. And if it is laid on thick enough in the record, with great lumps of prejudice showing through, it establishes a splendid booby-trap for Step II, unfriendly persuasion.

Unfriendly persuasion involves the use of a bludgeon wielded by the court—if a court can be found where the judges are not suburbanites privately sharing the views of their neighbors. (The opinion of Judge Hall, quoted in the previous article, pp. 97-102, is an example.)

In the fighting today, our troops sustained moderate losses

Let us now discuss in documented detail a recent skirmish in which local planners abetted by the feds stood firm against planned development. We move to a battlefront in the Washington metropolitan area.

The upper Rock Creek watershed in Maryland is one of the few relatively close-in undeveloped areas which has good access to the District of Columbia. Here is some general background, from which several morals can be drawn, on comprehensive planning for the Washington region as it affects upper Rock Creek.

The 1950 "Comprehensive Plan for the National Capital and Its Environs," indicated that in 1980 Montgomery County population would be 250,000, out of a total of two million for the region, which would have reached this number about 1965 and leveled off.[1] Single-family areas in broad suburbia dominate the map of the plan, with only

1. National Capital Park and Planning Commission, "Regional Aspects of the Comprehensive Plan, A Portion of the Comprehensive Plan for the National Capital and Its Environs," Monog. 6 (Washington, D.C.: The Commission, 1950), pp. 14 and 16.

a few multiple-family areas which existed at the time, and which it seemed too late to stamp out. The Rock Creek area was beyond the fringe, and would surely remain rural.

In 1961 came the "Plan for the Year 2000" for the Nation's Capital. Discounting two counties with small populations which had been added to the region, the population total was 2.1 million already with no sign of leveling off—in fact, growth to five million is anticipated by 2000, 2½ times the amount projected 10 years earlier. According to this plan,[2] "Most of the population growth will take place in the suburbs."

A third in the series, "On Wedges and Corridors—A General Plan for the Maryland-Washington Regional District," was published in 1964. Here it is reported that the 1960 population was 341,000 (as against the 250,000 estimated in the 1950 report for the year 1980) and 1966 population is indicated at 445,000, to climb to 640,000 in 1980, 995,000 in 2000.[3] This is four times the leveling off figure indicated in 1950, and current trends make it apparent that the estimates made after 1960 may be low.

The "Plan for the Year 2000" proposed the Rock Creek area for dairy and livestock use at the turn of the century—a rural wedge at the intersection of urban corridors. "Every effort should be made to preserve . . . the Piedmont dairy land in Montgomery County."[4] Urban sprawl was rejected as policy.[5] Two other policy statements in the plan were basic to the issues: "A variety of housing types and mixes is inevitable in each part of a large metropolitan area, and it is therefore desirable to guide this trend along sound lines."[6] "Land is not an unlimited commodity, particularly when that land makes up an area immediately subject to metropolitan growth. In a metropolitan setting, the more efficient use of land implies, for one thing, higher development densities in the suburban areas. . . . The creation and preservation of urban parks and open spaces which are appropriately sized and distributed particularly require that other land uses be accommodated in an efficient way."[7]

2. National Capital Planning Commission, "A Plan for the Year 2000" (Washington, D.C.: The Commission, 1961), p. 16.

3. Maryland-National Capital Park and Planning Commission, "On Wedges and Corridors—A General Plan for the Maryland-Washington Regional District" (Silver Spring, Md.: The Commission, 1964), p. 157.

4. *Ibid.*, p. 56.

5. *Ibid.*, p. 29.

6. *Ibid.*, p. 28.

7. *Ibid.*, p. 29.

It is highly unlikely that land this close to the center of the Washington region will be used for dairying in the year 2000. The imaginary crisis conjured up by those who worry about loss of agricultural land to cities has been put down by Marion Clawson in *Modern Land Policy.*[8]

"On Wedges and Corridors" is said to be in accord with "Plan for the Year 2000," but there are some curious interpretations. For example, the year 2000 plan strongly recommended *decentralization of federal office space* into corridor locations as an important part of the general scheme.[9] "On Wedges and Corridors" rejoices that "A recent decision by the President's . . . committee on Federal Office Space—*to concentrate Federal construction in a largely rebuilt downtown Washington*—has given strong impetus to the radial corridor and central core philosophy embodied in the year 2000 plan. . . . There will certainly be other such endorsements, and implementing actions, in the near future."[10]

Like the year 2000 plan, "On Wedges and Corridors" urges efficient use of land: "Extravagant 'leapfrogging' of development into the countryside and overemphasis on larger and larger residential lots wastes the land and establishes widespread patterns of land use which become obsolete before they are even fully developed."[11] "On Wedges and Corridors" urges a greater variety of living environments: "New towns staged in the corridor afford the greatest opportunity to create . . . a choice of living environments. Residential areas need not consist of row after row of houses on uniformly sized lots or unimaginative blocks of apartments in strict zoning categories. Cluster developments which compatibly integrate single-family homes on various sized lots, townhouses, garden and high-rise apartments, commercial and auxiliary uses can maintain strict density control of the cluster of uses."[12]

The idea in "On Wedges and Corridors" is to provide the kinds of residential environments indicated only in the urban corridors. On the wedges, the recommendation is to surround and separate the corridors with rural space, with recreational opportunities for present and future generations, "to provide a *favorable rural environment* in which farm-

8. Marion Clawson, "Land Use and Demand for Land in the United States," in *Modern Land Policy: Papers of the Land Economics Institute* (Urbana, Ill.: University of Illinois Press, 1960), pp. 12-14.

9. See *supra* note 3, p. 250.

10. *Ibid.,* p. 11.

11. *Ibid.,* p. 16.

12. *Ibid.,* p. 19.

ing, mineral extraction, fishing and other natural resource activities can be carried on without disruption, and to conserve natural resources and protect the public water supply."[13]

Residences will be allowed in the rural wedges, but only on large lots *individually developed primarily for the use of people whose livelihood is dependent on the rural area.* A specific type of zoning is proposed to protect these wedges.[14]

The general plan in "On Wedges and Corridors" shows the 18 square miles of the upper Rock Creek watershed as being rural. Other maps show dairy and livestock farms as the predominant future use,[15] but also indicate a population of 11,000 for the area,[16] no doubt as a result of a return to a type of dairy and livestock operation which requires substantially more labor and less land than at present. About half the land would be in two-acre lots for the rural workers, the rest available for roads, parks, dairy and livestock farming, and other activities.

Passing on hastily to the 1966 "Master Plan for the Rock Creek Planning Area," we find that it is stated to be in accord with the wedges and corridors general plan,[17] which was stated to be in accord with the year 2000 plan.

The "Rock Creek Plan" has admirable graphic analysis of the character of the land and its suitability for various purposes—there are maps on slopes, suitability for agriculture, for onsite waste disposal, for roads and homesite foundations, and on limitations for construction and agriculture. But the recommendations do not entirely coincide with those in "On Wedges and Corridors." Among minor differences:

1. No land at all is indicated as being in agricultural use. The entire area is divided into residential, commercial, and industrial categories plus public schools, institutions, a golf course, and public park land.

2. No proposal is made for the kind of rural zoning required in the "On Wedges and Corridors" plan as a prime essential for preservation of the rural reserve.

3. The population to be accommodated rises from 11,000, with

13. *Ibid.,* p. 44.
14. *Ibid.,* p. 78.
15. *Ibid.,* pp. 45 and 47.
16. *Ibid.,* p. 28.
17. Maryland-National Capital Park and Planning Commission, "Preliminary Master Plan for the Rock Creek Planning Area—A Plan for Stream Valley Protection and Development" (Silver Spring, Md.: The Commission, 1966), p. 6.

rural livelihoods, to 22,331[18] (note the precision), whose occupations will obviously be primarily nonrural.

4. In paying lipservice to the principles of "On Wedges and Corridors," there are proposals for scenic easements adjacent to scenic rural roads (which will be bordered by single-family detached houses on half-acre, one-acre, and two-acre lots to preserve the "rural" atmosphere). The cluster method (with no increase in density) may be employed "to create a network of such scenic rural roads," but the terrain is such that the open space would be largely invisible from the roads. An illustration entitled "Perceptual Survey" (see opposite page), taken in conjunction with other maps showing prime development areas, lowlands, public parks, and the like, indicates that for a substantial part of the road frontage, lands available for private development do not involve perceptual corridors, and under present cluster development regulations do not offer much incentive for design according to cluster principles. And under the zoning implementation, cluster development doesn't permit anything but single-family detached housing. Only with planned unit development is a variety of housing forms permitted under Montgomery County regulations.

Another illustration, "Application of Environmental Control Standards" (see page 114), reveals considerable wishful thinking. Conventional subdivisions are shown as occupying less land than would be required by zoning, with prime surrounding land gained by this understatement lying vacant to add to the appearance of spaciousness. One area will serve as an example. Compare probable subdivision layouts with a proposed planned development.[19] It is reasonably clear that the conventional subdivision pattern would not leave the open space indicated in "Application of Environmental Control Standards."

It should also be clear that the planned development is the best way to achieve conservation objectives, add to the public open system by coordinated private common open space, and make efficient use of the land with high amenity levels.

Under normal subdivision construction practices, there is occasionally some erosion. Under planned development, with the high degree of control possible if regulations are well written and well enforced, much of this sort of thing can be avoided during construction, and expert

18. *Ibid.*, p. 70.

19. Montgomery County Planning Commission, "Grantham, A Planned Neighborhood," Zoning Amendment Application E-670, Montgomery County, Maryland, 1966. (Copy on file at Montgomery County Planning Commission.)

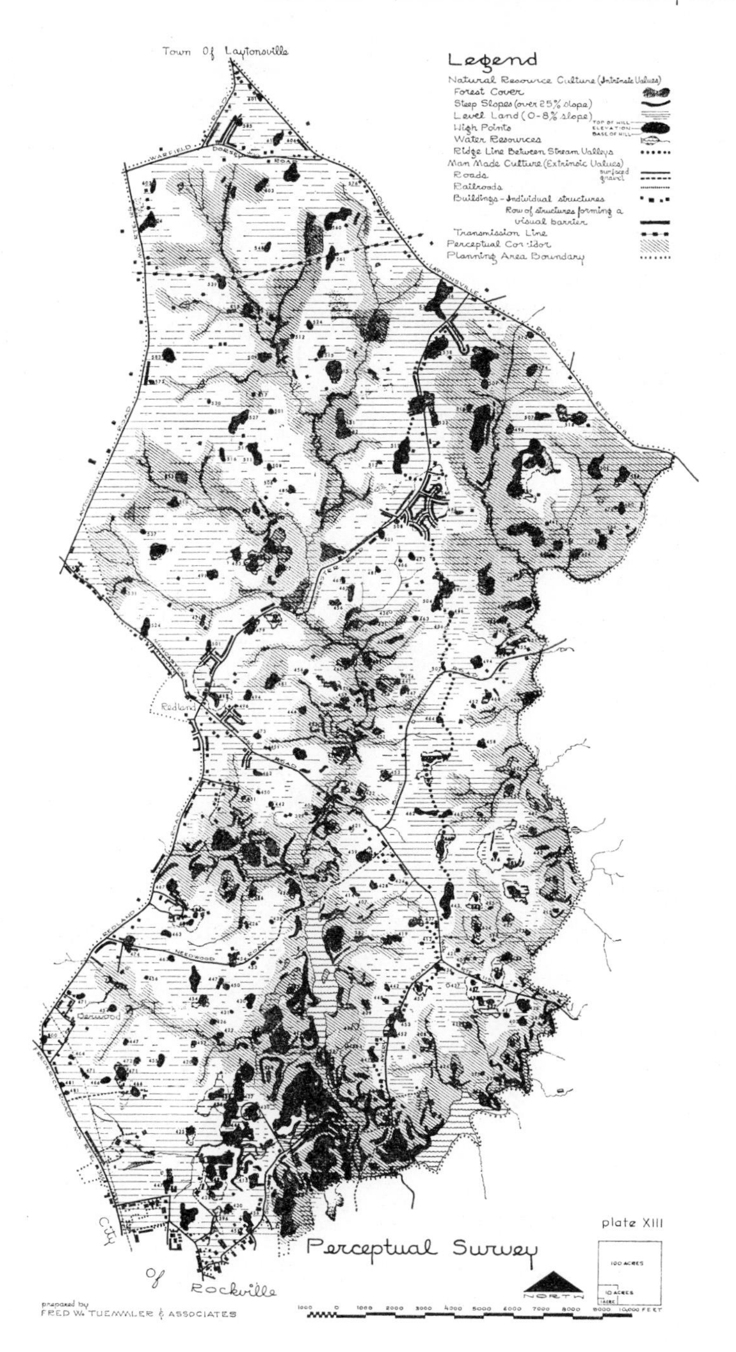
Town Of Laytonsville
Legend
Natural Resource Culture (Intrinsic Values)
Forest Cover
Steep Slopes (over 25% slope)
Level Land (0-8% slope)
High Points
TOP OF HILL
ELEVATION
BASE OF HILL
Water Resources
Ridge Line Between Stream Valleys
Man Made Culture (Extrinsic Values)
Roads
surfaced
gravel
Railroads
Buildings - Individual structures
Row of structures forming a visual barrier
Transmission Line
Perceptual Corridor
Planning Area Boundary
WARFIELD
LAYTONSVILLE
ROAD
Redland
REDLAND
NEEDWOOD
ROAD
Derwood
City
Of
Rockville
Perceptual Survey
plate XIII
100 ACRES
10 ACRES
1 ACRE
NORTH
prepared by
FRED W. TUEMMLER & ASSOCIATES
1000
0
1000
2000
3000
4000
5000
6000
7000
8000
9000
10,000 FEET

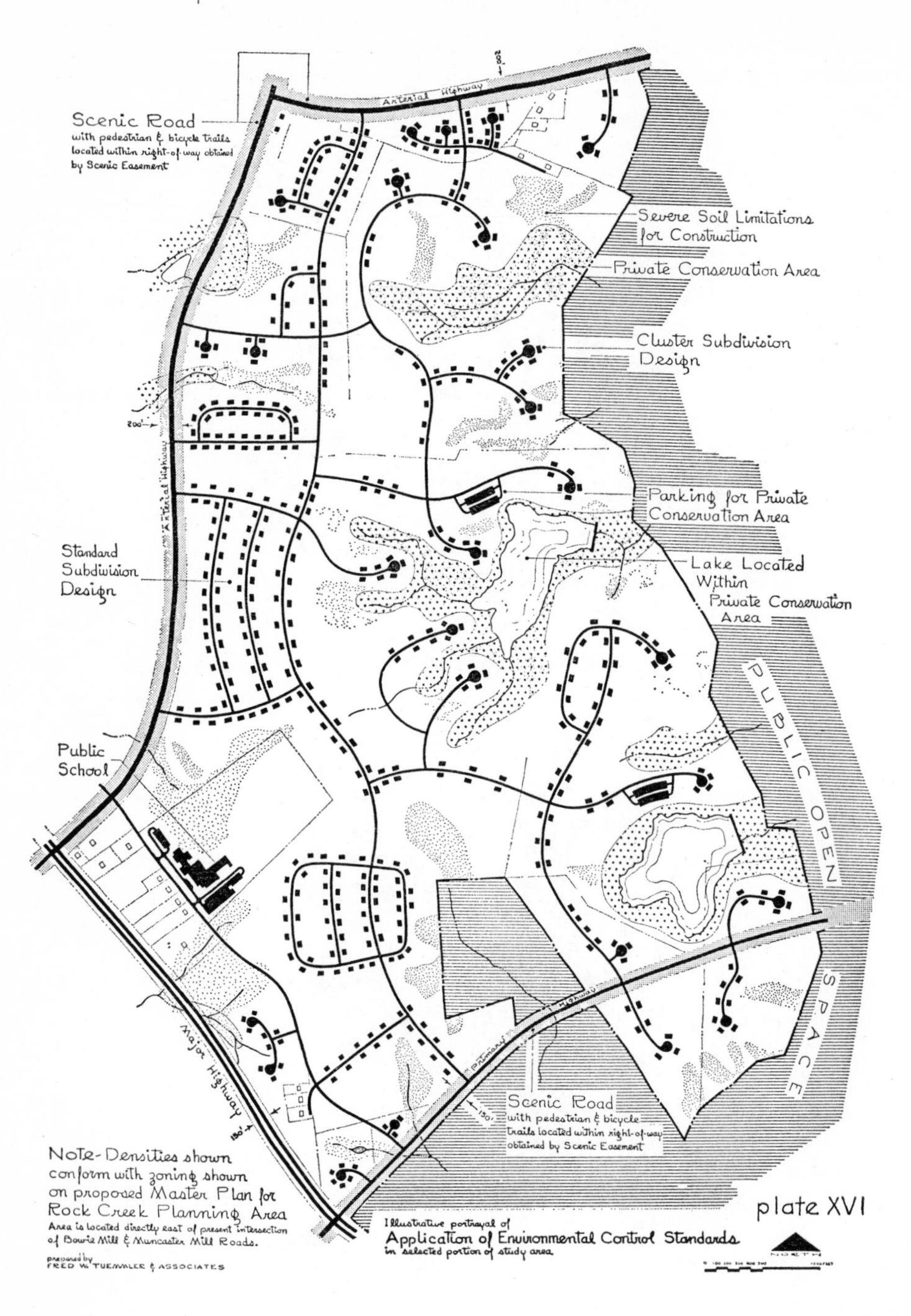
Scenic Road
with pedestrian & bicycle trails located within right-of-way obtained by Scenic Easement
Arterial Highway
Severe Soil Limitations for Construction
Private Conservation Area
Cluster Subdivision Design
Parking for Private Conservation Area
Lake Located Within Private Conservation Area
Standard Subdivision Design
Public School
PUBLIC OPEN SPACE
Major Highway
Scenic Road
with pedestrian & bicycle trails located within right-of-way obtained by Scenic Easement
Note - Densities shown conform with zoning shown on proposed Master Plan for Rock Creek Planning Area
Area is located directly east of present intersection of Bowie Mill & Muncaster Mill Roads.
prepared by FRED W. TUEMMLER & ASSOCIATES
Illustrative portrayal of
Application of Environmental Control Standards
in selected portion of study area

plate XVI

testimony in this particular case indicated that both during construction and afterward, erosion would be less under planned development than under general practice.

Do local planners in Montgomery County share this view? Apparently not. Two fairly sizeable planned developments are proposed for the Rock Creek watershed. In the master plan report, they are indicated as "The Threat to the Valley." What brings on this reaction? Both "On Wedges and Corridors" and the "Rock Creek Plan" are firmly opposed to urban sprawl in their statement of principles, but the actual plan proposed for Rock Creek is for urban sprawl in the form of 2,900 acres of R-A (two-acre) zoning, 2,400 acres of R-E (one-acre) zoning, 1,500 acres of R-R (½-acre) zoning, and 16 acres for townhouses. The other categories are single-family detached, and therein lies the apparent key to the problem.

The single-family-detached psychosis, the determination to defend present patterns against the needs of the future (and of the present as well), comes through clearly in "On Wedges and Corridors," the "Rock Creek Plan," and staff reports on applications for planned developments.

Having stated in "Goals"[20] that the cluster development can "compatibly integrate single-family homes on various sized lots, townhouses and garden and high-rise apartments," "Wedges and Corridors" later forgets its earlier statement and says, "The idea of planned community zoning is to promote variety in development and flexibility in urban design. These are valid objectives, but without careful coordination with a comprehensive public plan this type of zoning could lead to a continuation, or even an acceleration of all the unfortunate aspects of haphazard urban sprawl. Planned community zoning should not be used as the excuse for each sizable piece of property becoming an island unto itself. While this might result in some well designed neighborhoods, the urban pattern as a whole would deteriorate in efficiency, convenience and usefulness.[21]

"The recently adopted average density residential zones had the same objectives in mind as planned community zoning, but they are not so *bold or dangerous.* A more familiar name for the flexible type of building envisioned under these zones is cluster development, in which dwellings are grouped together on a small portion of the available land while the rest remains open for common recreational use. Planned

20. Maryland-National Capital Park and Planning Commission, "On Wedges and Corridors," p. 19.
21. *Ibid.,* p. 83.

community zoning *would allow a mixture of housing types* including both multi- and single-family, and maybe even a little commercial development. But the present average density zones allow only single-family housing."[22]

In proposed zoning amendments included in the appendix to the "Rock Creek Plan," the fixation is continued. In R-A, R-E, and R-R districts, cluster developments are to allow only single-family detached dwellings and accessory uses.[23] In a staff report recommending against the planned development application, it is stated, " . . . it is only necessary to visualize the probable reaction to a group of conventional zoning applications which might have been filed instead of this Planned Neighborhood application, permitting the same pattern of uses and densities. The mere facts that multiple-family dwellings were involved (indeed that multiple-family dwellings and townhouses are to constitute some 65 per cent of the total dwellings), that single-family densities of two units per acre were proposed, and that a commercial center was shown, would ensure denial for the entire project."[24]

There is considerable concern with the population densities which might be developed through planned development, although they are well toward the lower end of the LUI range indicated by FHA for outer suburbia. The present average density approach allows only the number of dwelling units which would be permitted in lot-by-lot zoning, but ignores the land economies and increased amenities possible through planned development and assures (in view of the red tape involved in using clusters) that they will be used only where terrain difficulties are substantial, rather than as a general rule.

There is nothing sacred about density as such. If we can have higher densities with greater amenities, we should not only permit but encourage them. This is one answer to urban sprawl. Large-lot zoning for as much area as can possibly be put into such categories is obviously not a solution, but a cause.

The "Rock Creek Plan" is not in accord with the general plan of "On Wedges and Corridors." It takes part of the "On Wedges and Corridors" argument for large lots for incidental residences for many times more rural workers than are likely to find rural employment, doubles the population and divides the entire buildable portion of the planning

22. *Ibid.*, p. 84.

23. Maryland-National Capital Park and Planning Commission, "Preliminary Master Plan for the Rock Creek Planning Area," pp. 72-74.

24. See *supra* note 19.

area into large lots for workers whose jobs will obviously be primarily nonrural, and eliminates the dairy and livestock farms on which "On Wedges and Corridors" depended for maintenance of rural character. Instead of a plan corresponding to the intent of "On Wedges and Corridors," a new plan is proposed for an urban sprawl metropolitan suburb predominated by single-family detached residences on large lots. Planned development for some 1,200 acres of the entire area is turned down, partly because it allows a density which is entirely justified by the location (if FHA experience is sound), but mostly because it allows something beside single-family detached housing.

Under the Rock Creek master plan, development is stated to be rural, a character which the plan uses repeatedly in describing it. However, with over 22,000 people in over 6,000 dwellings on the 6,800 acres zoned residential, if present policies are held, the appearance will clearly *not* be rural. It is true that there are 3,500 acres of public park, but this is already secured.

The real question is whether planned developments should be permitted in this area at all. About 1,200 acres (almost a fifth) of the entire residentially zoned area has had applications pending for planned development, and much of the remaining vacant portion could be encouraged to use this form. But the county says "No—urban sprawl is the optimum."

Has the federal government stood idle in this situation? It has not. It has taken a firm stand—on the wrong side of the barricade, which poses another powerful obstacle. Amid charges that "a dreary band of zoning lawyers" is wrecking the county (one of the dreary band is fighting for the two major planned developments proposed) the government offers to withhold federal grant and loan funds until things are straightened out to its satisfaction. Presumably, planned development is one of the threats to the valley to be stamped out, or perhaps the federal stand was merely singularly uninformed and unselective.

In *The Creek and the City,* a beautifully written and illustrated document produced by the Department of the Interior, the recent county council is excoriated for its zoning record, and charged with "opening the gates to high-density development on the critical 1,200 acres and to all the inevitable additional high-density zoning it would initiate."[25] The "high-density" development referred to is apparently the two planned developments shown in "The Threat to the Valley."

25. U. S. Department of the Interior, *The Creek and the City* (Washington, D.C.: U.S. Government Printing Office, 1967), pp. 27-28.

High density in this case is somewhere around 11 persons (four dwelling units) per acre in one planned development we have examined, somewhat less than that in the other. It should be repeated for emphasis that this is at the low end of FHA's land-use intensity scale for metropolitan suburbs, and might be typified by Reston. The density is high only in relation to large-lot suburban sprawl zoning, which in itself is high in relation to the pattern of landholdings in rural areas.

Elsewhere in *The Creek and the City* it is stated, "The belated and somewhat frenzied emphasis on planning around metropolitan areas, the growing respectability of 'green space' and the increasing numbers of trees spared the delicate ministrations of bulldozers, the evaluation of cluster housing and whole planned communities of various sorts, all testify to this effort 'to improve the rules.' So do burgeoning debates over the shortcomings of the standard zoning system, which often encourages sprawl by restricting densities of *population* in areas where a restriction of the *density and distribution of buildings and pavements* is actually the prime need."[26]

The kind of development regulations I have proposed here do regulate the density and distribution of buildings and pavements. They require a stated minimum of open space, and require moreover that a stated minimum of that open space be nonvehicular (primarily landscaped, with neither roads, parking areas, nor buildings). The method for plan review gives ample opportunity for local control of design to prevent excessive runoff and erosion. The common open space provisions allow for intelligent use of steep slopes, for valley bottoms, and soils that should not be built upon, for checkdams and recreational lakes, for protection of existing forested areas, for running private open space into the public open space net. If townhouses and apartments are allowed as part of planned residential complexes, it is possible to allow more density and at the same time to provide more open space. These facts have been adequately and repeatedly presented to the Montgomery County Council, and it is unfortunate that the Department of the Interior has apparently not heard of them.

In its conclusion to the chapter on "The Creek and Land Planning," the Department comes out in favor of urban sprawl large-lot single-family zoning in upper Rock Creek: "Leaning on such relevant facts as we do have, we know that time is short and pressure intense, and that an excessive density of buildings and pavements in the upper watershed

26. *Ibid.*, p. 31.

will work irreparable damage on the creek. Probably no one with present data can say precisely what a permissible density and pattern of development might be, but the area master plan makes as restrained an estimate as it can and seeks to implement it with the tools at hand. We can hope that the tools will be improved and honed and maybe new ones found and combined in new ways, and strengthened by new knowledge to come. But for the time being the master plan is the bulwark we have against chaos in the upper watershed."[27]

The master plan appears to be a bulwark against planned development and any form of housing except single-family detached on large lots. We know within the experience of FHA what permissible density might appropriately be. We have the potential for an improved tool in planned development regulation for substantial tracts, and we can to some extent apply it in other areas. We have the open space net concept as a means for developing an open space system of maximum utility.

In Montgomery County, the principal obstacles to the use of these tools are apparently the planners (backed by a local power structure intensely devoted to current developmental patterns and opposed to housing in forms other than single-family detached) and those branches of the federal government which use their extensive powers to grant or withhold funds to prevent planned development or which propagandize against it. Outside the Washington metropolitan area, the federal obstacle has not as yet become so formidable.

Conclusion

This has been a discouraging picture, but perhaps there is a useful lesson in it for those who seek to improve future residential environment. It's a rough obstacle course.

To do what needs doing (and we obviously already know more than we can apply effectively) a long program of demonstration and education is needed. In my experience, the chief and most effective opponents to planned residential development in suburbia are suburban professional planners. This is tragic, even though we can sympathize with their position under the guns of suburban planning commissions. To give suburban planners the relief necessary, the principal educational effort will have to be directed to such planning commissions and to the publics whose interests they defend so exclusively. The education

27. *Ibid.*

of planning commissions, to be effective, may require clear and enlightened court decisions, which means that cases in this field must be extraordinarily carefully prepared.

Probably the most effective work in development of ideas for planned development and in missionary enterprise using planned development to improve the residential environment has come from the National Association of Home Builders and the Urban Land Institute. Stimulus here has come from enlightened self-interest, of course, but the results have great promise.

Now we need able and extensive support from the planning profession generally. We need purposeful planning research on potentials for improvement, and we need a great deal more planning literature demonstrating the advantages of such improvement. Above all, we need stronger evidence that planners support planning for all the people, present *and* future.

These things I believe. The future is long, extending beyond the year 2000. The public welfare which suburban planners should serve is not so narrow as the local jurisdiction nor limited to our own brief time, but extends across the metropolitan area as it now exists and as it is to come. The public interest served includes the interest of the unborn (who cannot vote but are entitled to representation). If we are to plan honestly, we must plan for the future of suburbia as something other than a straightline projection and multiplication of what we now have. We should prepare to provide future population with the highest level of amenities we can achieve in the form of open green space and recreation areas, and we should do it systematically. And if we are to use land efficiently and economically, if we are to avoid infinite and monotonous urban sprawl, we should promote planned developments in suburbia and elsewhere with a variety of housing types and with the highest population densities we can achieve consistent with the amenity level we can supply as a result of combined public and private effort.

To the extent that these views are shared by others, we can build a far better suburbia, and we can use much of what we learn in the process to improve our central cities and opportunities for their citizens. But if local planners and federal forces combine to preserve and enlarge the suburban status quo, planning will become a mere provincial defensive exercise, betraying its promise for urban regions, for the present and for the future.

Planning for protection against difference?

On housing matters, most planners join likeminded laymen, legislators, lawyers, administrators, and courts in wielding public powers to defend the established folkways and current fashions of the majority of the affluent against the poor and against minorities.

Most planners express themselves as liberals. They favor a kind of comprehensive planning which limits private actions for the benefit of the general public. They say they are against racial segregation. They favor a federal Department of Urban Affairs. They back urban renewal and public housing. Surely these are the expressions of a liberal view.

The difference between what planners say and what they do has been comfortably rationalized into a "workable program" for using liberal cliches to support conservative values. Now the old order changes. Many planners are pushed toward the schizoid brink as the federal government insists, with formidable financial persuasion, that liberal principles must lead to liberal action.

Consider whence we have come and whither we are going. Bassett said in 1940: "A good zoning plan for a city furnishes harmonious regulations for every part so that the whole conserves the health, safety, morals, comfort, convenience and general welfare of the whole community."

As zoning developed, said Bassett, "The demand throughout the country for the segregation of detached, one-family houses from multifamily houses was so great, and the proof so clear that there were health and safety considerations that justified such separation, that courts gradually recognized as valid the graduations of residence districts according to the number of families per unit building. . . .

"As far as possible, it is well to segregate residential uses from business and industrial uses. [Note that this segregation is one-way.] Use districts are ordinarily residential, business and industrial. The district of less restricted use always admits the uses of the more restricted ones. . . .

"Many persons . . . consider that a business district is for business and nothing else. As a matter of fact, residences can be erected as freely in such districts as stores. . . .

"One of the earliest efforts in use zoning was to exclude residences from industrial districts. There was much to be said for this practice in that homes ought not to be among factories, and factory uses ought to be protected from constant complaints of common law nuisance. . . . However, on upland terrain—where homes can well exist until the land is needed for industry—it would be unreasonable to prevent residences. Then, too, an owner in such a locality might well say that his plot was too small for a factory, that owners of existing factories would not buy his land, that a store would be a total loss, and that to prohibit him from building a home would prevent his earning any return whatever on his land. Such considerations have prevented the widespread employment of this particular kind of exclusion. Under the usual zoning plan, where owners of land can build residences in industrial districts, whoever does so will assume the risk of having factories next door. Occupation for residence purposes will probably be temporary—until such time as the land can be used for factories."

That's where we stood less than 25 years ago. We started revising our thinking at the bottom of the zoning pyramid. It seemed that "harmonious regulations for every part for the general welfare of the whole community" might be more harmonious and more in keeping with the general welfare if residences were kept out of industrial districts, whether the landowner was willing to risk having a factory built next door or not. We noted that such housing was not likely to be occupied by the owner, and that it was generally anything but temporary—in fact it blocked further industrial development. Courts have gone along with these views, and even with the notion that housing may be barred from many commercial districts.

But what about the top of the pyramid? Is it still true that demand for segregation of detached one-family houses is so great, and proof so clear that *health and safety* considerations justify separation of detached one-family housing from all else, that courts should continue to recognize the validity of such exclusionary zoning?

Two questions get to the heart of the matter. *Who* demands districts of detached one-family houses? Is it only the people who live in exclusive districts of detached one-family homes or the far larger number of people who live in single- and multiple-family structures in other districts? And what are now the *health and safety* considerations that require the discrimination?

Evidence is overwhelming that Bassett, like most of the current crop of planners, kidded himself in order to protect middle- to high-income groups against the outside world. Perhaps Bassett, like most present planners, knew that regulations could be drafted to cover any real health and safety hazards likely to arise from mixing multiple-family housing into previously exclusive single-family districts. (Apparently there were no important health and safety factors to cause concern when single-family was mixed with multiple in the "lower" districts, or any housing with commercial or industrial uses.) Bassett, a highly sophisticated man, must have known that to support social and economic segregation it was necessary to bring in health, safety and "general" welfare.

Before zoning, we allowed economics and social controls to handle our social and economic adjustments. An individual sufficiently assimilated culturally (or so well off that his idiosyncrasies could be overlooked) was somehow admitted to the elite suburbs. More recently, we have tried to use public controls, racial zoning (stricken by the courts), zoning by minimum cost of housing (also stricken), and zones permitting only single-family housing (sometimes with high minimum floor areas) on very large lots. This latest effort sometimes gets by the courts and sometimes not, depending on how transparent the real intent became (and perhaps which side the judge was on before the case was tried).

Most public planners and most planning consultants now spend an inordinate amount of time devising means to use public regulation to defend the elite from the "different," who by unwritten definition are unsafe, unhealthy, immoral, uncomfortable, and inconvenient.* The present line of defense is to keep out "different" housing—apartments (garden, high-rise, condominium, and other), townhouses, and so

*Since this was written in February 1964, major developments have occurred which are promising. Some laws and court decisions have ruled against certain exclusionary practices.—Ed.

on—in order to keep out "different" people. Defense is on grounds of aesthetics, destruction of character of neighborhoods, overtaxing of schools, and of sewer and water facilities, traffic congestion, and so on. Most of the arguments can be refuted by facts, but few defenders of single-family suburbia are interested in the facts. Opposition to different forms of housing is merely the smoke. The fire is opposition to different *people,* to potential changes in the established social, economic, and political order.

"It is well known that residents of detached single-family homes are permanent, moral, and responsible; residents of apartments transient, immoral, and irresponsible; and residents of condominiums a little odd." "Apartments mean federal financing, and federal financing means open occupancy." These are the arguments in closed meetings. At well-regulated public hearings, expressions can be paraphrased thus (with some effort at exposing the fallacies by giving the whole inference of the declarations):

"It is less expensive to provide urban facilities and services to residences scattered all over the landscape than to the same number of people housed in a smaller area." "If apartments are allowed, there will be more children per unit than if the same number of families settled in detached homes." "There will be greater traffic congestion if high densities are permitted near principal destinations than if the same traffic passes the proposed site on its way from single-family residences in outlying areas." There are any number of "everyone knows" arguments which are equally fallacious, and when one is nailed, there is plenty of room for shifting ground.

Recent federal elections have not been swung by the suburban elite, and federal executives know it. The votes of labor, Negroes, Catholics, the poor, the unemployed, the underprivileged and the stomped-on have been counted, and the results appear in federal appointments and in federal policies. Thus it is increasingly difficult to maintain racial, economic, or social segregation through the use of local public regulations.

As the continuing compromise moves on, the results will neither be as bad as the single-family elite fear, nor as good as the determined reformers hope. Social controls and such laws of economics as are not repealed by federal action will continue to operate, even after discriminatory local public regulation has been upset by well-deserved federal intervention and more enlightened courts impressed by better prepared cases. The ignorant, the illiterate, the shiftless, the criminal of any race or creed will not be uplifted by federal edict. But for those of any race, creed, or employment, artificial local public barriers with no real relation to the general welfare will be removed.

For planners, the moral is this: Unless we practice what we preach, and take our thumbs off the scales, we do not deserve public esteem. It is time to mean what we have said, to serve *all* the people and not merely a select few. Consider all without giving *public* special privilege to any, to the end that there are good plans and harmonious regulations for every part of the urban area, "so that the whole conserves the health, safety, morals, comfort, convenience and general welfare *of the whole community.*"

Planning for people *or planning for taxes?*

Planning for people builds toward one kind of an urban environment. Planning for taxes, under current taxation systems of local government, builds toward another. The city for people and the city for taxes are not at all alike.

If planning is to be dominated by tax considerations, a tendency which seems to be increasing, it should be done by tax experts rather than planners. This would put the job in the hands of the appropriate profession. Most of the current crop of planners, whatever their other accomplishments, are not tax experts, and efforts to plan with one eye on taxes and the other on what they are trained to do produce predictable effects on planner and plans.

Planning for taxes, under present compulsions, under present systems of local government financing, and more particularly under present patterns of real estate taxation introduces an entirely new set of ground rules and objectives, some of which are diametrically opposed to those which govern planning for people.

Planning cannot operate successfully under two sets of rules so diverse in their objectives. There is of course a growing crisis in municipal finance. Should the city then be reconstructed to meet the financial crisis, or should there be financial reform? Many planners have apparently chosen the first alternative, and in so doing have abandoned planning for people.

Disenchantment with the kind of real property taxation we have is spreading rapidly. To date, few planners are in the forefront in seeking reforms, and many work toward the City of Taxes rather than the City of Man. Most pressures for improvement come from outside the planning field:

Three things, at least, are wrong with making present tax systems a major determinant in planning. (1) A city planned for taxes is likely to become a poor city for people. (2) A poor city for people becomes a poor city for taxes also. (3) A city twisted to fit present obsolescent and inadequate tax methods is likely to lose its "advantages" as tax methods change, and to be left with bad patterns of development.

Schizophrenic symptoms

There is nothing simple about the mixture of logic, nonlogic, fact, fancy, prejudice, conditioning, private advantage, public interest, rationalization, snobbery, science, art, and politics behind public policy decisions. It behooves the planner to know which is which, and to frame his recommendations as honestly as he can, within the public purposes of planning and within the constitutional framework of our form of government.

A "sophisticated" elite, with a whole range of legal private contracts and deed restrictions at its disposal for protecting its private values, chooses rather to misuse public controls. Municipal governments permitting themselves to be used to serve such ends seek circuitous means to accomplish objectives which have been declared unconstitutional if sought directly. And courts, because they are careless, because they are in sympathy with the elite, or because cases are poorly prepared or presented, permit themselves to see only the glittering public-purpose pinnacles of the iceberg and overlook the dark, submerged anti-public nine-tenths of the mass.

Things to look out for and look into

Planners who take time to find out where money comes from and where it goes in local government will not be so easily carried away by misleading propaganda.

Many planners and public officials take it for granted that property taxes in general, and residential taxes in particular, play a much more important part in local finance than is actually the case. This is a holdover from 30 years ago and before, when property taxes made up about two-thirds of city revenues, instead of the present (1962) one-third.

Planners should also be informed (and prepared to counter misinformation) concerning performance of and sources of payment for governmental facilities and services serving the local population. Many are provided in whole or in part through county, state, or federal sources or through special districts, thus spreading the tax base. The average citizen is not aware of the shift toward broader participation in providing and paying for such installations and programs—and this is true also of the average planner.

Tendency to plan for taxes rather than public need might be reduced if planners knew the present score on taxes. But this is not enough. Where public need is clear, planners should seek to meet it whether the scale or form or location of development is "profitable" under current revenue-producing systems or not, and then should join in the search for financial reforms which will make it possible to meet the need. On this, the help of competent experts in governmental finance will be needed. Planners should be certain that revised methods of revenue-production will not, in their turn, induce unsound planning.

Development policies for metropolitan suburbia

From metropolitan centers across the nation, outspreading waves of growth flood over farmlands and rural villages. Cities once isolated are swept into mainstream urban currents, and find that where they once measured population gains in hundreds per decade, they now count thousands per year. (The dangers of detailed prognostication are well known, but whether 50 million new metropolitan suburbanites are on the scene in 1975 or 1985, and whether the number is 25 million or 75 million, the problem of explosive growth is there—and it doesn't seem likely to stop when any of these figures or dates are reached.)

Massive population increase now just starting in metropolitan suburbia is not localized in a computer in the Bureau of the Census. It has started and is happening and will continue to happen to land and people and governments as fringe growth moves near them and to them and past them, a wave which spreads but shows little sign of receding. And it brings problems, financial and other.

Perspective on governmental finance

Urbanization in metropolitan fringes does not wait until financial problems are solved. It proceeds in spite of present means for collecting and disbursing governmental revenues, a hodgepodge of expedient piled on expedient.

Metropolitan areas on the current—let alone the coming—scale are something new. A hundred years ago, we had only 16 cities in the country with populations over 50,000, basic requirement now for the central city of a metropolitan area. In 1930, metropolitan districts reported by the Census numbered 96; in 1940, 140; in 1950, 172—and in that year more than half the population of the nation (for the first time) lived in metropolitan areas. In 1960, the number of metropolitan areas had risen to 212, and the proportion of total population living in metropolitan areas was almost two-thirds.

Metropolis is here in fact, but not here in government. There isn't even a generally accepted system for coordination between the multitudinous governmental units. But whether we like it or not, we are building a new America, a solidly metropolitan civilization. Taken individually, the problems of suburban Woodland are merely the problems of suburban Woodland. When the same thing is happening to hundreds of Woodlands, and is about to happen to thousands, the impact is of a different order and we will make adjustments in the traditional democratic manner, which means after the status quo becomes unbearable.

It is easily overlooked that we *have* been making almost revolutionary changes in the functions of government, the levels of government by which these functions are performed, and the way government is financed. At the national level, the income tax, a relative newcomer, is foremost among a number of federal taxes which were not there 40 or 50 years ago, and quite a number of people will remember the first federal billion dollar budget and the alarm it caused in 1917. It runs about two hundred times that now.

There have been, and will continue to be, major shifts in sources of revenue for support of local governmental functions. Total taxes now make up less than half of local governmental revenues, and property taxes, which contributed two-thirds of all local revenues 30 or 40 years ago now make up less than 40 per cent, with residential property taxes accounting for 25 per cent.

There is growing dissatisfaction with the effect of property tax on development, the way it rewards deterioration and penalizes building anew, encourages speculation and discourages constructive use.

We depend increasingly on national, statewide, and countywide measures which tap resources without allowing taxpayers to move a short distance across the line and escape paying a fair share of the bills. We move rapidly toward consolidation of functions and consolidation of the revenue-producing base, toward common action or sharing of financial responsibility in solving problems which can't be handled effectively at fragmented local levels.

As an example take schools. School revenues come increasingly from outside the immediate area. There is substantial federal aid for local schools. States have minimum foundation programs. And we are turning toward consolidated school districts (as we turned from the Little Red Schoolhouse to the consolidated school) in order to avoid situations where areas with concentrations of industrial development, school revenue potential high and school needs low, can thumb their noses at areas with low revenue potential and high school needs.

At local levels, we sprout nonproperty taxes like mushrooms—admission and amusement taxes, cigarette taxes, automobile license taxes, gross receipts taxes on businesses, business licenses (primarily for revenue), hotel and apartment occupancy taxes, income taxes, public utility taxes, sales taxes, and liquor taxes, to name some of the most important. These are all being used as municipal nonproperty taxes on top of state and federal taxes on many of the same things. As early as 1956, two municipalities had taxes on television antennas.

In addition, we are now levying direct service charges on things once assumed to be included in property tax—garbage and trash collection and sewerage, to name a couple. Almost all cities are in the water business and the parking business, and many are in the electric business using "profits" to help pay for deficits in other activities.

Robbing Peter to pay Paul has become a science. Sewer revenues are pledged to back bonds for parking lots, parking revenues to pay for water systems, water revenues to pay for city halls, gas tax to pay for schools, cigarette tax to pay for sewers, and anything not committed will be, most probably, to something totally unrelated.

The point of all this is that our systems for getting and spending for local facilities and services are changing rapidly even now, before more than the first stirrings of pressure from those 50 million newcomers. Change to come will be greater, and the pace of change will be faster. The revolution is just starting. Extensive and largely unpredictable changes are sure to come. Harsh economic forces shove toward painful decisions long deferred. Massive political pressures are building. Something new will emerge from present chaos, and it may even be related in some way to logic in finance. The Rube Goldberg school of municipal finance is passing—because it must.

This should make it clear that long-term development policies (or short-term development policies sure to have long-term effects) should *not* be based on current fiscal expediency. Yet current literature and loud local arguments suggest directly or by implication that the city of tomorrow should be shaped to fit the financial crises of today and yesterday.[1]

The scientific route to misguided conclusions

Studies of varying validity show that under current patterns of revenue and expenditure, this, that, or the other use, considered independently, produces net surplus or deficit for cities.

One conclusion which is general is that vacant land in surburban areas is most "profitable" in terms of municipal cost-revenue ratio. Planners and governing bodies alike have almost completely ignored the magnificent implications of this fact in creating urban development policy. The ideal city consists of vacant, taxable land. Some compromise would need to be made with legal necessity here. The *almost* ideal city consists of a luxury high-rise apartment containing the minimum number of tenants necessary to meet requirements for municipal incorporation (but no children), having the city hall in a room in the basement, and surrounded by vast areas of vacant taxable land owned by wealthy outsiders, who, for federal tax reasons, desire neither to use it nor to sell it.

At the other extreme, industrial development, considered as an isolated item, is usually highly profitable judged by the local cost-revenue ratio. Housing for employees of industry is not, since it normally involves relatively high governmental costs for schools and municipal facilities and services and does not, by itself, provide equivalent revenues. From this pair of carefully isolated facts, it becomes apparent that sound development policy for a community should encourage industry but discourage housing for the employees who make industrial production possible, since they don't pay their own way. Thus industry without employee housing might be added to the high-revenue high-rise and vacant land in the ideal city.

A scanning of recent speeches, articles, and studies gives more evidence than is really needed to back the argument that planners and city policy-makers are giving inordinate weight to current fiscal expe-

1. For more details on revenue sources and potentials, and for additional arguments against letting financial expediency dictate development policies, see "Planning for People or Planning for Taxes?", pp. 126-128.

diency in shaping developmental policies. In what follows, no mention is made of the kind of city needed to meet human needs in an evolving metropolitan environment. Total emphasis is on what pays and what doesn't under present revenue-production systems, and even here the economic interplay is lost, and the elements considered in magnificent isolation.

Through most of the items quoted, the emphasis is on means to achieve families without school children, or with as few as possible. Presumably the optimum goal here would be development policies to assure that the city of tomorrow will have no children. This fits well with other goals of the same kind—industry without resident employees, shopping centers without resident customers, and the like.

Architectural Forum, in April 1963, carried an article entitled "The Apartment Boom," which pointed out that "suburban communities have come to realize that apartment buildings pay more than their fair share of community costs, particularly for schools—whereas tracts of single-family homes invariably create deficits in community budgets."

A survey cited for Stamford, Connecticut, is quoted as giving apartment units a cost-revenue "surplus" of $33.34 annually on school costs only, a major item making up 40 per cent of total city budget. "High rise apartments attract young families without school age children, and older families whose children are on their own or in college." The single-family dwellings produce a school child from every two houses, as against one from every eight apartment units, according to the Stamford survey.

The *Forum* article goes on to point out that suburbs are beginning to realize that land is becoming scarce and that "apartments are valued as much as five times higher than single-family houses. . . . These statistics are not lost on the suburbs—zoning restrictions, which once were formulated to keep out high-rise apartments, are fast being shuffled to invite them."

In the general scheme of things, it appears obvious that high-rise and other apartments, along with high-density single-family dwellings—the townhouse, the patio house, the attached house—are all highly appropriate in close-in metropolitan suburbs. With the coming multiplication of population, permitting people who wish to do so to live as near urban centers as possible may be more than a matter of serving their convenience. It may be a way to stave off metropolitan bankruptcy—of which more later. At the moment, the point is that zoning ordinances and other regulatory devices must not be "shuffled" to invite this use or exclude that on the grounds indicated here. If they are, planning for sound long-range development is bound to fail.

Consider another planning study, "Land Use and Municipal Finance," from West Hartford, Connecticut. This one was done in 1960:

"Of the 11 tax-paying uses described, all but two contribute more in taxes than they receive in services. The two are single-family homes and two- through four-family homes. . . . The large portion of the Board of Education budget spent on these two uses is the critical factor causing this unbalance. . . . The other nine tax-paying uses combined make up the deficit created by these two uses and the three nontaxpaying uses.

"Vacant land is the most financially beneficial use. For every tax dollar spent servicing such land, $3.88 is received in tax payment.

"Although single-family houses produce the largest total deficit, they are not shirkers by any means. As a group, they contribute 90¢ of every tax dollar spent in their behalf. . . . Two, three and four-family homes, dollar for dollar, show up with the largest deficit. This use received a dollar's worth of service for only 68¢ in tax payment."

For each dollar in municipal costs, according to this study, there is a revenue return of $1.26 from retail establishments, $2.84 from wholesale, storage, and semi-industrial uses, $2.73 from all other commercial and service uses, and $2.71 for industrial property. In the case of retail and industrial uses, "the practice of assessing personal property is responsible for their financially advantageous position."

And in a singularly astute note: "Attempts to apply any of the foregoing results to any other community, *or to the same community during a different period of time,* would prove very misleading and frustrating." [Emphasis added.]

From a 1962 study, "Apartments—Analysis of Multiple Family Dwellings, the Prospects and Recommendations for the City of Falls Church, Virginia":

"On the basis of average figures compiled through a representative sampling, single-family residences yield an annual deficit . . . averaging $152. Multi-family garden developments yield an annual deficit of $115 per dwelling unit on the average. . . . An average surplus of $129 per dwelling unit is yielded by high-rise apartments. . . .

"The advantages of high-rise apartments far outweigh garden apartments because of (1) greater tax revenue; (2) greater purchasing power of tenants; (3) fewer school children; (4) a greater yield of revenue per square foot of land used."

From this and similar calculations, the inevitable conclusion concerning development policy is reached:

"Future apartment construction in Falls Church should be limited to high-rise projects since land available for this type of development is limited and this type of development provides a greater source of revenue."

Is this planning for a city or planning for a business? Curiously, the way to greater profits through prohibiting further single-family housing was not explored.

As an indication of how fast things are changing (or of how widely surveys of the same area may differ) here are citations of two studies of Prince George's County, Maryland. In an excellent Planning Advisory Service report, *Planning for Apartments,*[2] Jon K. Rosenthal mentions a 1959 analysis by the Maryland National Capital Park and Planning Commission which indicated that in Prince George's County "luxury and restrictive" (presumably high-rise) apartments yielded an average of .08 students per unit, standard or average apartments .15 students per unit, and single-family developments .19 students per unit. *Urban Land,* in January 1964, carried an item "A New Cost and Income Analysis of Family Dwelling, Apartment and Business Units" with a reference to figures for fiscal year 1963-64 produced by the Economic Development Committee of Prince George's County:

"Apartment units in Prince George's County pay more in taxes than they cost the county government for services, while single-family homes cost the County far more than the owners pay in taxes, according to the report.

"The report also maintains that the business community pays in taxes more than six times the cost of all services rendered, and carries the load to fill the deficit created by demands upon county government for services to individual homes. . . .

"The Committee's report concludes that 'apartment dwellers, for a change, can be recognized in the community as responsible taxpaying citizens who are more than paying their full share of the cost of all government services and actually return a surplus to the County of $18 per unit.'

2. American Society of Planning Officials, *Planning for Apartments,* Planning Advisory Service Report No. 139 (Chicago: ASPO, 1960).

"Stressing the high cost of education, which takes 70 cents from each tax dollar, the study shows that the average single-family home sends a statistical .943 students to school, while the average for apartments is only .242 per unit."

In the same county, then, studies less than five years apart showed single-family with .19 or .943 students per unit, and apartments with .08 for high-rise and .15 for standard as against .242 for all apartments.

Additional quotations to the same effect could be added at considerable length, but to little purpose. They would demonstrate a very broad range in cost-revenue balance for particular uses. They would generally show that single-family detached dwellings produce the greatest deficits, low-density residential uses—two- to four-family dwellings, garden apartments, and "standard" apartments—lesser deficits or small gains, and high-rise apartments the highest net gains in the residential sector. (In fact, a study on "High-Rent Apartments in the Suburbs" by Anshel Melamed, appearing in *Urban Land* for October 1961, states: "High-rise, high-rental apartments provide more than twice as much tax revenue per acre as any other suburban use surveyed." With service charges relatively low, this would mean that in the Philadelphia area he studied, net revenues for high-rise would top those for shopping centers, professional uses, or industrial uses.)

It would be ridiculous to conclude from these studies that single-family housing should be barred, and that only those forms of apartment housing producing a surplus should be admitted, along with commercial, industrial, and other producers of net revenues. It should not be necessary—but obviously is necessary—to consider alternative courses for shaping development policies for areas outside the metropolitan center, and where such courses are likely to lead as the 50 million newcomers (virtually all of whom will be children) appear in metropolitan suburbs.

None of the planning studies cited are directed toward correcting the obvious inequities and absurdities in the tax revenue producing system. All are efforts to warp the city of tomorrow to fit it.

Alternative A—planning to fit present revenue

If shifting and obsolescent revenue production and distribution systems of today are allowed to shape tomorrow's cities, tomorrow's cities will be ill-adapted to meet either the human or the revenue needs of their time. Once development takes place, the form of the city is relatively fixed, and can be changed only at great expense. Urban renewal in its current inadequate state makes this clear.

Where a metropolitan suburb is growing fast and has large areas of vacant land likely to have development character irretrievably fixed by tax-based development policy, the chances for error are multiplied, and so are the penalties.

Number of school children and costs per school child will continue to rise in the years ahead to the point where major shifts in financing methods are inevitable. The skills which build the nation's strength are increasingly acquired in the nation's schools, and we must also educate them longer and better. This means further increases in school costs.

Straws in the wind—in 1947, total school enrollment in the U.S. was 27.7 million; in 1952, 32.0 million; in 1960, 46.3 million; in 1963, 50.4 million. Out ahead, it looks like almost 75 million by 1980. We haven't located national figures on current expense per pupil (excluding capital outlay and debt service), but a recent study on elementary and high school current costs in Florida[3] indicates current expenditures per pupil rising as follows for the years cited above: 1947, $117; 1952, $194; 1960, $300; 1963, $342. Out ahead, $500? $600? $700?

Something has to give. We cannot sacrifice quantity or quality of education. To support education on the scale indicated, the financial base *must* broaden. Probably this means increased contributions from state and federal levels. Undoubtedly there will be increased financial interdependence within metropolis. Certainly it will be increasingly difficult for taxpayers in select suburban cities to build walls around themselves and remain unaffected by what happens elsewhere.

Many suburban areas are now holding to large-lot single-family detached housing in order to minimize number of school children. This saddles such communities with a form of development which is very difficult to change, which is not logical in terms of location within metropolis or in terms of metropolitan needs, and which is very expensive to service. When the inevitable change in school financing methods comes, the "exclusive" suburb will find that it has neither escaped its share of school costs nor avoided financial responsibility for damage its shortsighted policies have caused elsewhere. The problem of

3. Division of Research, Florida State Department of Education, "Current Expense Per Pupil in Average Daily Attendance," Research Brief #4 (Tallahassee, Fla.: Division of Research, March 1964).

dual payment for mistakes has been very well stated in the comments below.

In the lead article in *Zoning Digest* for August 1963, Henry Horowitz urges density zoning as a substitute for division into single-family detached, two-family, and multiple-family dwelling districts. "Of course," says Horowitz, "use of the density approach need not subject all one-family districts to 'invasion' by other than one-family houses . . . but the location of these areas should be based on due consideration of transportation, sewerage, water supply, trash and garbage collection, fire and police protection, and other municipal services." There should not be "buttering of mass slices of community with regulations permitting only one type of housing. . . .

"To zone acres upon acres of land to avoid a 'school problem' or to insure against the invasion of certain 'elements' is a luxury few communities can afford. The taxpayers will inevitably pay for the sprawl resulting from this type of zoning, but instead of bearing the ominous title of school tax, the payments will be called highway debentures, sewerage bonds, water rate increases, equalization rate adjustments, capital improvement assessments, and the like."

Alternative B—planning logical urban development

Development policies based on plans for logical urban development are likely to be far more useful in the long run than those based on planning for present revenue.

Details of planning for the metropolitan explosion on us and ahead of us are very complex, but they can be organized far more easily with the help of a few guiding principles:

1. In the metropolitan area as a whole, the public interest being protected and promoted requires that increasing population be provided with a favorable environment and appropriate public and private facilities related to each other, and to population and facilities in surrounding areas, in a manner which will be safe, convenient, comfortable, efficient, and economical.

2. For individual cities within the metropolitan area, the first consideration should be function appropriate to location in the metropolitan community. Planning within the city should then seek amenity, efficiency, and economy in the performance of that function. A city so planned and developed will weather growth in population and changes

in social and economic currents in the long years ahead. In contrast, the city which molds its permanent form on housing fashions of the past and fiscal emergencies of the present is in for trouble as housing fashions and fiscal arrangements change.

3. In terms of time and distance, accessibility to jobs, labor force, materials, markets, and major urban facilities is likely to be in direct proportion to distance from the metropolitan center. This gives close-in locations advantages which should be maximized rather than ignored or deliberately sabotaged. Since metropolis is likely to have a major center or centers and also outlying subcenters, the same principle should apply in satellite nucleations within the metropolitan area: We should make the most of nearness in time and distance.

4. Land close in to centers and subcenters in metropolis is an increasingly scarce resource, and it is *the* basic resource. With massive growth coming on, it follows that we should greatly increase allowable residential densities at close-in locations *if we can do so without sacrificing amenities.* We cannot leave amenities to chance. We must define them and require them. Having done so, if we are prudent, we will fix realistic *minimums* on land-use intensity in close-in areas, with maximums limited by detailed performance standards.

5. On vacant tracts of any size in close-in areas—and we should prepare to expand our concepts as to what is close in with population growth and improvements in transportation facilities—we should allow *only* planned development. There are now such vacant tracts. Present urban renewal programs and coming suburban renewal programs will make more available. We cannot indefinitely permit repetition of the mistakes of the past, the lot-by-lot approach to development in rectangular or can-of-worms patterns, with land needed for parks wasted in useless front and side yards on individual lots and in unnecessary widths and lengths of residential streets.

6. In planning developments for housing, we must demand a quality of planning we are only beginning to achieve—a relation of streets to structures in which streets are subservient rather than dominant, a relation of structures to space which makes space infinitely more pleasant and useful, a conservation of land area which increases population density and at the same time *adds* to amenities.

7. In cities and in major planned developments, we should demand a mixture of housing types. Given well-balanced and well-related housing for the newly-married, for families raising children, and for the elderly or single, the city or neighborhood improves its prospects for

sinking deep roots, for establishing lasting traditions. It is likely to become and remain a community. Given one-class housing, the result is likely to remain a housing development (however large) with relatively transient occupancy.

8. In planning regulation, we must substitute understandable and well-reasoned performance standards for vague language and for specification codes poorly related to basic purposes.

Chapter 3 *Planning techniques*

Planning for action

In 25 years as a planner, I have been exposed to vast amounts of windy oratory about how planning will create a brave new world. It is heralded as a miracle drug for all the ailments of the body politic, the most versatile and powerful patent medicine ever conceived by the mind of man or concocted by his hand. Generally it is sold and administered by plausible strangers, who explain that it is easier for them to come in and do the job for you than for you to do it for yourselves, with the help of somebody who knows the ropes. It's easier for plausible strangers that way, too. I make my living by being a plausible stranger, and I know. Plausible strangers in this field are called planning consultants.

The usual treatment goes like this. The Expert looks your town over and goes away and makes passes with colored pencils, zipatone overlays, and other mystic paraphernalia and writes reports in a language called Planningese. After longer than you thought it would take, he comes back with reports wrapped in a cover labelled MASTER PLAN, gives them to the planning commission, makes a speech, and leaves town. There, now. That wasn't too bad, was it? Your city will start getting better right away and keep improving itself until the magic potion wears off. At that point, or if it doesn't work, you can always try again. After all, if you go about setting things up properly, the federal government pays most of the costs with free money.

I have some radical notions about planning. I think of it only as a means for getting intelligent action, and not as an end in itself. I believe that it will work only in a framework of good local government, and that in many cases we would do better to improve the character of local government first, letting planning come when local government is ready for it. Little is gained by presenting cobblers with a turret lathe.

I believe that as much of planning should be done locally as possible, and by local people. Most of it can be. Of course there should be technical guidance and assistance, but planning which does what it is supposed to do is usually done with a maximum of local participation as it goes along, building in local understanding and support. Planning should be oil for the machinery of local government, not a brick dropped suddenly into the works.

I believe that as with other new functions of government (libraries, fire departments, police protection, schools, recreation, and other things which in historic perspective are recent additions), citizen boards are helpful in early stages of evolution. I believe that as planning proves itself as a part of good administration, and as planners develop knowledge and techniques toward which they are now groping, the citizen board should get out of the act. We aren't there yet, in most places.

I believe that if planning is going to do your city any real and lasting good, it should start from where you are and work forward, not from where somebody thinks you may be in 20 years and work backward. You need a comprehensive plan, of course—a plan which brings together the major patterns and elements of development in your town and makes them fit better into what you want your town to be. But to my way of thinking, it is better to have a current plan, covering things you know must be done soon and working them into a pattern which is most likely to fit things which may come later, than to spend undue time or money in attempting to structure a future far out ahead. Usually long-range predictions and projections made on the basis of common sense and without computer analysis are just as accurate as those made by complex means. Neither is much good. Which is why you should start with a current plan covering things you can foresee with some usable degree of accuracy and change it as you find out how to do things better, or as moving into the future gives you clearer vision as to which way things are moving, and how fast.

I have seen any number of cases where planning could have taken hold of a problem right under its nose and done something intelligent to solve it, but chose instead to engage in lengthy research as to the shape of things to come while the problem grew beyond manageable proportions. That kind of approach doesn't make much sense.

We need first to organize our tools, get them in shape for convenient and continuous use, and arrange to keep them that way. If this tooling up is done right, it will be useful to other departments of local government beside planning. If the tools are multipurpose, we can afford to spend more time and money making and maintaining them.

We need next to get an organized and coordinated *planned action* program (not just a planning program) and to keep it current after we get it set up. In promoting or guiding planned action, we need regulations which will encourage desirable action, and head off that which is undesirable. These include the whole range of planning controls—codes and ordinances—and some others we haven't started to use intelligently, such as taxation, business licensing, and so on.

If we bear firmly in mind that the end objective of planning is not the production of plans, but the production of informed, intelligent, well-organized action, we won't go far wrong.

With these generalities out of the way, here are some down-to-earth details.

Organizing help

The first step in organized planning is to organize people. The first step in organizing people is to decide who to organize. Here are some things to consider in setting up your steering group (whether you call it a development committee, a planning commission, or something else):

1. Get people who can cause things to happen tied in closely with the group which is going to decide what ought to happen.
2. Get broad representation of all groups which have a constructive interest in community well-being. Don't leave out a group unless you mean to.
3. Don't get overbalanced with people noted for public grinding of private axes, or with representatives of groups more interested in milking the town than in taking care of it.
4. Include some people who will work, or can get work done.

In the early stages, keep informal and flexible and tentative. Don't start off by adopting a final organization chart and a constitution and by-laws. Start a trial run on one or two simple and obvious things which need doing, and find out what (and who) will work, and what (and who) will not.

If you can't break through on doing one or two of the things which most obviously need to be done, either you have the wrong kind of committee or you have a town in which an organized planned action program isn't going to do much good. If the committee is the problem, strengthen it or fold it up and start over. If the town is the problem, you aren't ready to start a program which will call for action on a number of projects if you can't get action on one or two. You need to build up community planning. The problem isn't to get planning (at this stage in this situation). It is to find something which the community can and will do, and which it will be proud of when it is done.

Assuming that you can get the right people organized, and that the time is ripe to move ahead on an organized planned action program, what then?

What outside help will do for you depends on two things: (1) the kind you get, and (2) how you use it.

As a first principle on outside help, get good general guidance early. It will save a lot of time and mistakes and lost motion. A general consultant should help you sort out the things you can and should do for yourselves from things on which you need specialized assistance; he can tell you where to get specialized assistance; and he can help prepare instructions for local workers on things which can be handled locally.

As a second principle, use the general consultant to work *with* you, not to go off in a corner someplace and do the job *for* you, trying to explain it all at once when he is finished. No report is a substitute for understanding.

As a third principle, those things you can do well for youselves, do for yourselves. Stretch funds by hiring outside help only when you really need it. Don't import somebody at $10 an hour to do work that could be done by local volunteers or by people who could be hired locally at $1 an hour.

As a fourth principle, when you need specialized technicians, get the best you can afford, not the cheapest available. But be sure you are getting the best, not merely the most expensive.

There are national organizations to which you can turn for help, and there are federal and state agencies, universities, and power companies. And of course there are private planning consultants.

Among the latter there are numerous quacks who became planning consultants by the simple expedient of having it printed on their letterheads. If you are hiring a consultant, check to see whether he is a member of the American Institute of Planners. This isn't an infallible guide, but it does mean that he has had some screening by his peers. Of course the best test of the competence of a professional planner is to find out what happened after he worked elsewhere—not what the plans looked like, but whether they did anything.

Another source of help is written material. So many texts, manuals, guidebooks, monographs, and miscellaneous bits and pieces have been written on everything from aesthetics to zoning that some must be worth reading.

Before leaving the subject of outside help, let me urge you, as a most important middle-range objective, to get the outside help inside as soon as possible. Larger cities should have planning staffs of their own, depending on consultants only for special work. Smaller cities should try to get together with neighboring large cities or neighboring small cities to make joint arrangements for regular staff assistance. Sometimes counties can set up staffs to serve both the county and all or part of the cities.

Organizing facts

Good planning depends on good information, carefully selected, current to the degree appropriate to purpose, and organized for use.

Planners are merely an oratorical society if they assume that because they live in a town they know all about it. If, on the other hand, they get analysis paralysis, they will disappear beneath dead statistics and old newspaper clippings.

On collecting information, there is a simple rule. If you need it, can get it, and know what you are going to use it for, collect it. If you don't, don't.

Normally, local maps have been pieced together from old plats rather than drawn up on the basis of a general survey. It has been my experience that if you take enough old plats and try to piece them together, you'll wish you hadn't, and both your temper and your morals will suffer. After you get mad enough, you will wind up cheating.

Because aerial photography has been around quite a while now, and because it is now possible to get drafting film which is very close to the same size on wet days as on dry, here's a way to handle mapping when a city isn't in financial shape for a general survey but wants workable maps and wants to know what the score is on errors.

You start by getting tailor-made photography. Let's say we are using a scale of 200′ = 1″. The area should be flown down the center of half-sections—*not* down section and half-section lines—with plenty of ground controls. (This is not a job for a semi-pro with a crop-dusting plane and a Brownie camera.) Then you get film positives for atlas sheets. A film positive makes it possible to run all the prints you want on either blue-line or black-line paper for about two cents per square foot, or you can get it done for eight to 10 cents per square foot, if you don't have your own machine.

At the 200′ scale, on photo-atlas sheets covering quarter-sections (half a mile on a side) the primary areas will be 13.2″ square, but it's a good idea to leave a "convenience fringe" around the outer edges, so that the film positive sheets will be somewhat larger than that.

You draft your map atlas on tracing film over the photographic atlas sheets. Here, of course, you are working from plats, but when you run across mistakes in the original surveys you will usually know exactly where they are. Why? Because ground features shown in the aerials will fail to correspond to the plats. So instead of starting from scratch to locate a needle in a haystack, you know exactly where to start looking. When you get ready to make the corrections on the map atlas, you can do so easily by erasing on the film. It will stand a lot of erasures.

If you develop your material this way, you have a very valuable beginning on a mapping system which can be kept up to date, and which can be used in a variety of combinations. Since your base map and your aerial photos are to the same scale, and since both are prepared on transparent film, you can print the two as a sandwich and come up with a combined aerial photograph and base map. This is tremendously helpful, because it shows the location of every building, driveway, sidewalk, utility pole, and tree in relation to property lines.

What is more, it tells where unplatted roads are located, where roads which have been platted have been built and where they have not, where there are swampy areas, and even (in some cases) where the boundaries of flood plains lie.

But the utility of the system doesn't end there. If you will prepare separate additional sheets on sewer, water, and utility installations, you can sandwich them with the base map atlas sheets, the aerial photography atlas sheets, or each other to make prints with a variety of combinations. When you get new photography in four or five years, it sandwiches in without jiggering to give you an up-to-date combined base map and photo atlas. Elements can be added or subtracted from the sandwich material without extensive redrafting.

To go from the map atlas sheets to work maps for parts of the area, you simply run copies of the sheets involved and paste them together. To make a general map of the city, you paste up atlas sheet prints carefully and send the composite off to be photographed at set scales as a photopositive on film. If the area involved is too large to handle on one sheet at the 200′ scale, you can have a general map prepared at this scale in sections, and perhaps another at 400′ = 1″ and a third at 600′ = 1″. The photography doesn't cost much—$100 should more than cover the cost of three base maps in most cases, and you have the equivalent of three tracings on film. Incidentally, you can erase and make additions and corrections on these photographic film positives.

A great deal more could be said about this technique, but you probably get the point. It is possible for even a relatively small city to get its maps in shape and keep them that way without great expense.[1]

Other planning maps

After you get your base maps and aerial photography in shape, what planning information can you or should you put on maps? Bearing in mind the rule that you shouldn't collect and organize information you aren't going to use, here are some maps which you very probably could use. On a minimum basis, they would best be prepared on the combination base map-photo sheets. At an improved level, they could be prepared as sandwich sheets to be overprinted with the base map sheets, the aerial photo, or the utility sheets in any combination you want.

1. *Parcel map.* Most base maps show lots as they were platted.

1. For a fuller discussion of mapping see American Society of Planning Officials, *Coordinated Mapping and Aerial Survey System for Small Cities,* Planning Advisory Service Report No. 225, August 1967, and *Planning Maps for Small Cities: How To Make and Maintain Them,* Planning Advisory Service Report No. 227, October 1967 (Chicago: ASPO).

The parcel map shows actual patterns of ownership. Actual patterns of ownership are usually quite different from lot maps—people have bought combinations of lots and portions of lots, and the usual base map doesn't tell you this. It is something you need to know about for zoning, for studies of population density to guide in planning for water, sewer and streets, for tax purposes, and for a variety of other reasons.

The parcel map, in combination with the aerial photo, gives the truest picture of natural physical features and the things which man has added both in the way of physical changes and in the way of property lines.

2. *Land-use map.* This is a must in any planning program. It shows present use of land—residential, commercial, industrial, public and semi-public, vacant, and other important categories and subcategories. From this map you get essential information on the extent and pattern of present development, how much land is available for new development of different kinds, and where new development and facilities might be appropriate. This map should be prepared so that it can be kept current from week to week or month to month.

Because this map is so important, here are some suggestions on how it might best be made. Using prints made by combining the parcel map atlas sheets and the photo atlas sheets, indicate uses by color code (best for general reference) or symbols (best if reproduction is important). If reproduction is necessary, the symbols will need to be put on a separate sandwich.

If you use colors (and I much prefer them), put them on the buildings or portions of buildings involved in the use, or on land which is actually in use for the purpose indicated. This gets you away from the conventional system, where a small store in the corner of an acre of land is likely to get the whole acre colored in to indicate commercial.

3. *Development trends, buildings.* This shows when each building in town was constructed. Maintained on a current basis, it can be one of the most important tools in the kit. It spells out past and present patterns of growth and will help you avoid a lot of mistakes. On current growth, it tells you what is actually happening, so that you have a check on any predictions you may have made. This year's knowledge is better than last year's predictions. This map will keep the unexpected from being undetected.

4. *Development trends, land.* This tells when the various subdivi-

sions making up your town were created. Comparison of this map with the land-use map and the building trends map should show you some very important things about the need or lack of need for new subdivisions, may indicate areas where new subdivisions should be encouraged or discouraged, and should give you a firm foundation for subdivision regulation policies.

5. *Value of land,* and 6. *Value of improvements.* These show general value patterns useful in defining economic neighborhoods, estimating relative costs of lands for public improvements, and indicating values which should be protected and areas where slum clearance and urban renewal action may be indicated.

7. *Condition of buildings.* This shows general condition of each building in town, and is particularly important if you are going to work on an urban renewal program. If you are going to adopt and enforce a minimum housing code, this map plus the land-use map will show you where to start looking for areas where intensive code enforcement would be most productive.

8. *Public lands and buildings.* This would show schools and school grounds, parks, playgrounds and recreational areas, buildings and grounds of the city hall, the auditorium, the library, police and fire stations, municipal parking areas, etc., and also vacant lands or buildings owned by the city, with an indication of intended use if any. Vacant city property should be designated for desirable public use or used for trading stock.

9. *Streets.* This is not just a map showing the names and locations of platted streets. It should show streets which are actually in (whether they are platted or not), streets which are platted but haven't been developed, right-of-way widths, and present surfacing and condition. This will be a point of departure for a major street plan, a guide to planning maintenance operations, and if you are lucky and get at it soon enough, it may also lead to a street closing plan. Most cities have more streets and alleys than they need or can afford to maintain.

Other maps which are self-explanatory, and are likely to be needed, are:

10. *Water system.*
11. *Sanitary and storm sewer system and surface drainage system.*
12. *Electric, gas, and telephone system.*
13. *Topography.*
14. *Soils.*

Now you say, "Where are we going to find the time to get all that together?" I told you that there was work connected with practical planning—and so far you haven't started the planning itself. All you have done is to bring together and organize some of the material you should have before you go too far with planning.

Forget the word "planning" for a minute. You are faced, as a citizen or as an administrator, with the responsibility for good government of your city—for good, practical, businesslike administration. You want to spend what money you have for improvements wisely, to set sensible priorities. How much of the information which has been indicated can you get along without, and still do an honest and efficient job? Will you do better in the long run if you have to run down bits and pieces of information as the need arises, or will you do better if you have the information organized for maximum utility? Do you use a filing system for municipal correspondence, or do you just pile it up in a corner? What we have been talking about here is a sort of graphic filing system for information most likely to be needed.

I'm not ducking the question of where you get all this information. That comes next.

You already have most of the information, if your city is being run properly. If you don't have it, you ought to remedy the lack before you start planning on a more ambitious scale.

Take tax records, for instance. If you don't have reasonably current, well-organized, accurate property information, your town isn't being run right, and before you pursue planning much further you ought to plug this obvious hole. If you do have decent tax records, you are ready to make the parcel map, the land-use map, the map on development trends in the buildings, the maps on value of land and value of improvements, and the map on condition of buildings from those records with little strain. On the land-use map, you should make a supplementary field survey to catch recent changes and to double-check. On the building trends map, if you have building permits, you can update for recent buildings from the source, and the field survey for land use will give you a double-check.

Your plats give you the information you need for trends in land development. City records should certainly indicate the location of public lands and buildings—and in a number of cities, mapping vacant public land or buildings is an eye-opener to the governing body.

The street map is usually not a major problem, although you may have to get a field survey on condition. Water and sewer system maps you probably already have, but it's a good idea to get them redrafted to the same scale as your other maps so that they can be used as needed in printing sandwiches, and this is true also of the electric, gas, and telephone maps.

On topography, the problem is more complex. Here the U.S.G.S. quad sheets give general information, and you will probably find that you have some more detailed topo in connection with sewer and water installations and through highways. If you can't afford to have a topographic survey of the whole town—and don't jump to this conclusion before you find out how much it would cost as part of the aerial photography job—you can usually get enough of a start on it to have something to go on.

On soils, you should know character and location of those which are safe for virtually any type of urban development and those which impose limitations—the muck lands, the areas where poor absorption is likely to cause trouble, and so on. On this detail, the local Soil Conservation Service people can be most helpful.

Thus far, I have put a great deal of emphasis on laying the foundation for planning, and I have done so on purpose. Much of the talk about planning is in terms of what it will do for you on out ahead. I take the view, which I hope is practical, that if you start planning and planning doesn't start doing things for you in the present, it isn't likely to do much for you in the future. I have talked about tools which should be available to shape decision-making in the legislative and administrative branches of local government whether you call the process planning or not.

I have failed to mention population and economic base studies. Both of these should of course be handled as part of the preliminaries of the planning program, and both (in most cities) will be based on census information. About the only helpful hint I have to offer on this is that it is possible to purchase from the Bureau of the Census unpublished population, housing, and economic information broken down by enumeration districts. This breakdown of information by areas is likely to mean more in detailed planning than the total information for the entire city.

The plan itself

Now, very briefly, let's review some of the things which may go into the plan itself, and some of the means which can be used to make the plan work in guiding development.

1. *The land-use plan* is a compromise between what you have and what you would like to have, in which you give as much weight as possible to probable future needs of the city for public and private land in various categories, properly scaled and related to each other. This plan forms—or should form—the basis for zoning, and provides guidance on utilities installations, school locations, street planning, provision of recreational facilities, and many other things.

2. *The major street plan* is a design for moving from what you have to what you would like to have in the way of traffic arteries. In it you try to separate heavy traffic from residential areas, to make it possible for industrial truck traffic to reach industrial districts without extensive mingling with commercial and residential traffic, and to provide means by which traffic desiring to pass through your town can do so with a minimum of damage to your city and a minimum of delay in transit.

3. *The minor street plan* is one which should receive more attention. This has promise in two directions. Looking toward sound development in the future, if suggested minor street plans can be provided for unplatted areas, developers can frequently be induced to use them in planning new subdivisions. Thus—if the planning is good—the result is a coherent minor street plan properly related to major streets and to the total network, rather than a patchwork of minor streets which don't fit well into the community pattern. The second part of the minor street plan is remedial—an attempt to correct errors of the past. Here the idea is to close unnecessary streets (a major move toward economy in street maintenance), to redesign dangerous minor street intersections, and to develop means for discouraging through traffic in residential neighborhoods.

4. *The community facilities plan* is a proposal for moves from where you are to where you think you will want to be on buildings and grounds for municipal government, schools, parks, playgrounds, and the like.

5. *The open space net.* As a new plan element with great potential, I propose for your consideration the open space net.[2]

To these are added other plans, some providing detail within the general framework already discussed, others dealing with problems in particular parts of the city—plans for individual parks, plans for downtown improvement including parking, plans for housing and

2. For a full discussion of the open space net, see the article beginning on p. 161.

urban renewal.

I have a strong feeling that planning should also include plans for economic development—not merely industrial development in the narrow sense of manufacturing plants, but for general economic improvement by whatever means it can be achieved. This may mean boosting the tourist-attracting potential of your town, improving the quality of service and trade facilities to attract (or hold) business, developing wholesaling and warehousing potentials, and a number of other things.

All of these things, taken together, form something which has been called loosely a comprehensive plan, a guide for desirable public and private action to build a better community with a minimum of waste motion and mistakes and maximum returns from the tax dollar.

These things won't happen by themselves. Once the community has decided what its policies should be—and it should be the community which decides, not the plausible stranger—some controls are necessary. Part of these controls affect private actions, part public.

Planning controls

The zoning ordinance controls land use. In it the city is divided into districts, in line with the comprehensive plan, and the uses and characteristics of use permitted or prohibited in each district are set forth. This is primarily a restriction on private action in the interest of the common good. People who want to sell property in residential neighborhoods for filling stations don't like it, but if the zoning is sound, general public gains far more than compensate for occasional private losses.

Subdivision regulations govern the manner in which land is divided into lots and sold. This is another restriction on private activities, designed to keep the general taxpayers from having to subsidize newcomers who will probably add to per capita tax loads. When a poorly designed subdivision, with poor streets and substandard utilities, is foisted on a town, the developer may gain, but the town loses. Somebody has to pay the bill. Who? The people who buy the lots? No, there aren't enough of them. All the taxpayers pay the bill. This isn't right.

People who come into a town should pay a fair share, and the best way to get them to do it is by sound subdivision regulations in which it has been determined what a fair share is. Subdivision regulations are not universally popular with developers, particularly those who want to get out fast with as little investment as possible and as much return as possible. This is tough on them, but in the interest of being practical, from the point of view of the citizenry in general, this is the way it has got to be.

Building codes, fire, electrical, gas, plumbing, and housing codes are again regulations on private action; controls which the general public imposes because without them private gains would be greatly outweighed by public losses.

If you are going to be businesslike about local government, you will have these codes, ordinances, and regulations, and they will be sound, well drafted, and vigorously enforced. It is a proper objective of city government to provide the best possible city for the people who live in it, and to provide the kind of facilities and services needed or wanted by the taxpayers at the lowest possible cost. In the process of doing this, a bargain must be struck between private and public interest. Government is supposed to represent and protect public interest. What kind of representation does it give if it does not use its proper powers to adopt and enforce regulations which lead to improvement of the city and hold down city expenses and hazards to the citizens?

Control of public action related to planning lies in such devices as the capital improvement program, the capital budget, and the timing and conduct of programs for inducing public participation in action programs—donations of land, services, and funds on improvements where these are appropriate.

I have talked about planning as a practical operation, geared to the daily workings of local government. It is also—and I do not mean to slight the importance of this—the key to sound long-range development of our cities. But unless and until planning goes to work today, plans for tomorrow aren't likely to do much good.

A new element in land planning: *the land*

Most comprehensive plans, and most texts on urban land planning, neglect an important aspect of the land itself. There is of course recognition of land area, topographic form, and drainage patterns. But plans for land use, distributing activity by location according to increasingly sophisticated formulas, generally ignore completely the suitability of the soil for the uses proposed.

Overriding considerations may force solution of known soils problems regardless of expense. Planning fails if the expense comes as a surprise, and the failure is particularly painful if the expense could have been avoided by choice of an equally suitable location where the soils were appropriate to the use.

No claim is made here that soil characteristics should become the prime determinant of urban form. It should be clear, however, that soil factors affecting form or cost of development deserve as much consideration as other elements less crucial in shaping cities (but which are now getting a great deal more attention from planners).

Even in areas of relatively intensive settlement, soil analysis is useful in guiding redevelopment, in guiding location of major buildings, and in alerting builders to problems which may be anticipated. Certainly a soil map is helpful in selecting routes for major throughways (and in some cases in saving "cheap" park lands from invasion by highways, schools, and other public construction by demonstrating that costs of construction would outweigh "savings" in land expense).

In county and regional planning, where provision is made for inevitable outspreading of urban growth, the soil capability maps are even more useful. In advance of development, choices can be made which will not be available later.

For convincing arguments as to the importance of this approach, and a very short course in how to go about it, the 1963 *Yearbook of Agriculture* (a remarkable source document for articles on urban planning) contains a nine-page article by A. A. Klingebiel, "Land Classification for Use in Planning."[1]

Help is available

Before touching on other high points of the Klingebiel report, it should be noted that this is an area in which usual problems of shortage of trained specialists or major expenditure is not a bar to execution. More than 1,500 trained soil scientists, working in all states, are employed by the Soil Conservation Service and work cooperatively with state agricultural experiment stations and other local agencies. As part of the National Cooperative Soil Survey, there are now published reports for many counties, and preliminary reports and maps for other areas are available in unpublished form at offices of soil conservation districts or cooperating state agencies.

The Klingebiel article includes some horror stories. Septic tanks don't work, water supplies are polluted, walls crack, foundations slip, school buildings settle a quarter of a million dollars worth on a site within a few hundred feet of a good location, pavements buckle and sag, erosion and runoff create problems, pipelines break, water tables rise to damage basements, slabs heave, acidity or alkalinity affects pipes, cables, and concrete, landscaping doesn't work out, and so on.

As a guide to what to expect, where and where not to locate, and what to do, the soil survey is invaluable. It is not the sort of thing a planner—even with an M.A.—is equipped to handle. Let the soil scientists do it—if they haven't already. (In 1963, 55 million acres had been mapped and the work has proceeded rapidly since.)

Soil scientists have been helping farmers since 1900. In 1925, they began to work with civil engineers, and since then the results of the

1. U.S. Department of Agriculture, *Yearbook of Agriculture* (Washington, D.C.: USDA, 1963), pp. 399-407.

combined effort have been of increasing importance to urban planners and developers.

Urban land-use capability maps

Klingebiel indicates that soil maps are made at two levels of intensity, general and detailed. General maps show soil resources for broad areas for general planning of townships, counties, or regions, with as many as 10 soil associations on maps with a scale of one-quarter inch to the mile. (A soil association is a group of similar soils.)

Detailed soil maps are frequently at a scale of four inches to the mile, made on an aerial mosaic. Even at this scale, there may be areas of intricately mixed soils which can be described only as complexes, and the detailed maps do not pick up areas of a given kind of soil which are less than two acres in extent. Prudence dictates careful examination of individual small sites, but the detailed soil map shows which areas are definitely not suitable for particular structures and uses.

Neither the general nor the detailed soil map is in shape for urban planners to use directly without interpretation. The interpretation should take the form of an urban land-use capability map. Here soils are grouped on the map in a way related to urban requirements, so that planners may read directly suitability for potential structures and uses. One group swells when wet, shrinks when dry. If buildings or roads are to be built across it, construction will be expensive because of special measures needed. Another heaves during freezes, again posing construction problems, particularly in roadbuilding. Peat and muck soils have poor bearing properties. A number of soil types are undesirable for septic tank use because of low permeability.

There are combinations of soil types and other characteristics which should be mapped. Some soils are suitable for general urban use if on flatlands or gentle slopes, unsuitable if on steep slopes because of slippage or high erosion. Others are appropriate for general use in areas where the water table is low, inappropriate if the water table is high or fluctuates to include high cycles. There are flood plain areas in which no intensive urban use should be allowed regardless of soil type.

The urban land-use capability map should reflect all of these things, and soil scientists, given specifications as to needs of planners, can do the job.

With urban land-use capability maps, planners can work far more intelligently in determining appropriate land uses, and in devising regulations to control land use. Klingebiel cites an example:

> A planning group receives a request for development of a subdivision beyond present sewerlines. The soil map shows that some of the soils in this area are slowly permeable, others have a high water table part of the year, and still others are less than three feet deep over rock. The local officials can point out these limitations and suggest changes to fit the soils or reject the request for development on the basis that the soils are not suited for residential use.

Here trouble could have been saved if the plan had indicated the nature of the problem, and regulations related to the plan had indicated solutions acceptable to the body charged with protecting public interest.

The open space net

Urban open space is under increasing pressure. Providing it, conserving it, and using it wisely mount in importance as development intensifies and spreads and land costs mount.

The open space net, built by joining major public, quasi-public, and private open spaces into a continuous system, promises increased economy and efficiency through combined use, and increased amenity in the form of greenbelt parkways. Most of the gains can be achieved without major increases in public expenditures.

To be effective, the net must become a central coordinating element in planning—not something happening occasionally and in patches by fortunate accidents, but a sustained and purposeful combination of multiple means to meet multiple ends. Both means and ends must be examined in the context of the net system. When this is done, the system has dramatic promise, but it becomes apparent that some traditional planning concepts may have to be altered and improved.

Preoccupation with extensive long-range patterns can lead to astigmatism on more intimate relationships in the family and its immediate environment. For a balanced view, what follows begins with consideration of the open space net in broad city and suburban context, discusses potential improvements which the net might bring to the family and neighborhood level, and concludes with some notes on implementation.

Open space net considerations

OPEN SPACE IN THE CITY—CHANGING FUNCTIONS AND PATTERNS

Since cities began, the importance of urban space has been recognized. Form, function, and relationships have changed, but major open space was there. Sometimes it was public—the agora, the town square. Sometimes it was quasi-public—the temple or cathedral grounds, the campus. Sometimes it was private, surrounding the homes of the rich, the palaces of the mighty. Fortunately, it was usually distributed in such a way as to relieve the depressing density of urban development.

In time, many cities linked their major open spaces with boulevards or parkways, providing at least partial continuity and impressive vistas. Emperors and kings carried out grand designs with little concern for relocation of displaced persons, and Napoleon, in decreeing that old walls around inner cities should be replaced by parks, was uninhibited by concern over property rights or speculative values.

In the early 1900's, city planning in the U.S. moved toward classic revival:

> Plans were of colossal scale, with monumental proportions. Axes shot off in all directions, terminating with proposed buildings that put the visions of past kinds to shame. Great plazas and broad avenues, generously punctuated with monuments, were almost a civic obsession. The "City Beautiful" was the Grand Plan reincarnate; the *Ecole des Beaux Arts* in Paris was the fountainhead for the designers of this period and the plans had to be big to be beautiful. . . .
>
> All this activity was performed in something of a vacuum. An air of haughty detachment pervaded the planning, an isolation from the affairs of people and community activities. . . . It was as though the planners had determined that the people must adjust themselves to the mighty formal arrangement. It failed to occur to them that the entire development of a city was essentially a derivative of human needs.[1]

Since then, cities have become more complex, public services have increased in scale and scope, and human needs have become a major

1. Arthur B. Gallion and Simon Eisner, *The Urban Pattern* (2nd ed., New York: D. Van Nostrand, Inc., 1963), pp. 81-82.

consideration. The current move toward the open space net reflects this change.

MOVES TOWARD THE NET

In recent years, there is mounting interest in creating an open space system:

> We are groping here for a framework within which many kinds and varieties of public and private uses, balanced out in detailed short-range plans, can shift and change and mix and separate through the centuries. And we should start with public land.
>
> On this, we should move consistently toward an extensive and, where possible, continuous network of public land adapted to multiple purposes—open space, recreation, protection of watersheds and water supply, parks, schools, public and quasi-public buildings, transportation in whatever form it may take, and things as yet unknown.
>
> The public land net is the permanent objective, the historic goal. It can be achieved by pursuit of a series of short-range ends (which in relation to it become means). As present and future short-range public requirements unfold in a series of plans adapted to their particular times, lands contributing to the net should be acquired and held. Basic policy should be to add to the net by every appropriate device.[2]
>
> In the years ahead, continuing effort to relate public and quasi-public actions to building the public land net will multiply benefits (and particularly amenities), reduce costs, minimize the effects of errors in foresight, and provide for both present and future needs. . . .
>
> The land net becomes an organized public land reserve, built by combining uses involving substantial open space, growing gradually to completed form, and adapted to use and reuse in ways foreseeable and unforeseen as long as cities stand.
>
> Within the net, islands for private uses are served, interconnected, shielded, and buffered by the threads which set them apart. The existence of the net as a preferred location for land-consuming public uses gives private areas within its meshes security against

2. Frederick H. Bair, Jr., "Planning Ahead—Adventures in the Unexpected Obvious," *Florida Planning and Development,* Vol. XII, No. 1 (Jan. 1962), p. 5.

> disruption by unpredictable public action. The net makes logical major land use divisions easier—within one reticulation may be a regional commercial center, within another, an industrial park.
>
> Most spaces within the meshes may be used for balanced residential communities with supporting commercial and service facilities. Here the net provides access and a perimeter greenbelt, and the location of principal entries to the community from outside traffic arteries and transportation facilities sets the destination for internal collector streets and begins to establish a desirable internal pattern of land use.[3]

Emphasis above is on public and quasi-public uses inside the net. But there are obvious possibilities for inclusion of private uses involving substantial amounts of open space, if public controls can assure compatibility.

S. B. Zisman, long a proponent of more intelligent use of open space, observed in a paper in 1964:

> Open space in the past was, largely, a negative concept—the areas for non-building. It is now coming to be recognized as a positive element for urban growth. In the decades ahead open space as a system can become the means of control in development. If it is to achieve this role, a new text of planning policies and programs must be written—and followed into practice. The issues are not for planners alone. They will be fought in the political arena, and out of a public consensus may come the new tools and new means, both public and private.[4]

There are now gropings toward more definitive statements of the problems and potentials. In a recent symposium, the American Public Works Association outlined needs for research on better utilization of public space, including "the outlining of public space network possibilities to increase the output of public space for community life."[5]

3. Frederick H. Bair, Jr., "Future Town Forms—A Matter of Choice," *Florida Planning and Development,* Vol. XVI, No. 10 (Oct. 1965), p. 5.

4. S. B. Zisman, "Open Spaces in Urban Growth," *Proceedings of the 1964 Institute on Planning and Zoning,* The Southwestern Legal Foundation, Dallas (Albany, N.Y.: Matthew Bender and Co., 1965). The paper contains an excellent summary compendium of recent thinking on urban open space.

5. American Public Works Association Research Foundation, *Prospectus for Cooperative Research* (2nd ed.; Chicago: The Association, 1967). See particularly "Project 66-4, Better Utilization of Open Space," pp. 37-40. As background, see American Public Works Association, *Better Utilization of Urban Space, Summary of a Symposium on Research Needs* (Chicago: The Association, 1967).

Related matters included criteria for uniform identification of public space, dimensioning present and future space functions, determination of principles on optimum spatial distribution of socio-economic activities, interrelationship of public and private properties, and so on.

A related approach is systems engineering for satisfaction of open space needs:

> There is increasing demand for more extensive, and better quality, open space provision in all metropolitan areas. The provision of such space, and in particular its coordination with other facets of metropolitan development—transportation and land-use planning, water resources planning, residential and recreational development—may usefully be viewed as a problem in systems engineering.
>
> In this case, the "system" is the totality of urban open space—parks, freeways, streets, building surroundings. The "objective" is to satisfy a hierarchy of differential demands—open space for recreation, for civic design, for pollution control or as a device to define the physical structure of the urban community and add a sense of scale and direction—and at the same time to coordinate and make better use of the many different types of space which exist in an urban area.[6]

In essence, the current idea is to create an open space system by combining public and quasi-public open space wherever reasonably possible, and adding to the spaciousness and efficient functioning of the net by encouraging appropriate and controlled integration of significant private open space. Experience with planned residential developments suggests strong advantage in combining common open space with adjacent net lands, and the possibilities do not stop here. High-rise apartments, townhouse clusters, and other forms might well fit.

THE UNDIMENSIONED NEED FOR OPEN SPACE

Long-range need for open space is unknown, and will remain so. Research to refine the net concept, to determine what would build the net, reinforce it, enlarge it, protect it, make it more efficient and research to determine potentials and timing for action will serve a

6. Department of Civil Engineering, Technological Institute, Northwestern University, *Urban Systems Engineering, An Advisory Report to the Department of Housing and Urban Development* (Evanston, Ill.: Northwestern University, 1967), pp. 21-22.

useful purpose. Beyond this, *a priori* reasoning suggests putting the idea to work promptly.

As with a great deal of planning, exotic, complex, and futile research can be an expensive deterrent to needed action. The net concept is flexible, can accommodate to a wide range of errors in assumptions and forecasts, and can provide for a wide range of unknowns and unknowables. The nature of the problem assures that errors and uncertainties will be there, and on many of them elaborate research is unlikely to produce long-range answers of greater utility than those developed by simpler reasoning.

There will probably not be an oversupply of urban open space so long as we have cities. It is unnecessary to exploit all research potentials before proceeding to action which is obviously needed, and the sooner the better. For those still inclined toward elaborate detailing of long-range future requirements for urban open space (and other things) it may be well to underline the difficulties.

AREAS OF UNCERTAINTY

Changes in population. Thus far, we have been unable to forecast long-range changes in number or characteristics with any usable degree of precision. Check the record on items as "simple" as 20-year predictions.

Changes in public services. These have been rapid, and amount and scope will continue to increase, but only predictably within broad limits. What would be the effects of free and efficient mass transportation? Of economic "public service" in the form of a guaranteed minimum income?

Changes in standards. Look at the record for the past 30 to 40 years on amounts and kinds of recreational space which should be minimum or standard. As a more striking example, take schools—their size and place in the neighborhood or community, their space requirements, increased proportion of population attending as education lengthens, attitude toward general community use of buildings and grounds, past effect of auto and bus on size of service area, potential effect of bussing as a device to assure socio-economic homogeneity, possibilities for major educational campuses concentrating far greater numbers of elementary students and perhaps combining school levels which are now separate, and so on. Or review changes in standards for street widths, particularly arterials and the recently born system of freeways. What lies ahead will change rapidly. But how predictably?

Changes in tastes, customs, tolerance. The generality of the "general public welfare" is increasingly broad (metropolitan, regional, and beyond) and increasingly deep (including future as well as present generations). Recent decades have seen vastly altered tastes and customs, changes in what people want to what they will put up with. Changes in the future will probably be more rapid.

Changes in technology. The exponential curve of *physical* technology is taken for granted, but where it leads in terms of specific products, servicing, distribution, or processing is highly speculative. *Social* technology is also advancing, compounding problems of prognostication.

Thus long-range need for open space must remain in large measure undimensioned. The net concept is valid in spite of the uncertainties. In fact, it gains attractiveness because of uncertainties. Open space isolated is more difficult to reuse effectively as open space than open space integrated into a system.

Elements in the open space net

The net is intended to serve, to separate, and to buffer in areas where buffering is needed. Where it performs all these functions, its pattern is as follows:

Border Elements	*Buffer Elements*	*Linear Core Elements*
Collector or arterial street at outer edge of net forming boundary. Close to street, public, quasi-public, and private uses with substantial open space requirements, with space merged to contribute to buffer.	Parklike open space, preferably continuous with minimum of vehicular interruptions. May contain uses with only minor structures. Should contain pedestrian ways.	Limited-access highways, mass transit, major utility trunks, and the like.

All of these elements will not always be present. Thus through commercial or industrial areas, the linear core may suffice. And where parks or other open uses provide portions of the net, there may be no linear core.

These elements, illustrated in Figure 1, are discussed in more detail below.

LINEAR CORE ELEMENTS

One group of elements in the open space system is essentially linear, taking the form of interlocking corridors.

Limited-access highways, chiefly freeways and expressways with interchanges and access points in urban areas generally at intervals of half a mile or more, are prime determinants. They now tend to serve primarily as automotive arteries, but could often handle additional functions. Certainly they separate, in many cases into divisions of workable size for primarily residential neighborhoods, and into other divisions adaptable for major shopping centers, industrial parks, office complexes, civic centers, or institutional groupings. These arteries, as related to uses which now adjoin them, tend to create a need for buffering, rather than to provide it.

Mass transit rights of way should wherever practicable be combined with limited-access automotive systems. There are obvious reasons of efficiency and economy. Given two systems, automotive and mass transit, taking large numbers of people from the same general origins to the same general destinations and back, the same routes should serve. If properly designed stations (and parking areas) are integrated into selected prime interchanges in outlying areas, the highway system serves as a convenient collection device for mass transit customers. Use of mass transit from such points through the most congested part of the highway system should increase, and use of private automobiles should lessen. And if the noise of mass transit is a problem to adjacent uses, the same buffering used to reduce highway noises can serve a double purpose.

Some major utility installations require substantial open space, or would benefit from improved accessibility for maintenance if located in the net. High tension transmission lines and major sanitary and storm sewer, water, and gas trunks are the principal examples.

Some parks are linear, particularly those along the bottoms of stream valleys. They separate and buffer, but often serve and often should serve only park purposes. There are times when multiple functions are desirable and times when they are not. Adoption of the open space net concept does not imply that existing or proposed parks should be targets for freeways, mass transit routes, or visible utility lines. There will be times when a park can be created in connection with development of such facilities, but there are few cases when such facilities should be allowed to invade or destroy existing parks.

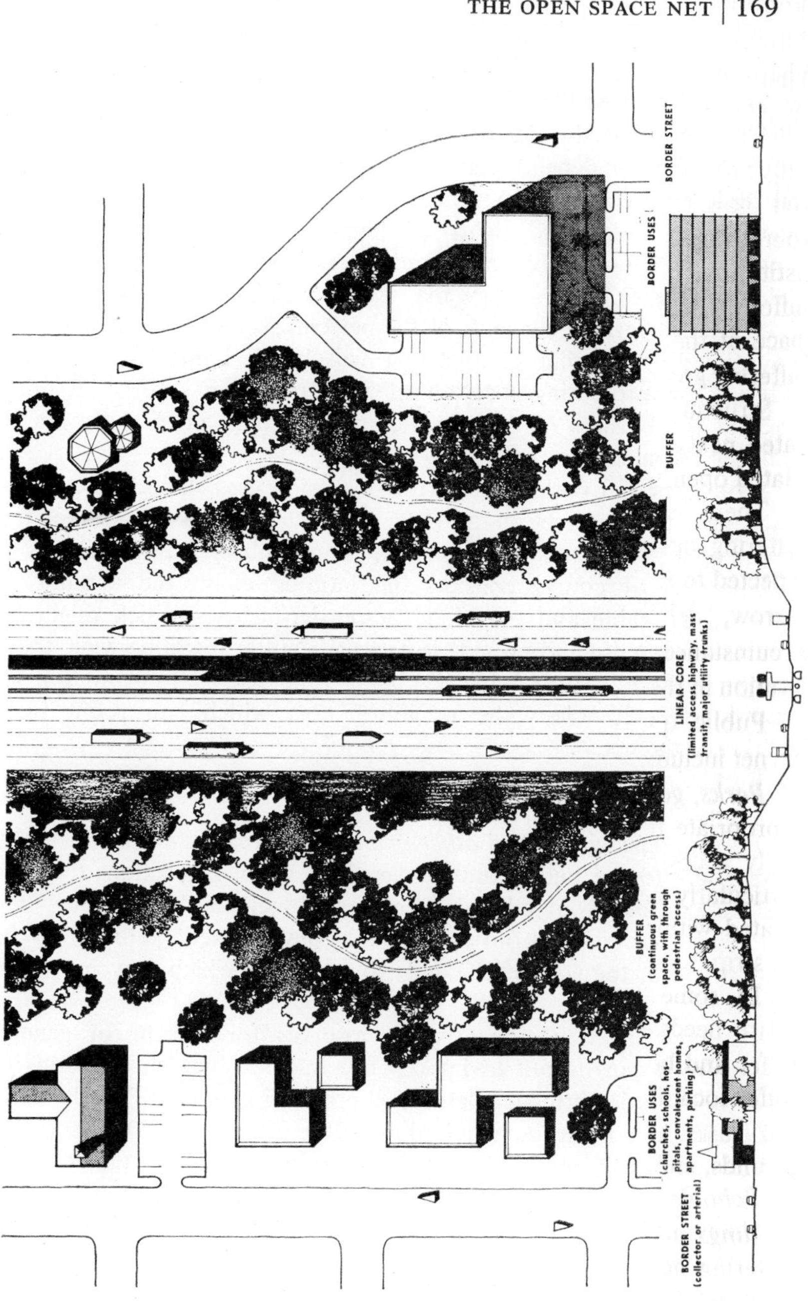

Figure 1. Detailed plan and cross section of net

BUFFERING AND BORDERING ELEMENTS

How and whether the linear core elements should be filled out with buffer and border depends on what lies within the meshes of the net. Where it embraces uses not likely to be adversely affected by the concentrated noise and lights of high-speed automotive or mass transport vehicles—heavy commercial areas, warehousing, and industrial uses, for example—there may be no need for greenbelting. But where traffic corridor elements of the net embrace areas of residential, institutional, or similar character it will be desirable to encourage buffering by promoting location of uses requiring substantial open space at the borders of the net and merging their open space into a buffering greenbelt.

Structures and parking areas for bordering uses should be concentrated next to the street at the outer boundary of the net, so that the related open space remains as continuous and unbroken as possible.

There is of course considerable latitude as to the amount of buffering desirable and the kinds of bordering uses which might be expected to require and provide it. Here the buffer might be wide, there narrow, depending on what is being shielded. This variation in circumstances broadens the range of uses which can profit from location in the net.

Public, quasi-public, and private buffer or border uses adaptable to the net include the following:

Parks, golf courses, and other open recreational uses are obviously appropriate to the buffer and border strip. In such locations they are easily accessible from adjoining residential neighborhoods. They are particularly accessible from multi-family developments which may be located within the strip itself, and from schools which may be within the strip.

In some locations, open space reserves for specific or general future needs can be put to interim use in a way which conforms to buffer and border principles and also provides revenue. Thus lands in buffer locations might be acquired early for future school or park sites and leased as private golf courses, driving ranges, riding stables, camp grounds, and the like.

Schools, institutions, churches, and other public and quasi-public buildings and lands offer a broad gamut of possibilities, adaptable to buffering needs and the kind of bordering structures and uses appropriate to space of such dimensions. The branch library, the local health and social service clinic, the fire station, the police station don't need much room but fit well into the logical pattern of neighborhood uses at the border.

Churches, with a wide range of space needs, make good border uses, and their green spaces (including perhaps cemeteries) serve effectively to build buffer. As multi-service institutions, churches will usually welcome accessibility to the general green area for outdoor functions, and where churches are located close to higher-density residential uses in the buffer-border strip, the pedestrian circulation provided should be helpful in building attendance.

Institutions of various kinds benefit from border locations and from combinations of their grounds with the green buffer strip. Hospitals, sanitariums, convalescent homes, homes for the aged, children's homes, and the like would obviously fit well.

Schools should be both a major contributor and a major gainer. Elementary school structures in border portions of the net, with grounds made part of the buffer, are logical in the open space system context, but require revision of some traditional ideas about the place of this kind of school in the neighborhood.

Since elementary schools are major users of open space, and could be major contributors to the net, the argument for a shift from central location in the residential neighborhood needs special emphasis. Increasing proportions of children are transported to school by bus or automobile, and for those who walk or ride bicycles automotive traffic is a mounting hazard. Moving the school to a border location in the net gives rapid vehicular accessibility from the boundary arterial or collector street, and for children going to and from school on foot or bicycles, the buffer portion of the net provides safety for at least that part of the trip. Reorganization of daily trip patterns which follows as a result of adoption of the net concept results in a more convenient and efficient combination of travel to school, commercial facilities, work, and other destinations.

There is also the matter of flexibility in use and reuse of school grounds and possibilities for expansion. In long-range perspective, a great many schools built a generation or two ago are no longer in the best functional locations, or have grounds submarginal by present standards. If the old school is vacated, its land is often isolated in locations not well adapted for open space reuse (or is "too valuable" for open space reuse). Learning from this experience, there is no assurance that schools being built now will meet future standards either as to size of plants or amount of open space. The possibility of campus-type elementary facilities mentioned earlier is only one clue to this type of obsolescence.

Given border and buffer location in the net, there is first the possibility that provision for future expansion would be easier; second, the probability that availability of parkway open space would reduce acreage requirements for a particular school; and third, an improved probability that should the school be found to be at the wrong location in relation to future patterns of development, the land remains available in the net for other uses requiring substantial open space.

Junior and senior high schools, colleges, and universities are excellent net uses, with locations close to interchanges giving easy accessibility from a wide service area. As tract requirements increase, it may be difficult in some instances to place the whole establishment in the border and buffer area, but divisions of functions adapted to the net idea make adjustments possible. Thus the physical education plan with its fields and stadiums, open-air amphitheaters and the like might form border and buffer uses, with more densely occupied portions of the establishment outside the net across the perimeter accessway.

Areas where slopes, soils, flood hazards, or similar conditions impede development are very often suitable for inclusion within the net. Sometimes such areas will serve as buffers to a traffic-handling linear core. Elsewhere they may separate neighborhoods without containing major traffic-handling facilities. If they can be tied into the net, it may be easier to protect them (as parks, small "wilderness areas," or wildlife sanctuaries) than if they remain isolated, and certainly inclusion as part of the net should increase their accessibility. The physical characteristics which inhibit urban development often provide a rich variety of plant and animal life and a taste of wild solitude rare in the city environment.

Watershed protection areas, water storage areas, and even some forms of sewage treatment may be included. To some extent, these may overlap previously discussed categories—parks, wilderness areas, wildlife sanctuaries, etc. But there are some special possibilities which might be overlooked:

Where there is high runoff and low absorption (as may often be the case along major freeways with their extensive paving) water-storage ponds can be provided in the buffer strip to contain and control runoff.

Some forms of sewage treatment may be appropriate in certain buffer areas. A conventional treatment plant might fit at the ends of buffer strips where pedestrian circulation is interrupted by interchanges, and sewage lagoons would be appropriate there and in other locations.

The serial ponding type of treatment being pioneered at Santee Lakes in San Diego County, California, is a particularly good example of a type of multi-purpose use adapted to inclusion in the net. Here a park area bordered on one side by a potential freeway right-of-way and on the other by a flood control channel is developed around five ponds. The first is an oxidation pond, followed by another pond continuing the oxidation treatment and acting as a separator between the first and three others used for fishing and boating. In the final lake, a swimming area is supplied with treated water recovered from sewage. Total water area in the five lakes is 30 acres, present land area in the park adds another 15 acres, and there is a total potential of about 300 acres.[7]

Open space around medium- to high-intensity residential uses and common open space in planned residential developments may fit well into the buffer greenbelt. In the neighborhood pattern discussed later, multifamily, townhouse, and similar forms would profit from location close to commercial and service facilities, from direct access to major open space, and from pedestrian ways with few or no vehicular interruptions.

Where the buffer must be narrow, townhouses or apartments constructed and oriented for noise resistance bordering relatively limited green space may be an answer. In more favorable circumstances, a high-rise bordering the park may considerably broaden it by merging its own green area with the strip.

Even in low-intensity areas, there are opportunities for broadening the scope and increasing the effectiveness of the open space system. As an example, in the Upper Rock Creek watershed in Montgomery County, Maryland, a stream valley public park is adjoined by largely undeveloped private lands which include tributary ravines and steep slopes unsuited for construction before rising to land well adapted for development. Here a logical solution would be to encourage planned residential development with common open space in the rough areas merging with the public park. This would protect lands highly sus-

7. John C. Merrell, Jr. and Albert Katko, "Reclaimed Wastewater for Santee Recreational Lakes," *Journal, Water Pollution Control Federation* (Aug. 1966), pp. 1310-18. See also, John C. Merrell, Jr. and Ray Stover, "Reclaimed Sewage Becomes a Community Asset," *American City* (April 1964).

ceptible to erosion, increase the visual effectiveness of the open space system, and provide easy access to the park from the planned developments.

In brief, there seems to be no shortage of uses adaptable to building buffer and border portions of the open space net. Anything providing (and requiring and benefiting from) substantial open space may be considered for inclusion, and the variety of opportunities within an urban area is such that careful planning should indicate an appropriate place and design for almost anything which would build the net.

Once the principle of the net is accepted as a basic consideration in planning, public uses can be located within it by direct public action. Quasi-public and private uses can be directed into desirable complementary patterns by a combination of regulation, the built-in inducement of advantageous location, and certain added attractions justified by both public and private interest. Before discussing implementation on the quasi-public and private fronts in detail, it is necessary to discuss some changes in neighborhood patterns which seem likely to follow as a result of application of the open space net concept.

The neighborhood revisited—by the family car(s)

The American wife and mother, in her role as taxi driver, often feels that nothing is near anything or on the way to anything else. Any thoughts she may have about planners in this regard are likely to be unkind.

There is reason for her distaste. Planners have virtually ignored her. The literature is full of all kinds of origin and destination studies except the one which traces the devious journey of the family car on its daily round (or family cars—having more than one may be evidence of urban disorganization rather than affluence).

Enough evidence can be supplied from personal experience to make the main point. Father to work (by car 1 or aided by Mother's Taxi Service to work or to the station). Children to schools—elementary here, high school there. Meeting at church. Shop. Pick up shoes left for repair. Something Committee lunch at civic center. Children from school—John to Little League Park, Deborah to Girl Scouts. Father home from work. Evening social or recreational travel.

The pattern will vary from family to family, from city to city, from central city to suburb. It will usually have one identifying characteristic: The destinations look as though they had been established with a shotgun. The elementary school is here, the high school there, the church in another direction, shopping and service facilities someplace else, and so on. And the random pattern often defies any linear shortcuts by which a number of places often visited could be reached along a single reasonably simple and direct route.

Considering the "neighborhood" in relation to the family automobile, social trends, planning theory, and the possibilities of the open space net, what improvements are possible?

ASPO's Planning Advisory Service Report No. 141, *Neighborhood Boundaries* (December 1960), surveys the neighborhood concept as it has evolved to that point. Crediting Clarence A. Perry with the origin of the generally conceived neighborhood prototype in a 1929 New York regional plan report,[8] this survey states that its six basic principles were:

1. Major arterials and through traffic routes should not pass through residential neighborhoods, but should provide the boundaries of the neighborhood.

2. Interior street patterns should be designed to encourage quiet, safe, low traffic volumes to preserve residential character.

3. Population should support its elementary school (about 5,000 persons when Perry formulated his theory; in 1960, "current elementary school size standards probably would lower the figure to 3,000-4,000 persons"). (What happens in the future, with changing standards and perhaps elementary campus-type facilities?)

4. The neighborhood focal point should be the elementary school centrally located on a common or green, along with other institutions with service areas coincident with neighborhood boundaries.

5. Radius of the neighborhood should not exceed one-quarter mile, the maximum distance a child should walk to school. "Perry calculated that an area of about 160 acres would adequately house the elementary school supporting population in detached single-family residences on 40 by 100 foot lots, provided a small proportion of the people lived in apartments bordering the shopping districts. Current practices of making larger individual lots, and proportionately lower

8. Clarence A. Perry, "The Neighborhood Unit," *Neighborhood and Community Planning,* Vol. VII (New York: Committee for the Regional Survey of New York and Its Environs, 1929).

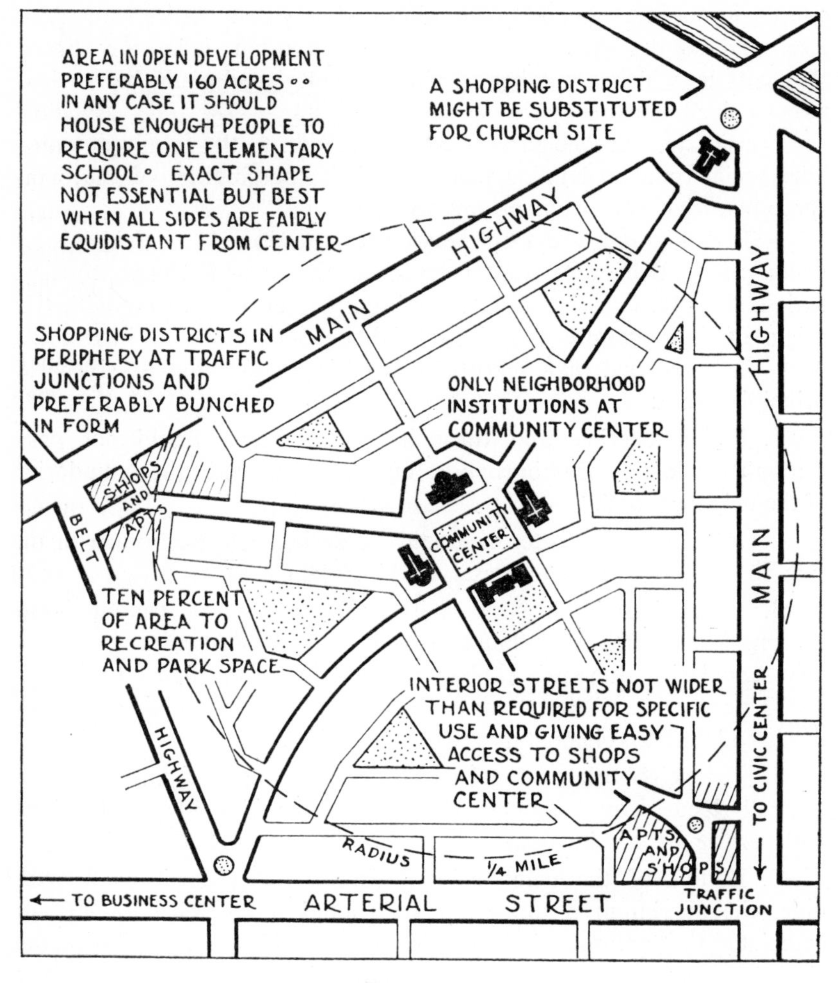

FIG. 33

Figure 2. The neighborhood unit as seen by Clarence A. Perry

Reproduced from Perry, *Neighborhood and Community Planning,* Vol. VII.

population densities, have increased the 'standard' neighborhood radius to one half mile."

6. Shopping districts should be at the edge of the neighborhood, preferably at major street intersections.

Perry's neighborhood unit appears as Figure 2. Given the kind of travel schedule assumed for the family car, the trip pattern is likely to be scattered.

Figure 3, an approach better adapted to the automobile, is for new development. It would obviously not fit for reworking old gridiron neighborhoods unless there was complete redevelopment.

The principles remain similar to Perry's, but the pattern differs from his in many ways. Perry had scattered small parks. The Urban Land Institute proposes consolidation. Perry's combined apartments and shops seem to be a minor and incidental consideration and are not shown as concentrated in what would now be considered the prime corner. In the more modern plan, although a minor shopping area appears at the upper right, the "strong" center and major apartment concentration is toward what seems to be the direction of the CBD.

"NEIGHBORHOOD" PRINCIPLES AND THE OPEN SPACE NET

The net offers new possibilities for gradual rebuilding of old "neighborhoods" (however called—residential units, development areas, service areas, or by other names), and for shaping new ones. Some accepted principles remain unchanged by the net proposal, others are challenged. Using the format of the Urban Land Institute illustration and notes, considerations on the neighborhood within the net would be as follows.

1. *Size.* The elementary school is losing its magic as a prime determinant of optimum neighborhood size and population. The family automobile and the school bus diminish the importance of walking distance to school as a criterion for school location or neighborhood extent. There may be continued gradual increase in the size of elementary schools as individual establishments, and there is at least strong possibility of super-consolidation in the form of campus-like school facilities.

The elementary school may also be losing its assumed importance as a rallying point for neighborhood identification, loyalty, and social action. This is particularly likely to happen if cross-bussing between

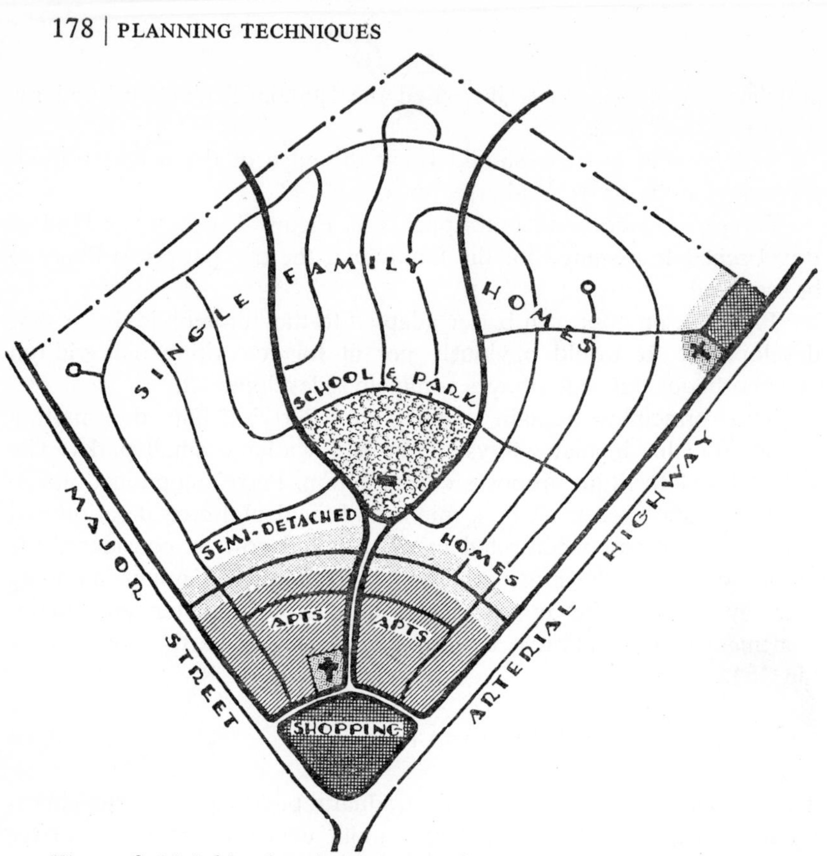

Figure 3. Neighborhood unit principles

1. *Size.* A residential unit development should provide housing for that population for which one elementary school is ordinarily required, its actual area depending upon its population density.

2. *Boundaries.* The unit should be bounded by arterial streets sufficiently wide to facilitate traffic by-passing the neighborhood instead of passing through it.

3. *Open Spaces.* Small park and recreation space, planned to meet the needs of the particular neighborhood should be provided.

4. *Institution Sites.* Sites for the school and other institutions having service spheres coinciding with the limits of the unit should be suitably grouped about a central point or common, and combined with the neighborhood recreation area, usually.

5. *Local Shopping Center.* If warranted by the population to be served the local convenience shopping facility should be located at the edge preferably at an arterial traffic junction and adjacent to similar commercial districts, if any, of adjoining neighborhoods.

6. *Internal Street System.* The unit should be provided with a special street system, each highway being proportioned to its probable traffic load, and the street net as a whole being designed to facilitate circulation within the unit with good access to main arteries, and to discourage its use by through traffic.

Source: Urban Land Institute, *The Community Builders Handbook* (Washington, D.C.: The Institute, 1960), p. 79.

school areas becomes common as a means for encouraging wider range of social exposure or if campus-type facilities become widely used.

Thus in the long view it might be better to consider optimum "neighborhoods" as service areas with populations sufficiently large to require and support a variety of both public and private services which could not be provided efficiently for smaller units. Until circumstances alter, the elementary school might well remain as one consideration, but it would be prudent to go beyond it and include some other things—the branch public service center, providing some localized city hall functions, fire and police protection, the branch library, the health clinic, general welfare services, and so on. The optimum "neighborhood" should have a population large enough to support its own shopping and commercial service facilities.

Obviously, the pattern of the open space net will not always produce optimum residential neighborhoods. Where the physical area set off by the net is small, it may be that concentration of relatively high densities will provide the necessary population, or that special attention should be paid to designing easy access to facilities in adjoining areas.

At the other extreme, areas too large to be served conveniently by one set of facilities might have secondary groupings of their own to be tied by easy access from more remote sectors to facilities in adjoining areas. Planning principles related to the net approach provide logical locations both for supplementary facilities in the same service area and for interconnections.

Such overlaps in areas larger or smaller than the optimum would to some extent reduce the sense of identification, place, and proprietorship resulting from facilities primarily for the service area and located within its boundaries. As a practical matter, this may be a marginal consideration. Most "neighborhoods" will provide their own facilities, or enough of them to serve as a focus. And there appear to be many people who are not greatly concerned about a sense of place and proprietorship so long as facilities are adequate and reasonably accessible.

2. *Boundaries.* It is accepted doctrine that major arterials should bound rather than pass through residential neighborhoods. As has already been made clear, the net concept adds the provision that the arterials should be limited access wherever possible, with buffer greenbelt added by systematic location of bordering uses requiring substantial amounts of open space.

3. *Open space.* Perry's diagram (Figure 2) indicates 10 per cent of the area of the neighborhood in recreation and park space, shown as a central community complex plus scattered small pieces for parks and recreation. Urban Land Institute, in Figure 3, calls for a central site for the schools and other service institutions, with a "small park and recreation site" for open space surroundings. The open space net approach would combine school, park, and other substantial open spaces (including private) in the greenbelt buffer at the edges of the neighborhood.

4. *Institution sites.* Perry and Urban Land Institute center the site for schools and other institutions. The net concept has such uses between perimeter streets and the limited access highway, adding their land to other open space forming the buffer, and so located as to provide safe access for pedestrians in a position to use the greenbelt and to facilitate automotive movements in a pattern well related to daily trips.

5. *Shopping center.* The shopping and commercial service area remains at the prime corner as indicated by Urban Land Institute.

6. *Residential types.* The ULI illustration has no specific notes on distribution of residential types, but the diagram makes the proposed pattern clear. Under the net concept, apartment locations would tend to concentrate along the greenbelt side of the border streets rather than forming a deep arc into the neighborhood as shown in the ULI plan. Some apartments might remain across the street from the shopping center, but it would seem preferable to provide for transition between the shopping center area and single-family detached sectors by townhouses, offices, and other public and private uses not requiring major open space and held reasonably low to avoid visual friction with the single-family detached area.

7. *Internal street system.* Certainly the principle remains valid that interior streets should have good access to major arteries and discourage through traffic. All of the plans used for illustration of neighborhood principles have street layouts which accomplish this objective with varying degrees of success. But the treatment of the neighborhood central area in each requires running collector streets through the interior of the neighborhood.

The open space net "neighborhood" moves principal collectors to the edges, eliminating even more traffic from neighborhood interiors and making a more convenient, better coordinated origin and destination pattern for daily trips. Even where existing collector roads remain, provision of new ones in the peripheral area during transition to full net potential would reduce interior traffic.

SCHEMATIC ILLUSTRATIONS

Figure 4 is an intentionally generalized and schematic illustration. It shows what might happen as a result of application of the open space net concept as limited access arterials cut through predominantly residential neighborhoods, and as complementary uses, open space, and principal peripheral collector streets are added.

Given a web of limited-access highways, interchange locations are key influences in neighborhood orientation. Four neighborhoods cornering at an intersection will usually not have the same design or facilities in relation to the corners because of the influence of direction of principal traffic flow toward major destinations in the morning, home from them in the evening. Each neighborhood will have one prime corner, toward principal destinations, and some will have more than one.

Of four neighborhoods cornered on an interchange, only two will normally have prime corners in that location. In terms of morning traffic flow, these will be "downstream." The remaining two will have their prime corners further toward mass destinations. In the diagram, "downstream" is toward the bottom of the page.

The two prime corners would have principal neighborhood shopping centers and other neighborhood service facilities for the areas they serve. The other two quadrants are available for supplementary facilities for their own neighborhoods, or for uses serving several (as for example a high school or a hospital).

This pattern suggests certain design requirements. In most cases there should be direct cross-connection at interchanges between the principal neighborhood streets bordering the net. This facilitates inter-neighborhood flow of local traffic without loading the limited-access system with short-trippers. It should not be necessary to swing onto the interchange to do comparison shopping in an adjoining commercial district or to reach a nearby high school, hospital, or other inter-neighborhood facility.

Where mass transit (indicated by the black dashed line down the center of the diagram) is part of the limited access system, stations should be in or close to the interchange to improve coordination of multiple-purpose trips for driver-commuters or for those taxiing commuters, and to consolidate commuter parking with other parking in the

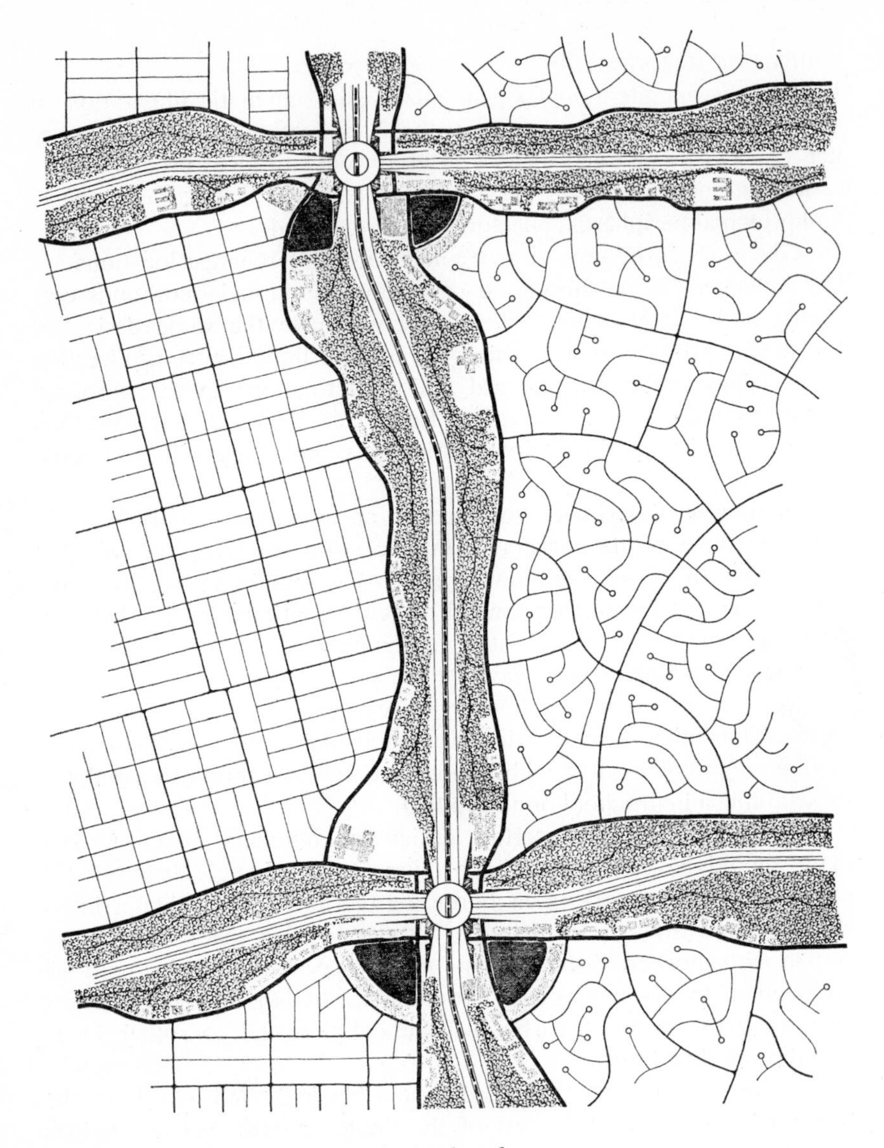

Figure 4. The net and neighborhoods

vicinity where this might increase efficiency of parking use. In some instances, commuter parking might be within the area or structure of the interchange itself.

As related to shopping centers, street design near the interchange should be so arranged that it is possible for drivers either to visit the center and its related services area or to bypass with a minimum of friction. The center should not interfere either with cross-connections to adjoining neighborhoods or with access to the interchange.

(It should perhaps be reemphasized that Figure 4 is schematic, intended merely to convey the general idea. No scale is given, specific building types are not identified, and the grid and curvilinear street patterns are as stylized as the tree symbols—which indicate only the open space within the net, and not that it is necessarily wooded. From the preceding discussion, however, it should be possible to detail the relationships.)

Notes on implementation

A number of actions toward building the net have already been suggested or implied, or become obvious when the principle is understood. This section reviews general types of implementation and proposes a few specific techniques.

THE COMPREHENSIVE PLAN

The comprehensive plan is obviously the place to start, since it states public intent and policies and lays the foundation for direct public action and for regulatory guidance of private action. Within the limits of current knowledge and foresight, the net should be generally located and dimensioned on the plan. Prime and other interchange locations should be identified in relation to service areas. The proposed interior pattern of the net (including uses in border and buffer sections) should be related to nearby uses outside the net.

From these initial efforts, necessarily fragmentary in some respects, it should be possible to assess priorities for needed action. With the net made part of the plan, next steps include detailed planning and programming for related public development, education to encourage public and private net-building moves, and specialized adaptations of the regulatory structure.

The long-range goal is to be achieved by short steps, of which the first should demonstrate that progress can be made and that the net is workable and has substantial advantages over more accustomed ways. Thus development action should start with what the military calls targets of opportunity, where current or impending programs are best adapted to achievement of net purposes. As examples, such demonstration sections might be created adjacent to new limited-access arteries, in connection with extensive redevelopment, or in open outlying sectors where it would be easiest to shape the emerging development pattern.

The planning commission has obvious leverage on items which they are required to review for compliance with the comprehensive plan, under relatively standard enabling requirements that after the plan has been adopted, "thenceforth no street, park, or other public way, ground, place or space, no public building or structure, or no public utility, whether publicly or privately owned, shall be constructed or authorized until the location and extent thereof shall have been submitted to and approved by the planning commission."

The scope and effectiveness of this power varies considerably. As examples of problems, school boards may be independent of local government. State or federal highway planners may ignore local plans, as may also special authorities of some kinds. "Higher" levels of government may pay no attention to local plans or regulations in locating structures and uses for performance of their governmental functions. In these cases, convincing persuasion may offset lack of direct control.

THE OFFICIAL MAP

Where state enabling legislation is adequate, the official map may be helpful in locating and holding future rights of way, in establishing a base for special zoning or subdivision requirements for net-related lands, and for other purposes. Effectiveness depends partly on how and how long lands may be reserved for public use.

THE CAPITAL IMPROVEMENT PROGRAM

In both its inclusive long-range aspects and in shorter-term capital improvement budgets, the capital improvement program offers recurring opportunities for providing and timing public improvements related to the net.

ZONING, SUBDIVISION REGULATION, AND SUPPLEMENTARY PUBLIC ACTION

Regulations can include a number of techniques for promoting appropriate development of and beneficial additions to the net, but there are limits to what regulations may be expected to do. Direct public action is often required as a supplement.

Buffer-border strips, particularly in areas not under direct public control, will be of major regulatory concern. In generally residential areas, the solution is probably special zoning for districts usually including all land within the border streets, and sometimes land across the border street from the net. Some effects of this zoning will carry over into subdivision regulations automatically, as in the case of lot sizes and dimensions.

Prefacing provisions dealing generally with such districts, a declaration of intent should state purposes, desired effects, and design relationships. Detailed regulations for buffer-border districts will vary according to location in the urban and urbanizing pattern, existing and proposed land uses in adjacent areas and in the strips, and other special considerations.

Adjacent to the border street, structures and intensive uses such as major parking areas should be restricted to a relatively thin strip in areas where sizable buffering is proposed. Setback from the border street should be adequate to assure safe and convenient access, but if held to reasonable minimums will increase the amount of interior space available for inclusion in the greenbelting.

The width of the buffer might be specified as a set distance, as a proportion of the depth of the lot between its front and the right of way of the limited access facility, or as a rear building line established on the zoning map.

Access to and through the greenbelt is important. In part, this access should be visual, in part pedestrian.

Much of the visual access from the perimeter street and property across it will be lost if it is blocked off by an unbroken structural wall of border uses. Zoning requirements for side yards will help, but should be supplemented by public action to provide uninterrupted exposure to the park in some areas, public parking areas along the border, and careful orientation of public buildings on their lands.

Pedestrian access to and through the greenway might be handled in part by subdivision requirements including public access easements under specified circumstances (perhaps combined with utility easements in some cases). Since action in building the net will often involve at some stage public ownership of at least strips of the land nearest the freeways, pedestrian ways might be designed and maintained in such locations as part of the redevelopment program. Given provision for pedestrian circulation as a stated part of the intent of the open space net plan, outright purchase or condemnation of title or easement for pedestrian use might be appropriate. And where rights-of-way for freeways are wide enough, there seems no reason why pedestrian ways might not be located along their outer fringes.

In outlying sectors through agricultural areas, if the strip can be located in advance of intensive development, land within it might be held in agricultural zoning with the proviso that it could be used for other than agricultural purposes only through planned development rezoning according to specified standards, and with uses and intensities as indicated in the comprehensive plan (which should in such case indicate prospective uses and intensities!). This gives maximum opportunity for public-private cooperation to assure solutions hand-tailored to local circumstances, and would probably present no legal difficulties if the provisions were carefully drafted and intent persuasively set forth.

Planned developments adjacent to the net, or on its fringes, should be encouraged to incorporate or merge their common open space with the buffer greenway, to maximize visual impact, and to increase accessibility and utility.

At interchange locations, prime and otherwise, boundaries for neighborhood shopping and office districts and for districts for inter-neighborhood public, quasi-public, and private major service facilities should be drawn to fit the cases and, if at all possible, only planned development should be permitted. One solution here would be acquisition of title or use rights by the public, covering the areas involved beyond the limited access and interchange rights-of-way, with passage of title or use rights into private hands only subject to planned development. Few localities are as yet in a position to move generally in this direction for legal, procedural, and financial reasons, but it seems inevitable that the time must come. When the situation has deteriorated to the point where urban renewal is justified for the entire area, the time has come.

Greenway uses close to interchange locations can be controlled with the stick, the carrot, or both. Near prime locations, the stick approach would prohibit uses which might be better located elsewhere, and would also permit certain uses desired within the greenbelt only in such locations. The carrot approach might take several forms. For example, uses permitted elsewhere only by special exception or other extraordinary procedures might be permitted by right only within the strip. Lot area requirements within the strip might be set somewhat lower than generally on grounds that proximity to permanent open space reduces need for lot size. As a case in point, a church might be allowed on three acres in the greenbelt rather than five elsewhere.

For multifamily uses, a provision with the same effect but stated differently might be effective. In connection with its land-use intensity rating approach, FHA allows extra land area credit where lands adjoin appropriate permanent open space. Thus a multifamily structure located within the net would get extra floor area. The special zoning regulations for net districts might specify that multifamily uses would be allowed only in specific delineated zones within the net, but that in such districts the extra floor area would apply.

BEYOND THE LOCAL SCENE—FEDERAL PROGRAMS

Fruition of the open space net principle can be hastened by astute use of federal programs already in being, and further encouraged by new adaptations. It is beyond the scope of this paper to explore these possibilities in any depth, but with focus on the net idea it is apparent that among others, urban renewal, open space, public facilities, planning, and perhaps even model cities funds might be effectively used. And given federal interest in the apparent advantages and economies of the net system, requirements and rewards recognizing the approach might stimulate better and faster net planning and development by such means as bonuses for location of mass transit in linear cores or increases in share of federal aid where the open space net is a goal in planning.

If the open space net concept can be incorporated into local planning even in the form of a relatively limited experimental demonstration, it seems highly probable that with the right start and continued public guidance and support the net should grow and spread under the impetus of its own merit.

High-level transportation nets for big-city CBDs

The electric elevator, first used commercially in 1889, was a prime mover in piling big-city central business districts high. Without it, new techniques for lifting structures skyward would have had limited application.

Population growth in sprawling metropolitan and megalopolitan areas intensifies land use at the urban center. Centripetal economic and functional forces limit outward expansion of the core. As a result, major CBDs are seeing a new upsurge of high-rise buildings. Old low structures on small lots come down in windrows to make way for massive tall buildings on substantial tracts. In city after city, gaps in rising skylines are filling in.

Congestion mounts. It is more and more difficult and expensive to get more and more people into and out of downtown. The battles of freeways, parking, and mass transportation continue with no end in sight. But it is also increasingly difficult to move around inside the core area. At or below ground level, sidewalks, streets, subways, pedestrian passageways are crowded. In buildings, entries and elevators are crowded. The lot of the downtown driver has been much discussed, but the lot of the downtown pedestrian is not a happy one either. Height adds distance of a new kind to local trips, and the distance is strewn with pitfalls, hazards, and delays.

Brown wants to visit Smith, 150 feet away as the crow flies, directly across the street and also on the thirtieth floor. Neither Brown nor Smith is a crow. A trip of more than a quarter of a mile is involved, 600 feet of it vertical. During the journey, Brown will wait for elevators and stop lights, add to pedestrian congestion on the streets and sidewalks, and impede the free flow of vehicular traffic.

Multiply these Brownian movements by the million, funnel them in and out at the bottoms of the buildings through dense pedestrian throngs, strain them through streams of automobiles, and the surviving Browns won't like it.

The very density of high-rise development downtown may help solve some of the problems created. With high buildings up, or soon to be built, in every block of the core, opportunity grows for a high-level transportation net supported largely by the buildings themselves and running partly through, partly between, the buildings.

Design considerations

The ultimate effectiveness of such a system will depend upon the extent to which it *is* a system. Bits and pieces will help, but they should be designed so that in time they can be put together to form an organized whole.

Substantial parts of such a system are already there—the elevators providing vertical transportation are in, or will be built as a matter of course in individual buildings. (The horizontal net would relieve elevator traffic to a considerable extent. In a 20-story building, the average elevator trip is about 10 floors. With a horizontal net at the tenth-floor level, the average trip would theoretically drop to five floors.) The hallways are in, providing horizontal "elevator shafts" for conventional pedestrian traffic. Hallways are usually under-used, and could be joined relatively easily by light, enclosed pedestrian bridges to provide a walkway net parallel to the sidewalks far below.

This would correspond to the minor street system in the high-level net, and even in early stages of development might include more than one layer. For example, pedestrian bridges might be started at the tenth and twentieth floor levels.

Early in the planning, it should be decided at what level (or levels) the system should be designed. As a practical consideration it will usually be necessary to determine the maximum height at which existing buildings will support a continuous network with minimum gaps to be spanned by special supports.

The collector system would consist of moving walkways, the

arterial system of monorail with pushbutton controls as in automatic elevators. These two elements of the net would require skillful adaption of design to existing structures to hold major alterations to a minimum, and careful planning of proposed buildings.

Theoretically, optimum location for moving walks would be through the midpoint of the long axis of blocks, and through the narrow dimensions of buildings close to the main elevator banks. This fits vertical and horizontal traffic systems in individual buildings. In practice, layouts of buildings and blocks will seldom fit this theoretical pattern. It will be necessary to design accordingly, bringing the moving walk net across each block as close as possible to a major vertical and horizontal circulation nexus. In some cases, these walks may have to be hung along the outer faces of buildings.

Moving walks could be constructed with movements on parallel belts in opposite directions on one level, or in an over-and-under pattern on two. Primary orientation would usually be either cross-town or longitudinally, with occasional feeders working across the prevailing direction of the net. Intersections would usually require two levels. Escalators would handle the short movement between levels.

The vehicular system might be in the form of a circumferential belt or belts, with crossing shuttles.

Putting these pieces together, the result might be something like this. Inside the beltline highway encircling the CBD would be a ring of high-rise parking garages, including perhaps helicopter landing areas, and high-rise apartments. The high-level monorail net would have a belt joining these structures, with cross-town and longitudinal connecting shuttles as required. Location of major ground-level mass transportation stations would be a primary factor in determining design. The primary function of the monorail net would be to move masses of people rapidly over relatively long distances. Supplementing this net with moving walkways would make it possible to spread monorail elements of the system relatively far apart.

Feeding and supplementing the monorail system, the moving walkway net should have its elements relatively closely spaced—generally through each block or alternate blocks in the direction of principal orientation, with cross-movement at longer intervals, with variations in this pattern to fit varying traffic flows. At the location of ground-level mass transportation stations, spacing would be closer, wider belts would be needed, and there would have to be major elevator facilities. The moving walkway net should extend to the peripheral parking garages and apartments. Its principal function would be to handle traffic of varying volumes for intermediate distances. The pedestrian net, tied at short intervals to the moving walks, would take care of short-distance traffic.

In cities with relatively compact CBDs, the vehicular net might be eliminated and its function taken over entirely by moving walkways, some of which could be designed for higher speeds.

Costs, revenues, benefits

The high-level transportation net can be built. Would it pay?

Probably yes in some cities now. Very probably yes in more cities in the not-too-distant future. Certainly it is time to start research, and if the research is favorable, to start planning.

Lack of experience makes some of the advance estimates difficult. Structural costs, costs of equipment, operating costs can be worked out from existing knowledge. Estimating "right-of-way" costs—routes through, over, and on the side of buildings, air rights, routes through buildings which are not yet there, provision for special supports where buildings are lacking now, but which can be made parts of buildings later—will require some pioneering in the field of cost analysis.

Estimating revenues will also challenge ingenuity. Should the system be free to users, with income from benefit assessments and general fund money? Would it be better to employ a turnstile system giving general access to the moving walkway and vehicular system? (The interconnected hallways for "pedestrian pedestrians" would almost inevitably have to be free, and provision would have to be made for cross-overs through paid parts of the system.) How many people would pay how much in fares for this kind of travel? What other revenues could be derived—for example from shops and eating establishments and other sales and service ventures paying a premium for being inside the system on a new Main Street, a pedestrian mall 10 or 15 floors up?

In assessment of benefits to individual properties, to the CBD as a whole, and to the general public, questions rank themselves row on row. The impressionistic general outlook from present ignorance is strongly optimistic, but needs careful testing.

The electric elevator multiplied the functional efficiency of downtown and of individual structures. It also multiplied the congestion problems of downtown. To what extent would the high-level transportation net further multiply functional efficiency and reduce congestion problems?

Here would be a system linking most downtown buildings together with a weatherproof circulatory network reaching out to parking facilities and high-rise apartments, and distributing from mass transportation stations. How much would it improve circulation of vehicles in the streets below and pedestrian congestion at the ground level? The system would reduce congestion in elevators—yes or no?

What happens to patterns of space-use in buildings and to lease charges per square foot at various levels? The ground floor areas remain. They have a head start on value for walk-in trade. If a second layer of prime frontage is created, what happens? It won't do to jump at conclusions. The second layer will not be created all at once, and the multiplication of intensity of use created by the net might quite possibly mean that adverse effects downstairs would be negligible—that the number of customers would increase fast enough to support both layers. Experience with businesses in bypassed districts might provide some leads. Very probably, as in the case of bypasses, some businesses would be improved and some would find it advantageous to move to new locations. Unlike the bypass situation, there will be few owner-occupants involved in CBDs.

To move ahead

The high-level transportation net could be built. It is very probably economically feasible now in a few cities, and will be in many. In time, something like this will be essential in metropolitan and megalopolitan centers.

A new CBD direction—up—calls for a new circulatory system—laterally. There is probably not room for it on the ground or under the ground, and in any event there are solid arguments for putting it near the middle elevation of buildings to free the streets and subground areas for movement of heavy goods, for vehicular traffic, for mass transport, and for ground-level pedestrians.

It's time now to move ahead. The action indicated is massive, on a wide variety of fronts, and involving a broad range of skills. Public interest and private enterprise will have to work closely together—neither can do the job alone on anything like the scale required.

Planners may lead off with initial demonstrations of potentials and needs and in bringing the team together, but the team will be essential however it is organized—architects, engineers, real estate economists, property owners, financiers, lawyers, traffic experts, public administrators, and a lot of other specialists, organizations, and interest groups. Local, state, and federal legislative, executive, and judicial bodies will inevitably be involved.

New kinds of laws will have to be passed, and old laws enlarged in their application. (How should condemnation powers be applied in the case of a recalcitrant property owner who refuses to negotiate for the use of part of the fourteenth and fifteenth floors of a building as a route for a public utility? How should offsetting benefits be appraised? May a building owner refuse use of elevators to non-tenants? What happens to the high-level right-of-way through a building if the owner decides to demolish the structure?)

All these things can be worked out and should be worked out. If they are not, the problems ahead will dwarf present troubles.

Ordinance establishing a planning commission

In getting planning under way, it is desirable to pass an ordinance giving the new commission formal status and indicating how it is to operate and what it is expected to do. A new commission is often at a loss as to procedures, powers, and duties, and many commissions which have been long established show some uncertainty.

The ordinance and commentary which follows provides at least a starting point for adaptation to local requirements where new commissions are being established, and such an ordinance might be considered for adoption, with modifications as local circumstances indicate, where existing commissions are operating informally or under ordinances needing amplification or revision.

A preamble is not essential in an ordinance, but can perform a very useful educational function. In the case of an ordinance establishing a planning commission, a large part of the purpose is educational. The preamble should indicate in a general way why planning is considered important, where it gets its authorization, and what function it is to perform. In addition to providing guidance for the commission, this kind of statement may also be useful if legal questions arise:

Whereas the City of______________desires to encourage sound and harmonious growth of the municipality and its environs and efficiency and economy in the provision of facilities and services, to insure maximum returns for expenditure of public funds, and to avoid errors and waste resulting from unplanned and uncoordinated development, and

Whereas, to these ends and for these purposes, it is necessary that there should be prepared and maintained in current form a comprehensive plan, with related studies, statements of policies, regulations and ordinances to guide the development of the City of____________, and

Whereas it is recognized that planning is a means to these ends, and

Whereas the City is authorized and empowered to establish a planning commission by the provisions of__________________ [here indicate provisions in the charter or in state law providing for the establishment of a planning commission],

NOW THEREFORE BE IT ENACTED BY THE____________ [governing body] OF THE CITY OF __________________:

In adapting this ordinance to local use, be careful that provisions concerning number of members, terms of office, method of appointment, inclusion of ex officio members, and other details are in accord with applicable charter provisions or enabling legislation.

How many members? Less than five seems too few. More than 10 becomes unwieldy. In the absence of specific guides in the charter or the enabling legislation, something between these two figures is desirable. An odd number is often used to reduce the likelihood of tie votes, but this is not a primary consideration.

It may be felt that a planning commission of 10 or fewer members fails to give adequate representation, but establishment of a commission is the beginning, rather than the end, of public participation in the planning process. The planning commission can serve as an executive committee for a much larger committee framework if this seems indicated. It should be kept reasonably small for maximum effectiveness.

Who should be on the commission? There are two questions here, one of which should be answered in the ordinance. The other need not be and probably should not be, but should certainly be settled before making appointments.

On the matter of residence, should membership be restricted to persons living within city limits? If the charter or the enabling act require residence, this question is settled. If not, there may be solid reasons for leaving the way open to appointment of some members from urban fringes outside the city. If annexation seems possible in the future, if there is to be extraterritorial jurisdiction on zoning and subdivision regulation (and requirements concerning extension of utilities often give extraterritorial "jurisdiction" even where the law does not provide it directly—water lines, sewers, or other city services and facilities may be withheld from new subdivisions outside the city which fail to meet city subdivision standards), if it would be helpful to establish direct liaison with the county, or even if it is hoped to accomplish extraterritorial planning objectives by persuasion rather than regulation, it may be well to allow for some representation on the planning commission from outside city limits.

The other question involves qualification of members. Here the goal is membership which will be honestly and broadly representative of the general public interest. The danger is that persons will be appointed to the planning commission who may have private interests conflicting with public. Under no circumstances should the ordinance require representation of special interest groups in a position to derive private profit if planning decisions, zoning, subdivision regulations, or other matters with which the commission may deal, can be warped in their favor, and such representatives or individuals should not be appointed to the commission unless there is assurance that they will subjugate private interest to public.

Ex officio members. In establishing smooth working relationships and a free flow of communication with the city administration and the governing body, it is often desirable to provide for ex officio membership. Ex officio members should not dominate the group, of course, so there should be a limit on number. Since there may be changes in the organizational set-up of the city or in personnel, it may be just as well to leave detailed determination of ex officio membership to be decided in the light of current circumstances.

Terms of office. One of the principal functions of the planning commission is to assure continuity in public policy. Terms of members, other than ex officio, should therefore be arranged so that they do not coincide with changes in the governing body due to local elections. Memberships should overlap so that a majority of the commission stays each year. Since membership involves considerable time and effort, it will be easier to get responsible people to serve if terms are limited (and if an occasional bad apple shows up in the barrel, it will be possible to remove it more quickly if there are relatively short terms). A good average is three years, but there is nothing sacred about this number.

The second part of the ordinance which follows illustrates how these points might be handled. Again, in making local adaptations be sure to comply with the charter and with enabling legislation which may apply:

Section 1. Establishing Planning Commission: Qualifications of Members; Terms of Office—There is hereby established a planning commission, hereinafter referred to as the "commission," which shall consist of_____members appointed by the__________[governing body] from among the residents of_____________. [This would cover a situation in which it is intended to limit membership to residents of the city. If it is desired to include fringe areas, eliminate the period and add: "and its environs, provided that not more than_____members shall be appointed from outside city limits."]

Among this membership, two shall be ex officio, one to be appointed from the administrative membership of the city government and one from the membership of the________ [governing body]. [As stated, this provision assumes two ex officio members. More, less, or none can be provided.]

Terms of office for members other than ex officio shall be for_______ years, provided however that in first establishment of the commission, ____members shall be appointed for terms of one year, ____for terms of two years, and_____for terms of three years. [This provision should be juggled to fit the number of members to terms of office so that an approximately equal minority will come up for reappointment each year.]

Ex officio members shall be appointed______________ [alternatives:] "for annual terms, provided that membership on the commission shall terminate with the office from which ex officio membership is derived"; "to serve during the pleasure of the__________ [governing body]"; or as may otherwise be appropriate.

[On the sticky question of personal qualifications, there may be no provision, or perhaps one like this would be helpful.] Members other than ex officio shall be appointed from among persons in a position to represent the general public interest, and no person shall be appointed with private or personal interests likely to conflict with the general public interest. If any person appointed shall find that his private or personal interests are involved in any matter coming before the commission, he shall disqualify himself from taking part in action on the matter, or may be disqualified by the chairman of the commission.

Removal from office; vacancies. Provision should be made for formal action by the governing body, but there might also be a provision for removal by less complicated means in cases where non-attendance by a commission member becomes a problem. If vacancy occurs as a result of removal from office, death, resignation, a move out of the area, or other reasons, appointment to fill the vacancy should be for the unexpired term. Otherwise the scheduling of normal replacements might be disrupted.

Section 2. Removal from Office; Vacancies—Any member of the commission may be removed from office for just cause and on written charges by a two-thirds vote of the entire ______________ [governing body], but such member shall be entitled to a public hearing before such vote is taken. In addition, any member may be removed for non-attendance at planning commission meetings without action by the ____________ [governing body], according to rules adopted by the planning commission.

It shall be the duty of the chairman of the commission to notify the ______________ [governing body] promptly of any vacancies occurring in membership, and the ______________ [governing body] shall fill such vacancies within ________ days for the unexpired term of the original appointment.

The next section is relatively cut and dried, and for the most part will normally require little variation. As stated here, it assumes ex officio members:

Section 3. Officers, Rules, Employees, Salaries, and Expenses—The commission shall elect a chairman and vice chairman from among those of its members who are not appointed ex officio, and may create such other offices as it may determine. It shall provide itself with a secretary, either by election from among its members or by appointment of an officer or employee of the city who is not a member of the commission. All members, including ex officio members, shall be entitled to vote, but a secretary who is not a member of the commission shall not be entitled to vote. Terms of all elected offices shall be for one year, with eligibility for reelection.

The commission shall adopt rules for its governance and for the transaction of its business, and shall keep a record of attendance at its meetings and of resolutions, transactions, findings, and determinations showing the vote of each member on each question requiring a vote, or if absent or abstaining from voting indicating such fact. The records of the commission shall be a public record.

Subject to approval of the ____________ [governing body] and within limits set by appropriations or other funds made available, the commission may employ such staff, technicians, and experts as may be deemed proper, and may incur such other expenses as may be necessary and proper for the conduct of its affairs. Members of the commission shall receive no salaries or fees for their services thereon, but may receive necessary travel, per diem, and other expenses while on official business for the commission if funds are available for this purpose.

The last paragraph above may be modified as necessary to fit local administrative practice on staff and consultant assistance, and on handling expenses. Planning commission members normally serve without salaries or fees, but should of course be covered on expenses incurred in their work. The language of the section which follows should also be fitted to local practice.

Section 4. Appropriations, Fees, and Other Income—The____________[governing body] shall make available to the commission such appropriations as it may see fit for salaries, fees, and expenses necessary in the conduct of its work. The commission shall have authority to expend all sums so appropriated and other sums made available for its use from grants, gifts, and other sources for the purposes and activities authorized by this ordinance.

In some ordinances, provision is made for the governing body to establish a schedule of fees to be charged by the commission. Usually it is better administrative practice to have any fees charged in connection with commission actions (normally to offset staff or other expense) go through the office of the city treasurer, city clerk, or other official charged with handling city money.

The following section is intended to be detailed enough to make it clear what the commission is intended to do but flexible enough to allow latitude for action which may be required.

For example, paragraph (h) is broad enough to allow the planning commission to be appointed as the zoning commission under standard zoning enabling legislation language: "Where a city planning commission exists, it may be appointed as the zoning commission." The commission might also be designated as the Local Planning Agency, under certain federal programs, assigned the job of reviewing subdivision plats, or given other duties under the umbrella of this language.

Section 5. Functions, Powers, and Duties—The functions, powers, and duties of the commission shall be, in general:

(a) To acquire and maintain in current form such basic information as is necessary to an understanding of past trends, present conditions, and forces at work to cause changes in these conditions.

(b) To prepare and keep current a comprehensive general plan for meeting present requirements and such future needs as may be foreseen.

(c) To establish principles and policies for guiding action affecting development in the city and its environs.

(d) To prepare and recommend to the ____________ [governing body] ordinances, regulations, and other proposals promoting orderly development along lines indicated as desirable by the comprehensive plan.

(e) To determine whether specific proposed developments conform to the principles and requirements for the comprehensive plan.

(f) To keep the ____________ [governing body] and the general public informed and advised as to these matters.

(g) To conduct such public hearings as may be required to gather information necessary for the drafting, establishment, and maintenance of the comprehensive plan and ordinances and regulations related to it, and to establish public committees for the purpose of collecting and compiling information necessary for the plan, or for the purpose of promoting the accomplishment of the plan in whole or in part.

(h) To perform other duties which may be lawfully assigned to it, or which may have bearing on the preparation or accomplishment of the plan.

In connection with its duties, and within the limit of its funds, the commission may make, cause to be made, or obtain maps, aerial photographs and surveys, and special studies on the location, condition, and adequacy of specific facilities of the city and, as appropriate, its environs, including, but not limited to: studies on housing, commercial and industrial facilities; economic development; parks; playgrounds and other recreational facilities; schools; public and private utilities; and traffic, transportation, and parking.

All city employees shall, upon request and within a reasonable time, furnish to the commission or its employees or agents such available records or information as may be required in its work. The commission, or its employees or agents, may in the performance of official duties enter upon lands and make examinations or surveys in the same manner as other authorized city agents or employees, and shall have such other powers as are required for the performance of official functions in carrying out the purposes of this ordinance.

The particular and central job of the planning commission is the preparation and maintenance of the comprehensive plan and the basic data needed to guide its adjustment to unforeseen circumstances. Hence there is need for a statement in the ordinance indicating how the plan should be prepared, what it should include, its purposes, the necessity for holding hearings, the manner of adoption by the commission, and the manner of obtaining recognition by the governing body.

The next section covers these matters. It should be noted that the requirement for making a plan is mandatory, but the language referring to the long-range financial program as part of the plan is permissive. This might be made mandatory also, and certainly one of the objectives should be to establish a long-range capital improvement program. In many cities, however, there will be officers in a better position than the planning commission to make a capital improvement budget.

Section 6. The Comprehensive Plan—When basic information has been compiled and analyzed, the commission shall make a comprehensive general plan for the physical development of the city, based on existing and anticipated needs, showing existing and proposed improvements, and stating the principles and policies according to which future development should proceed and the manner in which such development should be controlled and guided. The comprehensive plan may also include a suggested long-range financial program for public improvements.

The plan shall be made with the general purpose of guiding and accomplishing a coordinated, adjusted, and harmonious development of the city and its environs which will, in accordance with existing and future needs, promote public health, safety, order, comfort, convenience, prosperity, and the general welfare and efficiency and economy in the process of development.

The plan shall be adopted by the commission as a whole or as substantial portions, corresponding generally with functional or geographic subdivisions, are completed. Before adoption of the plan or portions thereof, a public hearing, or hearings shall be held, with due public notice.

The adoption of the plan, or a portion or portions thereof, or of any amendment or addition thereto, shall be by a resolution carried by the affirmative vote of not less than three-fourths of all the members of the commission. The resolution shall refer specifically to the maps, reports, descriptive material, and other matters intended by the commission to form the whole or part of the plan, and the action shall be recorded on the plan or parts thereof by the identifying signature of the chairman or the secretary of the commission, or both, together with the date of such action. A copy of the plan, portion of plan, or amendment shall be certified to the ___________[governing body].

The______________[governing body] may, by appropriate official action, formally approve the matter certified.

Note that there is no absolute requirement for approval of the plan or portion by the governing body. The planning commission adopts it. The governing body may approve it, and it would be well if it did so to indicate a consensus on the policies and programs involved. But the planning commission is, for the most part, an advisory body as will be seen in the next section, and the governing body may overrule its advice. Thus giving the commission power to adopt its own plan, with or without concurrence of the governing body, does not set the commission up as an appointed dictatorship in a position to impose its will on the elected representatives of the people. The "power" of the planning commission lies in its ability to give well-considered advice persuasively.

The next section makes three things clear. First, the planning commission's advice need not be requested until after it has prepared a plan or portion appropriate to the matter to be considered. Second, after a plan or appropriate parts have been adopted, the governing body binds itself by the ordinance to ask the advice of the planning commission on certain matters affecting the physical development of the city, and agrees further to wait a stipulated time for a report. Third, the governing body is not bound by the commission's report.

Section 7. Legal Status of the Comprehensive Plan—Whenever a comprehensive plan, or a portion of such plan corresponding generally with a functional subdivision of the subject matter or a geographical subdivision of the area, has been adopted by the commission, then and thenceforth, if the plan or portion thereof covers the matter involved, no street, park or other public way, ground, place or space, no public building or structure, and no city-owned water, sewer, electrical, or other utility system shall be constructed, altered, or authorized in the geographic area over which the city exercises jurisdiction unless and until the location and extent thereof shall have been submitted to the commission for a report thereon expressing approval or disapproval and the reasons therefore, or suggesting amendments or alternatives to the action proposed. Within 30 days after the request for such report has been received by the commission, or within such other time limit as shall be agreed upon, either such report shall be made or failure of the commission to report shall be deemed to be approval by the commission.

The report of the commission may be overruled only by at least a three-fourths vote of the entire __________ [governing body].

The last provision gives added weight to the advice of the commission, in that it requires more than a simple majority vote to override. For a lesser degree, the requirement might be for a majority vote of the entire governing body, which would mean that an extraordinary majority would be required only if a member or members of the group were absent. If a simple majority of the members present is all that is to be required, the provision should be dropped. If possible, it would be best to have it stand as suggested.

Comes now a situation in which the planning commission does have administrative powers. Here the commission becomes involved in plat approval, but only after it has adopted a major street plan and the governing body has adopted subdivision regulations. It would be most difficult for a commission to do an effective job on plat approval without knowing where major streets are proposed, and the usual result of efforts in the absence of a major street plan is that the commission has a tendency to penalize the subdivider by requiring wider streets than are necessary for minor street purposes simply because it hasn't made up its mind where major streets are to go. Moreover the commission without a major street plan has an inclination to insist on continuity of street pattern from one subdivision to another which may not be needed if there is a proper major street system, and which leads through traffic into residential neighborhoods where it does not belong.

In delegating plat approval to the commission, the governing body, by its approval of guides and standards in the form of subdivision regulations, has fulfilled its duty. It is not delegating legislative power, but saying in effect: "If a proposal meets these requirements, it should be approved. If it does not, it should not be approved." The act of the planning commission is thus administrative, no legislative power being delegated.

The other sections which follow are routine, and complete the ordinance. Section 9 is the usual language protecting against having the whole ordinance thrown out should any of its provisions be declared unconstitutional. Section 10 sets the effective date, and might be otherwise phrased if there is local reason for doing so.

Section 8. Plat Approval by Commission—As soon as a major street plan is adopted by the commission and subdivision regulations have been adopted by the ____________ [governing body] it shall become the responsibility of the commission to pass upon all proposed new or amended plats coming directly or indirectly under the jurisdiction of the city. No new plat, and no amendment or vacation of an existing plat or portion thereof shall thereafter be recorded without the approval of the commission.

The "directly or indirectly" language here is intended to cover situations like those where the city has adopted a policy of refusing to extend water or sewer lines to subdivisions outside its limits unless the plat is approved, or circumstances where a county has agreed to give consideration to recommendations from the city in approving or disapproving plats outside but near city limits.

Section 9. Conflicts with Other Ordinances, Separability of Provisions—All ordinances or portions of ordinances in conflict herewith are repealed. Should any section of this ordinance be held unconstitutional or void, the remaining provisions shall nevertheless remain in full force and effect.

On this provision, be careful that no existing ordinances or portions of ordinances which it is intended to retain are inadvertently repealed.

Section 10. Effective Date—This ordinance shall take effect immediately upon passage.

The major street plan—and ordinance

Every city should have a major street plan. And it isn't a bad idea to have a major street *ordinance* to go with the plan.

The major street plan

We don't want to shatter illusions about how complicated and difficult and mysterious and technical and expensive and expert-requiring planning is, but in a city of 25,000 or less, the kind of major street plan we are talking about can be drafted in the course of an afternoon by a group of reasonably intelligent people.

The major street plan we are talking about shows arterial and collector streets—where they are to be and what right-of-way widths they will require. The plan is made so that when construction engineering and traffic engineering gets under way, there will be right-of-way in the right places. This isn't a plan showing design of traffic separators at intersections, or paving specifications. All that comes later.

Drawing a major street plan for a small city can be a fairly simple operation which yields important long-range returns. To start with, there should be the basic planning tools—a good base map showing

This article originally appeared in *Bair Facts,* published by Chandler-Davis Publishing Co., West Trenton, N.J. (1960). Reprinted by permission.

right-of-way widths of existing streets, a land-use map, and if possible an aerial mosaic.

The purpose of the job is to devise a major street skeleton which will be functional and adequate, without running a lot of bones through areas which should be muscle and without leaving a lot of muscle unsupported by bones.

Arterial traffic will flow better, be easier to control, get involved in fewer accidents, and disrupt a smaller area of residential uses if it is concentrated on a few streets designed to handle through traffic than if it filters through a lot of streets which haven't made up their minds whether they are major streets or not, and which intersect each other at odd intervals and odd angles.

Of course you should know that if there is any way to reduce loads on streets inside the city by running through traffic on beltlines or bypasses around the outskirts, the city will benefit tremendously—and so will the through traffic. If you don't figure on bypasses and belt routes to fit your town some kindly fellow from a higher bureaucracy will come along and figure out a bypass or belt route which suits him, and when figuring is done at that level it is almost impossible to head off the disaster to schools, residential areas, or other vital zones which appear to be targets for high-level highway planning.

APPLICATION OF SOME PRINCIPLES

Consider now the major street plan in the illustration. The drafting of the illustration took considerably longer than the drafting of the plan in rough form.

Here is a town through which north-south traffic used to flow from the Old County Road route and up through the road marked (1) at the top of the map. East-west traffic used to concentrate along State Road 000 on the map, because US 00 (11) was developed to bypass the center of town. The road marked (7) in the middle of the southern section was built as a full-scale arterial from US 00 to State Road 000 a couple of years ago.

There will be extensive development inside this town in the northern sector, to the northeast of the school, and to the west of the school. The lakeside portion is already built up, as is the greater part of the south side of town.

Outside of town, to the west along the lake and above US 00 there will be considerable residential development, and north of town,

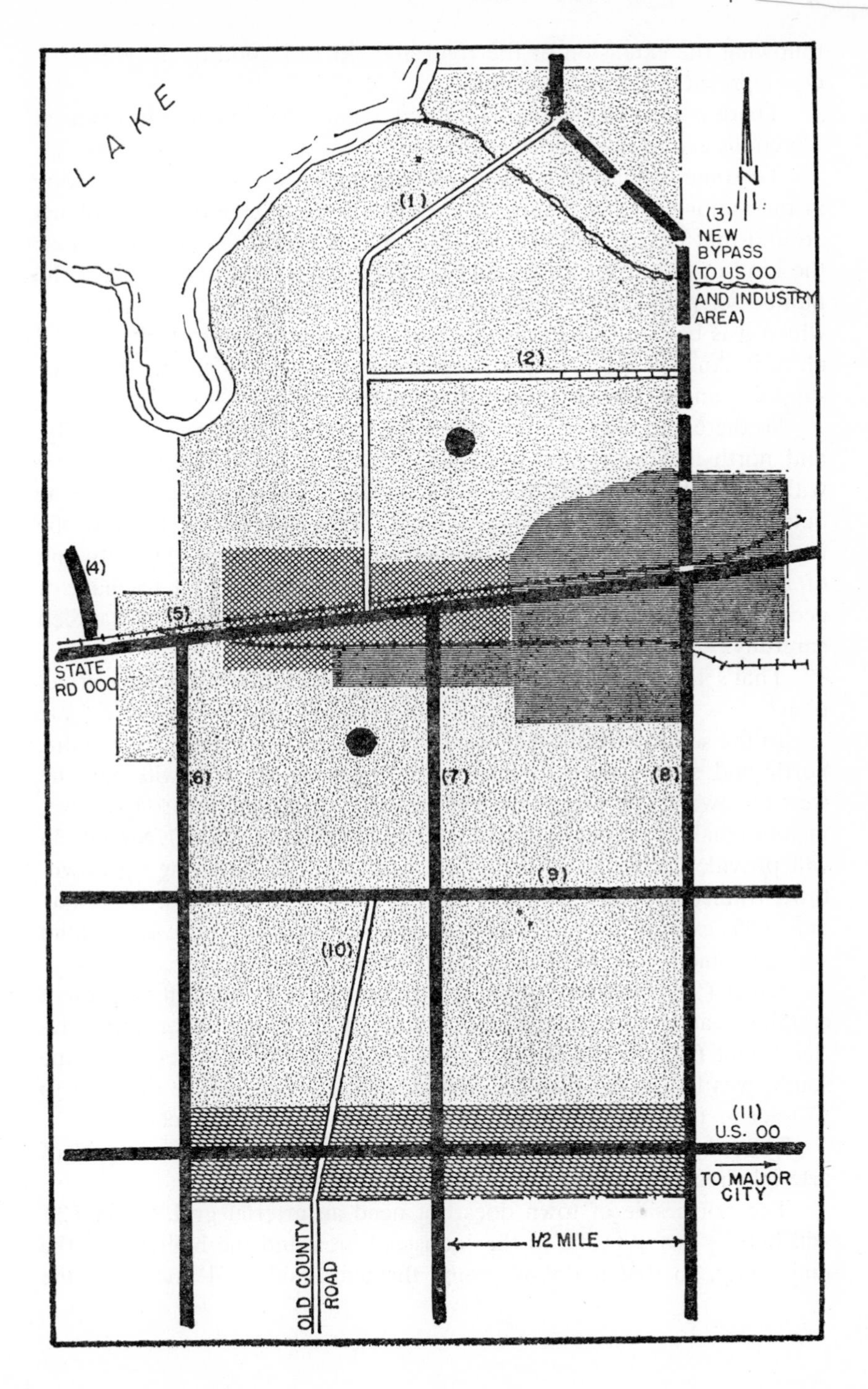
LAKE
(1)
(2)
(3)
NEW
BYPASS
(TO US 00
AND INDUSTRY
AREA)
N
(4)
(5)
STATE
RD 000
(6)
(7)
(8)
(9)
(10)
(11)
U.S. 00
TO MAJOR
CITY
1/2 MILE
OLD COUNTY
ROAD

following the extension of the road marked (1) good quality lakeside development is already in progress.

There is heavy trucking to the industrial areas, coming in from all directions except northwest.

To some extent this will be a "bedroom" town for people working in the major city a few miles to the east, and in the complex of plants around that city. It will almost have to be a "bedroom" town because the kind of industries it has, and is likely to have, will not support the number of people in the income bracket needed to buy the homes for which it is best suited. Retirees will take up some of the slack, but not all of it. And the major city is near enough so that it is an attraction for shopping and service and recreational activities.

So there will always be considerable numbers of people in this city, and north and west of it, who will want to get to US 00 and away without running through downtown traffic. Through traffic originating outside the area will go along US 00 without affecting local traffic much, although the roadside commercial development at the south end of the city may in time create enough marginal friction to make it necessary to build a bypass around the bypass, unless it is handled carefully.

That's the general picture. Now what did they do about a street plan?

In the south part of town, the streets marked (6) and (8), running north and south, were designated arterials. Street (6) will pick up west-of-town traffic bound for US 00 without running it through town, including lakefront development which will come in via (4). Street (8) will provide access to the industrial area without cluttering up downtown traffic, and will form part of the north-south bypass. Both (6) and (8) existed as relatively unimproved roads, and will require widening and paving to arterial construction standards.

Street (9), running east-west, is narrow and crooked in its present condition, and will require widening and straightening to form an arterial. Street (10), which is part of the habit-pattern of drivers from the south, was left in the plan as a collector road, but will be diverted to (7) across (9) instead of carrying through traffic past the school.

Thus the south end of town will be served by a half-mile grid of arterial streets, supplemented by one collector street.

The north side of town does not need an arterial grid. Street (3) will bypass heavy traffic to the industrial area and the highway to the major city, so that it doesn't come through residential areas and the business district. Street (1), now open, will serve the limited area it traverses as a collector street for north-south traffic, and (2) when opened across town (it now goes only to the end of the segmented section in the illustration) will take residents of the north residential area over to the bypass if they wish to avoid the business district in getting to the major highway.

Major street ordinance

Now that you have a major street plan, what are you going to do with it, and what, if anything, is it going to do to you? Something, somewhere, ought to indicate what the plan is for, why it was drafted, how it affects the city, and what it does to people and property along major and collector streets and elsewhere. Hence the major street ordinance:

Whereas the City of ____________________ desires to provide for orderly, efficient, and economical growth and to protect the safety, comfort, convenience, and general welfare of its citizens, and

Whereas the Major Street Plan, as adopted herein is a part of the comprehensive plan, and a means to these ends.

NOW THEREFORE BE IT ORDAINED BY THE CITY OF ____

____

Section 1. General Purposes and Intent—The general purposes and intent of the city in adoption of this official Major Street Plan are as follows:

(a) To provide a convenient and adequate major street network to meet the needs of residential, commercial, and industrial traffic within the city, and to facilitate flow of traffic through and around the city.

(b) By establishing a major street network, to reduce the use of minor streets for through traffic, thus contributing to the safety and comfort of dwellers along such minor streets.

(c) To give assurance and guidance as to intent concerning location of major streets in order that developers, residents, and commercial and industrial interests may be directed thereby.

(d) To provide a basis for city programs for right-of-way acquisition, and for design and construction appropriate to such streets.

(e) To guide planning and control of land use along such streets in order to minimize potential marginal interference with free traffic flow, and to protect the uses along such streets from potential damaging effects of concentrated traffic flow.[1]

Section 2. Existing and Proposed Streets Designated as Arterial or Collector Streets—The following existing or proposed streets, or portions of existing or proposed streets, are hereby declared to comprise the Major Street Plan for the city, and are hereby designated as arterial or collector streets as follows:[2]

(a) *Arterial Streets*

[List streets or portions of streets designated as arterial, including existing and proposed streets.]

(b) *Collector Streets*

[List streets or portions of streets designated as collector, including existing and proposed streets.]

Section 3. Effect of Designation as Arterial or Collector Streets—The streets designated, and no other,[3] shall be developed and maintained as arterial or collector streets, and shall be used as through streets for movement of concentrated flows of traffic.

(a) *Width of right-of-way*—Arterial streets shall have a minimum right-of-way width of____ feet, collector streets a minimum right-of-way width of____feet.[4]

(b) *Traffic Flow*—Except where traffic signals control flow, traffic shall have right of way in the following order, and stop signs shall be erected accordingly: Traffic flow on arterial streets shall have right-of-way over traffic flow on collector and minor streets; traffic flow on

1. Note that preservation of right-of-way for future acquisition is not one of the purposes of this ordinance. Courts have frowned on efforts of cities to protect right-of-way until such time as it is convenient to acquire it, on grounds that this is taking of property without just compensation. Note also, in what follows, that right-of-way is preserved for future acquisition, but only through legitimate exercise of the police power.

2. Where a listing is likely to be too long and cumbersome, and perhaps in any case, it might be well to include a Major Street Map by reference, either as a substitute for the listing or as a supplement to it. Use language similar to that for establishing the Official Zoning Map in the zoning ordinance.

3. "And no other" indicates that the city has made up its mind. Without this phrase it is not clear to residents, developers, or commercial or industrial interests whether this is really a major street plan or just part of a major street plan. Assurance as to the completeness and stability of this part of the comprehensive plan is important to a lot of people.

4. Where an honest effort is made to reduce number of major streets, there shouldn't be much objection to holding width and general quality high. HHFA, in "Suggested Subdivision Regulations," says: "Each community should consider street width standards from the point of view of its own experience and local conditions. However, 80 to 120 feet may be considered reasonable for arterial streets, and 60 feet for collector streets." In some cases, it might be desirable to have several classes of arterial and collector streets, with Arterial A at 120 feet, Arterial B, 100 feet, and so on.

collector streets shall have right-of-way over traffic flow on minor streets. Where streets of the same designation intersect, right-of-way shall be as determined in laws or regulations adopted by the city.

Section 4. Setbacks and Curb Cuts—In order to preserve free traffic flow on arterial and collector streets, to minimize marginal frictions caused by land uses bordering such streets, and to protect inhabitants of residences bordering such streets from hazards, noise, glare, and fumes arising from concentrated flow of traffic:[5]

(a) No portion of any residential structure shall be erected closer than_______feet to the centerline of any street designated as an arterial street, nor closer than_______feet to the centerline of a street designated as a collector street.[6]

(b) No curb cut shall be made in connection with any commercial or industrial structure or use unless plans showing the relation of the curb cut to the structures and parking area (if any) on the lot, and to structures, parking areas, and curb cuts on adjacent lots shall have been approved by the planning commission.

Section 5. Violations and Penalties—Any person violating the section of this ordinance relating to setbacks and curb cuts shall upon conviction be fined not more than $500 or imprisoned for not more than 60 days, or both, and each day's continued violation may be considered a separate offense.

Section 6. Separability—Should any portion of this ordinance be held unconstitutional or invalid, the remainder shall continue to have full force and effect.

Section 7. Effective Date—This ordinance shall be effective immediately upon becoming law.

---

5. This elaboration of the statement already made in Section 1 may be redundant, but it emphasizes that the purpose of the regulation is "police power"—protection of health, safety, etc.—rather than a subterfuge to keep land open for future acquisition. This is a particularly important consideration where proposed streets are involved.

6. Residential yard requirements which grow out of this provision should be tailored to fit the requirements on width of the streets. It is assumed that along major streets, it is desirable to have more separation between residences and the right-of-way line than along minor streets. Thus if the front yard required generally in a residential district under zoning regulations is 25 feet, it is logical to increase it to 35 feet adjacent to a major street. On a 100-foot arterial, then, the figure to go in the first blank of this section would be 85 feet, 50 feet for half the width of the right-of-way and 35 feet for the yard.

The minor street plan

Most cities have miles of minor streets they don't need. They don't do anybody any particular good, they are expensive to build and maintain, and they cause unnecessary traffic hazards.

Sometimes these streets exist on the ground, sometimes only on paper. In either case, if a street is superfluous, it should be eliminated. Cities have trouble enough financially without keeping up unnecessary streets, and the money which can be saved (often a staggering amount if you will figure it up for yourself) can be used for a lot of other things.

One of the most expensive mysteries of our time is why developers in the past (and a good many in the present) put so much land into unnecessary streets. The same developers quite frequently argue long and plaintively that they can't afford to make lots a decent size.

Horrible example

As an extreme example, we have before us a map of a city in which 176 300-foot by 230-foot blocks march with monotonous regularity up and down and across a 491 acre square. Each block has a 30-foot by 300-foot alley, abutting which on each side are five 60-foot by 100-foot lots. All streets, major and minor, are platted at 90-foot wide.

This article originally appeared in *Bair Facts,* published by Chandler-Davis Publishing Co., West Trenton, N.J. (1960). Reprinted by permission.

Things aren't as bad as they sound. This is actually a lovely little town. Very few people bought only one lot. The precise pattern of blocks is broken geometrically by squares and parks. Great live oaks sweep over the streets. Something less than half the blocks have been built on, and the rest can be replatted into a less wasteful pattern. A lot of the streets haven't been opened, and many of those which have been opened haven't been paved, so that a minor street closing plan, if adopted, can still head off a lot of future expense.

But unless . . .

But unless somebody does something about it, here is the score:

	Acres	*Per Cent*
Lots	242.4	49.3
Streets and alleys	229.1	46.6
School grounds	7.8	1.6
Parks and squares	9.8	2.0
Cemetery	2.4	0.5
Total	491.5	100.0

The streets and alleys figure is clearly way out of line—10 lineal miles of alleys and 17.7 lineal miles of streets are not needed to serve a little over three quarters of a square mile, but that's the way it works out as this city is platted.

Actually, only about 0.3 miles of alley is justified (to serve the business district). This leaves 17.4 miles of 30-foot alleys, or 34.9 acres, as surplus.

Five miles of 90-foot streets are also superfluous—another 54.0 acres.

In a 491 acre tract, then, 88.9 acres have been wasted in a manner likely to be a continuous drain on city finances. What can be done about it? What can the city do with the land?

Well, unfortunately, it can't do as much as if the area was being platted for the first time. It can split the alleys between abutting owners, after making necessary reservations for needed easements. This would raise lot sizes by about 10 per cent.

And the city has, if it can work out the legal angles, something over 200 90-foot by 155-foot lots which it can sell. These come out of the unneeded streets—and a major added advantage in the deal is that the lots would be bringing revenue in the form of taxes rather than draining taxes into maintenance and construction costs.

As we pointed out to begin with, this is an extreme case. Things probably won't work out in the same proportions in your town, but the same principles can be applied.

Another example

Figure 1 shows the street pattern of another town. Figure 2 indicates what the minor street closing plan turned up in this case. Here the saving amounted to only about three miles of minor streets. Only three miles? How much of your tax dollar do you want to spend in maintaining a mere three miles of streets you don't need?

In the first city discussion, a minor street closing plan is still in the conversational stage. In the city illustrated in the maps, the show is on the road. Here's the way the job was done.

First the city tooled up with a good base map and an aerial mosaic. A parcel map was drafted which showed land ownership patterns as well as lot lines. Then a land-use map was prepared on the parcel map base, and this map indicated both use of the land and location of principal buildings.

The planning commission drafted a major street plan and major

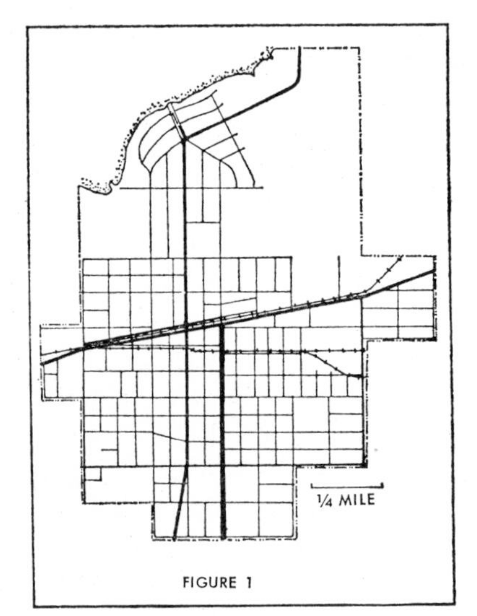

FIGURE 1

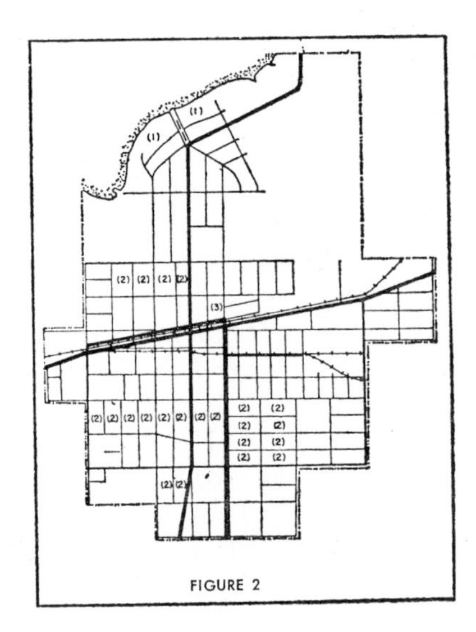

FIGURE 2

street ordinance, and the city commission adopted them.[1] Thus it was clear which streets were major streets, and which were minor.

And then the planning commission drafted a minor street closing plan, covering the settled areas of the city.

To decide which streets to close, the planners looked first at the general pattern. They noted that several streets seemed to be closer together than necessary for good traffic circulation, and working from this clue they examined the land-use map and aerial mosaic to find out whether property abutting these streets needed the streets for access. In some cases, where there had been lot splits or reversed frontage platting, it was impossible to close a street. But there remained a substantial amount of street which could be closed.

Figure 1, as compared with Figure 2, gives some idea of what was accomplished and how it was done. Note (1) indicates a street platted through a city park. It wasn't needed for access to the park or for general traffic circulation.

Street closing indicated by (2) involved considerable runs of street which served no traffic-circulation purpose and which were not used for access by abutting property owners. Note (3) indicates a one-block stretch of street which served no purpose whatever.

1. See "The Major Street Plan and Ordinance," p. 205.

Off-street parking: *public action on a private log jam*

Proposed here is a set of public actions to encourage desirable private improvements which might otherwise be blocked. Unless private action can proceed, substantial areas may deteriorate, with diminishing public revenues and increased public expense.

The city for which these solutions have been suggested is like other cities all over the country, and the solutions may have common application. Here are a couple of the problems.

Old outlying business districts

An old outlying business district is well located to meet current commercial needs. Buildings are solid and worth saving. Lots are small. Ownership is fragmented. Little off-street parking has been provided. On-street parking on axis streets has been eliminated to meet the needs of growing traffic. There is little chance for private action to get anything like the kind or amount of organized off-street parking needed.

Zoning (and common sense) demands that off-street parking be provided on the lot or within a reasonable distance in connection with new construction, additions, or major alterations. Left to their own devices, owners can't find much space on their small lots. If they could buy adjoining lots in the business frontage (which would be costly and involve demolition of buildings with substantial residual value) part of them could meet zoning requirements—but at the expense of diminishing the potential range of commercial facilities available and wrecking the continuity of concentrated pedestrian flow. If they proceed individually to attempt to buy lots to the rear of their establishments, some might be able to do so but most could not. The result would be a wasteful mish-mash of small, scattered parking lots mixed in among residences already of declining quality. Without some kind of public action to treat the problem as a whole, lack of off-street space will continue to drag this area down.

Behind the principal business frontages on the major intersecting streets is nondescript residential property. If accumulated, planned, and improved as a whole, it would provide 300 to 400 parking spaces within an L of business development, benefiting directly four blockfaces of commercial property. Location of a major parking lot would enable double-front development of adjacent business buildings, and customers moving from the parking lot through such buildings or pedestrian ways could get conveniently to establishments on the other side of the street. The plan looks solid, and the costs are not out of line. Public action seems to be the most practical way to handle the matter.

Before the public rushes in, however, there are some important policy questions to be answered. Since some of the questions apply equally in the next case, they will be discussed later.

Close-in residential conservation area

Within easy walking distance of the CBD is a substantial area of solid old homes, mostly large, mostly in good condition. Two opposing trends are running neck and neck—a move toward private improvement and a move toward private neglect and deterioration. The majority of the houses which are being improved are being divided into apartment units in the middle-rental range with a fair sprinkling of low and high rentals. Some are purchased as bargains in floor area for single-family use. In most blocks, there are spots of blight which give ample grounds for concern.

Lots are narrow and deep, and buildings run fore and aft, with narrow side yards or none and limited open space concentrated to the rear. Quiet streets bring steps to the sidewalk—front yards are minimal. There are trees. There are quaint and curious houses, late

Victorian and early 20th century, aging toward historic status which will some day be fiercely protected—but not yet.

Again, off-street parking is the drag. Streets and such off-street space as exists, ample when car ownership and population density were lower, now under heavy pressure, show signs of inadequacy if the desirable trend to conversion is allowed to continue. Under zoning requirements for off-street parking, the trend *can't* continue. The land for parking isn't there, and the slow move toward private removal of derelict structures isn't likely to provide it in time—before the cancer spreads.

In this area, the answer is not in massive parking lots, seas of cars overwhelming the neighborhood with blighting influences of their own. Here, what is needed is a planned complex of small parking lots, located near block centers, providing access to a few house-locked areas for on-site parking, convenient off-site parking for residents in the block not able to park on the lots on which they live, and as an important by-product, miniparks for greenery and relaxation next to the street.

Again, public action is the most practical answer. Some is under way in the form of neighborhood conservation projects, but unusual moves need to be made to make the most of the opportunity. If the worst of the old structures go out and new ones are built on their sites, the parking situation gets worse.

These two samples will do to get on with. Others might be cited. Now about policy.

Policy determinations

How far should government go in providing off-street parking in areas in trouble because they lack it? In both cases cited there is clear public interest in some kind of action. If none is taken, the public is very likely to be paying the bill for massive bulldozer operations after a long period of net public loss because of decreasing revenues and increasing costs (social and economic).

In the CBD, a precedent has been established—and probably a bad one. Zoning does not require off-street parking in the CBD in connection with new or expanded uses or major structural alterations. The CBD has been considered a special case, and massive public parking has been provided at general public expense.

It does not seem wise to eliminate all parking requirements outside the CBD simply to be equitable and make the error universal. Nor does it seem intelligent or equitable to eliminate parking requirements in selected areas outside the CBD which are in trouble because they lack parking as a joint result of private and public shortsightedness, and can't find a place to provide it. This might ease the problem of renovation conversion and rebuilding temporarily, but would merely make things worse in the not-too-long run. The parking shortage would mount.

Well, then, how about putting in public parking in areas of greatest need and then saying that owners within a certain distance of such lots are exempted from the off-street parking requirements of the zoning ordinance? Consider this from either the political or legal point of view. You are now at a public hearing on the proposal. You are one of the vast majority of taxpayers providing your own off-street parking as required by the zoning ordinance, and you are requested to state your views as to taking your tax money to provide public off-street parking which you won't use for people who haven't provided private parking for themselves and now can't. You and your lawyer will please limit your remarks to five minutes.

The series of commentaries may be long, but action by city council will probably be brief.

What's left is a modified benefit district approach, with private advantages apportioned and private costs assessed, but with the public agency taking action which private individuals could not or would not take, and with maximum latitude for private choice. Costs should be amortized by those directly benefited. Planning, construction, operation, and maintenance would be a public responsibility. Exemption from private provision of required off-street space should be equitably distributed, so that a few property owners cannot take action which would exhaust the supply.

Here's a tentative solution which can be adjusted to fit local circumstances, and which might even be applied to the CBD so far as zoning requirements for off-street parking are concerned.

A solution

Starting with zoning, provision must first be made to permit off-lot parking. It is desirable to specify maximum distance between such parking and the use it is intended to serve, and to leave a loophole for attendant parking. Normally parking to serve residences should be required to be closer to the use than parking to serve commercial facilities:

Section XX. Off-Lot Parking

Where off-street parking required in connection with a use cannot be located on the lot with the use, such parking may be provided off the lot, subject to the following requirements:

1. If the use is residential, hotel, motel, or tourist home, the off-lot spaces shall be within 200 feet of the principal entrance or the entrance for individual occupants for whom spaces are reserved.
2. If the use is other than residential, hotel, motel, or tourist home, the farthest portion of the parking lot shall be within 500 feet of an entrance to the establishment.
3. Distances indicated above shall be measured along routes generally available to the pedestrians involved.
4. If and so long as satisfactory attendant parking service is provided, or if for employees of the establishments, parking spaces may be at greater distances than those indicated above.

Note that distance with respect to residential and kindred uses is from the parking space; with respect to others, from the farthest portion of the lot. Spaces for establishments or individuals will be reserved for residential, hotel, motel, or tourist home uses, but may or may not be so reserved for other uses.

---

5. Such off-lot spaces shall be located only in districts in which similar off-street parking is permitted.
6. The off-lot parking area shall be:
   a. Held in fee simple by the same owner as the use requiring the off-street parking space, or
   b. Under lease, rental, or other form of agreement satisfactory to the administrative official as assuring continuing availability for required off-street parking for the use, or
   c. Established by the city for the purpose of providing such off-lot parking for specific areas and/or land uses, and with number of spaces allocated by specific individual lots. Where and to the extent that such lots serve residential, hotel, motel, or tourist home uses, spaces allocated shall be marked and reserved for individuals or establishments. Where and to the extent that such lots serve other uses, spaces allocated may be

similarly marked and reserved, in whole or in part, or may in whole or in part be made available for general public use.

The options available to the property owner under the general provisions of the ordinance and the section above give a reasonable range of choices. He can provide parking on the lot on which the use is located. If this can't be managed, he can provide parking within specified distances on another lot which he owns, by leasing or renting space, or (if it is available) he can pay for space on a public lot set up to help meet parking requirements in a specified area or even for particular uses within such an area. Or he can use any combination of these devices.

The last provision sets the stage for what comes next, procedures for providing and allocating public parking areas and for a form of financing which helps the city get its money back without loading the burden on the general taxpayers. First reaction of one attorney was that this was using zoning for blackmail. On more mature consideration, he agreed that it was rather a device for enabling property owners who might not otherwise be able to make the most of their property to proceed to do so, but only by paying the bill.

(It should be noted that *all* required parking must be maintained. It will not do merely to have the parking available at the time the occupancy permit is issued and then to discontinue it. This provision would normally come in the general preface to parking regulations and thus is not inserted in the off-lot language.)

Section XY. Procedures on Publicly Established Parking

Where an agency of the city proposes to establish parking lots to provide off-lot parking for specific areas generally, or for specified uses within such areas, and where off-lot parking spaces in such lots are to be allocated to lands within such areas in order to assist in meeting the off-street parking requirements of this ordinance, these procedures shall be followed:

1. A report shall be prepared by the planning commission for official action by city council, containing the following information and recommendations:

   a. Reasons for establishing the area [a statement of the arguments for public action in the case, including a recital of the peculiar problems of the area which make it difficult or impossible for individual property owners to provide parking as required by this ordinance and the public benefits to be expected as a result of public participation in the provisions for such parking].

This is a very important part of the recommendation, since it requires a statement of public purpose which may be vital in defense of the action.

---

b. Boundaries including all lands intended to be primarily benefited by the establishment of the facility, which boundaries shall not extend farther from any proposed parking lot than 200 feet in the case of residences, hotels, motels, and tourist homes, nor 500 feet in the case of other uses, as provided in Section XX, 1-3, above.

c. Boundaries and layout of the proposed lot, total number of parking spaces to be provided, and location of vehicular and pedestrian accessways and other features, including buffering, general landscape treatment, and the like.

d. Net area, within the boundaries established under (b) above, of lots on which uses requiring off-street parking under the terms of this ordinance exist or might be expected to be established, or net area of lots which are or might be expected to be occupied by particular classes of uses to which spaces are to be allocated.

e. Allocation formula to be applied, expressed as number of parking spaces per 1,000 square feet of net lot area. For any lot, fractions over one-half shall be considered one space.

The planning commission comes up with a specific plan for a publicly supplied parking lot, indicating location and number of spaces to be available. These can't be parcelled out on a first-come, first-served basis. Some kind of allocation formula is needed. The one proposed assures equitable treatment, and that the parking "account" will not be overdrawn.

It would be most unusual for such a lot to provide all the spaces which could be required by full development of all the benefited lots. It will alleviate the problem, but not completely cure it. In most cases, property owners will still have to provide some space on their own in order to make maximum use of their land.

Now what about the financial end of the deal? Should everyone in the district have to pay? This could be managed by making it a parking benefit district in states in which this is permitted by law, and might work particularly well for major commercial lots. For the kind of "spot" lots needed in residential areas, it doesn't seem such a good idea—the area is too small. Here's one way to do it.

---

2. Upon formal approval of such proposal by city council and completion of the parking lot, allocation of off-lot parking spaces according to the formula approved shall become effective. City council shall establish an annual fee per off-street parking space in such lot, and may from time to time amend such fee.

No owner of land shall be required to pay such fee except in connection with reservation or use of all or part of his allocation, but no portion thereof shall be alienated from the land to which it applies except on written consent of the owner if the fee has been paid or by consent of the city on payment of the fee if the owner has not paid such fee. Such alienation may be for periods of only one year, renewable for periods of only one year. Subject to these requirements:

a. An owner of land desiring to use all or part of the allocation running with such land to satisfy all or part of the requirements of this ordinance for off-street parking may do so upon payment of the annual fee per space established by city council.

b. An owner of land who has used all of the allocation running with such land to satisfy part of the requirements of this ordinance for off-street parking may use remaining unused allocations of others for temporary satisfaction of all or part of the remaining parking requirements, but only upon written consent of the owner or owners of other allocations who have paid the fee to reserve them but are not using them, or from remaining unreserved allocations upon which no fee has been paid. Written consent of owners assigning unused spaces shall specify number of spaces released, and that number of spaces remaining under the control of such owners is sufficient to meet the requirements of this ordinance for his use. Unreserved allocations may be assigned by the city upon payment of the annual fee per space. In either case, assignment shall be for a period of one year only, and the person to whom spaces are assigned shall agree that unless the number of off-street parking spaces required by the use is maintained, the nature or extent of the use will be changed to conform with the off-street parking provided.

Regarding fees, the amount set should be sufficient to amortize the public investment in the lot and cover the costs of management and maintenance. Because all of the spaces may not be taken up initially, even with the variety of arrangements indicated, establishment of fees should include consideration of a reasonable vacancy ratio.

The allocation formula insures that the number of spaces available in the parking area or areas will not be exceeded by individual reservations because if each lot used the maximum allocated to it, the total number of parking spaces would be filled, and no more.

Safeguards against over-allocation are not enough. There should be devices for encouraging maximum use. As set forth, these permit an owner who has reserved his spaces but does not need them to satisfy his present requirements under the zoning ordinance to "sublet" spaces on an annual basis. This introduces an element of equity. An owner who has provided all or part of required off-street parking on his lot is not left in the position of being penalized for his foresight. If he wishes, he may reserve his allocation by payment of the annual fee and sublet for whatever profit he can make.

On the other hand, an owner who does not wish to become involved in such an arrangement simply does not pay the annual fee for his spaces. The city is then in a position to permit such spaces to be used by others who need them, again on a temporary basis. In either case, it is essential that it be clearly understood that if spaces temporarily assigned become unavailable, those who have decided to gamble on their continued availability will either have to provide spaces of their own or cut back on their operations.

In the long run, it is probable that pressures on such lots will mount to the point where all of the spaces are in full use. At such time, it may be that an addition to the lot, or creation of another lot, will be justified. Or the planning commission may feel that land-use intensity in the area is as high as it should go, and recommend against such an addition as a way to hold the line.

One other detail might be added. In some cases, the gambling instinct of individual property owners without enough parking spaces of their own may be overdeveloped. In order to control situations in which one or two such owners might acquire an unduly high proportion of unreserved space, language like the following could be included:

---

c. In connection with temporary assignments of unused allocations of parking spaces, no owner of land shall be permitted temporary use of a number of spaces equal to more than his full allocation, or more than 25 per cent of the total number of unreserved spaces.

This cuts two ways. An owner with an allocation of 10 spaces in the lot could get temporary assignment of a maximum of 10 more either from another owner or from the city, or in combination. But if only 24 spaces remain unreserved, he cannot use more than six of them.

Action

Obviously, what is proposed here involves considerably more than zoning. Zoning is amended to permit use of a new technique in meeting demand for off-street parking space, but additional action will be needed to provide the space.

The best way to start would be to take the most critical areas. (Since the CBD is usually one of them, it might be well to start by inserting off-street parking requirements there if they do not already exist. This would remedy a common inequity, provide a source of income for providing space, and relate the expense to the area benefited.)

Outside the CBD, other areas should be selected on a worst is first basis. It is emphatically not recommended that the program start by putting in all the spaces which might conceivably be needed. Try it where the shortage of parking is most obviously related to problems of redevelopment. From there, spread out cautiously as funds become available, if the technique takes hold.

With sound planning and good execution, this approach seems to have a great deal of promise. As part of the execution, particularly in residential areas, it will probably be found that peripheral green space, particularly for yard depth usually required adjacent to streets, will result in an important secondary benefit.

Chapter 4

Toward a regulatory system *for use, development, occupancy, and construction*

In the regulatory field, planners tend to concentrate on zoning and subdivision controls. Administration of subdivision regulations is normally a planning responsibility. Zoning administration is commonly handled by the building official, who also handles building, plumbing, electrical and gas codes, and may handle the housing code (or elements of it included in the building code). The health officer is usually responsible for enforcement of health codes and may be responsible for the housing code (or the more inclusive occupancy code). Fire prevention codes are under the fire chief or head of the fire prevention bureau.

Added to general codes there are special local ordinances dealing with specific land uses or particular aspects of use, development, occupancy, or construction—anti-noise ordinances; smoke abatement or air pollution controls; regulations for gas stations, keeping of animals, signs, mobile home parks, excavation and filling, and so on.

Superimposed on these local controls are regulations from outside the jurisdiction, from state, federal, or other levels, controlling particular functions, uses, or characteristics of use.

The forms in which these regulations have been drafted; conflicting standards and other substantive requirements; differing procedures for preparation, referral, hearings, administration, and appeals; and meaningless variations between requirements or procedures in neighboring jurisdictions create problems for those who govern and those who are governed.

The expanding scope of planning makes it desirable that planners should participate, and perhaps lead, in systematizing regulations. Those who do will find tools adapted to planning purposes in regulatory fields with which many planners are unfamiliar.

Basic problems

Codes have been cumulative, imitative, and insulated. There are fashions in codes. Public enthusiasm for particular types crested historically at different times, in differing legal climates, in reaction to different crises. "Model" building codes, zoning ordinances, subdivision regulations, housing codes, environmental health codes, and similar controls tended to develop in isolation, without much attention to overlaps, gaps, or conflicts. The newer codes are overlaid on the old without fitting either to the other. To make matters worse, enabling legislation or charter provisions sometimes institutionalize these shortcomings, making improvement more difficult.

In localities which lack the whole array of codes, federal workable program requirements have exerted pressure for obtaining a complete set. Unfortunately, emphasis has been more on form than on content —on having codes with the right titles regardless of whether they fit together. Meeting deadlines often means adoption without adaptation. As early zoning "progress" was measured by number of cities adopting zoning ordinances (regardless of quality), so recent "advances" have been scored in number of places having approved or recertified workable programs. Thus there has been considerable proliferation of defective regulations, but only relatively minor efforts toward improvement.

Limited overall perspective, limited awareness of the purposes and working details of individual regulatory elements, and limited time are all part of the problem. Planners, ill-equipped by training or experience to go much beyond elementary zoning and subdivision regulation, find themselves responsible for preparation, implementation, and maintenance of workable programs, and when the need for a housing code arises, to maintain eligibility for federal loans and grants (the results may leave much to be desired). A not altogether hypothetical example would be a city with a building code making the building official responsible for, among other things, enforcement of standards on light, ventilation, sanitation, screening, ratproofing, and the like. The city has not adopted a housing code, although provisions of the building code have the same effect. When the need for a housing code arises, to maintain eligibility for federal loans and grants, a "model" housing code is located, with standards, enforcement, and appeals provisions quite different from those in the building code, and with administration by the local health officer.

Although the conflicts are noted, the governing body passes the housing code stating that there isn't time to eliminate the inconsistencies before the eligibility deadline. Undoing the damage is likely to be considerably more difficult than it would have been to avoid it in the first place, and conflicting standards and duplicated and diluted enforcement responsibilities weaken rather than strengthen the local program.

Regulations from outside the local jurisdiction have multiplied. State agencies, in particular, have expanded the scope and intensity of direct controls and now often regulate many of the same things which are regulated locally, but with varying requirements and administrative procedures. Thus there may be some form of state regulation of hotels, eating establishments, service stations, campgrounds, mobile home parks, apartments, schools, day nurseries, hospitals, nursing homes, convalescent homes, private sewerage and water supply systems above certain minimum sizes, water pollution, air pollution, and so on.

To the extent that state requirements are adequate and well enforced, confusion, annoyance, and wasted manpower and money can be avoided by eliminating overlapping portions of local controls.

Controls in neighboring jurisdictions may vary needlessly. In addition to conflicting requirements within a particular jurisdiction, there are often minor (and sometimes major) variations in requirements of adjoining jurisdictions. If there is sound justification for these differences, they should stand. Quite frequently, there is no logical reason for variation.

To the extent that state regulatory methods and requirements within a general area can be standardized, builders and developers active in several jurisdictions will benefit, and quality of administration may be improved by the possibility of areawide courses for training and retraining personnel.

Controls may have lost proper relationship to public purpose. Some regulations are vestigial, related to obsolete public purposes. A common example of obsolete control is the manner in which many zoning ordinances handle accessory buildings in rear yards, reflecting concern about keeping the stable and smokehouse away from the main dwelling. In subdivision regulations, a common minimum lot size for sewered, single-family residences is based on desirability of space for a subsistence garden to help meet food requirements during the Depression. And many housing codes and some building codes ignore the arrival of air conditioning, artificial ventilation, or improved artificial lighting.

There can be little doubt that many existing codes have the more than incidental purpose of making construction as expensive as possible to maximize tax returns or to benefit the building trades.

The examples above cover instances in which controls are exercised for public purposes which are no longer significant, for inappropriate public purposes, or for purposes which are, in effect, anti-public. In addition, public purposes are emerging which present regulations ignore or handle only in a very crude fashion. There is growing awareness of the public (and private) costs of urban and suburban development on soils poorly adapted to the purposes to which they are put. Yet few zoning ordinances or subdivision regulations relate uses or lot sizes to soils types. (Construction codes are more sophisticated regarding soils.) As land scarcity drives development to steeper slopes, public concern about slippage and erosion mounts, but there are as yet relatively few jurisdictions with regulations which deal intelligently with these problems. Protection of view is becoming a matter of growing public concern in many areas, but we are only beginning to move toward adequate controls in this field.

There are general rules in law that public regulation should have substantial relation to public purpose, and that the regulation should be the least reasonably necessary to accomplish the purpose. Current controls tend to violate both of these principles to some degree. Intent may be good, but performance is seriously defective. The first step toward improvement is a careful analysis of current purposes, with much more detailed and specific definition than is usually the case. With clearer understanding of objectives, regulations can usually be devised which perform more effectively but which leave wider latitude and flexibility for private action.

Controls should look to the future. In formulation of regulations, concern with keeping the status quo from deteriorating clearly has a place. It is important to avoid repetition of the mistakes and abuses of the past. But regulation should be more than a response to the past or even current problems. It must be better related to planning objectives for the future.

Among other things there should be devices for development timing. There should be means of encouraging appropriate mixtures of uses, replacing present controls which often prevent desirable integrations. There should be provisions for a wide variety of planned developments. There should be faster and more sensitive response to unforeseen public needs—given an unpredicted interest in particular forms of housing, for example, it should not take years to make regulatory accommodations. And there should be far more sophisticated use of regulation to encourage needed action in the private sector, and not merely to restrict it.

General plan of attack

The objective, stated simply, is to produce a system of regulations responsive to clearly identified current and future public purposes, internally consistent, and organized for efficient use and administration.

The scope of the system should extend well beyond zoning and subdivision regulation to include all codes and ordinances (or significant parts thereof) substantially related to use, development, occupancy, and construction. There are sound reasons for the enlargement. The general idea of the workable program is sound—there is a real need for an enlarged regulatory arsenal for effective guidance of urban development. The increased array of specialized tools makes for better performance of specific functions and should (although it has not yet) reduce the tendency to use a more limited number for purposes for which they were not intended. And consolidation offers major potentials for improving procedures for referrals, notice, adoption or amendment, administration, and appeals.

There is wide variation in grants of power in the form of state enabling legislation for planning and related purposes; in general or charter powers for local governments; in functions performed directly by states and the agencies, and methods for performance; and, of course, in local codes, regulations, and ordinances. Thus it is impossible to do more here than provide an outline of an approach.

The job breaks down into five parts: assembling materials; analysis; reorganization and improvement of regulations; reorganization and improvement of procedures; and determination of need for amendments in state legislation.

Outline of approach

I. MATERIALS TO BE ASSEMBLED

A. *State, general, and special enabling legislation of local application (including charter provisions),* to determine what the local jurisdiction is empowered to do, how, and for what purposes. Specifically:

1. General enabling legislation on planning, zoning, subdivision regulation, official maps, urban renewal, and so on.
2. Provisions concerning: building codes (including plumbing, heating, gas, electrical, and so on); housing and general occupancy codes; fire codes; health codes; and the like.
3. Provisions concerning local regulation of particular types of development or land use—gas stations, outdoor advertising, junk yards, inoperative automobiles, swimming pools, mining (including sand and gravel pits and quarries), well drilling, discharge into public waters, and so on.
4. Provisions concerning control and abatement of nuisances, and other general controls likely to be useful as supplements to specific regulations.

B. *State regulations,* to determine what controls state agencies exercise as related to existing or potential local controls, what agencies are involved, the purposes of state regulation, standards established, and inspection and enforcement procedures. Examples of such regulations are those affecting hotels and restaurants, mobile home parks, campgrounds, apartments, schools, fire safety, mining, junk yards, outdoor advertising adjacent to certain highways, limited access provisions, discharge into public water supplies, sewerage treatment and public water supplies, outdoor theaters, and the like. Agencies involved will usually include state education departments, state health agencies, state highway departments, and the state fire marshal's office, among others.

C. *Federal regulations,* to the same effect as above (e.g., Federal Aviation Agency, Federal Communications Commission, Corps of Engineers).

D. *Authority and special district regulations,* to similar effect (e.g., drainage districts, sanitation districts, school districts).

E. *Local codes, ordinances, and regulations.* In many jurisdictions, much more than a casual check of more obvious titles will be desirable, and it will be necessary to check carefully for amendments and additions not yet included in printed codes. As a specific example, material relating to the regulatory system discussed here was found under the following heads in one city code (with more obvious references eliminated): advertising and signs; animals and fowl; dredging or landfilling, docks, landings, and so on; excavations and soil removal; accumulation of garbage, refuse, waste, and weeds on vacant lots; licensing; streets; drainage easements—alteration or obstruction; water impoundment; obstruction of watercourses; nuisances generally; service stations; drive-in theaters; trailers and trailer camps.

F. *Codes, ordinances, and regulations from neighboring jurisdictions,* to be used in an effort to develop uniform requirements or procedures where there is no substantial reason for variation.

G. *Models, guides, and standards* to be used for comparison with local regulations and as a guide to possible refinements or improvements.

II. ANALYSIS

A. *State, general, and special enabling legislation of local application* (including charter provisions). Prepare detailed breakdowns on purposes, powers, and procedures, grouping material under each of these heads, but retaining identification of source to provide a cumulative and comparative listing of purposes and similar listings of powers and procedures.

B. *Federal, state, and authority or special district regulations.* Analyze to determine where there are substantial existing or potential overlaps in fields of control. In such areas, check adequacy of standards and administration. Appraise possibilities for:
   1. Relinquishing local controls where "outside" standards and administration are adequate.
   2. Improving nonlocal standards or administration where either or both are inadequate, to protect local interests but relieve pressures on local administrators.
   3. Coordinating local with nonlocal control. This may involve changes in local standards to come up to nonlocal requirements (which usually override in any case) or arrangements concerning inspection responsibility or scheduling, exchange of information on violations, and the like.

C. *Local codes, ordinances, and regulations.* Prepare detailed, cumulative, and comparative analyses by purposes, standards and other substantive requirements, and procedures. Relate substantive requirements to purposes, structuring analysis to group-related requirements from different codes. For example, zoning, building, housing, and fire codes will all have controls affecting building spacing, applying generally or to particular uses or types of construction.

Check substantive requirements for internal consistency and relation to public purpose. Compare with models and guides to determine whether the most effective techniques are being used. Where conflicting standards relate to same purpose, select standard to apply generally. Where standards vary for sound reasons, provide for cross-referencing. Check also against requirements in neighboring jurisdictions to avoid unnecessary trivial variations (and perhaps to prepare for interjurisdictional adjustments).

Analyze and compare procedures on preparation of original codes, ordinances or regulations, and amendments and on referrals, notice and hearing, and adoption. It may be very helpful at this point to appraise arrangements for keeping official documents updated and available to the public and to officials in current form.

Analyze and compare routine administration—applications, collection of fees, processing, inspections, actions to discover and abate violations, and so on. Analyze forms for adequacy and efficiency.

Analyze and compare appellate functions and procedures—number of appellate boards, functions, adequacy of limitations or guidance in ordinances or codes (and/or in enabling legislation), forms of applications or appeals, notice and hearing, findings required before making determinations, nature and effect of determinations, appeals from boards.

(In the analyses and comparisons indicated under C, there should be careful checking throughout as to conformity with enabling authority. The first purpose of this check is to ensure that the regulations or procedures are in accord with existing enabling legislation. There is a secondary purpose as well—to prepare for recommendations regarding changes in enabling legislation where there is justification for change.)

III. REORGANIZATION AND IMPROVEMENT OF SUBSTANTIVE PROVISIONS (STANDARDS)

A. *Eliminate from local controls provisions found to be exercised adequately by "higher" governments.* For public convenience, local regulations might well include cross-reference to such other regulations, but unless local standards are set higher, or nonlocal administration is defective, there is no point in duplicating jurisdiction.

B. *Determine where controls to meet specific purposes belong in the regulatory system.* Conventional divisions of subject matter will be continued—zoning, subdivision regulation, building codes, housing (or occupancy) codes, environmental health codes, fire codes, and so on, although there may be justification in some instances for combinations of previously separate codes. But within this framework, there will be prime and sometimes secondary locations where regulations relating to a specific public purpose should be concentrated. Such concentration should help to eliminate the conflicts, overlaps, and gaps which occur if provisions to the same general effect are scattered at random through the regulations.

C. *Reassemble standards and other substantive provisions* as indicated above, using "override" standards where they will meet all public purposes, and providing clear cross-references where it is necessary to have varying requirements in different sections of the system.

(Reorganization and improvement of standards and other substantive requirements can usually be made without adjustment in enabling authority. Major procedural changes, particularly on amendments, notice, and hearing and appeals, will probably require changes in enabling legislation.)

IV. REORGANIZATION AND IMPROVEMENT OF PROCEDURAL PROVISIONS

A. *Preparation of original codes, ordinances, or regulations and amendments,* and on referrals, notice and hearing, and adoption. Consolidate requirements and make uniform where appropriate.

B. *Routine administration.* Consolidate requirements, make uniform where appropriate, and establish clear lines of administrative responsibility.

C. *Appeals.* Consolidate requirements, provide introductory section applying to all appeals boards indicating general rules applying—

filing of appeals or applications, notice and hearings, findings required, limitations on powers, nature and effect of determinations. In addition, under sections on individual boards or in portions of the general regulations making reference to appeals or applications to such boards, spell out limitations and requirements in particular classes of cases.

V. DETERMINATION OF NEED FOR AMENDMENTS IN ENABLING LEGISLATION (CHARTERS)

Whether amendments will be needed, and what kind, will depend on what turns up as a result of the overview outlined above. Sometimes it will be possible to work effectively within the established limits, particularly if they are fully understood and liberally interpreted. Usually, some amendments in state legislation or charters will be found desirable. Such changes will be of one of the types indicated below.

A. *Changes in organization of statutes.* Most states now have systematized and coordinated legislation on planning, zoning, subdivision control, official maps, and in some cases urban renewal. There remains a need to bring together into the same general area within the statutes a variety of other enabling provisions now widely scattered. At present, few local planners, legal staff members, or other local officials are aware of all the regulatory tools available.

B. *Changes in powers.* Powers delegated to local governments vary considerably from state to state, but in most states specific or implied authorization somewhere in the statutes or the charter gives the necessary grant of power to do almost anything which reasonably needs doing—given a liberal and alert local legal department.

C. *Changes in procedures.* If there is systematic review of the enabling legislation for the wide range of use, development, construction, and occupancy codes discussed here, it will usually become apparent that there is need for more nearly uniform requirements on procedures for preparation of original controls and amendments, referrals, notice and hearing, administration, and particularly appeals. And there may be need for statutory authority to adopt standard codes by reference (including future revisions). Otherwise, localities may be left enforcing obsolete standards or revised provisions having no legal support until the governing body goes through the formality of adopting the revisions.

Extended comments

The outline above was kept brief. The comments which follow are in the nature of extended remarks.

REPORT ON LEGISLATIVE BACKGROUND FOR THE REGULATORY SYSTEM—POWERS, PURPOSES, AND PROCEDURES

At an early stage, it will be desirable to prepare a paper along the lines indicated by the title. It should include properly identified quotations or summaries from the charter and from state statutes. Statutory material will not be limited to the complex generally classified as planning enabling legislation, but should encompass general powers of local governing bodies, special statutory provisions relating to fields to be included in the regulatory system, and regulatory powers assigned to state agencies and special authorities and districts, with indications as to relation to similar local powers.

Some of this material will appear in obscure locations. Because of the unsystematic nature of most state statutes and the uncertainties of indexing, the best approach is probably a leaf-through. This will usually prove sufficiently rewarding to justify the effort because of unfamiliar material it turns up.

For example, in a review of Virginia statutes, it was found that cities have the same powers concerning limited access streets (planning, designation, regulation of use, and extinguishment of access) as does the state highway commission (Va. Stats. 15.1-16). This is a useful thing to know where plans for limited access streets are threatened by rising pressures for strip commercial zoning.

In the same statutes, cities are empowered to divide their jurisdictions into districts for the purpose of applying different building code requirements (Va. Stats. 15.1-863). Here is an extension of usual zoning powers which does not appear explicitly in the zoning enabling legislation. It might be useful in municipalities with extensive undeveloped areas where embattled *rurales* oppose full regulation. It might also be helpful in model cities areas, where code adjustment to needs for low-cost housing is a consideration.

In addition to locating and recording all relevant material, it is important to note override relationships and indications as to how conflicts are to be resolved (if indications exist). Do charter provisions or general legislative provisions prevail? Are powers granted generally cumulative to charter powers without indicating conflict situations, or must a choice be made as to whether charter powers or general enabling provisions will be used? Given varying provisions to the same effect in different parts of general legislation, is the choice as to which to use open or is there indication that one form or the other takes precedence?

Not infrequently, judicious selection of enabling authority may simplify local action, sometimes making it possible to improve substantive or procedural aspects of local controls without amendment of state legislation. This is true particularly where charter powers are broad and enabling legislation indicates that they shall govern in case of conflict with general laws.

REPORT II—GENERAL ANALYSIS OF EXISTING LOCAL REGULATIONS

This intermediate working document should facilitate reorganization and improvement of the system but should be kept as simple as is compatible with this purpose. It is a reference document, indicating general content of what is covered where, with detail included only as necessary to identify conflicts and with running commentary as to shortcomings, proposals for change in standards or techniques for control, changes in location within regulations, and so on.

A front-to-back leaf-through of the most complete available set of official records is the best way to be sure that amendments have been included with printed codifications. Since some codes may have been adopted by reference, the same kind of search is indicated on them, with a check as to whether recent amendments have been included.

On definitions and rules of construction, which could be a very bulky section, it is probably sufficient to develop a card file and refer to it in the report. The objective here will be to identify definitions and rules of construction appearing frequently in existing regulations and to decide on multipurpose forms wherever possible. It should be possible to develop a general section on definitions and rules of construction applying to the regulatory system as a whole, with definitions and rules applying only within one code appearing with that code and with highly specialized definitions applying only to one section of the code appearing where the term is used. (As an example of what may be expected, in one analysis of this kind the word *street* was defined six different ways in various local codes and ordinances.)

In the course of this analysis, checks against model codes, standards, and ordinances will suggest changes which might be noted in the commentary. A word of caution about models is in order. Usually they will be better organized than local regulations and will contain fewer internal contradictions. But some types of standards require local adaptation and there may be numerous contradictions between models. Thus far, there is little evidence that organizations producing building codes, for example, are closely in touch with organizations responsible for fire prevention codes, and a letter to either pointing out divergent requirements is likely to produce the response, "yes, we know," with little indication of concern about remedial action.

CROSS-BREEDING CODES

When the time comes to reassemble the elements of the various codes into a coherent system, there should be an appraisal both of prime functions for particular types of control and of advantages of combining the techniques available in various codes to get more flexible regulations better adapted to public purposes.

Thus the prime characteristic of zoning is that it provides for division into districts and for the application of regulations which vary from district to district. Typical enabling legislation indicates matters which may be regulated in very broad terms, indeed, and traditional zoning has not begun to push toward the outer edges of what appears to be authorized, nor have other forms of regulation taken advantage of some of the possibilities inherent in crosses with zoning.

As examples, jurisdictions containing both urbanized and relatively rural areas can establish an urban services district boundary and relate zoning and other regulations to this type of districting, giving some measure of control over development timing and setting requirements according to the types of urban services which will or will not be available. In subdivision regulation, not only lot sizes but the types of improvements required might well be related to the zoning.

Touched on earlier was a case in which special enabling legislation specifically authorized districting for varying building code standards. But standard zoning enabling language empowers regulation and restriction of "construction, reconstruction, alteration, repair, or use" by districts, and if there is sound public reason for varying building code requirements (as perhaps in model cities or rural areas) additional legislative authority may not be needed.

Where feasible, fire district boundaries might well be made to correspond with boundaries of certain types of zoning districts, with cross-referencing to make it clear that special construction is required in such districts.

Thus zoning principles may be advantageous in combination with other regulations. And principles in other regulations may be helpful in improving zoning.

As a simple illustration, usual yard, height, and building spacing requirements in zoning are notoriously crude and difficult to relate to specific public purposes in any but the vaguest terms. Techniques used in the better building and occupancy codes are an improvement. In the more advanced forms of planned development zoning, techniques borrowed from other types of codes relate separation of buildings on the same or adjacent lots to height and length of wall and window orientation. The benefits need not be restricted to planned development zoning.

Housing codes are typical of the ad hoc approach to regulation. Federal concern at first centered on housing as the prime element in urban blight and then broadened with the realization that slums include more than housing. The regulatory reflection of this increased scope will be the occupancy code. On building and occupancy codes, a decision should be made for combination or separation. Some standard building codes interweave occupancy requirements with other provisions and some have separate housing sections as part of the building code package. From the administrative point of view, combination has decided advantages. But if it is decided to separate the building code from the housing code, and to make the building official responsible for one and the health official for the other, the separation should be thorough, with conflicting elements removed from the building code.

Development of a coordinated regulatory system will probably suggest a number of ways in which administration can be improved and consolidated. One possibility might be a combined permits, inspections, and licensing division coordinating functions previously scattered. Another improvement might be in the appellate process, particularly in the matter of variances.

A single jurisdiction may have a board of adjustment (zoning), a board of adjustments and appeals (building code), a board of electrical appeals, a board of plumbing appeals, and a board of minimum housing standards. These boards tend to have two functions in common—expert interpretation of the particular code involved and hearing and deciding appeals for variances based on unnecessary hardship. For special expertise, perhaps the separate boards must remain. On variance matters, however, a consolidated board would be advantageous, particularly if the regulations defined and limited its powers with care. Under present circumstances, the codes in one jurisdiction may vary widely, spelling out findings required for a variance in zoning in great detail, but giving no guidance whatever (beyond the words "unnecessary hardship") as to variances from the plumbing code or housing code.

As a final note on appellate boards, it will be found that there is also wide variation in requirements concerning public notice and public hearings. Zoning boards of adjustment must hold hearings, with due public notice, on even the most trivial appeals. But the building code board of appeals may not be required to give any public notice or hold any general public hearing on an appeal coming before it. Here again the combined regulatory system should conform requirements.

Sign control

Signs irritate a lot of people. They also serve a lot of people. This leads to a lot of sadly unimaginative namecalling and to confusion in regulatory efforts.

A considerable amount of sign regulation is none of zoning's business. Physical standards for signs and the manner in which they are erected belong in the building code. Regulations for signs generally, without respect to zoning districts, belong in a separate sign ordinance. But it is proper that there should be some aspects of sign regulation included in zoning.

Public reaction to sign abuses is firmly rooted in aesthetic considerations (which have only recently been included among the elements justifying the use of the police power in zoning). There is no question that signs may affect the character of districts and the value of buildings, or that they are or are not appropriate in different parts of a town. So regulations intended to indicate what kind of signs may be erected and where may properly be included in the zoning ordinance.

Signs are erected by different groups, in different ways, in different locations, and for different purposes, and setting up zoning regulations on signs may involve reactions and compromises (or lack of compromise) between a lot of people. There are likely to be highly emotional conflicts between two extremist pressure groups: (1) people who have a direct economic interest in signs and what they do and want complete

This article originally appeared in *Bair Facts,* published by Chandler-Davis Publishing Co., West Trenton, N. J. (1960). Reprinted by permission.

freedom on sign erection because it affects their livelihood; (2) people who have no direct economic interest in signs and what they do, don't like them, and would like to see them eliminated for aesthetic reasons. Between these two extremes there are militants, moderates, and people who don't care one way or the other. Everybody but the indifferent group is likely to want to get into the act, sometimes openly and sometimes behind the scenes.

Thus in preparing sections of the zoning ordinance relating to signs it is particularly important to know what you are doing and why you are doing it and be able to defend your recommendations. This is not an area for fuzzy thinking or reliance on cliches.

Who erects signs and why

Generally speaking:

1. *Public bodies* erect signs to convey information to the general public as a matter of public convenience or necessity—highway markers, traffic control signs, public notices, identification signs, historical markers, directional signs, and the like.

2. *Quasi-public bodies*—for example, churches, noncommercial clubs, Little Theater groups, neighborhood associations—erect signs to convey information to a more limited segment of the public. These signs are usually for purposes of identification and announcement of events. Sometimes such groups will erect directional signs.

3. *Private individuals and organizations* erect signs for many reasons. In the most restricted residential neighborhood there will be signs to which no one objects—house numbers and modest name signs in front yards or on mail boxes. But when commercial overtones appear and signs become advertising, the demand for regulation and control starts to mount.

There are three major divisions of advertising signs to consider:

1. *Signs erected by or for specific places of business* to help sell whatever the place of business has to sell. These signs inform the passing public about a particular location and goods, services, entertainment, or accommodations to be obtained at that location. Signs of this nature may be divided into *on-site* and *off-site* with respect to their location. As to what the signs cover, a pyramid may be built up starting at the top with those covering only name and general nature of activity (Grace Blivet, Dressmaker; Jones Hardware Co.). The next

layer would consist of signs indicating name and nature of activity and major classes of goods, services, facilities, etc. (Warners Corners Tourist Stop—Motel, Filling Station, Rest Rooms, Restaurant, Cocktail Bar, Gifts, Souvenirs). And finally there comes the lowest layer, signs indicating name and nature of activity, major classes of goods, services and facilities details as to items with or without brand names, prices, sales pitch, and miscellaneous including very miscellaneous.

Off-site signs in this class do not necessarily describe what might loosely be called "attractions" in the immediate vicinity. Harold's Club, in Reno, Nevada, has signs in Florida, and it is not necessary to be anywhere near Silver Springs in Florida to discover that it ranks itself modestly with the seven wonders of the world.

2. *Signs promoting products and erected or controlled by the producer.* These can be identified by the fact that the same signs continue to boost the same product. Product promotion signs may or may not make mention of points of sale, but the emphasis is on the product rather than where to buy it. These signs come in all sizes and shapes, and are likely to appear almost anywhere unless something is done about it.

3. *Signs erected by the outdoor advertising industry* in the course of conduct of the outdoor advertising business. The outdoor advertising industry is not interested in the things being advertised, but in performing the advertising service. This industry is composed of many elements which should not be lumped together in appraising it.

One group of outdoor advertisers is primarily interested in standardized poster panels, and the organization to which most firms in this group belong (the Outdoor Advertising Association of America, Inc.) has a commendable set of policies controlling location, erection, and maintenance of signs. Some of the members don't adhere to the policies but at least the policies are there.

Other firms and individuals specialize in painted signs, novelty signs, and so on, and frequently appear neither to have policies nor to be guided by them.

Some basic principles

Zoning controls on signs should be limited to signs which can be seen from off the premises on which they are erected. In general, this means that the signs controlled are those which are visible from public ways, although there are circumstances under which visibility from neighboring private property would be a consideration.

By and large, so far as attracting general public interest is concerned, signs must be visible and legible from public ways. The public way creates the value for the person erecting the sign, and visibility from the public way (or from off the premises) creates the problems which give rise to the need for zoning controls.

Note that the controls should apply to all signs visible and legible from public ways or from off the premises, and not merely to exterior signs. A sign affixed to a window for the purpose of attracting attention of persons off the premises should not be excluded from control merely because it is fastened to the inside of the window rather than the outside.

Zoning control on signs should balance need in the various districts against the effect of signs on the character of the districts, on property values, and on aesthetic considerations. Real needs should be met with as little damage to the neighborhoods as possible.

So far as commercial signs are concerned, in residential neighborhoods there should be a bare minimum—small signs indicating the presence of permitted home occupations or giving notice that property is for sale, rent, or lease.

In certain special districts—buffer commercial-residential areas, multiple family-motel, neighborhood shopping centers, professional office districts, and the like—the primary residential character of the district or its intimate relationship to surrounding residential districts makes it desirable to restrict number, area, and type of signs visible from off the premises. Here signs should probably be limited to on-site notices identifying establishments by name and indicating the general nature of the business conducted. There should be no product promotion signs legible from off the premises, nor any general outdoor advertising signs.

In general business districts and in industrial districts, the picture changes. Here signs should be permitted with lesser restrictions, but there should still be some regulation in the public interest.

In such areas both on-site and off-site advertising is appropriate and it is logical that signs erected by or for specific places of business, product promotion signs, and signs erected by the outdoor advertising industry should be permitted. But even here it is desirable to establish some zoning controls on the number, gross area, and location of signs. Both in the general public interest and in the interest of the advertisers, it seems proper to prevent the multiplication of signs competing for public interest to the point of diminishing returns. If there are too many signs too close together, their very number defeats their purpose and the signs become a mere nuisance.

If it can be agreed that signs derive their value primarily from visibility from public ways, a standard set of rules can be evolved which meets public requirements without unduly restricting the needs of businesses or the choice of property owners or lessors as to the kinds of signs which may be erected on their property. Between general business districts and industrial districts of various classifications, distinctions may be made in the rules, but within each district the rule remains the same without discrimination as to the nature of development on a lot or the area of the front of buildings.

The rules as to number and area of commercial signs permitted might take this form:

"In a (strip commercial) district, one sign may be permitted for each five feet of frontage on a public street, and total area of all signs shall not exceed five square feet for each foot of frontage on the public street. In the case of corner lots, both frontages may be included in computing permissible number and area of signs." (Or, "in the case of corner lots, half of the longest frontage of the lot may be added to the shortest frontage in computing permissible number and area of signs.")

By varying the number and area factors, regulations appropriate to other districts in the general business or industrial categories can be developed.

Think this type of regulation through with respect to your local situation. It would probably have to be coupled to a firm drive for elimination of nonconforming signs, but the end effect would be salutary. The corner gas station on a 50-foot by 100-foot lot, under the first alternative above, could erect a total of 15 signs with a total area of 750 square feet. If this seems like a lot, count the number and area of signs displayed at such a filling station. If it still seems like a lot (which it won't if you figure in signs on the marquee, signs on the gas pumps, signs on the Coke machine, signs on the display standards, signs in the windows, signs on the walls, price signs, signs at the property line, dangling banners, and fluttering pennants) you can change the basic figures.

The interior-lot store with 25-foot frontage would be permitted five signs with a total area of 250 square feet. And so on.

So much for the general ideas, the preliminary sorting as to who erects signs and why, and principles which might be applied in the regulation of signs in various districts. Now it is necessary to define terms in such a way that we can make the language fit our purposes and try to develop a sample (*not* model, sample) set of regulations which communities can tailor to fit their needs.

Zoning is only one of a number of ways to control signs. It should be used in its proper place as a part of a whole kit of tools.

Zoning controls

What follows deals with zoning, but don't stop any genuine effort at sign control with zoning. Use all the tools you need.

DEFINITIONS

In zoning, special definitions concerning signs are important. They make it possible to include what you want to include and to leave out what you want to leave out without a lot of repetitive extra language in the body of the text.

Here are some definitions which might be helpful—but if they don't fit your requirements, don't use them. Make some which do.

SIGN—Any device designed to inform or attract the attention of persons not on the premises on which the sign is located, provided, however, that the following shall not be included in the application of the regulations herein:

1. Signs not exceeding one square foot in area and bearing only property numbers, post box numbers, or names of occupants of premises.
2. Flags and insignia of any government except when displayed in connection with commercial promotion.
3. Legal notices, identification information, or directional signs erected by governmental bodies.
4. Integral decorative or architectural features of buildings, except letters, trademarks, moving parts or moving lights.
5. Signs directing and guiding traffic and parking on private property, but bearing no advertising matter.

SIGNS, NUMBER AND SURFACE AREA—For the purpose of determining *number* of signs, a sign shall be considered to be a single display surface or display device containing elements organized, related, and composed to form a unit. Where matter is displayed in a random manner without organized relationship of elements, or where there is reasonable doubt about the relationship of elements, each element shall be considered to be a single sign.

The *surface area* of a sign shall be computed as including the entire area within a parallelogram, triangle, circle, or semi-circle comprising all of the displayed, but not forming part of the display itself, or frames surrounding display areas.

SIGN, ON-SITE—A sign relating in its subject matter to the premises on which it is located, or to products, accommodations, services, or activities on the premises. On-site signs do not include signs erected by the outdoor advertising industry in the conduct of the outdoor advertising business.

SIGN, OFF-SITE—A sign other than an on-site sign.

OUTDOOR ADVERTISING INDUSTRY; OUTDOOR ADVERTISING BUSINESS—Provision of outdoor displays or display space on a lease or rental basis only.

STATEMENT OF INTENT

Statements of intent in zoning ordinances serve two functions. The first, most obvious, and least important (if the ordinance is well drafted) is to guide those who will work with the regulations after they have been adopted—the public, the administrative staff, the board of adjustment, the courts.

The second, least obvious, and most important function of the statement of intent is that constructing it serves as a disciplinary exercise for those drafting the ordinance. Shaping the statement means pausing to think—defining what you propose to do, and for what reason, before you proceed to doing it. If you know, the intent will become clear in the ordinance whether it is formally stated or not.

Don't use the provision below if you can construct a better one:

"*INTENT*—Concerning signs, it is the general intent of this ordinance to prohibit signs of a commercial nature from districts in which commercial activities are barred; to limit signs in the most restricted commercial districts to those of an on-site variety and to control the number and area of such signs; and to control the number and area of signs in certain other districts."

SAMPLE SIGN-CONTROL PROVISIONS

Here are some sign-control provisions illustrating principles discussed.

Note that there is reference to other material necessary elsewhere in the ordinance, and that we haven't tried to run down all the cross-references here. Note also that we aren't attempting to provide regulations covering every conceivable situation. This is just a sample of *a* way to go about it, not a definitive statement of the only way to go about it.

In highly restricted residential districts:

1. In connection with a church, a school, a private club, or a community or neighborhood building, the following are permitted:
   a. Not more than two identification signs with combined surface area not exceeding 20 square feet.
   b. Not more than two bulletin or notice boards with combined surface area not exceeding 30 square feet.
   c. Not more than two temporary signs or banners with combined surface area not exceeding 20 square feet in connection with special events, provided that no such sign or banner shall be displayed for a period exceeding two weeks.

   No such sign shall be erected within 10 feet of any side or rear property line.
2. In connection with entrances to subdivisions and neighborhoods, identification signs not exceeding two square feet in area may be erected at each entrance.
3. In advertising property for sale, rent, or lease, any property is permitted one sign with surface area not exceeding four square feet and in addition, for each 150 feet of lot line adjacent to a public street, another such sign may be erected. No sign shall be erected within 10 feet of any side or rear property line.

In less restricted residential districts—As above, with the following addition:

---

4. In connection with guest homes, rooms for rent, and permitted home occupations, one sign with surface area not exceeding one square foot advertising such items, if mounted flat against the wall of the principal building.

In neighborhood shopping centers set closely in residential surroundings, the aim is to avoid damage to the character of the general area. The problem is complicated by types of centers—there are those which "just growed," and also planned neighborhood centers with an entirely different character.

For Topsy districts serving a neighborhood function (and this might apply both to those zoned neighborhood commercial and to nonconforming commercial uses with excessive signs being amortized) the approach might be:

Signs shall be permitted only as follows: Not more than three in number and not more than 100 square feet in combined surface area identifying the premises and the general nature of the business conducted. All signs shall be on permanent mountings, shall not be movable, and shall not extend into any public way, provided, however, that signs may overhang a public way if no portion is less than nine feet above such public way and extends over the property line a distance of not more than three feet.

This type of regulation would be highly restrictive. As an alternative for Topsy districts close to residential areas:

Signs shall be permitted only as follows: On-site signs with number and surface area limited by the following formula—for each five lineal feet of lot frontage on a public street (frontage being determined by the principal entrance to the premises) and for each 10 lineal feet of lot adjacent to a public street but not constituting frontage on such street, a maximum of one sign and 10 square feet of surface area is permitted. The total surface area permitted may be used in a lesser number of signs than the maximum permitted, but the maximum number shall not be exceeded even though the total permissible surface area is not used.

For planned neighborhood shopping centers a somewhat different approach seems appropriate. If the center is well designed, there should be good separation from adjoining residential districts, buffer landscape strips or walls, proper off-street parking, substantial setback from streets, and all the rest of it.

The most able shopping center designers will avoid voluntarily the types of errors zoning tries to prevent. But the most able shopping center designers are usually someplace else. So the zoning controls must be there. On signs, the following might help:

Only on-site signs shall be permitted in this district, in accordance with the following formulas and restrictions:

1. One identification sign structure, which may include up to three sign faces, with combined surface area not exceeding 100 square feet, for each side of the premises adjacent to a public street. No portion of

such structure shall be closer than 10 feet to any right of way line, nor closer than 25 feet to any residential district boundary. Lettering on such sign shall indicate only the name of the shopping center and the general nature of businesses conducted.

2. For each five lineal feet of frontage of principal buildings (frontage being determined by the principal entrance to the building) and for each 10 lineal feet of sides of principal buildings exposed to general public view from either the parking area or public streets, a maximum of one sign and 10 square feet of surface area is permitted. Total surface area permitted may be used in a lesser number of signs than the maximum permitted, but the maximum number shall not be exceeded.

Signs other than those indicated in 1 above shall be mounted only on the walls or roofs of buildings in the shopping center.

For highway commercial districts and strip commercial districts along city streets, if such districts are not intimately related to residential districts, the regulations can be somewhat relaxed and still serve their purpose. In these districts, filling stations will usually be permitted as a matter of right, and conduct of the outdoor advertising business is appropriate. There seems no reason to limit signs to those of the on-site variety.

The decision as to erection of off-site as against on-site signs may properly be left to those who control the street or highway frontage. But in view of the appearance of such districts when signs are not controlled, it is obvious that some control is still necessary.

Control through zoning here should concern itself with the number, area, and location of signs:

In this district, on-site and off-site signs are permitted, subject to the following formulas and restrictions:

1. For each five lineal feet of lot frontage on a public street (frontage being determined by the principal entrance to the premises) and for each 10 lineal feet of lot adjacent to a public street but not constituting frontage on such street, a maximum of one sign and 30 square feet of surface area is permitted.

   The total surface area permitted may be used in a lesser number of signs than the maximum permitted, but the maximum number shall not be exceeded even though the total permissible surface area is not used.

2. No sign shall be erected in or over any required front yard, or within 15 feet of any residential district boundary.

Controls other than zoning

The general sign ordinance should cover general sign regulations. The building code should handle structural items.

There are possibilities in licensing individual signs or sign erectors at the local level, and in performance bonds to guarantee that signs will be properly erected, maintained, and (if temporary) removed.

In areas where directional and informational signs are truly needed, but where they might be objectionable if erected in competitive splendor by private enterprise, local government might get into the sign business—for an appropriate fee and with proper restraint.

Miscellaneous notes

There you have something to get on with, so far as areas most likely to give trouble are concerned. If you want to control signs in other business districts or industrial districts, you can work out similar formulas. And don't forget the possibilities for eliminating nonconforming signs.

There are lots of details left out in the provisions above: "No source of illumination shall be directly visible from any public way or residential district." "No red, amber, or green illumination, fixed or moving, shall be mounted or used in such a location or manner as to create confusion with traffic lights or lights on emergency vehicles." (The latter provision probably belongs in the general sign ordinance rather than the zoning ordinance.)

"No sign shall be so erected as to be visible from a residential district unless a public street intervenes between the sign and the residential district."

And there are the provisions concerning administration of the sign portion of the ordinance, and other odds and ends which you can either put in or leave out depending on your own circumstances and inclinations.

If you really *want* to control signs, you can control them.

Subdivision regulations

What right have public agencies to regulate and control the use and development of privately owned land? There is constant erosion of the basic freedom to have and to hold, to keep or to sell, to use at will or not to use at all. Why do we not only tolerate this invasion of private rights by public action, but encourage increasing spread of controls?

There are two equations which help to define and explain what has happened to us:

1. Public right to control use of private land is equivalent to private right to create problems affecting public interest.

2. The degree of public interest (and hence the amount of justifiable public control of private affairs) is proportional to the density and interdependence of population in the social units involved.

Man is independent only so long as he is alone. As he becomes associated with other men, independence lessens, and interdependence grows.

In all the history of the human race, there has been a progression from independence to interdependence. In our own time, the process is accelerating with rapid concentration of population into larger and larger urbanized centers, with increased job specialization and with increasing demand for public services of ever-widening scope.

In urbanized and urbanizing areas, private rights of land ownership are diminishing and the public share in control of what are called

This article originally appeared in *Bair Facts,* published by Chandler-Davis Publishing Co., West Trenton, N. J. (1960). Reprinted by permission.

private lands is growing. A man may not be deprived of his property or its use without due process of law, but the legal processes available are increasing in extent and in kind.

In exchanging the independence of the cave for the interdependence of the city, something had to be given for what was gained. The consideration in the contract was a portion of the right to do as we pleased with what we owned. We are still giving up bits of our independence in order to gain things we want more, and we are doing it voluntarily—sometimes almost eagerly. In this country, we have driven some good bargains. We still have a sizable stock of independence left; we have a vast amount of benefits to show for what we traded off.

No law dictates where we must live. If we elect to live in urban areas, we are subject to more controls, and receive a great many more services, than if we live in rural isolation.

No law dictates that a developer must operate in urban or urbanizing areas. For him the benefits of such a location are overwhelmingly persuasive and far outweigh the price he must pay in submission to necessary controls. But if he prefers independence to the benefits, with the controls which are part of the bargain, he can find non-urban areas where there are very few controls indeed. (Unfortunately, he can also find a number of urban areas where such controls are inadequate. In the best areas for development, where such controls are lacking or weak, they are being strengthened rapidly.)

A primary function of planning is to determine what the public interest is and to devise means by which it can be served efficiently. Development of subdivision regulations is a job for planners, because subdivision regulations are one of the controls which promote the general welfare of the public. Before equitable controls can be devised, it is essential that there should be clear identification of the major parties in interest, the functions, problems, and objectives of each, and the manner in which each is affected.

Stated briefly, the job of the planner is to produce regulations which protect the public interest and balance controls and costs against benefits in such a manner that each of the parties involved carries his own share of the load, and none is left holding the bag.

Who wants what, and who pays?

1. The developer. The developer is primarily interested in deriving a profit from the performance of certain important functions. He is a land processor and marketer, and he may also be a home builder. The range of things which developers do varies widely.

There are those who merely buy land wholesale and sell it retail, adding nothing in the process except marking stakes and a few dim truck-trails. The buyer gets land and hope, and both are overpriced.

At the other extreme, there are developers who proceed with great care to assemble land suitable for residential use, study its potentialities, divide it into lots and streets, parks, playground areas, school and church sites, and commercial centers adapted to its needs. They install water mains, sewer mains, paving, curbs and gutters, sidewalks, street markers. They build homes, or work with home builders. Where they sell lots, they attach deed restrictions requiring a high quality of construction and architectural control.

There is considerable confusion as to who pays for what in this process, but the maze is not impenetrable. If the developer is successful, when he has finished his work he has his investment back, plus his profit. The amount of the investment, the time required, and the ratio of profit will vary considerably depending on subdivision regulations, the developer's approach to his problems, and the market for the product.

In most cases, the investment of the developer is for a relatively short term. His services and obligations cease when the property is sold or shortly thereafter and the homeowners, governments, and taxpayers in general take over the responsibilities and expenses.

The residential subdivider benefits the area by making property available in the form required for urban settlement. The urban area benefits the developer first merely by being there. The vast majority of subdivisions derive an important part of their value from location near cities, and certainly the salability of property is affected by its nearness to an urban center.

The second major benefit which the urban area confers on the developer is the promise of dependable government and continuing services. If buyers were not assured of schools, streets, hospitals, sewers, water, garbage disposal, police and fire protection, libraries, parks and recreational facilities, and the other things which government must maintain, sales and values would be seriously impaired.

2. The homeowners in the development. The people who buy homes or lots in the development pay for what the developer has done. In general, the price includes the cost of all of his work, all the land he has dedicated to public purposes, all the facilities and improvements he has installed, and all of his profits.

In the balance, then, the buyer gets a lot or a home and related public facilities for a price which reflects costs plus profits. He also gets the ancillary benefits of assured urban services which may be reflected in the price but are not provided by the developer.

In the interests of equity, it is important that the homeowners in new areas pay their individual shares of the costs they create. The cost of installation of the public facilities they require should be included in the price of the property they buy. The developer, in this case, is the logical collection agent for government.

3. Governmental bodies. It is up to the governmental bodies involved to provide services and find means to pay for them. Hence government seeks, or should seek, ways to assure that at least as far as original facilities are concerned, new subdivisions should as nearly as possible pay their own way into the urban circle.

Government will have to serve the new homeowners, and will be hard pressed to meet the cost of services and maintenance from available revenues.

The profits of growth accrue to a very limited group, and government is not in the circle. As cities grow, per capita costs of government rise.

Certainly local government is in a poor position to subsidize growth which increases its costs. If subsidies are necessary, they might better be for slum clearance and low-cost housing to reduce governmental costs than for middle- and upper-cost developments which raise them.

4. The general public. John Q. Taxpayer has trouble enough as it is. He does not benefit in any large measure from mere quantitative growth. His forlorn hope is for increase in the quality of his city and improvement and greater economy in its services.

He sees his city as a place of crowded streets and crowded schools, of inadequate parks and vanishing parking, of struggle against obsolescence and mounting costs, of increasing demands for services by the population already there. And he knows that, one way or another, he is going to have to pay the bill.

He welcomes newcomers—if they will carry their own share of the load. But he doesn't see why he should be expected to carry it for them.

What should be regulated

If defenders of the inviolable rights of the individual stood firmly against champions of the notion that individual rights are insignificant if not mythical, it would be much easier to sort things out. It is not so. People persist in taking both positions at once.

A man protests that controls deprive him of the right to develop his property as he sees fit. If he were not controlled, he could create situations which would add to the tax burden of others without giving them any voice in the matter at all. He is fighting for individual rights (his) and at the same time making it clear that individual rights (other people's) don't amount to much.

The need for regulation arises from situations like this. The basic and guiding principle on which regulations should be based is that *everybody's* rights should be protected or infringed equitably. Regulations are for the purpose of averaging things out so that as nearly as possible everybody pays for what he gets and gets what he pays for.

There is well-fertilized and poorly-weeded confusion about what the public has a right to regulate. As history demonstrates, sooner or later, in one way or another, *anything is subject to regulation if public interest demands it.*

Public interest

"Public interest" is a broad term involving but not restricted to those things which are referred to as police powers. It is getting broader all the time as our culture grows more complex and we become increasingly interdependent, as individual actions affect the welfare of the people as a whole in more and more ways. What should be controlled, and the manner and extent of regulation, changes from decade to decade, and even from year to year.

There is a subtle but vitally important distinction between things which should logically be controlled in the public interest and things which a particular public may be interested in controlling. For practical purposes, there is "working" public interest only when the public sees the need for and purpose of regulation. However necessary a control may appear to planners for the promotion of public health, safety, comfort, convenience, morals, or general welfare, it must be sold to the public before it is supported by the public.

Those burdened with responsibility for preparing regulations should be alert to this. They should first be sure themselves, and then should make it clear to others, that what they propose is in fact related to present or demonstrable future needs of the public they represent, and that it is an honest balancing of interests of the parts to benefit the whole. They should have defined public needs by a careful planning process, so that they themselves know what they are doing. They should be able to prove that they are not unnecessarily infringing private rights or penalizing private interests because they have not made up their own minds as to public requirements.

Once these things are settled, it is safe to impose regulations without fear of the courts. Reasonable controls which are clearly in the public interest have seldom been thrown out. Make your controls reasonable, be sure that you can prove they are in the public interest, and don't let the lawyers scare you. Let the courts have the final say, rather than the lawyers. In court cases generally, about half the lawyers involved are on the losing side.

Steady!

One set of proposed subdivision regulations contained the odd phrase, "No final plat shall be approved by the [Planning and Zoning] Commission unless the Commission first obtains the recommendation of the Planning Engineer, the County Health Officer and such other County Government departments, *but not including the County Board of Public Instruction,* which have jurisdiction or interest."

As we understand it, elimination of consideration of schools came about because the county attorney advised that a requirement for compulsory dedication of school sites without compensation was legally objectionable. It is, under certain conditions. But the commission came to the erroneous conclusion that it was improper to include any provisions concerning location of school sites in subdivision regulations.

School location is obviously a matter of paramount public importance. In writing subdivision regulations as part of the job of comprehensive planning, it is vital that appropriate sites be reserved for school use. The fact that there is a wrong way to do it doesn't mean that the problem should be ignored.

Items to be regulated

Among factors to be considered in subdivision regulation are the following:

1. Need. There are areas where the first determination should be as to whether the subdivision is needed. Is there already a sufficient supply, or oversupply, of available property of the class proposed? Premature subdivision has created tremendous problems in the past, and is still creating them.

Widely scattered houses are expensive to service. Speculative promotion of lot sales (which frequently is a matter of skimming off the cream and abandoning the rest) often leads to a shotgun pattern of lots with individual absentee owners, so that when the time is ripe for solid development, the area involved is difficult to handle.

2. Location with respect to existing development. Does the proposed subdivision fit into the general pattern of development so that the services it will require can be provided efficiently and economically? Unless it does, or is in a position to be self-sufficient on required services or pay the extra costs involved in providing extraordinary extensions of streets, water mains, sewers, and other facilities and services, development may be very expensive to the taxpayers in the area initially, and expensive to maintain.

3. Site considerations. Assuming that there is need for a subdivision of the type proposed, and that the area involved fits in well with the pattern of general development, the next question concerns the suitability of the site for the uses intended. As one of many subjects for investigation, consider flooding and drainage. Is the proposed subdivision in a general area which has been inundated? Have works been constructed by public bodies which will prevent future general flooding, or are such works in process of construction or in firm planning stages? Can the developer take independent action to insure that property in the proposed subdivisions will be protected?

Unless the site is protected from flooding, development should not be permitted.

4. Streets. The location and construction of streets should be regulated. Major streets should conform to the comprehensive street plan for the area, and should skirt subdivisions rather than run through them. Minor streets should be designed to discourage through traffic, and no more minor streets should be permitted than are necessary to serve the subdivision. Costs of street maintenance are high, and there is no excuse for adding to the burden without need.

5. *Easements.* Regulations should require easements for utilities along rear lot lines or side lot lines when necessary.

6. *Blocks.* Design standards should be appropriate to the needs of the area as to block layout. A common, costly error is to extend the established gridiron pattern which usually results in blocks which are too short, causing unnecessary expense for street construction and maintenance.

7. *Lots.* Regulations should set minimum size and design standards for lots, related to the purposes for which the lots are intended and their location within the subdivision. Considerations would include intent to use the lots for single- or multiple-family dwellings, commercial purposes, etc., and also special design requirements as indicated for waterfronts, lots adjoining major streets, and other special cases. Lot size might also be regulated according to soil and subsoil characteristics in areas where use of septic tanks and/or individual water systems in intended.

8. *Public sites and open spaces.* Where the comprehensive plan shows proposed parks, playgrounds, schools or other public buildings, beaches, or other public uses, regulations should require dedication or reservation of such areas for the intended use. In the event of extraordinary proposed developments of a nature or timing not anticipated in the comprehensive plan, public sites not indicated in the plan might be required. It would also be desirable to give consideration to the location of quasi-public buildings and to encourage provision of suitable church sites.

9. *Improvements.* Regulations should cover the nature and extent of improvements—design and construction of streets, curbs and gutters, public sidewalks, street markers, storm sewers and other storm drainage facilities, sanitary sewers, water supply including supply for fire protection, street trees, planting strips, street lighting systems, and such other items as may be required.

10. *General layout.* Over and above details, regulations should include provision for the control of general layout. Will the plan of the proposed development make for a good neighborhood? Can people get to the places they want to go by the means they usually employ? Children are likely to get around on foot or on bicycles. Can they go to and from school safely and directly with minimum interference with normal flow of street traffic? Are collector streets oriented so that they will best serve their purpose?

How much flood damage can we afford?

Rainfall during the recent damp spell was nothing spectacular in the light of past records and future certainties. We've had lots more rain than that, and we will again have lots more rain than that. This time, there wasn't even a hurricane to go with it—the rain came down vertically and spread in a slow and orderly manner.

Thousands of people had to move out of their homes through vast lakes of sewage-laden water. Thousands of miles of city streets and outlying areas became impassable, and will require extensive and expensive repairs. Tens of thousands of toilets refused to flush or bubbled their effluent into the surface water sprawled across low areas in the countryside and the urban landscape.

How is it that this little rainy spell caused so much disaster?

Reasons for the trouble

The reasons are obvious. Water runs to low areas. If the low areas are full of buildings, and the buildings are equipped with septic tanks, the buildings will be flooded, the septic tanks will cease to operate, sewage will mingle with the sheet flood, and things will be pretty much in a mess.

Even the most expensive promotional efforts fail to make septic tanks operate in areas where ground water is too close to the surface of the ground. And in road building, promotional optimism is a poor substitute for water-resistant construction.

Some building in low areas has been by people who were uninformed, misinformed, or not very bright. A great deal of it has been done by people who know better, but wanted to build on cheap land without making needed improvements, and to sell and get out before heavy rains came.

The man who subdivides a temporarily dry lake bottom and builds and sells houses on it is no asset to humanity whether he knows what he is doing or not.

To compound natural drainage problems, fills form dams which make lakes of property immediately above them, or choke drainage of extensive upstream areas. Drainage canals throw excess water onto lands already saturated. Roofs and pavements replace water-absorbing open land and multiply runoff.

The results are easily predictable. When it rains hard cries for help come over the stinking water. Federal, state, county, and local governments are supposed to rally round and move people out, provide credit, dig drainage ditches, throw up dams, install storm and sanitary sewers, man the pumps, patrol the area to protect against looting, fix the roads, and clean up the mess. After things have settled down a little, the demand mounts for multi-million dollar flood control projects on a grand scale.

Sooner or later we will ask ourselves the question: *"Why should we go on subsidizing people who persist in building on flood plains?"*

If we aren't moved by humanitarian considerations—retirees investing life savings in waterfront homes where the waterfront turns out to come above the furniture, kids exposed to typhoid, wage earners learning how liquid their assets really are—we should consider this: *Something we could stop is adding to the rate at which our taxes are going up!* There's an argument which ought to get action!

Things we should be doing

Some action can be handled rapidly, some will take time, but all of the following approaches should be started.

1. Flood plain zoning. In 1939, the Committee on City Planning and Zoning of the National Fire Protection Association issued a publication, *Flood Plain Zoning and Evacuation,* which referred to flood plain zoning as a comparatively new development prohibiting "all uses of land in certain districts subject to frequent and extensive flooding, except agriculture, orcharding, dairying, automobile parking, or recreation, while in other districts not so frequently or extensively flooded, certain commercial and industrial uses, subject to comparatively little damage by flood waters, would be permitted."

In 1940, the County of Los Angeles amended its zoning ordinance to provide that because frequent inundation made certain areas unfit for human habitation, "no building or portion thereof which is designed for living purposes or as a place of public assembly or for both may be built, and no existing structure altered, so as to be used either in whole or in part for such use" in such areas.

It may not be necessary to limit so severely. If there are proper improvements, flood plain lands may be used for residential, commercial, or industrial purposes without hazard. It should now be obvious, and it will become more so, that low-lying lands should not be used for such purposes without proper improvement. And it should be crystal clear that *if a developer elects to operate in low areas, the responsibility for necessary specialized improvements should rest on the developer, and the improvements should be made or assured before construction subject to damage from flooding is allowed.*

Otherwise, governmental agencies will be besieged during flood periods with demands for corrective action. Such action is inordinately expensive after the land is partially or completely built up, and the resultant burden on the general public is both onerous and unnecessary.

The special regulations needed to cover all aspects of the problem will normally be scattered through zoning, subdivision regulations, and building and sanitary codes, but one Florida area is making a substantial start in its zoning ordinance. The Sanibel Island Planning and Zoning Authority adopted a zoning ordinance which provides:

> On the Island, there exist areas which, in their natural state, are subject to frequent inundation of a kind which would make them hazardous for construction of buildings intended for human occupancy. For the most part, these are low-lying lands, below elevations of the Island now improved and developed, and these lands are more susceptible to dangers from wind-driven tides during hurricanes than most of the developed areas of the Island.
>
> Major portions of these areas are joined together and related in such a manner that drainage and improvement of part affects drainage and improvement of the whole.

For the purpose of promoting, protecting and improving the public health, safety, comfort, convenience, and general welfare, it is particularly important that as these lands are improved and developed they shall meet certain special requirements in addition to the general requirements indicated elsewhere in this ordinance and in other laws and regulations. These special requirements are related to facilitating adequate provision of sewerage and drainage systems, and to protection against the dangers of inundation during hurricanes and other periods of high water.

Therefore, in the Official Zoning Atlas, these areas have been indicated with a double symbol—a primary symbol, as for example R-1 or R-G, indicating the general classification for zoning purposes, and a suffix (PF), indicating Park and Floodway. Such areas may be used in their present state in the manner and for the purposes set forth in the Schedule of District Regulations under the heading "Park and Floodway." Such areas may also, after improvement as indicated below, and subject to the special requirements of the district indicated by the primary symbol and the general requirements of this and other ordinances and regulations, be used for the purposes indicated by the primary zoning symbol.

Any or all of any area designated as Park and Floodway by the PF suffix added to its primary zoning symbol may be used according to the regulations for the district indicated by the primary zoning symbol upon determination by the Sanibel Island Planning and Zoning Authority:

a) That the lands have a permanent elevation of at least 5 feet above mean low water [establishing minimum elevation of finished fill]; and

b) That in the opinion of the County Health Department, the elevation and soils characteristics of the site of the intended use will permit operation of septic tanks, or other sewage disposal facilities required by and to be installed for the intended use, without undue hazard to health; and

c) That the manner of development and fill does not constitute an impediment to the general drainage system for the Island or the drainage of adjacent lands susceptible to development.

2. *Subdivision regulations.* Florida does have some subdivision regulations designed to minimize flood damage. In 1956, Dade County

passed an ordinance requiring that low land in the unincorporated areas had to be filled to meet "flood criteria elevations" before it could be platted. The elevations were contours established by the water control division of the county engineer's office, the county health department, and the planning department, and in addition to filling, both the area to be platted and adjacent areas had to have proper drainage.

3. Building controls. On lands platted before proper subdivision controls were established, applicants for building permits were required to supply an elevation survey of the existing grade and to install a bench mark. From the marker and the flood criteria maps, the building division determined required elevation, and filling and construction had to be in accordance with elevations and other requirements established.

4. Sewerage and water supply. Here county health departments should be the source of guidance. No development for human occupancy should be permitted on low lands until adequacy of proposed sanitary facilities and water supply are approved. If there is to be much fill, septic tanks may give trouble.

5. General drainage plans. Just as a major street plan is needed before minor streets can be planned intelligently, there should be a general drainage plan for the whole watershed or subwatershed before minor drainage systems make much sense. This should set forth major natural channels, canals, and holding basins, and indicate the level at which ground water is to be held in various parts of the area. Major drainage works, beyond those required for individual projects, are of course a public responsibility—if it is determined that it is in the public interest to develop the lowlands in the first place.

6. Combinations of elements affecting the comprehensive plan. As with most planning, plans for flood damage prevention affect and are affected by other plan elements, and should be skillfully interwoven with other plan elements to get maximum benefits at minimum expense.

In extensive low areas, all or most of the following will be involved. To start with, there will be the major drainage plan. Careful on that—too much drainage can cause as much trouble as too little. Needed is a balance holding ground water at an optimum level for prevention of salt water intrusion in coastal areas, for maintaining adequate underground water for domestic, agricultural, and industrial purposes, and for preserving lakes and wildlife areas.

In connection with the major drainage plan and its canals and dikes, some important savings can be made in road construction by using the dikes for roadbeds. On the other hand, road construction which ignores the general drainage plan can raise hob with it.

Once the major drainage plan has been established, it is much easier to design subdivisions intelligently. Most subdivisions in low areas will be—or should be—created by digging canals and lakes and using the spoil for fill. The minor canal network should be as carefully designed as the minor street network. Unless sufficient width and depth of canals is provided, and a satisfactory flow pattern is established, they become stagnant slime pools. The shape of the bottom and the manner of stabilizing the shore line is also important—wash from passing boats eats away improperly designed shores, particularly in narrow canals.

Certainly the recreational values of the canal system should not be ignored. A well-designed canal system makes it almost as easy to get around by boat as by car, and travelling by boat is more fun for some people. How do the canals fit with water routes to good fishing areas? And how can "through" and "local" boat traffic be separated—it is just as objectionable to have major boat traffic tearing through a quiet neighborhood as to have major automobile traffic there.

We can do a great deal to alleviate the flood-damage problem, if we will. If we don't take action, it is going to get increasingly worse, increasingly expensive, and increasingly hard to solve. If we do take action promptly, we can save a lot of present and future expenditure of tax money, and at the same time enhance the livability of our environment.

Can we get zoning out of politics—or politics out of zoning?

Politics is not necessarily a dirty word. According to Webster, it is the science and art of government, the theory or practice of managing or directing the affairs of public policy, or "in a bad sense, artful or dishonest management to secure the success of political candidates or parties." We could do with a great deal more good politics (and less bad) in general government and in planning and zoning.

Current theory on planning and zoning is that the comprehensive plan indicates a desirable pattern of evolution. Zoning in accord with the plan helps guide development to fit the pattern.

The power to plan and zone and the process for adoption of either the plan or the zoning ordinance is set by state enabling legislation. Across the country, procedural regulations are reasonably standardized. Professional guidance in preparation of plans or zoning is not required by state laws, but is generally used in preparing the documents. The planning commission considers the material and holds public hearings on it, then makes its recommendations to the governing body. The governing body holds further hearings and takes final action, with or without changes in the material submitted. Amendment of either the plan or the zoning ordinance requires the same procedures as original adoption.

This is government in the democratic tradition, and few would urge that either the plan or the original zoning be dictated by professionals

This article originally appeared in *Nation's Cities,* November 1967. Reprinted by permission. Copyright 1967.

(however competent) without regard for the democratic process.

But there are those who suggest that zoning map *amendments* might well be handled by qualified professional staff members without referral to the governing body, thus removing opportunities for application of the wrong kind of politics. In the comprehensive plan and the zoning ordinance, public policy should be officially set by the elected governing body, with appropriate guidelines for administrative action and procedures for appeal of administrative decisions. From this point on, why shouldn't zoning map amendments be handled by trained and experienced professional administrators? If proposed changes in the zoning fit the plan, let the administrator make the changes; if not, let him deny them.

As things are now, Owner A has a house separated from a gas station only by a district boundary. He wants this property rezoned commercial. Owner B wants a tract rezoned for planned residential development. The Chamber of Commerce pushes for rezoning of an extensive vacant multiple-family area for a planned industrial park, and the Suburbia Heights Neighborhood Association wants the same area rezoned single-family large-lot. In each of these cases, and in others varying in all directions, consideration of the proposed amendment requires going through the same procedure as for adoption of the original ordinance. Thus elected bodies are spending what many people (including their members) consider to be inordinate amounts of time considering zoning details, and on occasion there are grounds for suspicion that the kind of politics involved is not of the character which might be wished.

Those who argue for map amendment by professional staff planners would say that at least some of the cases above could be handled without referral to the governing body. This is undoubtedly true—if state laws can be changed to allow it. The option isn't there now. And there would have to be limits as to how far the professional administrator could go. *Minor* changes, yes. *Major* changes, no. If a major change in zoning (or in the comprehensive plan) can be made by an administrative official without referral to the governing body, he might as well be empowered to draft, adopt, and enforce the original document.

As an alternate to giving staff planners map amendment powers (with all the sticky problems involved in getting enabling legislation changed), there are usually ways within present laws to accomplish at least some of the same results.

Take the case of Owner A. The ordinance might provide that where a lot in a residential district directly adjoins frontage in a commercial or industrial district, the residential lot may be used for a range of purposes much broader than generally permitted in residential districts. This kind of transitional zoning would give Owner A and others in a similar plight some relief without setting the stage for the kind of commercial creep likely to ensue if A's residential neighbor discovers that now *he* is next to a gas station—on A's property. A great many of our amendment applications are for cases like A's, and can be avoided if the transitional use approach is used.

Owner B's case can also be handled administratively without rezoning the property if ordinance language is changed to allow planned residential districts meeting stated requirements in specified existing districts.

Comes now the collision between the Chamber of Commerce and the Suburbia Heights Neighborhood Association. Neither owns the property in question, so the conflicting suggestions will probably come through members of the planning commission or the governing body. A change to industrial or large-lot single-family will be a major change. The interests of two "publics" are involved here, the issue is substantial, and there is justification for continuation of present procedures.

The professional staff would study the proposals and present policies, objectives, statistics, maps, and charts of the comprehensive plan. The planning commission, as a lay advisory body presumably outside politics of the wrong kind, will consider the matter, hold hearings, and make its recommendations to the governing body. When the recommendations are submitted, they have the force of professional opinion plus the endorsement (with or without modifications) of a lay body appointed to give impartial advice. The governing body, elected to guide local policy, will also hold hearings and make its decision. If the planners have done their homework well, if the planning commission is well-chosen and has earned respect, and if the members of the governing body are honest, the politics involved will work as politics should. If not, they won't, but it won't be the fault of the procedures and changing the procedures wouldn't change the results.

Given a governing body with a majority of members interested in playing dirty politics with zoning, there are many ways to separate the cat from its hide. The planning commission can be stacked to override the recommendations of the staff where this suits a questionable purpose. Or a "professional" planner can be found who will do what he is told. Or since the planning commission is merely advisory, its advice can be ignored, with or without bland comments to the effect that theory is all very well but that in the present case there are imperative practical considerations (or charitable—with benefits not necessarily restricted to widows and orphans).

It may be argued that even in the case of the Chamber of Commerce v. Suburbia Heights Neighborhood Association there is no need for the pushing and pulling. The issue has already been settled. The comprehensive plan shows the area as multiple family, and it has been zoned multiple family in accord with the plan. The planning director should at least be in a position to head off zoning changes which are clearly *not* along the lines indicated by the officially adopted plan.

Here we run into one of the discouraging realities. Contrary to the theory that zoning follows the plan, what often happens is that the plan follows zoning, both in time and in pattern. The city grew. Then it got zoning. The zoning for developed areas was largely a reflection of what was already there. (It could hardly be otherwise, considering the effects of nonconforming status on existing property. For example, try to zone miles of existing but surplus strip commercial development in the residential category it should logically have. The effort will be futile, and probably lead to short job tenure for the professional who recommends it.)

The zoning for vacant areas was usually a combination of extension of existing patterns and a means for establishing a sort of land reserve. Where there was no clear pattern, the land was placed in what was in effect a holding zone—in agricultural or large-lot residential categories.

Comes then the plan—or plans. Many cities have had several. On land use, neither existing uses nor existing zoning could well be ignored, although the zoning was sometimes refined. The result was frequently a comprehensive plan in accord with zoning, including the holding zones. When the time comes to make decisions as to what to do in reserve areas which have remained undeveloped, the plan echoes previous zoning uncertainty instead of giving firm, logical guidance.

Thus the existing plan is not always a dependable guide for zoning changes, although able planners will be working continuously to improve both, and to make them track more closely. On major items, there is probably more to be said for the present cumbersome amendment process (for either the plan or zoning) than against it. At least there is ample opportunity for public airing of the issues, and where the results become nauseating there are always the courts—and the next election.

To end on an up-beat, there is one approach which appears to fit within the framework of standard state enabling legislation and gives the planning director a chance to screen some of the applications for zoning changes—although if an amendment is processed it must follow the regular procedure.

In Honolulu, petitions for amendment (other than those originating with city council or the planning commission) are to be filed with the planning director. He may deny the petition, with a report for the record, and there's the end of it, unless there is an appeal to the zoning board of appeals. The board may reverse the director only if it finds that his action was based on an erroneous finding of a material fact, or was arbitrary, capricious, or an obvious abuse of discretion. Appeal from the board is to the courts.

Language in the ordinance limits the circumstances under which amendments can be justified thus:

> No amendment shall be recommended by the director or commission or passed by city council except on substantial proof that it is in accord with sound zoning practice and will serve to promote the public health, safety, convenience, or general welfare. With regard to changes in zoning boundaries, no change shall be made except upon demonstration that conditions and trends of development in the area have so altered since adoption of existing boundaries as to justify the change, or that existing boundaries, either through prior error or change in conditions, are unreasonable, and that the objectives of the ordinance will be promoted by the proposed change.

Is zoning a mistake? *thoughts on performance standards for performance standards for non-Euclidean non-zoning*

A thoughtful reader of Bassett's classic work on primitive zoning will be shocked at how little seems to have been learned since it was written. About 1915, when much of the urban crisis in New York City was blamed on an unwise mixture of conflicting land uses, our present form of zoning began to take shape. The first crude zoning provided for diminishing segregation from the "top" down. Most exclusive was the single-family residence zone, protecting the rich from association with the poor. At the other end of the scale, there was no segregation to amount to anything. Single-family residences, tenements, stores, warehouses, and boiler factories were permitted in the industrial district, where the poor could mix as much as they pleased.

Before this new control device could be tested by experience, it was widely "sold" around the country, much in the manner of present-day urban renewal. Progress on the municipal scene was measured in terms of how many additional cities had zoning each year, rather than by what was actually happening to cities.

There was (and still is) little rational appraisal of whether zoning was doing what it was intended to do, and whether zoning was the best way of doing what had to be done. As shortcomings became obvious, efforts were made to change details (largely in the direction of increased segregation), but change wasn't easy: It was easier to copy than to understand and improve.

Even today, with minor variations, we still imitate this regulatory device created for the nation's largest city almost 50 years ago, complete with all the crude complexities of a first effort at a complicated job.

Even where zoning has moved from its origins, the movement has not always been in the right direction. For example, take the board of adjustment. In New York, the board was required to be composed of paid, qualified experts. In most cities, however, the board is an amateur and inexpert quasi-judicial body operating in a nonjudicial manner, without properly prepared attorneys, without a judge to explain the points of law involved, and without proper attention to required procedures or to the limitations on its powers to dispense justice—or favors.

In theory, zoning is in accordance with a comprehensive plan intended to promote healthy urban growth. In fact, it is quite generally formulated in accordance with existing land use and obsolete tax systems. It often amounts to a delaying action to maintain the status quo except when amendments are forced through to increase speculative opportunity. The delaying action has not been spectacularly successful, and the amendments are seldom justified by the comprehensive plan—if one exists.

Aside from the fact that zoning has not lived up to its theoretical expectations, there is the worrisome possibility that it may have been the wrong approach in the first place. Zoning is a treatment of symptoms, rather than a curing of disease. We have not yet concentrated enough attention on finding the *causes* of frictions between land uses, or seeking regulatory remedies for incompatibilities. Instead we continue to classify and map a vast array of uses (the characteristics and relationships of which we have not found time to understand) and then sort them into separate bins of odd shapes and sizes.

Major overhaul of both intent and method of the land-use regulations now called zoning is long overdue. The improved model may be virtually unrecognizable as zoning. This doesn't matter, so long as the functions that need to be performed are handled effectively.

Before tinkering with the mechanism, it would be well to acquire a thorough understanding of what it is supposed to do. (Observation of past planning and zoning activities indicates that this need for understanding must be stressed.) First it is necessary to think. After thinking comes understanding. After we understand, and only after we understand, can we act with wisdom. So far, we show little indication of being well into the thinking stage, but we are acting anyway. Possibly we can do better.

Regulatory objectives and the failure of zoning

Assume that the fundamental purpose of land-use regulation is to erect a control framework within which continuing land-use developments can be induced to form patterns which are convenient, comfortable, healthy, economically feasible, and adapted to changing public and private needs, customs, value systems, and techniques of this and future times. (If elaboration of this statement is needed, add it.) Now, assume that regulatory devices are to achieve these purposes by as broad a range of methods as necessary, but that there shall be no more regulation than is needed to achieve these purposes—no regulation without a demonstrably useful purpose. Bear in mind that the regulations should so far as possible provide the flexibility needed to cope with a future that is unpredictable in many ways. To solve this problem, what should we seek in the way of solutions? What should we eliminate from present practice, and what should we add? What can we learn from previous experience in zoning or in other fields?

To examine these questions, let us now put a first-class factory on a sizable tract in a first-class residential neighborhood. Let us accept for the moment the purposes of zoning stated in the standard enabling act and see whether location of the factory in this neighborhood promotes or defeats those purposes.

The plant is a handsome structure with park-like landscaping and wide peripheral open spaces. It draws most of its employees from the general neighborhood. It does not require frequent heavy trucking. It does not create noise, dust, fumes, odors, vibration, electromagnetic interference, fire, or explosive hazards above normal levels in the residential area. It has concealed parking and service areas.

Would the location of this plant "lessen congestion in the streets?" Quite possibly. By bringing a place of employment closer to the residences of the employed, it would lessen traffic congestion in the general street pattern of the city. It might lessen neighborhood traffic congestion as well, or at least not increase it, particularly if most of the wage earners in the area now drive past the tract on their way to work across town. Congestion in the streets is a matter of timing as well as volume, and the times of peak locally-bound traffic probably would not coincide with peaks of principal in-bound or out-bound traffic. Trips to school and work could be combined. Some employees might even walk. Given the right circumstances, a plant in a residential district might well lessen congestion in the streets.

Would the plant in this location "secure safety from fire, panic, and other dangers?" As much so, certainly, as the same plant located elsewhere. More so if there should be a real civil defense emergency or natural disaster, since workers would not be jamming major arteries in long, frantic journeys home.

Would the plant "promote health and the general welfare; provide adequate light and air; prevent the overcrowding of land; avoid undue concentration of population?" Yes. Would it "facilitate the adequate provision of transportation?" Certainly, for reasons outlined above under congestion in the streets. What would it do toward facilitating the adequate provision of parks? It would provide park-like open space, which would not be there if the same land were used for residences.

What about the "character of the district?" The plant would be as much in keeping with surrounding residential areas as would a school. In fact, it would be far less objectionable in its operational side effects than most schools. Would such a plant be in keeping with the neighborhood's "peculiar suitability for particular uses?" Most assuredly. What about "conserving the value of buildings?" (This poorly worded phrase in the standard enabling act would mean more as "conserving the value of *property*.") Such a plant, in such a setting, should not only conserve but raise the value of surrounding property.

Is this plant in this location in accord with sound planning principles? Would it or would it not contribute to the declared purposes of the very zoning that bars it? Are we or are we not going to do anything about changing an obsolete system which often defeats its own ends?

An alternative approach

Most thinking planners rejoiced when building codes shifted from specification to performance types. Before this shift, the exact manner of structural fabrication was prescribed: the size of lumber, the spacing of supports, the manner in which bricks should be laid in a wall, etc. In a performance code, the wall or roof or door that provides safety, strength, fire protection, etc., is permitted, regardless of materials or assembly techniques.

Acting on this principle, we should work harder for land-use controls that operate in the same way. We have an entering wedge in our timid experiments with industrial performance standards. We might well move on to more general use of performance standards. These should do two things. First, they should control *characteristics* of use in such a way as to reduce neighbor-to-neighbor frictions. Second, they should control location, scale, balance, and timing of uses to the extent that we can honestly relate such controls to the public interest.

A performance-standards approach to land-use regulation seems to require greater use of development policy and less reliance on conventional master plan mapping. Suggesting this change will of course stir up a storm. One is needed to clear the air. As we have said in more detail elsewhere,[1] planning must sort out what it can and cannot do, and it must go about its job differently.

Performance standards

One of the first things which becomes apparent in any effort to think through the problem of improving present forms of zoning is that it should be possible to *lessen* land-use segregation and still protect the public interest. In theory, it might be possible to eliminate district boundaries entirely. In practice, we can certainly reduce the number of districts. Moves are on foot in this direction.

Working with a development policy statement prepared by Hugh Pomeroy shortly before he died, a village near New York City was considering establishment of a nonresidential district (rather than a patchwork of office, light commercial, general commercial, light industrial, and heavy industrial districts).

Pomeroy's policy statement is as follows:

Taking into account considerations of:

(a) the conservation of existing and potential property values in the Village;
(b) the character of existing development in the Village;
(c) the physical situation of the Village and the suitability of the Village for various uses;
(d) the physical situation of the Village and the functional relationship of the uses of the land therein to the existing

1. See "Planning Ahead: Adventures in the Unexpected Obvious," p. 3.

and prospective development of the inter-community area. . . .

It is determined:

(a) that the most appropriate predominant use of land throughout the Village consists of low-density one-family residential development, carefully regulated as to quality;

(b) that all other uses in the Village shall be either

1. related to such residential uses in a community sense, as schools, churches, and other community institutions; or
2. economically related to such residential use by reason of contributing to a tax base for the Village which will make possible the adequate provision of the public facilities and services that are necessary for sound residential development;

(c) that all such nonresidential uses shall be limited in location, size and character to the extent that they will satisfactorily perform their respective functions in a manner that will not detract from the predominantly low-density one-family character of the Village or hinder further development of like nature and quality.

We can treat one of the village's zoning problems as a test case. Separated from the rest of the municipality by a 500-foot, limited-access highway is a substantial area facing a tremendous plant on one side and surrounded entirely by major traffic arteries. The part of the plant property inside corporate boundaries is now zoned industrial. The remainder of the isolated area, now zoned single-family residential, is not suited for high-quality residential development, and the municipality has been trying for several years to make up its mind how to handle it. The owner of a considerable part of the problem area is understandably anxious to develop his property, but not for residential use.[2]

Using the Pomeroy statement of development policy as the primary guide, the area would be set aside as a nonresidential district. It would be open to nonresidential uses meeting certain requirements, without distinction as to whether these uses were commercial or industrial.

2. Pomeroy was not responsible for the delay. His brief work in inserting a solid patch on a weak zoning ordinance only serves as a point of departure for what has been proposed.

The first performance-standard screening to be applied would come directly from the statement of development policy. Does the proposed use relate to residential uses in the village in a community sense, as schools, churches, and other community institutions do? Or does it relate economically to such residential use by contributing to a tax base which will make possible public facilities and services necessary for sound residential development? Will the proposed use be limited in location, size, and character so that it will not detract from the predominantly low-density, one-family character of the village or hinder further development of like nature and quality? If the answers to these questions are affirmative, the first test has been passed.

The second performance-standard screening would be with regard to site planning. Although Pomeroy did not propose the nonresidential district as such, he set the stage with general language which can be borrowed for the new proposal. Nonresidential districts are

> intended to provide a means for the establishment of the types of use outlined . . . in a manner in keeping with modern practice as to group design of buildings . . . , provision of adequate off-street parking, and safe and convenient traffic access and pedestrian circulation, and in harmony with the character of the neighborhood in which such uses are located. . . . In considering any site plan hereunder, the Planning Board and the Building Inspector shall endeavor to assure safety and convenience of traffic movement, both within the limits of the site and in relation to access streets; harmonious and beneficial relation among the buildings and uses of the sites; and satisfactory and harmonious relation between the site and contiguous lands and buildings and adjacent neighborhoods; all in furtherance of the purposes of this ordinance.

This means, in effect, site plan approval of each project, extending beyond the project itself to the relationship of individual projects to each other. The generalized statement needs considerable detailing, some of which is provided in the third screening.

The third performance-standard screening would involve characteristics of use. Here the conventional industrial performance standards would be applied (with appropriate ranges selected—proximity to New York City eases instrumentation and administration problems), plus some additional ones—standards relating to timing of principal traffic impact with respect to existing peak loads on surrounding major streets; standards for off-street parking, loading, and service areas; standards with respect to signs and lighting.

There would also be yard requirements, here again in relation to function rather than in the form of arbitrary figures picked out of thin air.

There are several noteworthy things about the approach sketched briefly here. It abandons extreme segregation in favor of controlled integration. It allows each case to be considered on its merits, but states what merits are to be considered. It encourages site planning and development in relation to surrounding planning and surrounding development—not in accordance with fixed rules having little demonstrable relation to public benefits.

Developing detailed standards

Turning now from the general to the particular, the same approach can be used on details. Take yards as an example.

Why is a yard? What do we expect it to do? If the things a yard is expected to do are done otherwise—by walls, air conditioning, location of windows, location of use areas in and out of buildings on adjacent properties, etc.—the yard is not needed. If the things a yard is expected to do are not done otherwise, the yard should be designed and shaped to do them.

Some functions of yards are: to satisfy aesthetic requirements and provide room for greenery; to prevent overcrowding of land;[3] to prevent spread of fire and facilitate firefighting; to afford general and service access; to accommodate landscaping and outdoor facilities (including outdoor storage, off-street parking, and outdoor recreation); to provide the visibility necessary for traffic safety; and to provide view. There may be others. If so, they should be considered in establishing yard dimensions and orientation. But unless the regulation is related to some logical function, it is arbitrary.

Many of our present yard requirements make little sense in terms of yard functions.

In a multiple-family residential district, side yards shall be a minimum of 3 feet in width, and combined side yards shall be a total of 12

3. What exactly is "overcrowding of land" under existing technology? Is it two people per acre or a thousand people per acre, and by what standards may the first be too many and the latter below the permitted maximum?

feet in width, provided however that combined width of side yards need not exceed 20% of the width of the lot. Rear yards shall be a minimum of 40 feet in depth, provided however that accessory buildings may be constructed in a required rear yard if no portion is closer than 20 feet to the main building, nor closer than 5 feet to any property line. Buildings exceeding 35 feet in height shall provide 1 foot of additional side or rear yard for each foot that height exceeds 35 feet.

Given two 35-foot buildings six feet apart, with overhanging roofs cutting the sky opening to three or four feet, the space provided is totally inadequate for most of the stated purposes. It might be far better to permit row housing with appropriate firebreaks. Why require a high building next to a low building to have a larger side yard? The number of people exposed to views of each other is not increased. The noise levels on the lower floors remain the same. The amount of light and air available will still be inadequate.

There was once a sound reason for the large rear yard requirements. Stables *should* be separated from houses. In our times, for architectural flexibility, it would be far better to reduce minimum rear yard dimensions and thereby increase the buildable area, using lot-coverage requirements to assure open space greater than that provided by the presently required yards.

To assure adequate light, we would do well to consider drafting regulations based on solar orientation. To assure adequate air, there is promise in a combination of air conditioning devices and housing code requirements, with additional controls relating to privacy (location of windows *a la* FHA's techniques on multiple-family structures). For functional open space, there is the possibility of regulating the shape and location of such space above and beyond yards and lot-coverage requirements, if we choose to go that far.

In summary, we have too long been hypnotized by a specification-type code filled with complexities which fail to achieve basic purposes. Indeed, some present regulations actually work to the detriment of sensible land-use control. Zoning in its present form has moved generally toward more and more segregation as a means for reducing frictions between uses. We have failed to seek basic causes for frictions and means to remove them.

It is possible to move toward performance-type land-use controls which would give greater flexibility of land use and still protect the public interest. It is past time to do so.

Zoning—a mad tea party?

> *"I want a clean cup," interrupted the Hatter. "Let's all move one place on."*
>
> *He moved on as he spoke, and the Dormouse followed him. The March Hare moved into the Dormouse's place, and Alice rather unwillingly took the place of the March Hare. The Hatter was the only one who got any advantage from the change, and Alice was a good deal worse off than before, as the March Hare had just upset the milk jug into his plate.*
>
> —Alice in Wonderland

In recent years, in response to impulsive suggestions from a variety of Mad Hatters, there has been a considerable amount of moving "one place on"—or two or three—in zoning. Confusion mounts when a participant insists on occupying several seats at the same time, and becomes compounded when simultaneous moves take place in all directions. It isn't quite clear who, if anyone, gets any advantage from the change.

What is said here is not a plea for the status quo. Zoning will not stand still, and considering the shape it is in, nobody in his right mind should want it to. But the change should be in the direction of improvement, rather than a move from occasional mild disorder to universal chaos.

As a matter of law, practice, court interpretation, and tradition, zoning has rules. The rules are generally similar across the country. They are similar because local zoning is permitted by state enabling acts, and the enabling acts are largely derived from a common ancestor. The usual zoning rules (what might be called "Euclidean" zoning) fit reasonably well into the American system of government, with its division of functions and its checks and balances. They fit well because they were designed for that form of government, put together and applied in that form of government, and tested by the courts of that government.

There are plenty of problems in current zoning. Does this mean that Euclidean concepts and principles should be overhauled? Obviously they should—*if* the problems arise from the rules, if changing the rules will solve the problems, and if the new rules can be fitted into the larger framework of American government and the democratic process.

However, the vast bulk of evidence indicates that most current zoning problems do not arise from application of conventional rules, but from failure to apply them. The failure usually does not arise from defects in the rules, but from impatient unwillingness to stop long enough to find out what they are or certain conveniences inherent in not knowing (or appearing not to know) what they are. Under these circumstances, a mere change in the rules isn't likely to help much.

To take one prime example: in conventional zoning it is clearly the intent to provide for a division into separate legislative, executive, and judicial functions. This is familiar and traditional in American government, and a statement of specific rules, as we understand them, comes later in this article.

The "new look"?

Consider now some examples of the Mad Tea Party approach, none of which is hypothetical. Obviously none of these cases fits conventional zoning rules. The real question is whether they spell out a new pattern that will be an improvement over Euclidean zoning and will fit well into our governmental system.

A city commission directs a building inspector not to issue a permit for a use the zoning ordinance allows in the location proposed.

A zoning ordinance provides that churches may be built only if the legislative body issues what amounts to a special exception, which it may grant or refuse without reference to any standards.

A state supreme court declares use variances by boards of adjustment illegal on grounds that such actions represent legislation by a nonlegislative body. So one city in the state gets a local act passed in the legislature permitting its board of adjustment to issue use variances anyway, and in other cities boards of adjustment continue to issue use variances without bothering to get special acts.

A local governing body adopts a comprehensive plan, showing an area as intended for multiple dwellings. It adopts a zoning law based on the plan, indicating the area as zoned for multiple dwellings, subject to limitations on density, yard sizes, off-street parking, and related matters. It establishes a board of adjustment with the usual powers, including the handling of special exceptions. But it requires that before a multiple dwelling can be erected in the area planned and zoned for multiple dwellings, a "use permit" must be obtained—not from the administrative official nor from the board of adjustment, but from the governing body. By way of explanation, a member of the governing body states publicly that his group hasn't really decided whether multiple dwellings belong just anywhere in the area zoned for multiple dwellings or not, and proposes to consider each individual case as it comes up instead of making any general rule.

A governing body operating under the standard zoning enabling act secures from the state legislature an amendment inserting the governing body in the appeals procedure between the board of adjustment and the courts. The amendment further provides that there can be no appeal to the board of adjustment from an act of the administrative official when he is carrying out a specific order from the governing body, and gives these elected officials the power to do anything the board of adjustment might do (without the restrictions applied to the board of adjustment) and "to take or direct to be taken such further proceedings or action as in its judgment should be taken"—without any restrictions whatever.

The new policy?

If these interminglings of function are a good thing and result in better government, it is time to develop a set of basic principles that fit the new approach. The improved framework, if that is the word, would permit the amorphous remnants of erstwhile legislative, executive, and judicial bodies to float about freely, performing or not performing their own or each other's functions—if they feel like it.

Conservatives may feel that this would add confusion to a situation in which there is already evidence of an oversupply. But if this kind of arrangement is needed to improve zoning, let's have it. Certainly in our complex society there will be a few proponents of the anarchistic philosophy of operating with no governmental principles at all, or of making up new principles for each case as it comes up.

A parting (?) look at established rules

It might be well to look once more at the existing rules before we abandon them. As we understand them, this is their intent:

1. Zoning law shall be passed, amended, or repealed only by the governing body. This power may not be delegated to an administrative official or agency, nor to an appointed board. It is reserved to a legislative body elected by and responsible to the people.

In the law, standards and procedures shall be provided to guide the administrative official or agency, the planning commission and staff, and the board of adjustment as to their respective parts in the zoning operation. The law, and any standards or procedures included in the law, shall be in accordance with the enabling legislation empowering the governing body to act in zoning matters, the Constitution of the United States, the state constitution, and any other laws limiting or defining the powers of the governing body and protecting the rights of individual citizens. The zoning law shall also conform to any clear-cut interpretations of enabling and related legislation by the higher courts.

Having passed the zoning law, with standards and procedures for administration, neither the governing body as a whole nor any of its members shall interfere with its application in particular cases. If the governing body desires to change administrative procedures or standards, or to alter other provisions of the law, the change shall be made in the form of amendment to the law.

2. The administrative official shall be guided by the letter and clear intent of the law. Where he is in doubt, he will let the board of adjustment make the interpretation. He will not "correct" or "improve" the law independently, nor adopt administrative procedures at variance with the requirements of the law as written, nor issue permits or certificates other than in accord with the law. If it appears to him that the law is defective or not clear or needs elaboration or improvement, in the course of good administration he will see to it that the matter is brought to the attention of the governing body for action.

3. The board of adjustment shall be guided by the letter and clear intent of the law. Part of the board's operations (concerning special exceptions) may be considered to be of an executive or administrative nature. Part of its operations (involving variances and appeals from acts or interpretations of the administrative official) may be considered to be of a judicial nature. None of its operations shall be of a legislative nature.

The board of adjustment shall not issue use variances amounting to amendments of the zoning ordinance, nor issue special exceptions not specifically provided for in the zoning ordinance or not meeting the conditions required in the zoning ordinance, nor shall the board depart from the procedures and requirements of the zoning law in any matter before it.

If inability to grant relief or to take other action that appears proper to the board indicates a deficiency in the law, the board will see to it that the deficiency is brought to the attention of the governing body for action, but it will not exceed the powers granted to it by law, regardless of the circumstances of a case or class of cases.

4. The planning commission and staff shall be responsible for the development and maintenance of the comprehensive plan. Zoning should be in accordance with the comprehensive plan. Therefore, when changes are made in the plan, the planning agency shall advise the governing body of any corresponding changes that should be made in zoning. The governing body shall refer any proposed changes in zoning originating outside the planning agency to the agency for study and recommendations. And the board of adjustment shall refer all proposed special exceptions or variances of a nature likely to have substantial effect on the comprehensive plan to the planning agency for its recommendations.

(In the zoning law, the governing body may desire to set apart classes of special exceptions and variances most likely to affect the comprehensive plan for study and recommendations by the planning agency before final action can be taken by the board of adjustment, using language similar to the following: "Upon favorable recommendation by the planning board, the board of adjustment may permit. . . .")

These rules seem to be a common-sense application of the familiar principle of division of powers. Like most of the rules of Euclidean zoning, they work rather well—when applied. Certainly they appear to be good enough to build on. Surely they are not so defective that they should be abandoned in favor of the Mad Tea Party approach.

If the principle of division of powers is good, the rules should stand. If the rules stand, they should be observed. If they are observed, there will be a great deal better zoning and a great deal less litigation.

Contract zoning? *it's all "contract" zoning*

All legal zoning is contract zoning; all contract zoning is conditional. Approach the matter on the basis of common sense. This is where law begins, regardless of where it may get to in the hands of practitioners expert in the art of purposeful confusion.

Blackstone defines a contract as an agreement upon a sufficient consideration to do or not to do a particular thing. It doesn't stretch this too much to include permitting the doing or prohibiting the doing of a particular thing. The consideration is the condition in the contract. If the parties agree upon the conditions and the terms are met, the contract becomes effective, if not, not. There is an exchange of one thing for another, a *quid pro quo*.

The state legislature, from its established position in the governmental chain of command, says to local government: "You may zone, if you will do it for the following purposes and use the following procedures." The city or county usually signifies explicit agreement with these terms: "Whereas Chapter 999, State Statutes, empowers. . . . Now therefore, in accordance with the purposes, requirements, and procedures set forth therein, be it enacted. . . . " The party of the first part (the state) grants to the party of the second part (the local body) the right to zone, conditioned upon considerations involving purposes, methods, administrative procedures, etc. Whether or not the party of the second part indicates explicit agreement with these terms, the terms are enforceable. Zoning not in accord with enabling legislation is headed for trouble in the courts.

Local zoning may be said to be the result of a contract between state and local government, and courts have both upheld this arrangement and indicated that zoning in its absence is unlawful.

In day-to-day workings, zoning actions seem similarly in line with the Blackstone definition of a contract. A man wishes to build. He submits an application and plans demonstrating compliance with the pre-set conditions of the city, and the permit is issued. If he builds without a permit, or fails to conform with the conditions of the ordinance regarding uses, building height, lot and yard size, signs, off-street parking, and so on, he is in violation of the ordinance. To the extent that he may not build without the permit, with all that the permit implies concerning agreement with the considerations established, he must contract with the city, and the zoning is obviously conditional. Without such contracts and conditions, zoning would be meaningless and ineffective.

Perhaps these two basic examples are sufficient to support the initial statement—all legal zoning is contract zoning; all legal zoning is conditional. The second statement may be superfluous—there can be no contract without conditions, or considerations, as Blackstone calls them.

This is not to say that *all* contract zoning or conditional zoning is legal. The point being made here is that in essence zoning is contractual and contains conditions. The reason the point is being made is that the average lawyer (and on occasion an above-average lawyer) fills the room with ominous thunderings when contract or conditional zoning is mentioned. This has caused many a planning commission to flee a perfectly safe and sane position to seek shelter from threatened judicial lightning. Planning commissions and city councils and county commissions should stop being frightened by tag lines and law book labels for indexing and sort out what seems legal from what does not on the basis of understanding equity and common sense. Usually the courts will go along with this approach.

We no more believe that contract or conditional zoning is illegal, in itself, than that touchdowns became illegal during the current football season because a large number of apparent touchdown plays were called back by officials for infraction of rules.

In zoning, as in football, there have been violations of the basic rules. In zoning, these violations involve trading the wrong quids for the wrong quos, the wrong quids for the right quos, the right quids for the wrong quos, and using the wrong methods of exchange. Various combinations of these basic errors are committed, and any one of them, or any combination of them, will cause the courts to call foul. The judiciary normally indicates with varying degrees of exactitude wherein the error lay, but the results get more notice than the explanation. Hence there is a too prevalent impression that all contract zoning and all conditional zoning is in a class with murder, arson, and grand larceny. Planning commissions are generally opposed to murder, arson, and grand larceny, from which it is made to follow that they should be opposed to contract or conditional zoning. Somewhere in this reasoning there is a fallacy. If contract zoning involves elements of grand larceny, an honest planning board should be opposed to it, but the two things should not become inextricably intertwined.

Quids, quos, and exchange methods

A helpful article on whither things have drifted appeared in the November 1965 issue of *Zoning Digest*. In "Contract Zoning and Conditional Zoning," Enos P. Schaffer distinguishes, with hypothetical illustrations and case citations, between what he calls "true contract zoning, conditions before zoning, and conditional zoning." The article is useful as a framework for discussion, as a warning of some things to avoid, and as a point of departure for some observations about how things might be done legally without all this claptrap.

"True contract" zoning is exemplified by Schaffer as a hypothetical case involving a request for rezoning for an apartment development which the city would very much like to have. So that he can obtain a mortgage committment, the developer asks the city for assurance that, once granted, the zoning will not be changed for four years. The city rezones, making a separate agreement not to change the zoning for four years, or including language to this effect in the ordinance.

Either course is void, says Schaffer, citing C. J. S. *Municipal Corporations* §139 (1949):

> A municipal corporation may . . . [not] surrender or contract away its governmental functions and powers, and any attempt to barter or surrender them is invalid. Accordingly, a municipal corporation cannot, by contract, ordinance, or other means, surrender or curtail its legislative powers and duties, its police power, or its administrative authority.

There is more to this iceberg than shows above the surface. Assume in the circumstances above that the city has officially adopted a comprehensive plan, after careful consideration of a broad range of public needs and objectives. In the general plan it is made clear that more apartment housing is needed in the city. The land is in the middle of an area where apartment development is entirely logical. The proposal meets criteria adopted earlier for apartment rezoning and is in accord with the district regulations in existence for apartment zoning. There is nothing arbitrary or capricious about either the plan or the zoning proposed. The city has well and truly exercised its legislative powers and its administrative authority and proposes to continue to do so.

It would appear desirable in the public interest (as well as the private, in this case) for a city to be able to make a formal declaration that for a reasonably limited time it believes its plans, and ordinances based upon them, to be solid. For example, we believe that a city should be able to say: "We have enough land now zoned commercial to meet requirements for the next 20 years, and half of it is vacant. Therefore we will not grant any applications for commercial rezoning for two years."

Or to take an example closer to the hearts of planners: "Any rezoning must be in accord with the comprehensive plan which the city has officially adopted," a broader generalization which might include the former.

Not mentioned by Schaffer, but perhaps offering some hope, is the observation by Charles S. Rhyne in *Municipal Law* (1957, p. 261):

> A municipal governing body may bind its successors by contracts for a reasonable length of time for public purposes, but generally it may not bind its successors for personal or professional services; or abrogate or forego, for itself or its successors, any of its legislative functions.

If the local body formally declares its intent to *hold* to its legislative determinations (for public purposes clearly demonstrated, set forth, and defined) for a reasonable period (which may include some succession in membership of the governing body) does it "surrender or curtail," "abrogate or forego," any of its legislative functions, powers, and duties, or may it truly be said to be *exercising* them in a manner promoting public ends?

One supporting case cited by Schaffer provides a clearer distinction between blacks and whites. A city rezoned property from residential to commercial on recorded condition that the use to be made would be only for a funeral home, with automatic reversion to residential zoning if other use was made of the land. The court said that in giving commercial zoning, the legislative body may not act in this manner. The Schaffer article does not indicate the reasoning, but valid arguments are not hard to supply. If the applicant gets commercial zoning, he gets all of it, otherwise he is deprived of rights available to others in the same district. "All property zoned alike should be treated alike."

And of course the automatic reverter clause won't hold. It violates state procedural requirements for notice and hearing in connection with zoning amendments. Here there was the wrong method of exchange, and undue limitations on the quo. The quid may have been all right.

(The unfortunate thing about cases like this is the mechanical ineptitude of the solution. Presumably the funeral home was at the edge of an existing commercial district, otherwise the spot zoning issue would have been raised. In such a location, the ordinance might well have provided for funeral homes, certain types of professional and business offices, and certain other relatively innocuous uses as logical buffering operations within a set distance from the common boundaries of commercial or industrial and residential districts subject to detailed requirements. Funeral homes might have been permitted outright in certain residential districts, again with detailed requirements relating to major streets, lot and yard sizes, location of functions and related buffering, hours of operation, off-street parking space and space for forming processions, signs, lighting, and so on. Or funeral homes might have been made permissible as special exceptions in certain residential districts, subject to similar guides and standards and with the possibility of adding appropriate conditions and safeguards. With all these perfectly legal solutions available, the city in question chose one which was not.)

Conditions to be met before rezoning, in the Schaffer article, include situations in which the city indicates (without guarantee) that if certain conditions were met, it would probably consider rezoning proper. Some of the conditions appear to us to be appropriate, others seem to be a form of blackmail, including measures for forcing the owner to remedy defects of the ordinance, but only with regard to his own property.

The narrow line dividing these from "true contract" cases is that here the city merely says that if the owner "voluntarily" does certain things, his chances would be better. Nothing is guaranteed.

The initial example is an application for change from residential to commercial zoning. The tract is on a minor street, backing without an alley upon a residential district in which there are private homes and a girls' school. The city suggests that dedication of land for street widening and an alley would make the land more appropriate for consideration for commercial use. The owner dedicates. The city suggests further a restrictive convenant on the land, prohibiting liquor establishments, bowling alleys, and buildings over 20 feet high. The owner goes along. "Then the city adopts an ordinance rezoning the property, without any mention of conditions in the ordinance, or denies the rezoning." This is legal.

The blackjack is effective here, but the manner in which it is swung lacks finesse, and one of the reasons for swinging it is at least dubious. Matters get worse in an elaboration of the case discussed later, but alternative approaches based on this much of it will serve to indicate that there are ways to handle everything which was done which are more equitable and open and which are clearly within the rules. We think there is major opportunity for abuse in the method used, and that this sort of thing should be discouraged, whether or not it is technically legal. The city might also have hinted that it would consider the proposed zoning more proper if the owner bought tickets to the Policemen's Ball, gave half the land for a park, or guaranteed support for the present administration in the next election, "without any mention of conditions in the ordinance."

The conditions could have been handled in a more businesslike and forthright way. In the amendment section of the ordinance, it might have been provided that no land would be considered for rezoning to commercial unless it was on a street with stated minimum right-of-way and was served by an alley (and was either adjacent to an existing commercial district or contained X acres, plus whatever other specifications make sense in terms of public interest). This sets terms under which *all* applications for commercial zoning will be considered—not granted, necessarily—and avoids the appearance of having the city make up its rules as it goes along. The conditions are set openly in the *ordinance,* and are demonstrably related to zoning purposes and sound planning policy.

The second set of considerations seems both unfair and unnecessary in the form proposed. Here the applicant is caused to do to himself what the law could not do to him. If the city may not reduce one man's rights by contract as a condition for rezoning, where is the equity in reducing another man's prospective rights as a sort of under-the-table means for insuring merely that the zoning application will be more favorably considered? The city feels that it is necessary to protect this particular girls' school, these particular residences, against deprivation of light and air (the 20-foot height limitation—which would be extraordinarily low for a *residential* area, let alone a commercial district) and against noises (liquor establishments and bowling alleys). If such regulations are in the general public interest, why not make them general regulations? If they are not, why stick this applicant with them?

Assuming general desirability, the situation could be handled (as in the preceding instance) in a much more open and direct manner and without raising any hair-line legal issues. The answer is transitional zoning:

> Where a residential district adjoins a commercial district for a distance of X feet within the commercial district from the boundary, uses shall exclude liquor establishments and bowling alleys, and height limitations and yards adjacent to the residential district boundary shall be as for the residential district.

Purists may argue that this violates the requirement that regulations shall apply equally within the commercial district. As a practical matter, the transitional area is a district unto itself, with regulations applying equally within it. If it makes anybody happier, draw a line around it and give it a separate designation.

Schaffer's summary on conditions to be met before rezoning points out that here persons other than the city take actions which would make their proposals more acceptable, but without assurance of rezoning, whereas in "true contract zoning" the city limits its power to legislate. He says that since the applicant has no recourse for breach of contract (there is no contract), he "would not 'deliver' the deeds of rights of way to the city, but would merely hand them to someone in the city for 'delivery' to the city on passage of the zoning ordinance or for return should the ordinance fail, the person holding the instruments acting as escrow agent."

Whether such courses are legal or not, a pious hope is in order that more open, direct, and equitable methods will find increasing use. Our own summary would be somewhat different from Schaffer's:

1. Conditions to be met before rezoning may extend beyond anything stated in the ordinance and may be arbitrarily attached on a case-by-case basis without any stated general policy. The city doesn't guarantee that the zoning will be granted if the conditions are met, but makes it moderately clear that the zoning won't be granted unless the conditions are met, whether they are equitable or not.

2. It is legal, by this informal process, to induce an owner to place restrictions on himself which could not be imposed by the zoning sought, so long as all that is offered by the city is enhanced hope. In contrast, it is illegal for the city openly and formally to deprive the applicant of rights generally available to others in a district, or to guarantee rezoning in exchange for abandonment of such rights.

3. It is best not to mention any such deals in the ordinance. On the contrary, have all records indicate that deeds, covenants, dedications, etc., are not conditioned on rezoning and have nothing to do with it. Having the lie in the record makes it all right. If any note is made in the ordinance relating to such matters, make it a disclaimer of any relationship between the boodle and the action taken.

4. To avoid misunderstandings, the payoff should not be made until after the rezoning is consummated. Manage this so that nobody can welsh. Since the lid would blow off if there were recorded agreements, do it in a roundabout way through a satchel-man both sides can trust.

Conditional zoning in Schaffer's article uses the same example as the one on conditions to be met before rezoning, but with a further element. This time the city is concerned about the fact that there is already an adequate supply of vacant commercially zoned land in the area. "The city does not want to give existing owners of vacant business land a monopoly, nor does it believe the public will be served by aiding land speculation if there is no good faith intent to develop the land for business use. If the owner, however, improved the land as proposed, the public welfare would be served."

Before getting into methodology, how's that again on purpose? Schaffer doesn't cover this, but we propose to. There is already an adequate supply of vacant commercial land in the area, but the city doesn't want to aid speculation or give a monopoly so it proposes to zone more land than is needed because of the ownership pattern, land prices, and the intent of individuals to sell for what the market will bear. Thus land-use planning becomes an element of reduced weight in the comprehensive plan. Where land prices are high and the ownership pattern is monopolistic or speculative, the overriding consideration is creation of a sufficient surplus in the category involved to bring prices down. Never mind what it does to the plan.

Such enabling legislation as we have seen doesn't include language making control of land prices one of the public purposes of zoning. Nor is it generally considered in the public interest to bust the plan in order to bust speculators. (The action here apparently didn't involve the usual inverse relationship between available land and public interest. Where there is more commercial land than is reasonably needed, the price is low and there is a tendency for everybody and his brother to establish suicidal business enterprises and go broke, blighting the landscape with dead or dying enterprises.) So in this case, it appears that the objective was wrong. Now consider two methods for attaining it which Schaffer offers for purposes of discussion.

Under Method A, the city rezones, with the ordinance *to take effect* only if a building permit is issued:

(a) for construction of improvements according to plans submitted; and
(b) within a year from the date the ordinance is adopted; and
(c) if the required right-of-way is dedicated for street widening and the alley and the restrictive covenant is recorded prior to getting the permit.

Under Method B, the city rezones immediately, but provides that the zoning *shall not remain in effect more than one year,* unless a building permit has been issued with conditions as above.

Discussing Method A first, Schaffer says:

> This type is an extension of the situation in which the owner met conditions before rezoning. It merely extends the time the conditions must be met to some date after the city has acted. . . . The advantage of the Type A conditional ordinance is that rezoning never goes into effect until the conditions subsequent are met. Thus there is no ordinance to revoke, either by action or by implication. It stands on firmer legal ground than the ordinance that goes into effect and provides for automatic repeal upon failure of the conditions subsequent to be met (Type B).
>
> For either type no further action is required by the city. There is no written agreement, and there is no provision in repealing the conditional ordinance at any time or from further amending the zoning. . . .

The conditional ordinance does, however, give the owner a greater amount of security. If he makes the building and financial commitments and proceeds as proposed, his rezoning will be forthcoming, since the only act required to put the rezoning into effect is his act of getting a permit.

There are some things about these conclusions which deserve discussion. As a minor point, it would hardly be true that no further action is required by the city under Method B. The land has been zoned. If it is to be rezoned at the end of the year, it seems essential that full amendment procedures be followed.

As a second point, Ernest Bartley, in looking over our draft notes for this article, observed that both procedures suggested appear to delegate legislative power to an individual. Whether the ordinance takes effect (Method A) or remains in effect (Method B) depends on whether an individual gets a permit. Related to this, Rathkopf, at 29-1, *The Law of Zoning and Planning* (3rd ed.; 1960), states:

> The rule generally followed in deciding the validity or invalidity of consent provisions is that if the action or inaction of the property owners has the effect of legislation, then the consent provision is deemed to fall within the forbidden delegation of legislative power and such provision is invalid.

To the bartering or surrendering of powers about which Schaffer expressed alarm in relation to contract zoning, it appears that delegating powers should be added as a source of concern, and delegation of power is what is done by either of the methods proposed.

Perhaps the most important point of all is that both approaches seem to us to involve the kind of contracts which *are* illegal, and not merely because of the delegation of power. This is not a situation in which it is suggested that the applicant do something to improve his *chances* of getting zoning. The city has made it clear that the zoning is granted, provided the applicant does certain things. There is no question that if the applicant conforms to the requirements, he gets his zoning. The contract is explicit.

Under these circumstances, the city imposes directly the limitations on bowling alleys, liquor and height, and the requirements for rights-of-way, and these are a binding part of the contract. The quids and the quos are clearly set forth, together with the method of exchange.

What then is the substantial difference between this approach and any other by which the city itself applies, as an inseparable part of the zoning, limitations which do not apply generally in the district? The zoning is ineffective *until the special requirements set by the city for this particular parcel are met*.

A perspicacious court might see a persuasive parallel between this case and the one in which the applicant got commercial zoning—but only if he erected a funeral home. Here the applicant gets commercial zoning—but only if he builds within a specified time, stays below 20 feet, and avoids bowling alleys and liquor establishments. In either instance, the regulations applying to one piece of land within the district are different from those applying generally, and the differences are the direct result of city action setting terms for granting or withholding the zoning. Land zoned only *if* is in effect not zoned *unless*.

Morals and advice

Perhaps too much space has been devoted to legalistic hairsplitting. These complex rituals can obviously lead to trouble. If at all possible, they should be avoided. Usually they can be. Most of the things which should be done can be done in a forthright and clearly legal manner, and the things which shouldn't be done, shouldn't be done at all.

The meat of the matter is this. General rules for zoning are set by the state and can be changed only by the state. Local governments must work within them, creating detailed zoning with demonstrable relation to the purposes set forth in the state act, applying equitably in the manner required by the state act, adopted, amended, and administered according to methods and procedures outlined in the state act.

So long as the game is played well within the rules, courts aren't likely to blow the whistle at local government. When the play is marginal or worse, the referee will step in. On borderline cases, officials make some bad calls and aren't always consistent. When fouls are really foul, the courts are sound in their judgments.

The safest and best approach to local zoning is first to know the rules and second to stay well within them. Local governments which know the rules and don't abide by them deserve to get into trouble. In most cases, local government gets into trouble because somebody who was supposed to know the rules didn't.

Don't worry about judicial interpretation of fine points on contract zoning, conditional zoning, or other esoteric matters unless you have studied the rules carefully and find there is no clearly authorized way to operate. If what you are trying to do is fair, if it well and truly accomplishes one or more of the public purposes of zoning, if you follow the procedures prescribed in the rules, it will be found in almost every case that there is a way to do it without running along the outer edges of the enabling legislation or beyond.

If what you are trying to do won't fit the rules, it is very likely you shouldn't be doing it. In those rare cases where the rules can't be made to encompass clearly appropriate action, get the rules changed at the state level—don't try to change them locally. The rules won't let you.

How to estimate chances for getting necessary zoning and how to make a successful zoning presentation

First we will arrive at an exact answer on your chances for getting necessary zoning. I now take the role of the local planner, and as the local planner I say to you:

"You don't have to estimate. You have a 100 per cent chance of getting the necessary zoning.

"Zoning is in accord with the comprehensive plan. I developed the comprehensive plan (or it was developed by consultants, or we really don't have one but I'm not going to admit it). I am pledged to protect and defend the comprehensive plan (whether we have one or not) which zoning is in aid of, and I'll explain to you what the plan is.

"The comprehensive plan (whether we have one or not) is a carefully reasoned scientific admixture of projects and related policies, reports, maps, and charts, all being continuously revised and therefore not available in current form for public consultation, which determines with admirable precision how the future should be structured. To help in this monumental task, we have computers into which we feed whatever information we can get, and which tell us (after a year or two of care and feeding) that whatever it is we were going to do anyway was right.

"Implementing planning, we have the zoning ordinance. As a developer, sir, all you have to do to get the necessary zoning is to select

This article was first presented to the National Association of Home Builders, School and Workshop Conference on "Keys to Successful Multi-family Housing," June 13, 1966.

land which is *already* zoned for the purpose for which you intend to use it. No strain—100 per cent. Well, mark that down a little because some of the neighbors out that way may put on pressure to get the zoning changed when they find out that you propose to use the land for a purpose the ordinance allows but they didn't know about."

With this, I relinquish the role of the local planner, having laid more groundwork than we can use. Now let's look at what a lot of developers are up to, and the way the planner can be expected to react to it.

The developer is interested in making a profit. To many planners, who get paid regularly whether they produce or not, making a profit is automatically sinful. If a profit is made, somewhere or other community virtue has been (to use a technical term) besmirched.

For maximum besmirchment, the developer starts by seeking land where the zoning is right (from the planner's point of view). That makes the price right from the developer's point of view because the price doesn't reflect the intensity of use the developer proposes. Then the developer comes to the planner and says: "What are my chances for getting the wrong zoning (from your point of view) so that I can make a profit because I paid a price reflecting zoning you thought was right?" Here again, there is no strain in arriving at an answer. Zero per cent. Well, mark that up a little because the planning commission or the city council doesn't always go along with the planner.

So there's your answer. Add 100 per cent to zero per cent (or 95 per cent to five per cent) and divide by two—50 per cent. This is the wrong answer, of course, and wrongly arrived at, but it is precise.

A very able lawyer once stated the moral to what I have just told you, and if you will be guided by it, your chances of having the necessary zoning, or of getting it, will be much better: "Never fight zoning. Always try to improve it."

The lawyer's record is instructive. First he lost most of his cases before the planning commission and the governing body and then won them in court. Then he lost most of his cases before the planning commission and won them before the governing body. Then the governing body decided he was improving the ordinance too much, hired a competent planning staff, and got the ordinance rewritten. From the lawyer's point of view, this was too bad. But a lot of his previous clients liked the new order of things. They now *had* the zoning they had had to fight for previously.

In a nutshell, your chances of *having* the zoning you need are excellent if you have a good zoning ordinance, based on a really intelligent comprehensive plan—and if you have a good project in a proper location. If you have a good ordinance and a bad project, your chances should be very bad indeed. That's why we have zoning. One question is of central importance: Do you deserve the zoning which you think is necessary?

If you have a bad zoning ordinance—and we have entirely too many of them—and a good project, you have a real problem.

How to make a successful zoning presentation

The best way to make a successful zoning presentation is to do it long before you need the zoning for a particular piece of land. Promote good local planning. Push for a good planning staff and planning commission. See to it that you get a good, modern zoning ordinance, and after you get it, support it. Given these things, if your proposal is appropriate, the land will be zoned for the purpose for which you intend to use it.

Most planners, planning commissioners, members of governing bodies, and judges (particularly those in the higher courts) believe that the general public welfare can be reasonably well defined, and that it should be defended against individual actions which might damage it. In defining patterns of desirable physical development, a sound plan defines the public welfare. A good zoning ordinance protects it. And a bad project—which can be conveniently defined as one which doesn't fit a good plan and zoning ordinance—is what the zoning ordinance is intended to protect the public welfare against.

On occasion, developers have been known to think: "I have my private rights, and among them is freedom to make a bundle, so to hell with everybody." It you have such thoughts, keep them well concealed, particularly when trying to get zoning. Big brother and little brother are watching you (and are paid to do it, partly with your money) and they have wide support from those you are saying to hell with.

Most developers make some kind of market analysis before they become committed to a project. This is good sense. There would be less concern at this session about how to make a successful zoning presentation if more developers made another kind of analysis before getting involved. It might be called a public interest analysis. The first part should be an honest appraisal of the plan and ordinance—from the point of view of the general public welfare. If you find that the plan and ordinance do what they should and the action you are considering doesn't fit, drop it. You'll be doing a public service, and you will also be saving yourself a lot of money and time.

If you find that the plan and ordinance don't do what they should—again in terms of the public welfare, not yours, and with public welfare extending to the future, and not merely stopping with the present—and that if they were properly amended, your project would fit, go on to the second part. This lays the foundation for a zoning presentation which is likely to be highly successful if the spade work is well done.

In specific terms, indicate what changes should be made to make the plan and ordinance serve the general public interest better. Appraise your chances for mustering support for the general change, and weigh the probable effectiveness of the support. If things look favorable to this point, check the attitudes of the planning staff, the planning commission, and the governing body about the proposal (making it clear while you are talking that there is broad support for the change). At this point, if the outlook is auspicious, venture a small option on the property, and continue to promote the change which is in the general public interest (and which, incidentally, will allow you to do what you want to do *because it is in accord with the general public interest*). This is a very strong position.

Now let's get to some nuts and bolts. Assuming that you have a sound proposal, and that you can prove it is in the public interest as well as your own, what's the approach? The first thing you should do is to decide what kind of a change you need. Usually the application is for a map change. Quite often a map change isn't the answer at all, and may be harder to get than something simpler and more effective.

Consider the following case. A developer wants to build townhouses in a single-family district. The ordinance defines multifamily structures as containing three or more dwelling units. Therefore, the townhouses must go in multifamily districts. The developer applies for a map change making his land multifamily, in the middle of a single-family district. The battle is on—the natives hit the warpath against apartments in their midst, attorneys call attention to the obvious spot zoning character of the proposed change, and the case is lost. There's no use going to court about it. The court won't reverse the decision.

Now consider this alternative. Propose that the definitions section of the ordinance be amended by the addition of the following:

Dwelling, one-family attached: A building containing not more than one dwelling unit, attached at the side or sides in a series of three or more buildings each containing not more than one dwelling unit. At points of attachment, such buildings shall be separated from each other by fire walls extending from footings through roofs without openings which would permit the spread of fire from one building to another. Such buildings shall each have a separate lot with dimensions meeting the requirements of the district, or be so located on land in the same ownership that individual lots meeting district requirements could be provided, in which case dimensions of such land shall not be reduced below those required for provision of separate lots. The term attached dwelling is intended to apply to townhouses, patio or atrium houses, or any form however termed which conforms to this definition.

To go with this, there would also be proposed amendment of certain district regulations, including perhaps the addition of cluster zoning provisions and some adaptation of side-yard requirements. I belabor the obvious point of side yards because I am currently helping to improve a zoning ordinance which permits townhouses if each (not each group, each townhouse) has 50-foot side yards.

Amendments of definitions and district regulations are often easier to get than map changes. If such changes have obvious merit (and particularly if they get planners, zoning administrators, or the governing body off hooks on which they have been often and painfully impaled) the formal proposal for amendment may come from within the governmental structure. This is an easy way for you to make a successful zoning presentation. All you have to do is to show up at a hearing (which somebody else has arranged) with as many supporters as you can muster and applaud the wisdom and foresightedness of the course your local government is planning to take.

Before promoting a zoning change, examine *all* the possible solutions to your problem, not just the one which seems most obvious. Weigh the amount, and more important the quality, of the support you can get for each. Given anything like equal choice, select the answer which has the strongest relation to general public interest.

If the change in definitions or district regulations will serve your purpose, it has these advantages. It has nothing to do with anything that looks like spot zoning. It doesn't identify a particular piece of property, and certainly can't be claimed to single it out for special privileges. And if you are after limited objectives, it doesn't create difficulties like those in the townhouse example, where rezoning for multifamily use turned loose a verbal lynching party because the neighbors knew that multifamily zoning would open up the land to the whole range of multifamily uses, and not merely to townhouses.

As another suggestion, if you must go in for a map change, don't walk alone. Look at the entire area as it relates to the rest of the city, and as it relates to the plan and to zoning. If you find that a general map change is logical for the area in which your tract is located, make a strong case for a general map change. If the case is strong enough, you may again be able to get the amendment proposed by local government, or you may have to join with other property owners involved. In either case, you are trying to make a logical improvement on the zoning pattern, and not merely to get zoning for your own particular piece of land. Unless you take the general approach, you will be fighting for spot zoning for your tract alone, and it's an uphill struggle. Usually you won't win it, and usually you shouldn't.

If your land is outside but immediately adjacent to a district which permits the use you are after, you can avoid the spot zoning problem by merely asking for an extension of the district boundary to include your land, but here again you would be on better ground if you can take a more impersonal approach and propose a remedial change which includes other land also, to create a better zoning pattern, not to make you rich.

One of the most obvious ways to prepare yourself to make a successful zoning presentation is to go to the planning director and ask him what he thinks should be demonstrated in your case, and how he would like to see the material presented. You may have a rough time with some planning directors, but I think you'd be surprised at the number who will welcome you with open arms. Here's someone asking a planner for advice, rather than sniping at him from the brush. It may move him to tears. It may also make your case. Or it may lead to some changes in what you had proposed to do.

Another approach (or a supplementary approach) is to go through the recent record of zoning changes. Who has asked for what, why, what kind of presentation was made before the planning commission and the governing body, what form do planning commission recommendations take and what reasoning does the commission use in suggesting approval or denial of an application, what seems to move the governing body, and does the governing body often reverse the planning commission? If so, what reasons are given?

Scan the written record first. If the pattern which emerges is fairly clear, you have enough to get on with. Otherwise, you may want to listen to the recordings of the hearings. You may find (and often will) that the written record is in the form of abbreviated and stereotyped phrases. One of my planning director friends is threatening to set up a file to simplify preparation of recommendations. "After the public hearing, the planning commission voted to recommend ( ) deny ( ) (check one) granting of the application on grounds 1, 4c, 6, 9, and 11."

The stenographer would then type in language from cards keyed to the numbers, with entries along the following lines:

---

1. This is a logical extension of a zoning boundary which would improve the pattern of uses in the general area and conform to the comprehensive plan.

4. This is an illogical extension of a zone boundary which would intrude a damaging salient of (a) commercial, (b) industrial, (c) high-density apartment use into a stable neighborhood of well-maintained single-family homes, and would be likely to lead to neighborhood deterioration, the spread of blight, and requests for additional zoning of a similar nature which would expand the problem.

6. This is spot zoning generally unrelated to either existing zoning or the pattern of development of the area, and contrary to the intent of the comprehensive plan. To grant this request would extend to the applicant development rights denied to others similarly situated in the same area.

9. Intensive traffic created by the proposed use or other uses permissible under the zoning sought would traverse established single-family neighborhoods on minor streets, leading to congestion, noise, and traffic hazards.

11. The proposed zoning would permit uses which would overload both existing public facilities and those proposed in the comprehensive plan.

That's a fair sample of stereotypes. If you knew about them to begin with, you'd be in better shape either to avoid getting involved in the wrong projects or to prove your case where you think your project is right. It is almost essential that you use arguments and demonstrations of a kind intended to fit the thinking of the people you will be working with. Many applicants fail to do it (and many inept lawyers fail to do it when they represent applicants). Applicants or the people representing them do best when they have a good case to begin with and present it as if they were staff planners, checking well-organized facts against specific public interest points or general policies related to the public interest.

(I might note as a point of useful information that in many areas, recommendations of the planning commission are prepared in tentative-draft form by the planning director or a staff member *before* the public hearing, presented to the commission after the public hearing, and rarely modified by the commission. This is to underscore the importance of working closely with the director or key staff members before you put in your application, and up to the time of the hearing.)

I might also note that if there is good staff, a good commission, and a good governing body, you won't do much for your cause by the shotgun approach, although some lawyers insist on it just in case it might help. It is more likely to irritate and alienate, particularly when there is nothing but noise unrelated to the central issues. With this warning, I leave it to you whether you want to bring in widows and orphans, the fact that anything would be better than what's there (well calculated to enrage any of the neighbors who happen to be at the hearing), the sound moral fiber and civic virtues of the applicant, the need for haste to keep the whole deal from falling through, or the allegation that zoning is probably fundamentally unconstitutional.

If you have a good case, it may be just as important to get a planner to help you with the preliminaries and the presentation as to get a lawyer. Good planners won't work with you on bad cases, and good lawyers will usually want planners to help them.

A word of caution on this. There have been instances where the phone rings just as I am leaving my office for the happy hour. The caller says: "We've got this case coming up day after tomorrow and we need an expert. Can you get here by tomorrow noon so our lawyer can tell you how he wants you to testify? And maybe if there's time, you could look at the property, just to be able to say you have seen it. You don't need to worry about exhibits—they're all prepared."

A number of people have been profoundly shocked before they were temporarily deafened by my response.

The best time to involve a planner in the preparation of the case is before you take an option on the land. Maybe it will turn out that you don't have a case, but you'll save yourself a lot of time and money if you find it out early.

The best planner to involve in the case, and the first, is the local planning director—if he is a competent professional. I'm not suggesting that you involve him in a moonlighting operation or in any other way which would involve conflict of interest. What I am saying is that he is charged with guiding and promoting sound development, and if your development is sound, he might well give you valuable guidance as part of his job. This doesn't mean that he is obligated to give you an infinite amount of time or detailed assistance, of course, but he should be willing to talk about the situation. And if he talks to you about it, he's likely to wind up knowing more about it.

If you bring in an outside planning expert, get one who is respected and give him enough lead time. He will want to prepare a planning case that will hold water with planners. He will want to talk with the local planning staff. He will want to prepare detailed studies and exhibits, material to present verbally and succinctly at the hearing, and material to be handed out which expands on important points. He will also want to work with your lawyer, and unless you have a good zoning lawyer (and they are not numerous), the lawyer, if he is wise, will learn at least as much from the planner about presenting the case—and about what to present and how to present it—as the planner learns from him.

There is one nasty and unfortunately not-infrequent situation which will take more than ordinary preparation. This is where you have an incompetent planning staff and/or commission and a butt-headed governing body, and where politics rather than merit governs the outcome of the case. If there is substantial opposition, the answer is no, no matter how good the argument, unless there is equally vociferous support (in which case the matter is likely to get tabled until after election, with all hands making speeches out of both sides of their mouths to make sure that the issue is firmly in doubt).

What you should do here—again assuming that you have a good project and can prove it on public interest grounds—is to prepare the case for the courts. And here, in addition to being particularly careful to be on firm planning ground, you will want to be well attuned to court decisions and to trends in such decisions. The lawyer-planner team must work very closely together, both to avoid entrapment and to allow the opposition every opportunity to exhibit symptoms of foot-in-mouth disease.

So long as you are being tromped on with asininities largely unrelated to planning and zoning principles, with arbitrary rulings, capricious decisions, and unreasonable regulation, lie there and squirm, concealing your satisfaction with a look of anguish. This is where meekness pays off. Your turn will come. Every hoof mark on your prostrate carcass may become grounds for branding with a hot judicial iron the mavericks who have stampeded across you.

I am not urging endless litigation in dubious minor cases. But where there is adequate justification, cases should go to the courts. If we had had firmer court tests of bad zoning, with cases well organized and well presented, we wouldn't have nearly as much bad zoning.

Chapter 5

Zoning details

The ABCs of zoning

The feature distinguishing zoning from most other forms of regulation is that it divides jurisdictional territory into districts or zones. Within each district, the controls must be uniform as applied to each class or kind of building. But the regulations may vary from one district to another.

In 1926, the U.S. Department of Commerce released the revised edition of the Standard State Zoning Enabling Act, which has been adopted with variations ranging from minor to major by most states. Before getting into mechanical details, it would be well to get a firm grasp on the purposes of regulation, and what may be regulated to accomplish these purposes.

Purposes of zoning

The first purpose listed in the Standard Act is in general police power language: "Promoting health, safety, morals, or the general welfare." Following this, the Act calls for regulations to be made in accordance with a *comprehensive plan.* The drafters of the Act did not mean by this what we mean by "comprehensive plan" today, but only that the entire territory within the jurisdiction should be zoned. Edward M. Bassett, one of the fathers of zoning, and a member of the Department of Commerce Advisory Committee on zoning, states in his classic reference, *Zoning,* that zoning has been upheld by the courts because it is *comprehensive* and not piecemeal, that *comprehensive* zoning ordinances should be adopted, that "piecemeal zoning" makes it difficult to attain "a comprehensive and coordinated *zoning* plan."

At this point, the statement of purposes becomes more detailed: to lessen congestion in the streets; to secure safety from fire, panic, and other dangers; to promote health and general welfare; to provide adequate light and air; to prevent the overcrowding of land; to avoid undue concentration of population; to facilitate the adequate provision of transportation, water, sewerage, schools, parks, and other public requirements.

The regulations are to give "reasonable consideration, among other things, to the character of the district and its peculiar suitability for particular uses" and are to be drafted "with a view to conserving the value of buildings and encouraging the most appropriate use of land throughout such municipality."

Those are the stated purposes, and they are broad enough to cover most of the things we *should* do with zoning.

There are some things for which zoning should *not* be used, and which the statement of purposes does not authorize. The courts have said it should not be used for racial segregation, nor to set the cost of housing. It should not be used to make housing in some districts more expensive than in others, an objective sought in some ordinances by extraordinarily large-lot requirements in "exclusive" districts, or by sliding-floor-area minimums. Generally applicable minimum residential floor areas, related to number of occupants, are appropriate as related to health and general welfare, but belong in housing or occupancy codes rather than zoning. There is strong objection, however, to thinly disguised efforts to make housing costs in some areas high by public regulation requiring more floor area than required to meet the needs of occupants. Economic segregation, like racial, is not a proper function for zoning.

There is no objection to otherwise lawful deed restrictions establishing minimum costs, floor areas, or lot areas above those needed to meet public objectives, but public regulation should not be used to protect an elite minority, and courts are likely to strike down "snob zoning" where public power is obviously used for this purpose.

Enabling act language on what may be regulated

Standard enabling act language indicates what may be regulated "for any or all of said purposes" and places some limits on how it may be regulated. Any and all zoning should have demonstrable and substantial relation to the purposes stated in the act, and the limits on form of regulation and procedures for adoption should be strictly observed. Government bodies may regulate and restrict: the height, number of stories, and size of buildings and other structures; the percentage of lot that may be occupied; the size of yards, courts, and other open spaces; the density of population; and the location and use of buildings, structures, and land for trade, industry, and other purposes.

For any and all of said purposes the local legislative body may divide the municipality into districts of such number, shape, and area as may be deemed best suited to carry out the purposes of this act; and within such districts it may regulate and restrict the erection, construction, reconstruction, alteration, repair, or use of buildings, structures, or land. All such regulations shall be uniform for each class or kind of building throughout each district, but the regulations in one district may differ from those in other districts.

With this background on the purposes of zoning and what may be regulated to accomplish the purposes, it is time to proceed to a discussion of how to prepare a zoning ordinance, and how to relate regulations to purposes.

Preliminary steps in drafting zoning regulations

Over an extended period of time, zoning can improve the situation, but it will not cause a miraculous reformation overnight. Nor is it possible to create a revolutionary plan for future development and zone according to it. Practical planning, like zoning, begins with what is and works forward. And unless there is wholesale clearance and redevelopment or other massive governmental action, the change is likely to be slow.

Zoning in most cities preceded the making of what we now call a comprehensive plan, usually as a stopgap emergency action to keep things from getting worse. It will usually be found that the land-use patterns shown in comprehensive plans conform closely to the zoning in effect when the plan was adopted. Thus as a twist of the familiar cliche that zoning must be in accord with a comprehensive plan, what usually happens is that planning is in accord with earlier comprehensive zoning.

Since zoning starts with what exists, seeks to prevent present unfortunate situations from getting worse, and is designed to create a better balance of land uses in the future, the first steps in preparing a zoning ordinance are to analyze the existing situation, define what's good or bad about it, and decide what action should be taken to correct current abuses and provide for future improvement.

The land-use map, showing how each piece of property is used, is a basic essential. It should be prepared on a parcel, rather than a lot, base to reflect actual ownership patterns rather than platted to lot sizes. It shows the existing patterns of development—residential, commercial, industrial, public and private, open use, vacant areas, and so on, with as many subcategories as are needed to suit regulatory purposes.

Before making final decisions on the land-use map, a quick general survey will give guidance as to how much detail is likely to be needed, so that the result will give necessary information without needless elaboration. It is better to have too much detail than too little, but going completely overboard is a waste of time and makes the map hard to follow.

As examples of decisions to be made early, consider the varieties of housing. Will it serve to identify only single-family, duplex, and multiple-family or will it be necessary to distinguish one-family detached, mobile homes, one-family semi-detached, one-family attached (row houses, townhouses, patio houses, and the like), duplexes indistinguishable from single-family detached in exterior appearance, two-family detached (visually identifiable as two-family), two-family semi-detached, two-family attached, and multiple-family by number of dwelling units and type (garden apartments, intermediate apartments, and high-rise)? Should guest houses and servants' quarters be identified? What's to be done about special forms of housing, the residence hotel, the retirement home, the rooming house, the tourist home, the hotel or motel available for long-term housing in the off-season?

Similar decisions should be made about commercial categories. Which are neighborhood oriented and which highway oriented? Should those creating special problems be separately identified? Examples of the latter are drive-in eating and drinking establishments and filling stations.

To what extent should the broad category often identified as "industrial" be broken down? Should uses primarily for major storage (with or without extensive distribution activities) be designated separately from manufacturing and processing? What industries should be identified as "light," with relatively minor nuisance characteristics, and "heavy," involving activities creating substantial environmental problems if they are in the wrong place?

In brief, it is suggested that if making the land-use map begins with some common sense assumptions as to what it should show in final form, there is likely to be less wasted motion. It is to be used for zoning, and it might as well start out in the form most useful for zoning.

Other map studies may include delineation of neighborhoods, development trends for buildings and land, land values, value of buildings, condition of buildings, utilities, soils, slopes and drainage, and so on depending on the circumstances of the case. In relatively advanced zoning, all or most of these maps may be made. Their purpose in refining district designation and regulations is clear without extended discussion.

Analysis of this material will indicate what the current situation is. Usually it will be found to be far from ideal. Land committed to commercial use (by extensive commercial development) will normally exceed by far any conceivable need for land for commercial purposes. Industry already located may have sterilized or severely limited the development potential of surrounding vacant property. General mixtures of commercial and industrial use with residential may assure both residential slums and low-grade commercial and industrial development—if any. Small spots of commercial or industrial development in predominantly residential neighborhoods are seeds for spreading blight, and small spots of residential development in predominantly commercial and industrial areas present their own obstacles to desirable development, particularly where the low price of available vacant land makes it unattractive to remove the residential structures.

These are only samples of common ailments. There are many more which plague cities and hamper desirable development—apathetic absentee ownership, clouded titles, inadequate facilities, crises in local government finance, and so on. Zoning can help on some of them, but zoning should not be expected to be the solution to all of them. Zoning can contain slums, but it can not cure them. Zoning can provide opportunities for sound private development, but it can not create the development. Zoning it all for oil wells won't produce the oil wells.

For some problems, controls should be sought in other regulations —health codes, occupancy codes, building codes, subdivision regulation, or even special licensing. For some, governmental reforms or reform of taxation policies may be the answer. For some, extensive clearance and redevelopment may be the solution. And for some problems, we just do not seem to have any workable answers yet.

Analysis of the existing situation will identify and define many problems. Do not overload zoning by trying to make it solve all of them.

Looking to the future, zoning may provide an improved pattern of land use, particularly where there is a significant amount of uncommitted area, or where there is to be substantial clearance and renewal. Where plans are known for new traffic arteries, new utilities, new industry, or other city-shaping influences, zoning can avert repetition of the mistakes of the past, make the most of opportunities, and assure that new development meets reasonable standards.

A comparison of existing land-use commitments with existing and estimated future requirements will provide important guidance to zoning policy, although it will usually be impossible for zoning to result in an ideal balance. Consider the common case where an excessive amount of land is preempted by strip commercial uses (with large numbers of substandard or vacant establishments, a substantial scattering of vacant lots, and trapped residences deteriorating in an environment hostile to good residential use). It is usually economically, politically, and perhaps legally impossible to draw boundaries in such a way as to undo the damage, throwing the excess into a residential category, for example. But zoning can be drafted in such a way as to discourage additions to the oversupply.

As an example on the other side, considering existing and probable future needs, there is often a shortage of land suitable for housing in other than single-family detached forms. Here zoning can have important remedial effects, designating land in suitable locations for townhouse, apartment, or mobile home park use. Merely zoning an area mathematically adequate for such uses will not insure that they can be provided, since there is rarely such a thing as an exclusive district for such purposes. To illustrate this point, the usual district designated multifamily in the zoning ordinance will contain substantial proportions, and often a majority, of single-family residences, which may make it difficult to assemble land for new multifamily use.

Similarly, there may be a shortage of land suitable for desirable industry, and mere zoning of run-down areas of mixed occupancy does not provide appropriate sites. If vacant land in prime industrial locations exists, some of it might well be zoned for industry, with restrictions to reduce potential adverse impact on adjoining uses of different character.

Division into districts

How many districts should there be, for what purposes, how bounded, and how related to each other?

The purposes should determine the number. As a guard against extremes, there are two rules. Enough districts should be established to serve substantial public purposes. No district should be established for trivial reasons. Eight or 10 districts may be too many, 39 or 40 not enough, depending on what it is proposed to accomplish, the size and complexity of the area, and the general approach to zoning.

Some years ago, there was an ordinance with a large number of single-family residential districts. All required 5,000-square-foot lots with 50-foot minimum frontage and all had identical other requirements with one exception. The sole variable was floor area of dwelling units, starting with 1,650 square feet and dropping in 25-foot increments to 600. Aside from the impropriety of zoning for sliding scale residential floor area (a particularly acute problem in this case because the special local enabling act inadvertently omitted size of buildings among the items to be regulated), there seems absolutely no justification for such minute distinctions.

At the other extreme, Hugh Pomeroy developed an ordinance with only one district—residential. Considering the circumstances, this may have been justified. The jurisdiction was small, had uniform development, and was occupied largely by retirees. Commercial and service facilities were available in a nearby area. Why have more than one district?

Statements of intent. In writing or rewriting an ordinance, preparation of statements of intent will always be helpful. These can be general for major groups of districts and detailed for individual districts, indicating the prime function of each, the reasons for establishing them, and the characteristics which distinguish them from the others. The purposes must have substantial relation to those for which zoning is intended.

The mental discipline involved in this exercise may have several results. Sometimes it will be found that there is no real reason for having all the districts initially proposed—the minor differences between some of them do not accomplish any real purpose except to make the ordinance more complicated. On the other hand, desirable refinements may appear.

Take the case of land along major streets, with spotty commercial development apparently committing it to conglomerate strip commercial zoning. Instead of lumping it in one general category, study of emerging patterns and potentials may indicate the possibility of subcategories. Sectors already developed as neighborhood, community, or regional shopping centers might be zoned, with adjacent frontage restricted to uses which will support, or at least not injure, the centers. Areas may be set aside for general or medical office complexes, with commercial and service facilities limited to those needed as accessory uses. Some lands may be zoned for wholesaling and distribution. Districts can be set aside for automotive and trailer sales and service, concentrating these facilities in their own areas rather than permitting them to spread indiscriminately along arterials. Part of the frontage might be zoned for industry, ranging from light (with requirements which produce an industrial park appearance) on down.

To the extent that uses can be sorted and grouped in this way, what might have been merely a strip commercial area can be regulated for both public and private advantage. Instead of a hodge-podge of mixed uses with little relation either to public convenience or intelligent grouping to maximize drawing power, the refined regulations encourage useful organization. Even where only part of the usual strip commercial district can be subjected to such refinement, there is substantial advantage in that area of conglomerate scatteration is reduced accordingly.

Statements of intent serve another very important purpose. In case of legal attack, the courts are often in the dark as to the purposes for specific regulations. Well-prepared statements of intent often serve as justification for what might otherwise be considered to be arbitrary, capricious, or unreasonable controls.

District boundaries. District boundaries and the way districts are related to each other must of course be tailored to the local situation, but there are some common sense guides. Boundaries should wherever possible follow property lines, center lines of streets, shore lines or center lines of bodies of water, or other clearly definable physical or cultural features. If they do not, their location should be indicated by reference to such features, as parallel to or extensions of them, with distances clearly indicated.

The ordinance should contain rules for interpretation of district boundaries, provisions for flexibility where a district boundary divides property, and procedures and guides by which the board of adjustment may settle uncertainties.

In ideal situations, the district pattern will be such that each will blend into the next without potentially adverse effects. There are few ideal situations. It thus becomes necessary to regulate in such a way as to minimize what may be strong interdistrict frictions.

In cases where commercial or industrial areas adjoin residential, one obvious possibility is to draw the boundaries at the back lot line, so that the activities face away from each other, rather than in the center of the street. The boundary in the street not only creates visual conflicts, but subjects the residential district to commercial or industrial traffic.

Where the boundary must separate activities in a side-by-side relationship, some other considerations come into play. In those fortunate situations where there is a logical buffer—a park, a river, a cemetery, an institutional use, a governmental building or the like—the division is easy. Where there is no such logical breakpoint, there are some very real problems.

Where residential districts must be separated from commercial or industrial along the same street frontage, an intersecting street sounds like a good divider, but this solution must be used with some caution. Given one corner of an intersection zoned commercial as part of a logical pattern, with the other three in residential classifications, there is a better chance that the zoning will hold up in court than if three corners are zoned commercial and the other corner residential. This follows from the stated rule that property which is similarly situated should be zoned alike, combined with an unstated rule that court challenges are more likely on behalf of zoning down than zoning up. The gas station wanting the fourth corner when the other three are already occupied by gas stations is likely to appeal to the courts and to win. The residential occupants of three corners are not likely to go to court to have the fourth corner removed from a commercial classification.

But the problem of commercial creep must be met some way. Given a drive-in eatery next to a residence, the odds are that sooner or later the residential property will apply for commercial zoning on grounds that it is next to a drive-in eatery. The argument is persuasive, the zoning is granted, and a filling station occupies the lot, whereupon the next residential owner applies for commercial zoning with the persuasive argument that he is next to a gas station.

One solution is to create buffer districts, relatively narrow bands of uses with only limited adverse effects on residential occupancy. Such uses might include offices, clinics, commercial establishments restricted to those conducted within completely enclosed buildings, and so on.

Another possibility is a form of regulation not requiring a separate district but having the same effect. Thus, where a commercial district adjoins a single-family residential district along the same frontage, for a stated distance within the commercial district, certain uses are barred—for example, gas stations and eating and drinking establishments. And for a certain distance within the single-family district, certain uses not generally permitted within the district are allowed—for example, small offices and clinics, two-family dwellings, or small apartments.

Considerations other than use are involved here, particularly yard and height regulation. These too can be handled in a way which provides a smooth transition.

Purists may object that this kind of transitional zoning violates the rule that "all such regulations shall be uniform for each class or kind of building throughout each district." Two answers are available. The regulations *are* uniform for each class or kind of building with a stated relationship to the district boundary. If that isn't convincing, there is still the possibility of setting up separate transitional districts with boundaries shown on the map.

Planned development regulation

In lot-by-lot development, the lot is the framework for design, timing may be haphazard, and regulations are usually designed to keep the worst from happening, which doesn't necessarily encourage the best. Planned development, as defined below, reduces uncertainty as to what will happen and when. It should improve design and function and produce a higher level of amenities. Planned development regulation can, therefore, encourage flexibility and allow greater freedom of design without erosion of public purposes. And some of the lessons learned from planned development regulation can be applied to improve lot-by-lot controls.

The material which follows suggests procedures and requirements for planned developments generally, gives details on one method for controlling planned residential developments, and indicates some spin-offs applicable to conventional zoning. In this article, no attempt is made to cover detailed regulations for other types of planned development districts—neighborhoods, community and regional shopping centers, planned office districts, planned industrial districts, planned resort districts, or districts providing for planned mixtures of uses (which might include new towns).

This composite article includes portions of "Improving Zoning—Some New Approaches," in *Land-Use Controls,* Vol. 2, No. 4 (Fall 1968), pp. 1-16, and "How to Regulate Planned Unit Developments for Housing," a two-part series appearing in the June and July, 1965, issues of *Zoning Digest,* Vol. 17, No. 6 and No. 7. For added detail, consult the original sources.

Planned developments generally

Definition. For regulatory purposes, a planned development may be defined as:

1. Land under unified control, planned and developed as a whole,
2. In a single development operation or a definitely programmed series of development operations, including all lands and buildings,
3. For principal and accessory structures and uses substantially related to the character of the district,
4. According to comprehensive and detailed plans which include not only streets, utilities, lots or building sites, and the like, but also site plans, floor plans, and elevations for all buildings as intended to be located, constructed, used, and related to each other, and detailed plans for other uses and improvements on the land as related to the buildings, and
5. With a program for provision, operation, and maintenance of such areas, improvements, facilities, and services as will be for common use by some or all of the occupants of the district, but will not be provided, operated, or maintained at general expense.

That definition covers all forms of planned developments. As a matter of regulatory mechanics, it is helpful to insert a general section on planned developments of all kinds, covering definition, intent, and processing procedures, and then to provide detailed subsections on specific types of planned developments—for housing, shopping centers, office centers, resorts, industrial parks, etc., and for appropriate combinations of these.

Intent. The statement of intent is an important element. Here is one from a recent ordinance proposal:

> Within districts now existing or which may hereafter be created, it is intended to permit, on application and on approval of detailed site, use and building plans, creation of new planned development (PD) districts for specialized purposes where tracts suitable in location and character for the uses and structures proposed are to be planned and developed as units. Suitability of such tracts for the plans and development proposed for the PD district shall be determined by reference to the comprehensive plan and the existing and prospective character of surrounding development.

Within PD districts, regulations adapted to such unified planning and development are intended to accomplish the purposes of zoning and other applicable regulations to the same degree as in districts in which regulations are intended to control development on a lot-by-lot rather than unified basis, and to promote economical and efficient land use, an improved level of amenities, appropriate and harmonious variety in physical development, creative design, and a better urban environment.

In view of the substantial public advantages of planned development, it is the intent of this ordinance to promote and encourage development in this form where appropriate in location and character.

General requirements. The regulations should establish guidelines as to where (and in some cases when) planned developments will be permitted. Location should fit the pattern of development indicated in the comprehensive plan. Most PD districts (except those for very low-density housing) should have access to major streets without creating traffic on minor residential streets outside the district. And there should be requirements concerning utilities, public facilities, and services, perhaps along these lines:

PD districts shall be so located in relation to sanitary sewers, storm and surface drainage systems, and other utilities systems and installations that neither extension nor enlargement of such systems will be required in manner, form, character, location, degree, scale, or timing resulting in higher net public costs or earlier incursion of public costs than would development in forms generally permitted under existing zoning for the area.

Such districts shall be so located with respect to necessary public facilities as to have access in the same degree as would development permitted under existing zoning, and shall be so located, designed, and scaled that access for public services is equivalent to, and net cost for such services is not greater than, access and net costs for public services for development as permitted under existing zoning.

To permit development which might otherwise be inhibited by these requirements, provision may be made for private facilities, utilities, or services approved by appropriate public agencies, or for offsetting any added net public cost or early commitment of public funds.

Procedures. Under the arrangement suggested here, planned developments involve amendment of the zoning map in accordance with general amendment procedures, but with some special details. Material submitted with the application for amendment includes a report indicating unified control of the property, agreement to proceed according to the regulations established when the map amendment is passed, provision for agreements, contracts, deed restrictions, and sureties acceptable to the governing body for completion of the development according to approved plans and for continuing operation and maintenance of facilities not provided by the public, and agreement to bind successors in title to commitments made.

At this point, a preliminary plan may be submitted. In its initial stage, it may be very general indeed. Before the planning commission hearing on the proposed amendment, the staff and the applicant confer in the same general way as for subdivision approval, ironing out as many differences as possible and defining remaining issues for consideration and decision by the governing body. The staff has a chance to work with the developer on improvements in the plan.

After the planning commission hearing, specific findings are required. Among these may be a recommendation that PD or general regulations as applied in the particular case should be modified because the applicant's solution to a problem meets the public purposes of the regulations to a degree at least equal to what would be accomplished if the controls were enforced strictly as written. (In effect, this is an admission that somebody might come up with something good which the planners had not anticipated.)

On the basis of such findings, the commission recommends approval of the amendment as proposed, approval conditioned on stipulated modifications, or disapproval. The governing body then acts on the proposed amendment, including the preliminary plan in whatever stage it has reached. If there are to be modifications of the PD or general regulations in the particular case, the governing body makes them, as a legislative act.

As parenthetical comment, preparation of detailed final plans is obviously costly. Normally, the applicant will not want to go to this expense until he knows whether he is going to get the zoning he is seeking. Hence the provision for the preliminary plan, indicating generally what is proposed. The important thing for the applicant is that if he wants modifications of standing regulations, he must get them at the time of the amendment, and the preliminary plan must therefore be in sufficient detail to justify his position.

If the amendment passes, development must be in accord with final plans, meeting guides and standards generally applicable to the class of planned development, as specifically supplemented or modified in the amending action, and must conform to time limitations established by the governing body for beginning and completion of the development as a whole or in specified stages.

After land is rezoned to PD status, the planning department must approve final plans for the development as a whole, or for stages or portions, before building permits may be issued. The planning staff may permit changes from approved preliminary plans which are in accord with the guides and standards, but other changes require new amending action by the governing body.

Moving on from these general provisions, following are some controls which might apply to planned developments for housing.

Planned development—housing (PD-H) districts

Planned unit developments for housing and related facilities should become more numerous. Well done, this form of land use is far more efficient than the usual lot-by-lot approach. It conserves land, reduces urban sprawl, maintains or increases amenities, and offers substantial economies in initial and continuing costs (public and private).

One of the principal advantages of planned unit development is flexibility—in building forms, relation of buildings to each other, relation of buildings to open space, use of open space. To promote this flexibility while retaining protection of the public interest, relatively sophisticated and complex regulations are needed.

In lot-by-lot development, primitive and simple regulations provide a rigid framework. Relatively standardized lots are required to be laid out for eventual construction of relatively standardized residences. Standard yard dimensions fragment open space on the lot and diminish its utility to the point where larger lots are needed than would be the case if some relation were established between yard dimension and yard function. The required yards leave a relatively standardized buildable area somewhere toward the middle of each lot. When each lot has been built upon, each house will have minimal protection from its neighbors, and each will be in about the same position on its lot.

In planned unit developments, land under unified control is to be planned and developed as a whole. The plan is comprehensive, including not only the features common in subdivision plats, but also details on buildings indicating heights, location of principal window areas, use areas within buildings, and relation to adjacent open space and to other buildings. *Common open space,* another distinguishing feature of most planned residential developments, is indicated in the plans as it is to be located, improved, and used, and provision is made for its maintenance, preferably as a responsibility of management or residents of the development, and not as a burden on the taxpayers. In addition to the comprehensive physical plan, there is a program for development of the project as a whole or in stages.

Because of this detailed knowledge of what is to be done and when, it is possible to allow considerably more latitude in *how* it is to be done while still maintaining control equivalent in effect to usual regulations designed to protect the public interest.

The Federal Housing Administration has made possible a major breakthrough in regulatory techniques. Two FHA documents contain most of the basic information: *Planned-Unit Development with a Homes Association*[1] covers the general approach and indicates in general how occupants can handle maintenance of common facilities within the development; *Minimum Property Standards for Multifamily Housing*[2] provides a wealth of detailed standards in a form well adapted to use in planned developments.

A third, a joint effort by FHA and the Urban Land Institute, entitled *The Homes Association Handbook,*[3] gives detailed information on a number of ways in which homes associations can provide for maintenance of common facilities.

Use of the FHA approach, adapted to local circumstances, is strongly recommended for two reasons. First, the standards, based on extensive experience, are excellently drafted and organized and provide a wide enough range so that they can be used in almost any situation. Second, since a very substantial amount of new development will be financed with FHA insurance on mortgages, use of the standards will reduce the complications which arise when several sets of regulations, all for approximately the same purpose, are slightly at variance with each other.

1. Federal Housing Administration, *Planned-Unit Development with a Homes Association* (Washington, D.C.: U.S. Government Printing Office, Dec. 1963), 64 pp.

2. Federal Housing Administration, *Minimum Property Standards for Multifamily Housing* (Washington, D.C.: U.S. Government Printing Office, Sept. 1965), 119 pp.

3. Urban Land Institute, *The Homes Association Handbook* (Washington, D.C.: ULI, 1965), 406 pp.

Without going into great detail, what follows covers preparation for regulation of planned unit developments for housing—ordinances, guides, standards, and procedures.

Establishing land-use intensity areas (or districts)

Zoning regulations covering lot-by-lot development establish different districts. Residential districts usually have a wide range of requirements. In outlying areas, large lots, large yards, and low building coverage, plus limitation to single-family detached housing, produces very low density (or intensity) of land use. At the other extreme there are high-density (or intensity) residential areas where lot area per family is small, yards are small, and multiple-family or other dwellings permitted produce high building coverage in relation to ground space.

Land-use intensity areas (or districts) perform the same general functions, plus some others. They are established in the same way, by placing boundaries on the zoning map either directly or by overlays. Usually land-use intensity area boundaries will coincide with other district boundaries to some extent. Sometimes they will coincide entirely.

Land-use intensity areas, thus distinguished, form the basis for establishing regulations for planned unit developments. As in the case of other zoning districts, regulations apply equally anywhere within one land-use intensity area, but vary from one area to another.

For its mortgage insurance purposes, FHA describes the means by which its insuring offices assign land-use intensity ratings to specific projects. Under the adaptation proposed here, the governing body assigns land-use intensity ratings by area within its jurisdiction, and these become binding. (Of course, if FHA assigned a lower rating to a specific project than had been assigned by the governing body to the area, the developer would have to go by FHA's rating in order to get mortgage insurance, but if FHA's intensity rating were higher than that set locally, the local regulations would govern.)

Because of the increased efficiency of land use under good planned unit development regulations, a higher potential population density should be permitted in such developments than in lot-by-lot areas. Otherwise, planned unit development merely leads to an improved kind of urban sprawl, and doesn't diminish it.

To give some idea of what land-use intensity ratings mean in terms of other matters related to them, and the range which can be established using the FHA approach, here are some examples. To simplify presentation (and language) from here on, LUI will be used to identify land-use intensity.

How land-use intensity ratings relate, and what they do

As a practical matter, LUI 3.0 would be below the lower limit likely to be applied in outer metropolitan fringes. (Reston, the planned development well out into the farmlands of Fairfax County, Virginia, from Washington would probably rate about 3.5.) For demonstration purposes, assume that LUI 6.0 is the highest rating to be allowed. (The FHA chart on the next page reads in tenths of the LUI scale, so fine adjustments are possible in establishing LUI area classifications. It also extends upward well above the 6.0 used in this example.)

For simplicity, assume that land area of 1,000,000 square feet is involved in each case (about 23 acres).[4] Some other assumptions will be made where they seem desirable.

AT LAND-USE INTENSITY 3.0

Maximum residential floor area permitted is established by the floor area ratio 0.1. Multiplying by land area of 1,000,000 square feet gives 100,000 square feet of residential floor area as the maximum allowed. Used in residences averaging 2,000 square feet each, 50 would be permitted (or about two per acre). If average size increased, total number would decrease, and vice versa.

Minimum open space required is based on actual residential floor area used. Assuming that the full 100,000 square feet of residential floor area is used, application of the 8.0 open space ratio for LUI 3.0 calls for 800,000 square feet of open space.

(On this detail, the FHA chart contains an unimportant defect. If all the residential floor area were used in one-story buildings, it would leave 900,000 square feet of open space. Even allowing for garages, carports, and other accessory structures which don't count as residential floor area, it would be most unlikely that as little as 800,000 square feet of open space would be left.)

Livability open space is open space for other than vehicular use,

4. This should not be used as an example for setting area minimums, which probably should vary from one LUI area to another. (In one set of regulations now being considered, LUI 6.5 requires only one acre; LUI 5.5, five; LUI 4.5, ten.)

including such space on lots and in common open space areas. This too is related to residential floor area actually used. At LUI 3.0, the livability open space ratio is 6.4. Multiplying 6.4 by the full 100,000 square feet of residential floor area allowed, livability open space comes to 640,000 square feet.

Figure 1. Land-use intensity standards

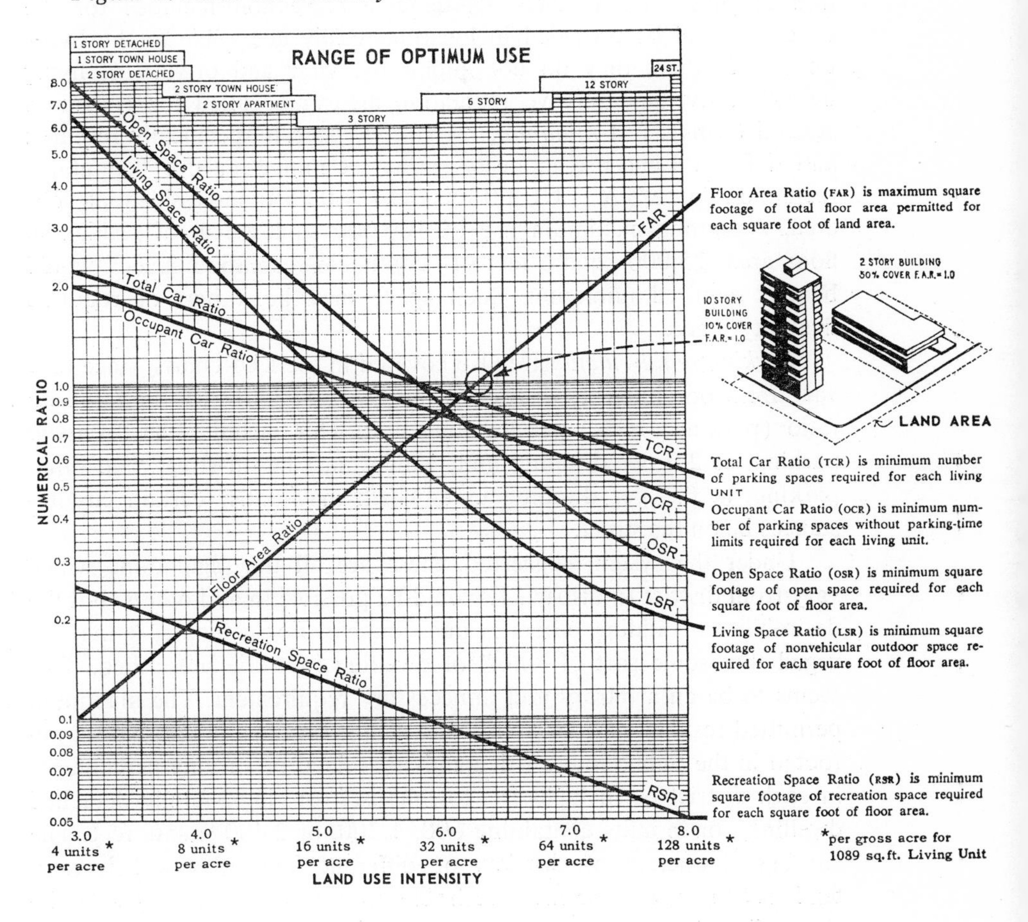

Vehicular space is not expressed in the ratios, but a rough approximation can be derived. If full use is made of residential floor areas and 20 per cent is added for accessory buildings, ground story coverage by single-story buildings would come to 120,000 square feet. To this must be added the 640,000 square feet of livability open space, for a total of 760,000 square feet, leaving 240,000 square feet for streets, parking bays, driveways, and open parking areas on lots.

Recreation space is required in planned developments. In generalized language, FHA states: "Adequate recreation facilities for the residents shall be provided in locations easily accessible to the living units and where they do not impair the view and privacy of living units." Active and passive recreation areas are called for (again in general terms). But *minimum recreation space* is specifically required and defined. Land-use intensity ratios set minimums for "countable recreation space." At LUI 3.0 the ratio is 0.25 times residential floor area. Assuming maximum use of 100,000 square feet of residential floor area, 25,000 square feet of "countable recreation space" would be the required minimum. Such space may be a part of required livability space.

Parking requirements are also covered in the LUI charts, since they vary from one intensity district to the next. At LUI 3.0, the *total* car ratio (parking) is 2.2 per dwelling unit. This includes the *occupant* parking, at 2.0 per dwelling unit, which must be off-street, and other parking, at 0.2 per dwelling unit, which may under certain circumstances be on the street.

Under the system suggested, these are all the regulations which vary from district to district. It would be possible to add others, but the desirability of adding others is questionable. For example, it may be urged that some sort of "mix" of dwelling types be prescribed. This seems to be an arbitrary and unnecessary requirement. The maximum permitted residential floor area sets a ceiling on the amount. No reason rooted in the public interest demands that fixed or varying percentages in each district be in high-rise, townhouses, or single-family detached dwellings, or in units containing 600, 1,200, or 2,400 square feet. The varying characters of districts of different intensities will have a tendency to suggest the most desirable mix, and the planning commission will review proposals under an arrangement to be discussed later. Beyond that, it appears desirable to leave as much flexibility as possible.

AT LAND-USE INTENSITY 4.0

Maximum residential floor area permitted is set by floor area ratio 0.2 (double that for LUI 3.0). In the case of the 1,000,000 square feet example, 200,000 square feet of residential floor area would be the maximum. With residences averaging 2,000 square feet each, 100 would be permitted (or about four per acre). In practice, as land-use intensity increases, average floor area of dwelling units tend to drop. Hence it might be considered that 1,500 square feet would be more probable at LUI 4.0, giving a total of 133 units, or about 5.7 per acre.

Minimum open space required in LUI 4.0, set by a ratio of 3.9 times residential floor area (actual floor area would be used in computation, but assume the full 200,000 square feet), comes to 780,000 square feet.

Minimum livability space required (again, this is nonvehicular space) is set by the ratio 2.6 times residential floor area. With maximum use of permissible floor area, the livability space minimum would be 520,000 square feet.

At this intensity (4.0), the relation between permitted residential floor area and required open space is such that if all the floor area were used in one-story buildings, with a reasonable percentage of additional nonresidential area in accessory buildings, required open space and permitted floor area would about balance out. (Open space required, 780,000 square feet, plus residential floor area permitted, 200,000 square feet, plus 20,000 square feet of nonresidential floor area in accessory buildings equals 1,000,000 square feet.) To the extent that the developer goes to buildings two stories or more in height, the total amount of open space increases. In the highly unlikely event that he elects to go to a high-rise with 20 floors and 10,000 square feet per floor, he has used up his maximum floor area on 10,000 square feet of ground, leaving 990,000 square feet of open space.

Vehicular space can again be roughly estimated. Given one-story construction throughout, covering 200,000 square feet of the tract, plus a requirement of 520,000 square feet of nonvehicular open space, 720,000 of the 1,000,000 square feet would be accounted for, leaving a maximum of 280,000 square feet for streets and parking areas.

"Countable recreation space" required as a minimum at LUI 4.0 is set at 0.18 times residential floor area. Assuming maximum use of the permitted 200,000 square feet, 36,000 square feet of "countable" recreation space would be required. (The figure for LUI 3.0 was

25,000 square feet, lower because of the general availability of more open space.)

Parking requirements are 1.65 *total* spaces per dwelling unit; 1.50 *occupant* spaces.

AT LAND-USE INTENSITY 5.0

Maximum residential floor area permitted is set by floor area ratio 0.4 (again doubling that of the previous intensity). This would give 400,000 square feet. At 1,500 square feet average per dwelling unit, this would work out to about 267 units, or a little less than 12 per acre. (At 1,250 square feet, the number of units rises to 320, or about 14 per acre. At 1,000 square feet, the number of units is 400, or a little over 17 per acre.)

Minimum open space required at the ratio of 1.8 times the full 400,000 square feet of residential floor area permitted would come to 720,000 square feet.

Minimum livability space required, at 1.1 times floor area, would amount to 440,000 square feet.

At this point, the relationships between maximum permitted floor area and minimum open space and livability space requirements begin to push strongly toward some multi-story structures.

Here, for the first time in the intensities discussed thus far, single-story coverage of the land won't work if the full permitted floor area is used. Maximum permitted residential floor area, 400,000 square feet, plus minimum open space, 720,000 square feet, comes to 1,120,000, or 120,000 over the total land available. In this kind of district, it would be likely that plans would call for a majority of the units in two-story townhouses and garden apartments, with some in single-family detached and some in higher apartments.

It is no longer possible to estimate how much vehicular space would be available by adding building coverage at single-story levels to required livability space. Building coverage will not be at single-family levels.

Required "countable recreation space" rises again (with a ratio of 0.13 multiplied by assumed maximum use of permitted residential floor area at 400,000 square feet) to 52,000 square feet. This rise is appropriate because of the increase in number of dwelling units.

Parking requirements drop to 1.25 per dwelling unit total; 1.1 per dwelling unit for occupants.

AT LAND-USE INTENSITY 6.0
Maximum residential floor area permitted doubles again, with the floor area ratio rising to 0.8. The 800,000 square feet allowable would permit 640 units averaging 1,250 square feet (about 28 per acre); 800 units averaging 1,000 square feet (about 35 per acre).

Minimum open space required, at a ratio of 0.86 times the full 800,000 square feet of residential floor area permitted, would come to 688,000 square feet.

Minimum livability space required, at 0.5 times floor area, would be 400,000 square feet.

Here the push toward multi-story becomes stronger. Subtracting required open space, 688,000 square feet, from the total 1,000,000 square feet in the tract leaves only 312,000 square feet for building coverage. Even if it were all two-story, it could not be squeezed in. Much of it is likely to be three-story and up at this intensity.

Required "countable recreation space" at this intensity is based on a ratio of 0.095, which on an assumed maximum floor area use at 800,000 comes to 76,000 square feet, again up from the next lowest intensity. By this time, such space is required at a minimum to occupy 7.6 per cent of the total site.

Parking requirements are .95 spaces per dwelling unit total; .80 per dwelling unit for occupants.

Regulation of yards, courts, and building spacing

Space around dwelling units performs various functions and should be related to the performance of such functions. In lot-by-lot development, this is not the case, or at best regulations handle relation of exterior to interior areas and spacing of buildings very crudely.

On these matters, the planned unit provisions here are the same for all land-use intensity districts, but allow flexibility without loss of protection of the public interest.

---

1. *Living rooms are required to have exterior glassed areas* equal to at least 10 per cent of floor area. (There is nothing new or startling about this. Most housing codes require it.)

(The requirement above provides for orientation of interior to exterior space. The idea behind the provisions which follow is that

SUMMARY—SELECTED LAND USE INTENSITIES AND STANDARD RATIOS

Computations with Standard Ratios

FLOOR AREA RATIO*	×	residential land area	=	maximum permitted residential floor area
OPEN SPACE RATIO	×	actual residential floor area	=	minimum total open space required
LIVABILITY (nonvehicular) SPACE RATIO	×	" " " "	=	minimum livability open space required
RECREATION SPACE RATIO	×	" " " "	=	minimum "countable" recreation space
TOTAL CAR RATIO	×	actual number dwelling units	=	minimum parking spaces required (total)
OCCUPANT CAR RATIO	×	actual number dwelling units	=	minimum off-street spaces required

Ratios Applied to 1,000,000 square feet (23 Acres) of Residential Land Area

(Assuming maximum use of permitted residential floor area)

		LUI-3	LUI-4	LUI-5	LUI-6	
FLOOR AREA RATIO		0.10	0.20	0.40	0.80	
× 1,000,000 sq. ft. = floor area		100,000	200,000	400,000	800,000	Sq. ft. maximum
Dwelling Units @ average						
2,250 sq. ft.	Total no., and per acre	44(1.9)				Total and per acre (Most probable extreme high and low ranges)
2,000 " "		50(2.2)	100(4.3)			
1,750 " "		57(2.5)	114(4.9)	229(10.0)		
1,500 " "		67(2.9)	133(5.8)	267(11.6)	533(23.2)	
1,250 " "			160(6.9)	320(13.9)	640(27.6)	
1,000 " "				400(17.4)	800(34.8)	
800 " "					1000(43.5)	
OPEN SPACE RATIO		8.00	3.90	1.80	0.86	
× floor area = total open space		800,000	780,000	720,000	688,000	Sq. ft. minimum
LIVABILITY SPACE RATIO		6.40	2.60	1.10	0.50	
× floor area = total livability space		640,000	520,000	440,000	400,000	Sq. ft. minimum
RECREATION SPACE RATIO		0.25	0.18	0.13	0.095	
× floor area = total recreation space		25,000	36,000	52,000	76,000	Sq. ft. minimum "countable"
TOTAL CAR RATIO per d.u.		2.20	1.65	1.25	0.95	Including on-street
OCCUPANT CAR RATIO per d.u.		2.00	1.50	1.10	0.80	Off-street only

*Maximum number of dwelling units is not fixed directly, but depends on size of dwelling units. The total residential floor area of all dwelling units may not exceed the maximum permitted residential floor area. This permits a range in size of dwelling units.

yards adjacent to substantial portions of the required glassed area of a dwelling unit should be wider than those which are not. Here principal functions to be performed by the yards are privacy, view, light, and air.)

---

2. *Yards, courts, and other open spaces are related to glassed areas and to walls,* need not be "ground-to-sky," and may in some cases be partly off the building site. Thus:
   a. *Where a wall contains less than 25 per cent of total required glassed area* of any dwelling unit at or below the third floor, up to half of the required yard depth may be in the adjacent half of a street.

(Here the street is allowed to perform another function of usual yards—building spacing—but only if the walls most directly affected do not contain 25 per cent or more of required glassed area.)

---

   b. *Where a wall contains glassed area for dwelling units at or above the fourth floor,* up to half of the required yard depth may be in the adjacent half of a street regardless of orientation of required glassed areas.

(Here the vertical distance is taken into consideration. Elevation cuts down on street noises as much as would extra yard depth at lower levels, the view is now more of distance and less of ground next to the building, and adding to on-site yard depth would not add materially to privacy.)

---

   c. *Where a wall contains 25 per cent or more of total required glassed area* of a dwelling, up to half of the required depth may be in the adjacent half of any common livability space of suitable character, such as a park, a stream, a lake, or other open space of a similar nature.

(Such common open space contributes to view, light, and air, and may be credited in part to what would otherwise be on-site yard requirements. Moving the walls toward such space gives opportunities to provide more on-site space next to other walls of the building, or to walls of other buildings, where orientation is not so fortunate.)

---

3. *Building height and building length relate to exterior space requirements, walls, and glassed areas as follows:*

a. *Where two opposing walls contain no glassed areas* (required or other), separation shall be as required by fire regulations.

(Separation here is strictly for fire protection. There is no need for spacing for other purposes.)

---

b. *For other walls, related exterior space requirements are as follows:*

(1) *Where a wall contains 25 per cent or more of required principal glassed area* of any dwelling unit, depth of yard shall be 10 feet plus 2 feet for each story in height plus 1 foot for each 15 feet of building length.

(2) *Where a wall contains some, but less than 25 per cent,* of required principal glassed area of any dwelling unit, depth of exterior space shall be 5 feet plus 1 foot for each story in height plus 1 foot for each 15 feet of building length.

(3) *Where a wall contains none of the required glassed area* of a dwelling unit, no yard is required except for compliance with fire regulations or if the nature or location of any other glassed areas involves loss of reasonable privacy for interior space requiring such privacy.

(A kitchen or bathroom window in a wall is not part of the required glassed area, but if the nature or location of such windows affects loss of reasonable privacy either within the dwelling unit or in adjoining units, extra space may be required as appropriate.)

---

(4) *Distance between buildings* shall in no case be less than the sum of the required depths of adjoining yards.

Preceding material is a generalized summary of the way land-use intensity areas should be established and how regulations for such areas work. It should now be apparent why complexity is necessary for flexibility.

PD-H ordinance provisions

Given the principles and regulatory details relating to planned residential development indicated above, and the section of the ordinance covering planned development procedures and requirements generally, details on PD-H might be fitted into the regulations thus.

1. *The intent statement* might well be very brief, i
section covers planned developments, as described gene
_______, primarily for housing.

2. *Definitions,* where of limited application, should app
of the sections or subsections to which they are applicable.
planned development—housing, would again be relatively brief,
the master definition covers planned developments in general:
planned development for dwellings and related facilities."

3. *Establish land-use intensity bands* (or area boundaries) on the official zoning map according to the same procedures used in establishing zoning district boundaries. It should be indicated that within the boundaries of such land-use intensity areas, planned unit developments for housing may be established as districts, subject to the requirements of the ordinance applying to such districts, upon applications, and according to procedures required generally for zoning map amendments as modified to meet special processing requirements for planned developments.

4. *Establish minimum area requirements* for planned development districts. As suggested earlier, these should vary from one land-use intensity classification (or group of classifications) to another. If planners believe in planning, planned unit developments should be encouraged, not inhibited. In high-intensity areas near city centers, a 10-acre minimum requirement, which might be quite appropriate on the outskirts, may virtually prohibit a development which would be a major asset.

5. *Set general requirements on suitability of land* as to physical character and location:

a. *Physical character of the site.* Suitable for development in the manner proposed without hazards to persons or property, on or off the site, from probability of flooding, erosion, subsidence, or slipping of the soil, or other dangers, annoyances, or inconveniences.

b. *Locational requirements.* Must have direct access to major streets or highways without creating traffic on minor residential streets outside the district. Must either be so located in relation to utilities and public facilities existing (or to be developed by the time they will be needed) that no additional public expense will be involved—or developer must off-set added public expense. Must be appropriately related to the existing and probable future urban pattern. (In the last sentence above, language might take the more specific form that no planned development district for housing may be established in specified commercial and industrial districts.)

6. *State requirements concerning site planning relationships at edges of planned development districts.* The purpose here is to provide mutual protection for the development and its surroundings from potentially adverse influences. Matters to be covered include at least the following:

a. *Vehicular and pedestrian access points.*

b. *Yards.* At edges adjacent to other residential districts, yards within the planned development might well be required to be the same as within the adjoining district, unless planned development regulations call for deeper yards.

c. *Screening.* Within the development, extensive parking areas, service areas, and other specified items likely to have adverse effects on surrounding property should be screened against viewing from ground level or first stories outside the development. Screening should also be specified against adverse views from within the development, and against lights, noise, or undesirable elements in the surroundings.

d. *Height limitation* should be set in such a way that heights of buildings adjacent to planned development district boundaries will relate properly to heights permitted outside such boundaries. One method is to hold to the same height limitation within a specified distance of the district boundary as for the adjoining district. Another is to limit by height planes starting at the same level as in the adjoining district, and rising as portions of buildings are set back farther from the perimeter of the planned development district.

7. *Establish requirements applying within portions of planned development districts other than at the edges, or generally within such districts:*

a. *Applying equally to all planned development districts:*

(1) *Uses permitted.* These will normally include most uses permitted in usual multifamily residential districts plus provisions for planned shopping centers or convenience establishments under specified circumstances, and for offices, buildings, and facilities required for operation, administration, and maintenance of the development (if these are not already included by reference from multifamily districts).

(2) *Site planning—general internal relationships.* Material here should start with general intent: "The site plan shall provide for efficient, safe, convenient, and harmonious grouping of structures, uses, and facilities, and for appropriate relation of space inside and outside

buildings to intended uses and structural features." But language should not stop with these platitudes. There should also be general-to-specific guides on such matters as street layout, block size (the maximum consistent with use and shape of the site and the convenience and safety of the occupants), vehicular access to streets, pedestrian ways, protection of pedestrian and traffic visibility, location of common open space (particularly park and recreational areas), and the like.

(3) *Regulation of yards, courts, and building spacing.* This is handled as indicated in the discussion beginning on page 335.

b. *Varying according to the land-use intensity area in which the district is located.* This series of provisions is handled as indicated in the discussion beginning on page 330. Set here, according to LUI rating, are maximum residential floor area permitted, minimum open space, livability space and recreation space required, and total and occupant parking requirements.

8. *Indicate contents of preliminary plan and report,* which may include everything to be required later in the final plan and report, but should include as a minimum:

a. *Proposed land uses and types of structures,* with approximate locations of buildings of major importance because of their functions (churches, shopping centers, convenience establishments, schools, management headquarters, community recreational buildings, and the like) or their form (high, massive, or extensive buildings likely to have strong visual impact). Relation to existing or probable future development outside the district.

b. *Proposed automotive and pedestrian circulation systems,* including designation of streets by type, and any existing or platted streets to be vacated. Major off-street parking and service areas.

c. *Proposed parks, playgrounds, school sites, pedestrian parkways,* and other major open spaces not for automotive traffic.

d. *General location of utilities, easements, and installations.*

e. *If development is to be in stages, indication as to location, order, and timing.*

f. *Proposals for expediting (or providing substitutes for) public facilities, utilities, or services.* Here would be indicated proposals for extending, at the expense of the developer, public facilities which would not normally be available at the time needed, and for handling common open space, maintenance of private streets, and similar matters.

9. *Indicate required planning commission recommendations and findings, to cover the following points:*

a. Suitability of the area for the proposed development.
b. Time limitations, if any, for the entire development and for specified stages.
c. Proposed agreements, declarations of intent, or specifications concerning dedications, deed restrictions, contracts, sureties, and provision, operation, and maintenance of common areas, facilities, and functions not to be a public responsibility.
d. Conformity of the latest draft of the preliminary plan and report with requirements of the zoning ordinance and subdivision and other general regulations of the jurisdiction.
e. Upon affirmative findings that the public purposes of such regulations are served to at least an equivalent degree by specific alternate proposals of the latest draft of the preliminary plan and report, suggested specific modifications of the zoning ordinance and subdivision and other general regulations as applied to the particular planned development, provided, however, that permitted residential floor area shall not be increased, nor shall required livability open space be diminished.

10. *Indicate requirements of final plan and report,* stating that no building permit shall be issued in the planned development until the planning department (or planning commission) has approved the final plan and report, which is to include:

a. Maps as required by subdivision regulations for final plats, but with such modifications of subdivision requirements as are provided generally for planned development, or as permitted or specified by the governing body in its zoning action in the particular case.
b. A final general plan indicating the location and purposes of all features and improvements, including items required to be included in the preliminary plan and report as specified above, but with such added dimensions and details as will permit the planning department (or commission) to make its determinations concerning conformity with regulations.
c. Proposed final drafts of all agreements, contracts, dedications, deed restrictions, sureties, or other instruments to be provided.

d. Detailed plans of individual buildings and groups of buildings and their sites. Such plans are to include floor plans and elevations and indications as to yards, courts, and open spaces between buildings or portions of buildings to the extent necessary to permit the commission to make its determinations. Such detailed plans may be submitted with the general material indicated in (a) through (c) above, or as separate sections of the final development plan and report, but if submitted as separate sections shall conform to (a) and (b) above.

11. *Indicate action required by planning department (or commission) on final plan and report.* The department (or commission) is to make a detailed review of the final plan and report to determine compliance with requirements applying in the case, making sure that all agreements, contracts, deed restrictions, dedications, and the like are in acceptable form and have been executed, all sureties provided, and all payments due made. With these things in order, the commission certifies its approval. As indicated in the preceding section, this approval may cover initially only the first three items, leaving reviews of detailed site and building plans for later actions. But no building permit may be issued by the administrative official until after the planning department (or commission) has reviewed and approved plans for the building involved, as related to surrounding buildings, and indicated that the plans conform to the requirements for the development.

One loose end remains. Provision should be made for further zoning action by the commission if for any reason the development does not proceed as required by time limitations. (In such cases, other action would be taken by other agencies of the local government on performance bonds and the like.) On zoning, what happens if nothing happens? A final provision along the following lines might be helpful:

12. *Planning commission action on expiration of time limits.* If development does not proceed within the time limits set, the commission shall be required to examine the circumstances and make recommendations to the governing body:

a. To extend time limits for all or part of the planned development, indicating suggested length of extension, or

b. To rezone all or part of the development to its former status or such other status as appears appropriate under current circumstances.

To the extent that any of the matters detailed above as PD-H ordinance provisions have been handled adequately in the general PD section of the ordinance, it would be unnecessary to repeat them in the PD-H section.

Planned development spin-off for conventional zoning

Several features from the PD-H approach have application in conventional lot-by-lot zoning. In multifamily districts (and in others, with appropriate adaptation), the LUI system of interrelated controls can be used. Transitional regulations at district boundaries where frictions are likely to occur have great promise. Yard and building spacing requirements can be refined to include consideration of window exposure. And there is a way to permit some of the flexibility of planned development where lots remain in individual ownership.

Adapting multifamily zoning to the LUI approach. Regulations for the Honolulu ordinance give a specific example of how conventional multifamily zoning can be adapted to the LUI approach, and some of the advantages. There are three multifamily districts, rated at LUI 50, LUI 63, and LUI 73. Following through on the LUI 73 district, the full rating applies only where lot area is 15,000 square feet or above. Below that area, the LUI drops on a graduated scale. So there are no "nonconforming" lots, but there is incentive for combination of small lots.

At LUI 73, the floor area ratio is 2.00. On a 15,000-square-foot lot, this would allow 30,000 square feet of residential floor area. This solved a previous problem. Prior regulations had required a certain lot area per dwelling unit, which resulted in fractional remainders. Using floor area instead of number of dwelling units both eliminated the fractional remainders and gave a closer control of residential density. If the dwelling units were large, the floor area allocation would be used in a smaller number; if small, in a larger number, with population remaining about the same.

At LUI 73, the open space ratio is 0.36. This is applied against actual floor area used. Assuming maximum use of the 30,000 square feet, 10,800 square feet of open space would be required. This does not mean that only 4,200 square feet of the lot would be available for building, because improved open space on the structure may be counted. To avoid crowding lot lines with structures, minimum ground-based landscaped yards are required, 10 feet in minimum dimension at front, side, and rear of the lot.

The livability space ratio (nonvehicular open space) is 0.23 at LUI 73. This too is applied against the actual floor area used. Again assuming the full 30,000 square feet of floor area, 6,900 of the 10,800 square feet of total open space would be required to be barred to vehicles, leaving 3,900 square feet for vehicular use.

The off-street parking ratio in this district was set at one space per dwelling unit. Assuming an average of 800 square feet per apartment, about 38 spaces would be required. It seems fairly obvious that 38 parking spaces cannot be provided in 3,900 square feet of vehicular open space; hence decked parking is indicated at this density. (Parking area in structures, along with areas for storage and for mechanical equipment, is excluded from the residential floor area limitations.)

Transfer of development rights. Even where zoning is on a lot-by-lot basis, with the lots remaining in individual ownership, transfer of development rights can achieve some of the advantages of planned development. Given a substantial tract in one ownership, under conventional regulations the potentials for development are usually more flexible than if the same land is in the hands of several owners. Public interest, so far as land-use regulations are concerned, is not in the pattern of ownership but in the pattern of development. Hence a combination of owners should be allowed to do anything an individual owner can do. The following statement of intent (again from the Honolulu ordinance) indicates the approach:

> Where development is on a lot-by-lot basis, rather than in planned developments as specially regulated by this ordinance, it is intended to permit joint action by adjoining property owners which allows greater flexibility in the use of land but accomplishes public purposes to an equivalent or higher degree than regulation on the individual lots. Such development . . . shall not alter the effect of regulations applicable in the district to the area under agreement as a whole, but may alter the effect on individual lots within the area under the agreement, provided, however, that at the edges of such area, the relation to adjoining property shall be the same as where regulation is applied on a lot-by-lot basis.

The agreement binds property owners and their successors in title to maintain the pattern of development so that the area as a whole will be in conformity with applicable regulations. Enforcement of such agreement includes the city.

This does more than permit mere density transfer. Toward the center of the combined lots, higher buildings would be allowed than would be possible on any of the individual lots. The development pattern would allow better combination of open space, perhaps eliminating some interior "strip" side or rear yards. (Percentage of lot which may be covered with buildings is limited in the Honolulu ordinance, so that elimination of such yards would not lead to excessive land coverage.) Off-street parking and loading arrangements can be more efficient.

Transitional requirements. In the planned development regulations, special requirements apply at the edges of the districts. The same approach can be used in conventional districts, easing the transition from one to the next and reducing the tendency for less restricted districts to encroach into adjoining areas.

Zoning ordinance checklist

Introduction

Most zoning ordinances have in them something old, something new, and something borrowed, and these ingredients are in a state of sporadic addition, adulteration, deletion, dilution, refinement, and/or reconglomeration under varying heats and pressures. Ordinances relating to fall-out shelters and trampolines leave traces understandable to any adult, but only people aging with the regulations can relate more obscure provisions to specific origins. Curious language was added after the "temporary" exhibition of a semipreserved whale at a shopping center. More went in when a hobbyist in a single-family district converted his small pigeon coop to a high-rise multifamily aviary.

Provisions to require re-subdivision of long strings of nonconforming lots now have a complicated addendum because a widow of limited means (but good connections) was being forced to maintain 150 feet of frontage in a district requiring 60-foot minimum lot widths. Her house was centered in a three-lot row of 50-foot frontages.

Those living intimately with zoning can supply innumerable similar examples, some of which are real improvements and refinements but many of which are not. As a result of repeated traumas, the anatomy of any zoning ordinance at or beyond middle age is likely to be warped, paunched, and complexioned in a manner reflecting excessive indulgence in ad hockery.

The best of new ordinances will in time be exposed to the same hazards. There must be adaptation to the unforeseen; adjustment to experience; correction of errors, omissions, and inequities; adoption of improved techniques; and reactions to large and small crises. Whether the ordinance ages and improves or becomes a creaking, misshapen monstrosity depends on how the changes are made, and why.

This report offers a series of suggestions for preparing and maintaining a zoning ordinance.

Format and other mechanical details

The zoning ordinance may be divided into three parts: the text, the schedule of district regulations, and the zoning map or map atlas.

TEXT FORMAT

Numbering sections. Looking forward to revisions, loose-leaf form is preferable for the text, and the numbering system should be logical and flexible to allow for additions or deletions.

The text should be divided under principal heads and subheads, each with a title which makes elements easy to identify. An ordinance so organized may not need an index, because the table of contents will be sufficiently detailed. Section and subsection heads should be assigned numbers in a logical decimal system rather than in the clumsy alphabetical-numerical progression [1-A-1-a-(1)-(a)]. And since decimals proceed in familiar progression, page numbers may not be necessary, simplifying later insertions.

As an example, if Chapter 10 of a code deals with zoning, and numbers in the 100 series are used for general provisions, the table of contents might be as follows:

CHAPTER 10. ZONING
10-100 GENERAL PROVISIONS
10-101 *Statement of legislative intent*
10-102 *Provision for official zoning map*
10-102.1 Authentication
10-102.2 Amendments to official zoning map
. . . . . . etc. . . . . .
10-103 *Rules for interpretation of district boundaries*
10-103.1 District regulations extend to all portions of districts
10-103.2 Where uncertainty exists as to boundaries on official map

10-103.2.1 Boundaries indicated as following center lines of streets or alleys
10-103.2.2 Boundaries indicated as following lot lines, public property lines, and the like.
. . . . etc. . . . .

The last entry above might appear as 10-1-C-2-b in an alphabetical-numerical progression, demonstrating one advantage of the decimal approach.

Amendments. To keep track of text revisions, a key indication in the table of contents will be helpful, with dates on the bottoms of revised contents and individual insert pages. Using the illustration above, change in the provisions on authentication would be indicated in the contents line thus:

10-102.1 Authentication (Ord. 11, 265, 11/16/71)

The bottom of the contents page would have a line indicating the latest amendments covered: "Including amendments through 11/16/71." And the bottom of the page of the text carrying the change would be annotated 11/16/71.

Given the latest revision of the table of contents, it would thus be possible to go through a copy of the ordinance to determine whether all of the necessary insertions had been made. Given a complete new edition of the ordinance, amendment details could be included, to give the full history from date of first passage, or a new series of change indications could begin.

FORMAT FOR THE ZONING MAP OR MAP ATLAS

Procedures and forms for preparing and maintaining zoning maps are well enough known so that only brief comment is called for here. The scale used should generally permit clear identification of lot lines, with 1″=600′ about the limit, and 1″=400′ or 200′ preferable.

Zoning boundaries should be shown with a line weight or line pattern easily distinguishable from other boundaries shown on the map, and letter-number symbols indicating district designation in the body of the map (R-1, C-2, and the like) should be so located and repeated within district boundaries as to make it easy to identify the zoning of individual property without threading a maze to find the district indicator.

Where district boundaries are not coterminous with, clear extensions of, or midway between other lines, it is best to indicate exact distances from those lines rather than require referral to the scale of the map.

Where a zoning atlas is used, orientation should be the same on all sheets. In odd-shaped areas, drafting convenience may suggest pointing the top of a sheet in a direction other than north, but the temptation should be resisted. If it can't be resisted, a north arrow should be prominently displayed.

Similarly, the scale *should* be the same on each atlas sheet. If there are overpowering reasons for variation (large areas with large property holdings might justify a smaller scale than usual, or areas with very small lots, a larger scale), graphic or other scale indicators should be prominently displayed. Use of the graphic scale avoids misinterpretations if the sheets are reduced or enlarged for special purposes.

Map amendments. Space should be provided on single-sheet zoning maps and on the key map and individual sheets of the zoning atlas for entries identifying date, ordinance number, and property description for each change. Keeping official map entries current is very important, particularly in those jurisdictions where a map change does not become effective until it has been posted on the official map. This is a sound requirement, since persons relying on the map may otherwise be misled as a result of administrative inaction.

FORMAT FOR SCHEDULE OF DISTRICT REGULATIONS

Purpose of the schedule. The purpose of the schedule (chart) of district regulations is to bring together in convenient, logical, and coordinated form the more important regulations applying to conventional zoning districts. (For certain types of special districts, e.g., planned developments, the schedule form may not fit, so that it will be necessary to carry such regulations in the general text.)

Main heads and subheads. A fairly complete schedule might have the following column and subcolumn headings across the top of the page, with district regulations in horizontal bands below them.

Schedule of District Regulations

Column	*Main Heads*	*Subheads*
1	*DISTRICTS, Designation and Intent*	
2-6	*USES AND STRUCTURES*	

2	Permitted principal uses and structures
3	Permitted accessory uses and structures
4	Uses and structures permissible only by special exception
5	Uses and structures requiring special administrative permit
6	Transitional uses and structures
7-9	*LOT, YARD, AND OPEN SPACE REQUIREMENTS*
7	Minimum lot requirements (area and width)
8	Minimum yard requirements (depth of front and rear yards, width of side yards)
9	Maximum lot coverage by all buildings
10	*MAXIMUM HEIGHT*
11	*SIGN LIMITATIONS*—No sign intended to be read from off the premises shall be permitted except . . .
12	*OFF-STREET PARKING AND LOADING REQUIREMENTS*

As part of the heads or subheads, certain columns would have cross references to detailed procedural or substantive regulations in the text. Thus, special exception or special administrative permit headings would direct attention to portions of the text dealing with procedures and detailed requirements for such permits.

There can be more or fewer heads than indicated in this sample. A column on prohibited uses might be added to itemize uses which otherwise might be interpreted as permitted by right. If off-street parking and loading requirements do not vary from district to district, but apply generally by class of use, there would be no point in having the off-street parking column on the schedule. In some schedules, a column headed "Notes" is added at the right edge to provide space for explanatory detail.

To keep track of schedule revisions, a date and ordinance indication is included in the block of text affected, and a date at the bottom of the schedule sheet indicates the latest amendments covered by the sheet.

Given such a schedule, a person who knows that his property is zoned R-3 can look across the R-3 band on the schedule and determine

Figure 1. Schedule of District Regulations

DISTRICTS	USES AND STRUCTURES			
Designation and Intent	Permitted Principal Uses and Structures	Permitted Accessory Uses and Structures	Special Exception Uses and Structures (See Section 21-402)	Special Permit Uses and Structures (See Section 21-403)
B-1: Neighborhood Business	B-1: Neighborhood Business	B-1: Neighborhood Business	B-1: Neighborhood Business	B-1: Neighborhood Business
This district is intended for application in locations where groups of small establishments may be appropriately located to serve frequent commercial and personal service needs of residents within convenient travelling distance. It is not intended to permit major commercial or service establishments in such districts nor any automobile service stations.	1. Bakery, confectionery, delicatessen and the like, provided that products prepared or processed on the premises shall be sold only at retail and only on the premises. 2. Barber shop, beauty shop. 3. Churches. 4. Drug store, newsstand, tobacco shop. 5. Eating and drinking establishments, except drive-in and those serving liquor. 6. Florist, gift shop, stationery store and the like. 7. Grocery, supermarket, meat market, fish market and the like. 8. Laundry and dry-cleaning establishments including self-service, provided that no such establishment shall employ more than 5 persons. Laundry and dry cleaning agencies. 9. Liquor stores, package only. 10. Public buildings and uses appropriate to the character of the district or requiring location within the district. 11. Public utilities installations and substations, provided that offices or storage or maintenance installations shall not be permitted. Utilities substations other than individual transformers shall be screened from R or A districts by a masonry wall or a fence with a properly maintained screening hedge.	Uses and structures which are customarily accessory and clearly incidental and subordinate to permitted or permissible uses and structures, including as accessory uses only: 1. Dwelling or lodging units for occupancy by owners or employees of principal uses only, provided that such dwelling or lodging units shall be located above or behind principal uses in such a way that they do not interrupt commercial frontage.	1. Private clubs, lodges, social centers, athletic clubs and the like. 2. Medical offices and clinics.	None.

Figure 1. Schedule of District Regulations (cont.)

LOT, YARD AND OPEN SPACE REQUIREMENTS			MAXIMUM HEIGHT	SIGN LIMITATIONS	OFF-STREET PARKING REQUIREMENTS
Minimum Lot Requirements (Area and width) (See Section 21-405)	Minimum Yard Requirements (Depth of front and rear yard, width of side yard) (See Section 21-406)	Floor Area Ratio	(See Section 21-410)	No Sign Intended To Be Read From Off The Premises Shall Be Permitted Except (See Section 21-415)	(See Section 21-420)
B-1: Neighborhood Business	B-1: Neighborhood Business	B-1: Neighborhood Business	B-1: Neighborhood Business	B-1: Neighborhood Business	B-1: Neighborhood Business
Minimum lot area: 5,000 ft. Minimum lot width: 50 ft.	Front yards adjacent to R or A districts: Where a B-1 district adjoins an R or A district without an intervening street or alley, and where lots separated by the boundary have adjacent front yards, the first lot within the B-1 district, or 100 ft. of such lot (whichever is less) shall provide a front yard of the minimum depth required in the adjoining district. Such yard shall be landscaped, except for necessary access drives and walkways, and shall not be used for parking. Other than as indicated above, all yards adjacent to streets: 10 ft., which shall be landscaped except for drives and walkways necessary for access. No such yard shall be used for parking. Side and rear yards adjacent to R or A districts without an intervening street or alley shall be of the same minimum dimension as required for the adjoining yard in the R or A district. The area within 5 ft. of the property line shall be landscaped with a properly maintained screening hedge, except for walkways necessary for access. No such yard shall be used for parking.	No floor area ratio is directly established for this district. Limitations on floor area maximum derive from height limits, yard requirements, and off-street parking requirements.	25 ft. above any portion of the lot within buildable area boundaries, provided however that where a lot in this district adjoins a lot in an R or A-1 district without an intervening street or alley, the Plane II height and light angle for the adjoining R or A-1 lot shall apply to the adjoining portion of the lot in this district	All permitted commercial uses. 1. One wall sign per street side for each ground floor establishment not to be directly illuminated and not exceeding 1 ft. of sign area for each 1 lineal foot of building frontage. No sign shall exceed 100 ft. in sign area. No illumination for any sign or premises shall be directly visible in any portion of a residential district after 10:00 p m , or from any room used for sleeping in any district. 2. One non-illuminated ground sign, for identification only, may be erected provided: a. All buildings are set back a minimum of 50 feet from the public right-of-way. b. No portion of the sign located in or overhanging any required yard area or right-of-way. c. The sign area does not exceed 12 ft.	Accessory dwelling and lodging units: 1/unit Eating and drinking establishments: 1/100 ft of floor area or 1/4 seats, whichever is greater. Other commercial uses: 1/400 ft. of floor area

what major regulations apply, without flipping back and forth through pages of text. If the principal uses permitted are indicated "As for R-2 and in addition . . . ," the R-2 uses are immediately above in the column, rather than several pages away.

For the public, the schedule is easier to understand and more convenient than regulations in page form. For administrators, the schedule is preferable. Some lawyers don't like it; cynics say this is because it makes the regulations clear, but lawyers have been known to object to the indignity of unfolding and refolding schedules in court or at hearings, or to raise convoluted questions as to the legal mechanics for amendment of items on the schedule. Given sheets in the neighborhood of 21 by 28 inches, handling problems are minimal. The dimensions are smaller than the 22 by 34 inches of an opened newspaper. Ease in reference outweighs minor difficulties in handling, and legal technical difficulties concerning amendment are more imagined than real. Particular sections on the schedule can be clearly identified by column and district coordinates, or by assigned section and subsection numbers for each box.

Even in cases where there are several districts with detailed requirements, the schedule form can be used to advantage. For example, a proposed schedule for the City and County of Honolulu had 23 districts on five sheets. In this relatively complex situation, the first sheet covered three preservation and agricultural districts; the second included seven single-family and two-family districts; the third, four apartment and two hotel districts; the fourth, four commercial districts; and the fifth, light, heavy, and waterfront industrial districts. The proposed schedule, however, was rejected and the information recast into 78 pages of single-spaced text. As a result, to find out what uses are permitted by right in an R-7 district, it is necessary to turn back from page 73 to page 72, then to page 70, then to page 68, then to page 66, and finally to page 61, with similar backlash on a number of matters other than uses.

Reproduction. Preparation of the schedule presents few problems if verbiage is held to a minimum (a virtue which the schedule form encourages). Where the schedule is set in type, a good printer will know how to hold material for future amendments without excessive costs, but the original job may be relatively expensive.

As an alternative to typesetting, schedule sheets can be reproduced photographically. Column heads are lettered and boxed in, with vertical lines drawn between columns. Regulatory material for each district is then typed and fixed in appropriate columns with rubber cement. When all typed material is attached for the first district, a horizontal line is drawn in at the bottom (with the depth of the band determined by the longest entry) and material is inserted for the next district.

Usually the schedule will be originally prepared in rough-draft form. With this as a guide, column widths of the final draft can be adjusted to the amount of text to keep the finished product fairly compact.

The final draft is then photographed at full scale or reduced (not more than one-third generally) on photopositive film for Ozalid, offset, or similar reproduction. If the originals are carefully preserved, when amendments are necessary old material is peeled off, replacement language inserted, rephotographed, and the revised copy printed as before.

In some jurisdictions, where land area is small and the number of districts limited, it is possible to print the zoning map on one side of a single sheet and the schedule of district regulations on the other, combining the information most users want on one large sheet. In cases where a proposed ordinance is reproduced in the newspaper in preparation for public hearings, the entire ordinance, text, schedule, and map can sometimes be printed on four newspaper pages, with reruns for later use on better paper. (This is useful and economical where few changes are made in the ordinance, but runs into trouble where there are numerous amendments in the first year or so.)

Districts: how many and what kind?

There is no easy way to determine how many zoning districts a community should have. The town of Jupiter Island, Florida, has only one district—single-family residential. In the case of *Gautier v. Jupiter Island* (142 So. 2d 321 Fla. App.), the court upheld this arrangement. Performance of a single function by a small town may make sense, depending on the regional context.

Another community has over 40 residential districts, identical except for a 25-foot variation in minimum floor area requirements. Quite apart from the dubious legality of sliding-scale minimum floor areas, so minute a distinction makes no sense at all.

The appropriate number and kinds of districts for a particular jurisdiction depend upon what the districts are intended to do under existing local circumstances and local plans.

INTENT STATEMENTS

The first, and perhaps major, virtue of intent statements is that they force drafters to relate regulations to defensible public purposes. They also serve as a guide to the courts, and may be both a guide and a defense for local legislative bodies. In the absence of such statements, courts are hesitant to speculate as to any special intent of the legislative body.

Where district regulations are in schedule form, an intent clause appears for each district or group of districts. For example, in conventional residential zoning, one such provision may cover all single-family and two-family, or all multifamily, districts. In commercial or industrial zones, a brief statement of intent may be needed for each.

Such statements may indicate policies on proposed containment or expansion, or reasons for special limitations. Thus where there is an oversupply of strip commercial zoning or areas with substantial overcrowding of residential use, zoning can hardly provide a cure, but it can discourage spread by including in the statement language along the following lines:

> This district is created in recognition of the existence of substantial areas presently committed to a form of development which is undesirable in the following respects. . . . It is not the intent to create additional districts of this type, nor to enlarge the limits of such districts.

Such treatment may be a practical compromise, avoiding creation of large numbers of nonconformities (with all the difficulties involved in limitations on structural alterations and the like) and containing the problem until further action can be taken to solve it. Such a holding zone might be established for a residential area slated for redevelopment or for strip commercial areas where public action to provide parking (through a parking authority, benefit district, or other approach) seems to be the best cure for slow commercial decay. The intent statement has the effect of drawing lines around mistakes that have already been made and indicating that they are not to be used as argument for repetition elsewhere.

SOME SPECIAL DISTRICTS

Intent provisions should be stated particularly carefully where there are special districts performing specialized functions not distinguished in familiar, older districting, for example, the commercial district catering primarily to through traffic, the office district, or the waterfront industrial district.

Thus cities with major waterfront activity may find that the provisions contained in conventional warehousing and light and heavy manufacturing districts are inadequate. Limited waterfront areas are occupied by uses which do not need to be there, preempting space that should be available for those that do. So a special waterfront industrial district is created. In Norfolk, Virginia, the waterfront industrial district (WF-I) entry on the schedule reads as follows:

> These regulations are intended to set apart and protect areas considered vital to performance of port functions, and provide for their efficient operation, continuation and expansion. To these ends, it is intended to permit in such districts the full range of facilities necessary for successful and efficient performance of their functions. In order to reserve such areas for port-related activities only, it is intended to exclude both uses which could equally well be located elsewhere and uses inappropriate in districts of this character.

The permitted principal uses column then lists uses generally permitted (piers, wharves, docks, ship terminals, shipyards, etc.) and certain others which are permitted only if port-related (warehousing, manufacturing, etc.).

Other possibilities for special districts will be discussed in context with permitted principal uses.

PLANNED DEVELOPMENT DISTRICTS

In theory, this rapidly emerging form should be highly attractive to planners, since development within each district is in accord with a predetermined comprehensive plan. In practice, such districts have not fared so well with planners, many of whom tend to be conservative about new ideas. As experience mounts, opposition declines.

Thus far, there has been heavy emphasis on planned residential development, but preoccupation with this form is giving way to a more general application. There can and should be a wide variety of planned development districts. In addition to those for housing, there can be planned neighborhood, community, and regional shopping centers, planned office districts, planned industrial districts, planned resort districts, planned development districts providing for mixtures of uses, and other forms.

As indicated previously, regulations for planned development districts do not fit the form of the district regulations schedule and will normally be carried in the text of the ordinance. Where there are to be several types of planned development districts, an introductory section will set forth general intent and the definition of planned development and procedures, and following sections will cover detailed requirements for each type of planned development district. Intent provisions should make it clear that where planning and development proceed as a package, there are sound reasons for regulatory forms and requirements to differ from those in lot-by-lot zoning.

HISTORIC AND CULTURAL CONSERVATION DISTRICTS

Historic districts have become increasingly common as cities become alarmed at the disappearance of landmark structures or whole areas of buildings and grounds of historic significance. Regulations for such districts usually include most of the following elements:

1. A declaration of intent, stating purposes and indicating criteria by which such districts shall be established.
2. Provision for protection within the district and in transitional areas visually related to it.
3. Provision for a special commission to advise on and administer detailed controls.

In some jurisdictions, a single building and grounds can be set aside within an historic district boundary. This does not constitute spot zoning, because it is for a public purpose and is (or should be) in accord with the comprehensive plan.

Historic zoning techniques and administrative devices are well adapted to application in the case of buildings and areas which are of major cultural significance, even though they may be relatively new. Thus enlarging the title, intent, and other details of historic district regulations to include cultural conservation may provide protection for civic center complexes, major institutions, and the like.

In some circumstances, separate districts for historic preservation and for protection of civic centers and other important cultural buildings or complexes may be necessary, but the combined approach has merit where it can be applied appropriately.

FLOOD HAZARD DISTRICTS AND OTHER FORMS OF FLOOD PROTECTION

Flood hazards come in a variety of forms: in floodways where rushing water is constricted in narrow channels; along coasts where tidal waves or wind-blown high tides may be equally destructive on a broad front; and in flood plains where the upward creep of water is less imminently hazardous but may cause tremendous property damage and the threat of epidemics. Areas threatened by any of these dangers should have regulations to minimize them, and the regulations should be carefully tailored to local circumstances, making distinctions as necessary between floodways and flood plains. They should relate to observed or "design" floods (maximum floods which may be expected to occur within specified periods) and include special limitations to fit anticipated problems.

In some areas, the district designation need not include flood hazard indications, but the regulations should recognize them. In one coastal resort area, the statement of intent generally refers to protection against "hazards to persons or property as a result of flooding due to windstorms and high tides," but the districts are resort residential, limited resort commercial, and intensive resort commercial. Protective provisions require that first floor elevations of any portion of a structure intended for human occupancy be above a stated safe level and that filling stations be barred from locations where breakthrough of a narrow peninsula during major storms might cause fire or explosive hazards "by reason of exposure, rupture or displacement of containers or lines holding flammable liquids due to erosion by high-velocity water flow and strong wave action."

Other coastal protective requirements might include establishment of bulkhead (seawall) lines, prohibition of construction or limitations on types of construction on the seaward side of dunes, prohibition against lowering dunes below a specified level, and requirements for filling where the dunes are lower than a specified level (and thus might form a breakthrough point during a hurricane). In some areas, strict limitation is placed on disturbance of native vegetation on dunes in an effort to preserve stability.

In summary, there is no magic formula setting the number and kinds of districts. Public purpose should be clear in setting up any district; no district should be established which does not relate to such purpose, and any district which does relate should be established. There has been an unfortunate tendency to cause proliferation of conventional districts which vary insignificantly and an equally unfortunate reluctance to develop significant new and special districts where there is real need.

District regulations—generally

District regulations should have legitimate, recognizable public purposes, should be clearly related to achievement of those purposes, and should be the simplest regulations which will achieve them effectively. These truisms, too often ignored by drafters or redrafters of regulations, are stated here as broad performance standards by which the controls themselves should be judged.

A simple illustration of one form of abuse is the use of zoning to make housing unnecessarily expensive by requiring value or construction cost to exceed given amounts. Zoning is also being misused where sliding-scale minimum size (square feet of floor area or cubic content) is used to set limits above those needed for health. And where extraordinarily large lot requirements are obviously set for the purpose of "snob" zoning, zoning abuse is evident.

In some cases, controls must be relatively complex in order to effectively achieve their purposes. Thus conventional yard requirements are unnecessarily rigid because they are simple; it is preferable to relate them to window exposures, a detail to be discussed at greater length later. And although it is simpler to bar gas stations from neighborhood shopping centers, it might be more in the interest of public convenience to develop regulations which would permit them subject to stringent limitations on location, appearance, signs, and manner of operation—which gets more complicated.

Some regulations are superfluous because of inadequate weeding as ordinances are brought up to date and new types of controls are added. For example, where floor area ratios and height envelopes are used, there is little point in retaining controls on number of stories, and elimination of limits on number of stories makes unnecessary a whole battery of definitions of story, half-story, basement, cellar, mezzanine, attic, and so on.

A great many ordinances are unnecessarily restrictive because there has been more emphasis on naming uses to be permitted or prohibited than on the regulation of use through performance standards. Performance standards are increasingly used in industrial zoning. They should be used increasingly in the regulation of other kinds of uses. The case of the gas station in a neighborhood commercial district has been cited above. As another example, consider the home occupation in a residential neighborhood. Is there any legitimate public reason for barring from a residential district a home occupation (whatever its specific title) which has absolutely no external evidence of its existence?

District regulations—details

The following material discusses column headings 2 through 12 of the schedule of district regulations cited earlier. (Intent in establishing districts has already been discussed.)

PERMITTED PRINCIPAL USES AND STRUCTURES

In the schedule, the listing of uses and structures should be general and should emphasize performance characteristics as appropriate. If it is felt that very detailed listings are needed, an appendix or supplementary regulations may be used, but no such listing is likely to include everything which may come up. Generalized listings will take care of the vast majority of cases and serve as a guide to whether specific uses should be permitted or prohibited.

Some ordinances attempt to use Standard Industrial Classification groupings and subgroupings as a source for detailed listings, partly because of the convenience in using computerized tabulations. This must be done with great care, since the Standard Industrial Classification is not designed with zoning in mind.[1] Thus for zoning purposes, drive-in eating and drinking establishments, gas stations, miniature golf courses, and perhaps even drive-in banking facilities have much in common, although they are widely separated or in some cases not distinguished in SIC classifications.

In drafting or redrafting ordinances, the yellow pages of the telephone directory or a city directory may serve better than the Standard Classification Manual as an initial source or a checklist to determine possible difficulties in general interpretation. The SIC or other codes can be used in computerization, but probably add little to public understanding or convenience in use of the ordinance.

1. Cf. Erling Helland, "The Standard Land Use Coding Manual in Preparing Zoning Regulations," *Land-Use Controls Quarterly,* Vol. 2, No. 4 (Chicago: American Society of Planning Officials, 1968), pp. 17-22.

Here is an example of generalized language used to describe one principal use in a preservation district:

Open agricultural uses not requiring intensive cultivation, including the raising and grazing of livestock (but not feed lots), orchards, vineyards, and the like.

For a strip commercial district, a principal category might be generalized thus:

Retail stores other than those dealing in second-hand merchandise, including those with incidental manufacturing or processing of goods for sale only at retail and only on the premises; *retail sales and display rooms and lots,* not including yards for the storage or display of new or used building materials or for any scrap or salvage operation, storage, or sales.

If these or similar general indicators need elaboration, elaborate. But it should not be necessary to list in detail every conceivable open agricultural use or every conceivable type of retail store, retail sales, or display room and lot, and still conclude by saying "and the like" to cover cases omitted because they weren't thought of when the regulations were written.

Definitions should be carefully coordinated with use listings. Thus if "intensive cultivation" is not considered clear enough in local usage, it should be defined to indicate its connotations as to plowing, harrowing, and the leaving of bare, fallow ground for extensive periods.

In the residential categories, correlation of definitions with listings of permitted uses may be particularly important. Single- and two-family dwelling forms should be defined to include detached, semi-detached, and attached, and, if it is intended to distinguish between mobile homes, other forms of prefabricated or modular housing, and conventional dwelling units, a distinction should be made in the definitions section and in the use listing.

Cumulative vs. "exclusive" listings. Antiquated ordinances use the pyramidal form, starting with the "most restrictive" district and permitting in each "lower" district all the uses permitted above plus new ones. The heavy industrial district becomes a catch all for residential, commercial, industrial, and miscellaneous. Few cities with such conglomerate "industrial" districts can be proud of the results. In effect, these are unzoned areas.

Most multifamily districts permit detached, semi-detached, and attached single- and two-family dwellings in addition to multifamily structures (in fact, they contain more single-family and two-family dwellings than multifamily structures). This seems to indicate a policy approving mixtures of housing types except among the self-elected elite. There does not seem to be any compelling public reason for the general use of a multifamily district that excludes single- and two-family dwellings.

In conventional commercial districts, there are sound reasons for the exclusion or careful control of residential uses. Detached and semi-detached single- and two-family dwellings are particularly prone to blight in commercial environments, and any residential use tends to break commercial continuity in a way that may contribute to commercial decay. Exclusive commercial zoning may limit applications for speculative amendments. ("If we can't find a commercial occupant, we can always use it for apartments.")

Such districts may allow accessory residential uses, permitting owners or employees to live on the site of a commercial enterprise. And if there is microzoning, with residential uses limited to the rear of the lot or above commercial enterprises (and with appropriate restrictions on off-street parking, vehicular access, and open space adjacent to residential windows), new residential uses can be protected from blighting influences and commercial continuity retained.

In planned commercial districts, where location of residential uses can be carefully integrated and controlled, there may very well be a place for apartments or townhouses in peripheral sectors and for apartments and perhaps office uses above the ground floor.

In central business districts, there are possibilities in stratified zoning, with ground and contiguous lower floors reserved for highly intensive walk-in commercial, service, and similar uses, intermediate floors for office uses of a less intensive nature, and apartments only in the higher portions of buildings. The apartments provide downtown living at elevations where street noise is unobjectionable and the view is best. They also reduce traffic congestion by allowing people to live near their work—and in some cases to reach it by elevator. The office uses do not require a sidewalk level location and are not allowed to interrupt sidewalk continuity. The ground floor is reserved for those uses which depend most on sidewalk-level entrances.

"Industrial" is a many-faceted term. In its broadest sense, it includes "any branch of art, occupation, or business." In the minds of some, it means only manufacturing. "Industrial" districts in zoning should be neither so broad nor so narrow. Primary activities should include bulk storage and warehousing, distributive operations, wholesaling, packaging, major repair and maintenance, processing, and light and heavy manufacturing.

A zoning ordinance responsive to modern needs and emerging urban patterns will sort these things out according to desirable location of functions within the local complex. Thus on the fringes of the CBD there will be some activities which belong in that and few other locations. There may be specialized distributive or production complexes which would fit best near major interchanges of limited access highways or at places where rail, water, air transport, and highway combinations offer particular advantages.

The ordinance should encourage desirable specialized industrial concentrations and protect them from undesirable or unnecessary intrusions. Commercial activities other than those supporting the principal function might well be barred, along with residential uses other than those necessarily accessory to the principal use.

It may be inevitable that some residual "industrial" districts will be too conglomerate for zoning to shape them into something more useful. Even here, new residential uses should be prohibited except in connection with large-scale redevelopment (and if there is to be large-scale redevelopment including residential use, it might well require planned development processing).

For "industrial" districts (and for other districts as much-needed standards are worked out), performance standards should back up general descriptions of types of activities permitted. This eliminates the long and incomplete listing by name of industries permitted or prohibited. Except where compatibility with district function is concerned, the name of the product produced or the process by which it is produced is not a matter of public concern. The thing that matters is whether it can be produced within tolerable limits on noise, glare, smoke and other particulate matter, vibration, fire and explosive hazards, and the like. The limits should be stated and administrative devices established for enforcing them.[2]

2. On administration of performance standards without extraordinary local expertise or specialized equipment, see "Performance Standards: Evolution, Administration, Instrumentation and the Gambling Instinct," p. 452.

ACCESSORY USES AND STRUCTURES

Simple ordinances in uncomplicated jurisdictions once handled accessory uses and structures by permitting "uses and structures which are customarily accessory and clearly incidental to permitted or permissible uses and structures."

Later, or in more complex situations, this was expanded by adding an illustrative list of the more common accessory uses, and the words "and the like."

In further evolution, many ordinances have come to include substantial detail as a result of experience with problems. The home occupation in a residential neighborhood, discussed earlier, is one, and a rather long list of others could be tallied. In residential areas, there are questions about private swimming pools; the breeding or keeping of pigeons, chickens, dogs, cats, horses, and cows; storage of major recreational equipment; guest cottages and servants' quarters; the height of fences; air conditioning equipment; and noisy hobbies. Should a hospital in a single-family residential area be permitted to have living quarters in the form of multifamily dwellings or rooming houses as an accessory structure, and, if so, what safeguards should be employed to protect neighborhood character? In agricultural areas, should roadside stands be permitted and, if so, with what restrictions?

It is generally agreed that if a use is permitted as a principal use in the district, it should usually be allowed as an accessory use. But what about accessory uses of a character not generally permitted as a principal use? For example, motorcycle sales and service are first permitted as principal uses in C-3. A major department store in a C-2 district has a small subdepartment selling motorbikes. Should this store be forced to discontinue its sales? Eating and drinking establishments, news stands, and self-service laundries are not allowed as principal uses in multifamily and hotel districts. Should they be allowed as accessory uses? If allowed as accessory uses, should they be allowed generally or only in establishments above a stated size? Should any external evidence of their existence be permitted? What percentage of total floor area may be occupied by such uses? (As a simpler problem, if such accessory uses are not permitted, should coin-operated vending machines be allowed?)

The best current ordinances spell out details, requirements, and limitations on accessory uses and structures, including, as appropriate: scale (percentage of floor area or lot area which may be occupied), location, manner and in some cases hours of operation, buffering, signs, and other items.

SPECIAL EXCEPTION AND ADMINISTRATIVE PERMIT USES AND STRUCTURES

Under the Standard Zoning Enabling Act, the board of adjustment was the only body empowered to act on special exceptions. In some jurisdictions, the governing body has moved in on this function, acting on what are called conditional use permits, special use permits, or something similar. This is unfortunate in terms of separation of powers but has been sanctioned by state legislation in some states. Since the board usually has no technical staff and may lack expertise in technical planning matters, a favorable recommendation from the planning department or planning commission is sometimes required before the board can act favorably on certain types of applications for special exception. And in some jurisdictions, action by the board does not become effective until it has been approved by the governing body.

The special exception or conditional use typically involves cases in which the use would not generally be appropriate within a district but might be allowable in certain locations within the district if specific requirements were met. Too often, the requirements of the special exception device are inadequately stated because drafters of the ordinance could not decide what the specific requirements should be, or because there was a desire to test neighborhood sentiment before allowing the use in a particular location. In general, special exceptions should be kept to a minimum. However, when they are used, the requirements and limitations should be specifically stated.

The administrative permit is partly an alternative to the special exception and partly a device for expeditious handling of relatively minor matters requiring more than routine consideration. To make the distinction clear, in one jurisdiction special exception uses in residential estate districts include airports, cemeteries, and extractive industries (among other items).

Administrative permit uses in the same districts include carnivals, circuses and fairs, private piers and boathouses accessory to dwellings, and temporary structures and uses connected with land development and building construction. The ordinance specifies in considerable detail the procedures and requirements for both special exception and administrative permit uses so that there is no question as to delegation of legislative authority.

TRANSITIONAL USES AND STRUCTURES

Interdistrict frictions are highest at district boundaries, and more intensive uses tend to invade less intensive districts by amendatory creep. A gas station at the edge of a commercial district is next to a house on the same frontage in the adjoining residential district. The homeowner asks for commercial rezoning—who wants to live next to a gas station? The boundary is moved, and he sells his property for a drive-in Chicken Shoppe. Now his neighbor, newly adjacent to the commercial boundary, wants it extended to include him—who wants to live next to a Chicken Shoppe?

To ease this friction, ordinances have been providing recently for transitional uses and structures (with some additional transitional provisions on buffering, yards, heights, etc.). As an example, where a commercial district adjoins a single-family residential district along the same frontage, without an intervening street, for a stated distance within the commercial district, no gas stations or drive-ins are permitted. For the same distance inside the predominantly single-family district, two-family dwellings are permitted. If the joint boundary divides single-family residential from industrial, the range of uses near the industrial district boundary may be decreased to exclude uses which might be most objectionable, and those within the residential district may be increased to permit, for example, small apartments and clinics.

Where such districts adjoin along common frontage, height limits may be increased slightly in the bordering residential sector and diminished in the commercial or industrial, and front yard requirements in the first 100-150 feet of the commercial district may be made the same as for the residential district, with parking barred from the transitional front yards. Side yards in the commercial or industrial district adjoining the boundary can be required to be of the same minimum dimensions as in the residential district, or fences or vegetative buffering can be required, or both the increased side yard and the buffering can be called for.

In some recent ordinances, there are also transitional protections where the common boundary between commercial or industrial and residential districts is at the rear lot line. Here the commercial or industrial property is required to provide a deeper yard than is generally called for within the district, to maintain it in landscaping, and/or provide a fence, wall, or vegetative screening to shield residential property from views of the back sides of nonresidential property, and from noise and lights on such property.

LOT, YARD, AND OPEN SPACE REQUIREMENTS

Minimum lot area and width. Such specifications are generally controlled only in residential districts and, in many cases, only with respect to residential uses. For residential uses, the requirements on lot width and area should be so related to definitions as to include corner lots, "irregular" lots (those inside the row adjacent to the street), and lots on curvilinear streets and culs de sac, and to provide against inclusion in required minimum lot area of portions of the property which are connected incidentally but cannot properly serve a function in relation to the structure. (As an example of this kind, consider lots in common ownership on opposite block faces overlapping only for 10 feet at a rear corner. If a structure taking credit for the total area of the two lots is built on one of them, the one built upon is very likely to be overcrowded.)

If yard width and area are controlled for residential uses in residential districts, it is only equitable to require minimum lot widths and areas for other uses permitted by right. Thus, where churches or hospitals are permitted principal uses, specific minimum lot widths and areas for churches and hospitals should be prescribed (as well as other special requirements on minimum yards, open space, lot coverage, and other matters). Where only a general minimum lot width and area is indicated, without reference to the use involved, it is of general application. In the absence of specific requirements related to other than residential uses, a church, for example, could be located on a lot of minimum dimensions intended to apply (but not indicated as applying) to single-family residences only.

In multifamily districts, improved control of population density and desired flexibility in development can be achieved by substituting floor area ratios for the more traditional (and less satisfactory) requirements as to lot area per dwelling unit. Under this arrangement, the developer can respond to market conditions by providing a variety of units—more small ones or fewer large ones—and the population housed remains about the same. The occupancy (or housing) code should control abuses which might otherwise arise as a result of efforts to make units or rooms too small in order to maximize the number of rental units.

In commercial, industrial, and other nonresidential districts, although no minimum lot area or width is generally required, the floor area ratio approach is increasingly used to control land-use intensity and combined with height and other regulations to control shape and spacing of buildings.

Yards.—Considerable advances have been made in relating yard requirements to yard functions, although the millennium has not arrived. In single-family detached districts, the front yard limits tend to reflect a Victorian front-porch-rocking era, and rear yard requirements are concerned with keeping the stable and smokehouse away from the main dwelling. There is hope for progress in a few provisions which allow carports or garages to project into required front yards provided suitable visibility for traffic is maintained. Anchorage and Honolulu permit such uses. One result in Anchorage has been a reduction in snow shoveling. Where such leeway is implemented systematically in development, front yards are no longer sterile decorative areas, but with the increased privacy gain utility as areas for sitting, play sites for children, and places for barbecues and family parties.

Fenced or walled front yards, again with requirements for visibility triangles for traffic protection, would provide still further privacy and utility for this area of the lot. And planned residential development lessons could be applied in lot-by-lot zoning of areas not yet built up by allowing the house to back close to subservient rather than dominating streets, placing car storage, service areas, and kitchen exposures on the street side, and facing living areas to expanded rear or side yards. (The more functional side yard will be discussed under transfer of development rights.)

In a number of recent ordinances, required rear yards become true yards, unoccupied by accessory structures, and of the same minimum dimensions as the side yards. If the side yard provides adequate separation of bedroom windows on adjacent lots and sufficient access, light, and air, the same separation should be sufficient at the rear. (There are also provisions allowing garages or carports to have party walls at certain locations on the lot, reducing fragmentation of open space.) By reducing rear yards to the same dimension as side yards, the buildable area of the lot is substantially increased. This allows a greater variety of building forms, with a potential for L or U shapes wrapped around private open space. With such reduction, it is also no longer necessary to indicate what accessory buildings may occupy what portions of the rear yard, and for what uses, of what heights, and at what distance from the principal building they may be.

As an example of what this kind of change might mean, one existing ordinance requires 75 feet of frontage and 10,500 square feet of area in a single-family district, making minimum lot depth 140 feet. Minimum yards are: front, 30 feet; sides, 8 feet each; and rear, 35 feet, with accessory buildings permitted to occupy up to 30 per cent of the rear yard. The minimum front yard area required is 2,250 square feet, or 21.4 per cent of the total minimum lot area. The minimum combined side yard areas come to 1,200 square feet, or 11.4 per cent of minimum lot area. The minimum rear yard required is 2,625 square feet, or 25 per cent of minimum lot area. Allowing 30 per cent of rear yard area for accessory buildings reduces required open space on the rear yard to 1,837.5 square feet or 17.5 per cent of total lot area. Thus 5,287.5 square feet of the total 10,500 square feet (50.4 per cent) is required as open space. The fixed buildable area for the principal building is 59 by 75 feet, 4,425 square feet. There is a secondary buildable area for the accessory building which is more flexible in location, but the building itself may not occupy more than 787.5 square feet.

Changing to an eight-foot minimum rear yard enlarges and unifies the buildable area, making it 59 by 102 feet, 6,018 square feet, up about 14 per cent from the present figure. But it also reduces required open space to 4,482 square feet, or 42.7 per cent of lot area, which appears inadequate. Measures to counter potential excesses are discussed in the section on maximum lot coverage by all buildings.

Relating window exposure to required exterior space.—As a further refinement, after minimal side and rear yards have been established, additional spacing can be required according to exposure of principal windows. Building or occupancy (housing) codes usually indicate that, for residential uses, glassed areas equal to 10 per cent of floor area (with adjustments for special situations) must be provided for habitable rooms, but specify only that such glassed areas must open on "approved" open space. Somewhere, either by amendment to the codes or by language in the zoning ordinance, the dimensions and character of "approved" open space should be indicated. Given this improvement, the minimal yards would be allowed only in relation to nonrequired windows or where there was a blank wall or carport. The width of adjacent open space would have to be increased if required glassed areas faced into it—a very desirable form of performance regulation.

This approach would solve the problems of some jurisdictions, where front, side, and rear yard requirements relate only to the orientation of the lot rather than to orientation of uses within the building. Under this crude form of control, apartments are sometimes built lengthwise on relatively narrow lots, with entrances and principal glassed area exposures of most of the units oriented to narrow side yards. Such structures meet the letter of the zoning ordinance. The "front" yard, toward the street, is deep enough and the side and rear yards meet minimum requirements. But most of the units face (or back on) space substandard with respect to exposure. The cure is in yard regulations based on orientation of principal glassed area of the units.

Maximum lot coverage by all buildings. In the example above, where the rear yard was reduced from 35 feet to eight feet, the potential lot coverage was increased to 57.3 per cent from 49.6 per cent. It is unlikely that a single-family residence, including attached or detached carport, garage, or other incidental buildings, would have a ground floor area of anything like 5,212.5 square feet, as theoretically allowed under the existing controls, or 6,018 square feet with the suggested rear-yard reduction. But should such buildings be constructed, lot coverage would obviously be excessive. As a preventive measure, limits can be placed on maximum lot coverage by all buildings. In this case, a maximum of 25 to 35 per cent might be appropriate, allowing 2,625 to 3,675 square feet of ground coverage.

Where uses are more intensive, the maximum lot coverage limitation is of greater practical importance. Thus in cases where no yards as such are required, an 80 per cent limitation on lot coverage would assure some open space, leaving the building's location optional.

Relating coverage to slope.—Sliding-scale lot coverage limitations related to slope have considerable functional utility. Thus in the preservation (open space) district in Honolulu, maximum lot coverage drops by stages from 10 per cent on base line slopes of less than 20 per cent to one per cent where slopes are 40 per cent or over. In apartment districts the coverage ranges from 50 per cent on slopes of 20 per cent or less down to five per cent on slopes of 40 per cent or more. This discourages excessive disturbance of the natural terrain on hillsides and seems to be a more practical and direct approach than requiring hillside lots to be larger than those in flat lands.

MAXIMUM HEIGHT

As development moves into the hills, there is considerable advantage in a form of height limitation which does not encourage cuts or fills, helps to protect the view, and is functional in protecting light and air. It works equally well on level ground.

Starting from Plane I, an artificially established base plan, Plane II is set parallel above it, with height varying by districts. From the intersection of Plane II with the vertical projection of the buildable area boundaries, light planes extend inward (with the angle varying by districts) from side and rear buildable area boundaries. No portion of any building may extend through these light planes.[3]

The effects are to place the higher portions of buildings toward the middle of lots, to relate required on-ground and above-ground open space to building form, to place higher portions of hillside buildings down the slope where they will interfere less with views from overlooking property, and to relate height to an artificial plane which gives a premium for building in portions of the lot below it and sets a penalty for building in portions of the lot above it.

There are a number of other height control devices relating to light and air, height bonuses for diminished ground coverage, and averaging arrangements which allow part of a building to go higher if the remainder is correspondingly lower.

View protection. In addition to the view protection features indicated above, proposals covering both height and axial orientation have been suggested. Here height limits related to elevation above a set ground level may be combined with restrictions as to degrees of horizon arc which may be obscured by higher portions of buildings with principal public viewpoints established as a basis for making determinations. Under this arrangement, where portions of buildings in strategic locations extend above the elevation set as a general maximum, there is some pressure to turn them so that their slim side is toward the public view.

SIGN LIMITATIONS

Sign control in residential districts is generally handled by specifying number, character, location, and size for specific uses permitted. In commercial, industrial, and other districts where use-by-use specifications are impractical, one technique used increasingly relates number and area of signs to frontage adjacent to streets. As one example:

3. For a detailed description of this approach, see Frederick H. Bair, *Height Regulation in Residential Districts,* Planning Advisory Service Report No. 237 (Chicago: American Society of Planning Officials, August 1968).

> Number and area of signs intended to be read from any public way shall be limited as follows. Minimum sign allotment shall be two signs and not to exceed 100 sq. ft. of sign surface area. Maximum sign allotment shall be not to exceed one sign, and not to exceed 30 feet of sign surface area, for each 10 feet of property constituting frontage on a street, and for each 20 feet of property adjacent to a street other than at the front.

Since there are three elements which can be adjusted, the device has wide flexibility. Units of frontage, square feet per unit, and number of signs per unit can be set to meet the circumstances of particular districts. Such limitations would of course be reinforced by necessary language concerning limitations on off-site versus on-site signs, general location of signs on property, definitions of sign, number of signs, surface area, and perhaps specific prohibitions against orienting signs to face residential districts.

OFF-STREET PARKING AND LOADING REQUIREMENTS

There appear to be no revolutionary advances in this field, but one caveat might be noted concerning loading requirements. A number of ordinances are so worded that a little old lady who makes hats and delivers them in a Volkswagen would be required to provide off-street loading space for a tractor-trailer. This might be construed to be excessive.

Nonconformities

There is an increasing tendency to divide nonconformities into appropriate subclasses, moving away from the old practice of lumping everything under the heading of nonconforming *uses*. Regulation can be simpler and more functional where division along the following lines is made:

Nonconforming lots
Nonconforming structures
Nonconforming uses of land with minor structures only
Nonconforming uses of major buildings and premises
Nonconforming characteristics of use

There seems to be increasing awareness that some nonconforming uses will not go away as a result of wishful thinking and that perhaps it is not in the public interest to require them to continue in obsolete and often unsightly structures. Take the case of old gas stations in neighborhood commercial districts from which new gas stations are barred. Some of them have had sustained good business because of their convenient and monopolistic locations. The outlook is for virtual immortality. But they may not be enlarged or structurally altered, and, from the point of view of appearance, structural alteration may be essential.

In such situations, if there are no realistic amortization provisions in the ordinance, consideration is being given to the idea that upon a finding that the nonconforming use is likely to continue, structural alterations and even some enlargement may be permitted as a special exception, subject to limitations and requirements including maximum lot coverage, controls on curb cuts, removal of nonconforming characteristics of use (such as excess signs), buffering, and so forth. The practical improvement outweighs the violation of the questionable principle that nonconforming uses will go away.

Transfer of development rights

Many of the lessons learned from experience with planned development regulations can be applied directly in lot-by-lot zoning. Some should be applicable, but need adjustment of lot-by-lot controls. Transfer of development rights is a means to this end.

The basic theory is that the public interest rests not with accidental patterns of ownership but with the pattern of development. If a row of lots on the same frontage are thrown together into a single tract, a number of things can be done which could not be done if they remained in separate ownership. There could be a higher building toward the center of the tract (assuming plane controls) than on a single lot in the same location. The spacing of buildings and portions of buildings might be varied. Intensity of use could be concentrated in one portion of the tract, leaving the rest relatively open. Off-site parking would become on-site parking.

Thus some ordinances are permitting transfer of development rights—not merely density, but the whole range—where owners of land in an appropriate pattern get together and record agreements, with the governing jurisdiction included in enforcement. The application of regulations remains the same at the exterior boundaries of the area of agreement, but elsewhere within it anything can be done that would be allowable if it were in one tract.

Some of the more obvious possibilities have been indicated generally above. One might be developed in detail. In single-family detached areas in planned developments, there is growing use of a design technique which places one side of the house on the lot line, and at the other side provides a yard which is the full combined width of what would have been the individual side yards, perhaps 15 to 20 feet or more. Spacing between buildings remains the same. But instead of two narrow side yards with limited utility, the combined yard is wide enough to be used for a variety of purposes.

Under transfer of development rights, where lot owners could agree on the arrangement, they could take advantage of the improved design.

The board of adjustment

Boards of adjustment in some areas continue to make decisions which are a matter of concern to planners, administrators, and governing bodies. It has been pointed out that there should be specific guides and standards in the ordinance concerning special exceptions and not mere listings of uses which the board can grant or deny depending on its mood or the personalities or pressures in the case.

It is at least as important that the board be given specific guidance in connection with the issuance of variances. General guidance from state enabling legislation has been improved in a number of recent legislative amendments, but where this is inadequate the local ordinance should set forth findings in a particular case. It will be helpful if the findings include guidelines derived from court tests in the state and around the country. Thus personal hardship should be distinguished from hardship running with the land, self-inflicted hardship should be barred as grounds for a variance, and, above all, use variances should be prohibited. In addition to indicating what the board may not do and the reasons on which decisions should not be based, it is helpful to indicate the kind and limits of variances which may appropriately be granted.

Definitions

Preparation of definitions for a new ordinance, or review of definitions for an ordinance being overhauled, should wait until the rest of the language has been completed, so that words which need to be defined can be identified and no space is wasted defining words that are not used. In cut-and-paste efforts involving extensive borrowing from other ordinances, definitions are frequently included for words which do not appear elsewhere in the ordinance.

Common words, used with their common meaning, need not be defined. Groups of words or terms referring to the same subject might well be defined under one head with subheads, rather than in alphabetical order (e.g., the various forms of dwellings and lodgings). And if a word or phrase is only used in one special section of the ordinance, it would be best to insert the definition at that point, rather than to include it in the definitions section.

Zoning: *notes on new approaches*

In an ordinance drafted for Anchorage, Alaska, some approaches were worked out which may be useful elsewhere. Here are a few with supporting reasoning and comments on technique:

1. Exploitation of natural resources, with emphasis on putting the land in shape for re-use.
2. Convenience establishments, a device for getting the corner grocery and similar convenience facilities back into medium- and high-density residential areas, with controls on location, grouping, and operational characteristics.
3. Extensions of commercial development, a means for permitting controlled expansion in depth from strip commercial areas.
4. Townhouses, as distinguished from row housing.
5. "Profession; professional office" defined. A new attempt to cope with an old problem.
6. A special district for public lands and institutions.
7. General residential development districts.
8. Flexible building spacing.
9. Planned shopping centers.
10. Commercial open recreational uses.
11. Private and quasi-public playgrounds, playfields, and children's camps, not operated for profit.
12. Residual lot area—specifications for administrative leeway.

Exploitation of natural resources

In many areas, exploitation of natural resources is a temporary use of land which presents problems because the land is left in such shape that re-use is difficult or impossible. This contributes to urban sprawl, raises costs for extending facilities and services, punches a hole in the tax base, and may contribute to blight.

Ordinarily, it is demonstrably in the public interest to apply controls to such use, permitting it in areas where it is an appropriate temporary use only if the land will be left in a condition which won't cause continuing problems. The controls proposed here are framed to fit a situation in which there are already some nonconforming uses causing difficulties, and new uses are to be permitted only as special exceptions. The ordinance provides that any use which would be permissible in a district as a special exception shall not be considered a nonconforming use in the district, and the second item indicates a way around this.

---

1. *Definition.* For purposes of this chapter, exploitation of natural resources is defined as commercial or industrial operations involving removal for sale, processing, or use of timber, native vegetation, peat, muck, topsoil, fill, sand, gravel, rock, or any mineral.
2. *Amortization of nonconforming uses and uses permissible but not specifically permitted by special exception.* Where exploitation of natural resources exists as a nonconforming use, or has not been approved as a special exception in accordance with the provisions of this chapter in a district in which such exploitation is permissible as a special exception, notwithstanding any other provisions of this chapter concerning such uses and their continuance, the following regulations shall govern:
   a. *Time limitation.* Within three years from the effective date of this chapter, either such use shall cease or the owners thereof shall prepare a Plan for Development, Exploitation Phase, providing for orderly progress according to a time schedule which will result in phasing out the operation within a period of not less than five years, and a Plan for Re-Use, indicating a proposal for re-use of the property in accordance with the regulations of this chapter for the district in which the property is located. Such plans shall be in accordance with the requirements of item 3c, below.

   The Plan for Development, Exploitation Phase, shall have as one of its final objectives the preparation of the property for re-use in accordance with the Plan for Re-Use. Such plans, with other necessary documents, shall be presented to the Board of Adjustment as an application for special exception, at least 90 days in advance of the expiration of the three-year period. If not so presented, continued operation after the expiration of the three-year period shall be a violation of the terms of this chapter.

These provisions offer inducements for preparing the land for re-use. Unless the requirements as to the plans for exploitation stage and for re-use are met, the use must stop in three years. If the requirements are met, it may continue for as long as eight years. (The periods may of course be varied to fit local circumstances.)

---

b. *Action by planning commission, board of adjustment.* Upon favorable recommendation by the Planning Commission, the Board of Adjustment may issue a special exception permitting continuation of the operation according to the Plan for Development, Exploitation Phase, to result in the accomplishment of the objectives of the Plan for Re-Use.

The Board shall not grant such special exception unless it has received a favorable or conditionally favorable report from the Planning Commission, and if conditions are attached by the Planning Commission, such conditions shall be included in the special exception, without alteration except upon agreement in writing by the Planning Commission. The Board may add other conditions and safeguards not in conflict with those proposed by the Planning Commission. The Board may require posting of a performance bond to assure that the property will be left at the end of the period specified in the Plan for Development, Exploitation Phase, in the condition specified in the Plan for Re-Use, and such performance bond may include provisions for removal of all or any part of any building or other improvement.

Here procedures remain within the limits set by standard zoning enabling legislation. The board of adjustment is the only agency empowered to issue special exceptions, but planning commission approval, outright or conditional, is required before the board may issue the exception, and the board must include any conditions set by the planning commission. In jurisdictions where the planning commission is empowered to issue special use permits, the board action would not be necessary. The same game can be played by any rules, but it should be played according to rules laid down by the state legislature, and not by rules invented locally on the spur of the moment.

It seems logical and within reason to require posting of a performance bond (or other acceptable surety) in connection with a special exception of this kind. The special exception is issued only if there is an acceptable plan for re-use. Unless the plan is followed, the public is not protected. The surety makes it certain that whether the applicant follows through or not, the public will not be left with a liability on its hands.

---

c. *Effect of denial of special exception, or failure to conform to requirements.* If the special exception is denied, the operation shall cease at the end of the three-year period specified in 2a, above. If operations fail to conform to the Plan for Development, Exploitation Phase, or if there is violation of any of the conditions and safeguards attached to the special exception, continued operation shall be considered violation of the terms of this chapter.

3. *Special exceptions in districts in which permissible generally by Board of Adjustment.* In any district in which new exploitation of natural resources is permissible by the board of adjustment by special exception, such special exception shall be issued only upon favorable recommendation by the Planning Commission, with limitations and additions as indicated in 2b, above. In addition to other considerations, the following guides and standards shall govern:

a. *Location* shall be appropriate to existing development and development which may reasonably be expected within the time limit set for the special exception. The site shall be so located with respect to roads and other transportation facilities as to make it unnecessary to conduct trucking operations on minor or collector streets through established residential or neighborhood commercial districts, or similar districts which may reasonably be expected to develop during the period of the special exception. Operations in the location proposed shall not create unusual traffic hazards, or the need for special public improvements or special public maintenance of public streets, bridges, drainage or flood control works, or any other facilities, provided however that the applicant may, by suitable agreement with the city, assume the costs or an appropriate share of the costs for such public improvements or maintenance.

b. *Dimensions of site: relation to performance standards.* The site shall consist of a minimum of five acres, with dimensions adequate to accommodate the operations proposed in the Plan for Development, Exploitation Phase, and the Plan for Re-Use. Dimensional requirements shall be increased as required to meet performance standards as set forth in Section XXX for light industrial districts, and shall apply at all boundaries of the site adjacent to lands on which there is development as permitted in residential or neighborhood commercial districts, or on which such development occurs during the period of the special exception, or at the nearest lot lines of such permitted development as exists or occurs during the period of the special exception.

In the proposed ordinance, performance measurements covering noise, vibration, smoke and other particulate matter (including dust), odorous matter, toxic or noxious matter, radiation hazards, fire and explosive hazards, humidity, heat, and glare are made at lot lines in light industrial districts. Thus increasing the dimensions of the lot at critical points permits a higher intensity at the source, since the added distance acts to reduce intensity at the point of measurement. In the special exception provision above, the same performance standards are to be applied as in the light industrial area, but points of measurement are defined in a way which gives the operator a break so long as all or part of his operations adjoin vacant land or land in uses other than those permissible in residential or neighborhood commercial areas. He is placed on notice, however, that if development occurs, he will have to adjust his operations accordingly.

---

c. *Plan for Development, Exploitation Phase; Plan for Re-Use.* In addition to such other studies, surveys, and reports as may be required in connection with applications for special exceptions in this class, applicants shall prepare and submit a Plan for Development, Exploitation Phase (the period of exploitation shall not exceed eight years in the case of new developments) and a Plan for Re-Use.

The Plan for Development, Exploitation Phase, shall show the proposed development as planned and staged, in relation to surrounding property within 300 feet, or such greater distance as may be required in the circumstances of the particular case, including topographic surveys indicating present conditions (including drainage) and the conditions (topographic, drainage, and soils) to be left at the end of the exploitation phase. Contour intervals for topography shall be not more than two feet, and one foot contours may be required in relatively flat areas.

The Plan for Development, Exploitation Phase, shall demonstrate the feasibility of the operation proposed without hazards or damage to other properties by reason of increased flooding or rise in groundwater levels, erosion caused by increased rate of flow or redirection of flow in flood channels, deposition of debris from flood or erosion, excessive slopes remaining at cuts or fills, or for other reasons. This plan shall also show important locational aspects of the stages of exploitation, where and how traffic on and from the development is to be handled, where equipment will be operating, the location and dimension of structures, and the like. The final stage shall indicate how the project is to be finished in accordance with the Plan for Re-Use.

The Plan for Re-Use shall indicate how it is intended to leave the property in its entirety in a form suitable for re-use for purposes permitted or permissible in the district, relating such re-use to uses existing or probable for surrounding properties. Among items to be included in such plan are feasible circulation patterns in and around the site, the treatment of the exposed soil or subsoil (including measures to be taken to replace topsoil in excavated areas) in order to make the property suitable for the proposed re-use, treatment of slopes to prevent erosion, and delineation of drainageways and flood plains to be maintained in open usage. In such plans for re-use, where conditions are suitable, permanent lakes may be permitted, but intermittent lakes and marshes shall not be allowed except in areas designated in the comprehensive plan as flood plains, or swamps or overflowed lands, and limited to open use only.

Convenience establishments

In the early days of zoning, someone decided that commercial and residential uses don't mix, and that commercial establishments should be barred from residential districts. Bassett's famous work on primitive zoning relates that: "The exclusion of business from a residence district was the most serious of zoning problems for several years."[1] Finally, a doctor testified that flies spread disease "by lighting on sick persons and then lighting on meat and vegetables in stores, thus infecting the food supply which went out to the neighborhood. He showed that other vermin could and did in this way spread disease. The court decided that the segregation of stores from residences was substantially related to the community health and safety."[2]

1. Edward M. Bassett, *Zoning, the Laws, Administration and Court Decisions During the First Twenty Years* (New York: Russell Sage Foundation, 1940), p. 64.
2. *Ibid.*, p. 67.

Thus the store was excluded from residential districts. The application of logic was neatly compartmentalized, however. Residences were permitted near stores. "The district of less restricted use always admits the uses of the more restricted ones," said Bassett.[3]

Since those days, we have learned a great deal about merchandising and about protecting health and about flies and vermin. Perhaps it would be safe now to allow stores to move back into certain kinds of residential neighborhoods. A lot of them have been there all along, as nonconforming uses which refused to die. This proves something about them.

In residential areas with medium to high population density there is a place for the small convenience establishment. If its location, size, and operational characteristics are properly controlled, it need not blight the neighborhood. It depends largely on walk-in trade (which is why it won't work well in low-density areas). Given a reasonable assortment of such establishments, properly grouped, a lot of families which can't afford two cars won't have to have them, resident housewives will be a lot happier, and when the old man comes home at night he can occasionally settle down with his beer without having to drive two miles to get a loaf of bread.

We aren't talking here about something as imposing as a neighborhood commercial district. This is smaller and homier, and it develops in a different way, mostly through the efforts of people who want to run their own businesses. What's wrong with that?

As handled in Anchorage, the schedule of district regulations indicated as an item under "Special Exceptions Permissible by Board of Adjustment" in the appropriate medium- to high-density residential districts, "Convenience establishments, subject to the requirements of Supplementary Regulations, Section YYY." These are the provisions of such a section, as proposed in rough-draft form.

---

1. *Convenience establishments defined.* For the purposes of this chapter, convenience establishments are defined as small establishments designed and intended to serve the daily or frequent trade or service needs of immediately surrounding medium- to high-density population. Such establishments include groceries, variety stores, drug stores, coin-operated laundry and dry cleaning establishments and laundry and dry cleaning agencies, tailoring and dressmaking shops, beauty shops, barber shops, cold storage lockers, medical

3. *Ibid.*, p. 63.

and dental offices, and the like. Specifically excluded are filling stations and repair garages and drive-in eating and drinking establishments.

The listing of kinds of uses permitted should be adjusted to fit local needs. Cold storage lockers appear here because in Anchorage a substantial portion of the population will have fish or game in cold storage. Medical and dental offices might be either included or excluded, but since they are often permitted in districts of this kind there is no reason to leave them out of the listing.

Since these facilities are intended primarily to serve walk-in trade, there is no reason for permitting filling stations, repair garages, and drive-in eating and drinking establishments.

---

2. *Distance to alternate facilities or locations.* No such convenience establishment shall be permitted closer than 1,000 feet to the boundary of any district where similar facilities are generally permitted, nor shall any new establishment of a specific kind be located within 1,000 feet of an active establishment of the same nature found suitable for supplying the same needs for the general area involved, provided however that medical and dental offices may include groups or combinations of physicians and dentists. Measurement of distances indicated shall be along usual routes of pedestrian travel.

This provision and the next make it clear that convenience establishments are not to be scattered at random all over the place. Under the special circumstances in which they are to be allowed in residential areas, there appears to be ample justification for limiting number and location. The public purpose of providing convenience establishments must strike a balance with the public purpose of protecting the residential character of the neighborhood. If there is a nearby commercial district, there is no need for convenience establishments in that portion of the residential district. If there is already a grocery within walking distance, there is no pressing need for another.

---

3. *Grouping of convenience establishments.* Strong preference shall be given to location of complementary additions in the immediate vicinity of existing convenience establishments of other types in patterns which facilitate easy pedestrian circulation from the surrounding area and from one establishment to another, and to

arrangements which encourage joint use of parking areas and automotive entrances and exits. In cases where a proposed location is more than 1,000 feet from an existing grocery store, variety store or drug store, and from any boundary of a district in which such establishments are generally permitted, if the location is suitable for later addition of other permitted convenience facilities, an isolated new grocery store, variety store, or drug store may be permitted. No new laundry or dry cleaning establishment or agency, tailoring or dressmaking shop, beauty shop, barber shop, or cold storage locker shall be located other than within 250 feet of a grocery store, variety store, or drug store. Measurement of this distance shall be from the principal entrance of the grocery store, variety store, or drug store along the usual routes of pedestrian travel. Separate offices of physicians and dentists (other than professional offices conducted as accessory uses in residences of such physicians and dentists) shall also be so located unless substantial public advantage can be demonstrated for other locations.

The idea behind this provision is that grocery stores, variety stores, and drug stores are likely to attract enough trade to encourage location of the other types of enterprises near them. It is intended to promote such groupings, rather than scattered establishments. The 250-foot requirement would mean that other facilities would normally be on the same block face, across the street, or around the corner, rather than in the block behind.

---

4. *Maximum size of establishments.* In the environment in which convenience establishments are intended to be permitted, it is the intent of this chapter that no such establishment or group of establishments shall be of such size or character as to create the impression of general commercial development. Therefore, in addition to other limitations designed to achieve these ends, no individual convenience establishment shall have a gross floor area exceeding 5,000 square feet.
5. *Minimum lot requirements.* Other than as required to meet other requirements of this chapter, no minimum lot requirements are specified.
6. *Minimum yard requirements.* A front yard 20 feet in depth shall be provided, and where the lot adjoins a street on more than one side, a yard 20 feet in depth shall be provided adjacent to all streets. *Side yards* shall be 10 feet in width adjacent to residential lots, but where the side of the lot is adjacent to a lot on which another

convenience establishment is located, or is being constructed, or is definitely to be constructed, no side yard need be provided if the structures involved are to have a common or party wall, or are to have no space between their walls. If there is to be space between the walls of adjacent structures housing convenience establishments or their accessory uses, such space shall be at least five feet in width. *Rear yards* shall be 25 feet in depth.

The front-yard requirement generally in the districts in which these provisions would be applied is 10 feet so that the buildings would be recessed behind the usual building line. The side yard is double the width which would be required generally for residential uses, and the rear yard is two and a half times the general depth.

---

7. *Landscaping requirements; buffering; control of appearance.* As minimum requirements: except for drives and walkways, any yard adjacent to a street shall be landscaped and maintained in a manner appropriate to a residential neighborhood for a distance of 10 feet from the lot line adjacent to the street, except for portions which adjoin lots in residential use, which shall be so landscaped and maintained for the full width or depth of the required yards within 25 feet of adjoining lot lines. Side yards adjacent to lots in residential use shall be similarly landscaped and maintained for their full required minimum width. No such required landscaped area shall be used for off-street parking or loading. No landscaping adjacent to a street shall be of a nature which impairs visibility of or from approaching traffic, or creates potential hazards for pedestrians.

   Where the site plan indicates potential adverse effects of parking or other characteristics of use on the lot on which the convenience facilities are to be located, a wall, fence, or appropriate vegetative screening shall be required to be erected and maintained in such manner as to eliminate such effects or reduce them to an acceptable level. Such buffering shall at a minimum prevent lights from automobiles parked or maneuvering incidental to parking from shining across adjacent residential property below a height of five feet at the residential lot line, or from shining into any residential windows if there is to be parking on the premises after dark.

   There shall be no garbage or trash containers, exposed garbage or trash, or outdoor storage in any portion of any outdoor space about the premises of any convenience establishment.
8. *Maximum lot coverage* by all buildings shall not exceed 40 per cent.

9. *Maximum height of structures.* Except as provided in Section 000,[4] no portion of any structure housing a convenience establishment shall exceed two stories or 25 feet.

10. *Minimum off-street parking and loading. Grocery stores, drug stores, variety stores, laundry and dry cleaning agencies,* and the like shall provide one off-street parking space for each 300 square feet of gross floor area. *Coin-operated laundry and dry cleaning establishments* and the like shall provide one off-street parking space for each two washing machines (drying machines and dry cleaning machines are not to be included in computations). *Barber shops* shall provide one off-street parking space for each barber chair. *Beauty shops* shall provide one off-street parking space for each barber chair, plus one for each hair dryer other than those used while patrons are in barber chairs. *Tailoring and dressmaking establishments* shall provide one off-street parking space for each 500 square feet of gross floor area. *Medical and dental offices* shall provide one off-street parking space for each physician, dentist, or employee, plus one for each 500 square feet of gross floor area. *Cold storage lockers* shall provide one off-street parking space for each 500 square feet of gross floor area.

    Where practicable, off-street parking facilities for groups of convenience establishments shall be combined, but the total number of spaces required in such combination shall equal the sum of the numbers required for each of the individual establishments or uses. Spaces for the patrons or employees of individual establishments need not be marked as so reserved, but the site plan shall show spaces as related to uses in such a way that it can be determined at any time that individual responsibility for provision of space has been met and maintained.

    There shall be no on-street loading in connection with any convenience establishment. Either separate off-street loading shall be provided in spaces marked and reserved for such purposes and not used to satisfy minimum off-street parking requirements (although such space may be used for off-street parking when not in use for loading) or required off-street parking space may be used for loading before 8:00 a.m. or after hours of closing for normal business.

    Off-street parking areas shall be designed to provide convenient and efficient parking and maneuvering incidental to parking and unparking, and parking layout, loading facilities, entrances and exits shall be approved by the traffic engineer before any permit is

4. The section to which reference is made provides the usual exclusion of chimneys, antennas, ventilators, etc.

granted, shall be paved with an asphalt or concrete surfacing, shall be properly drained, and shall be maintained in a sound and orderly condition.

11. *Lighting.* During hours of darkness when convenience establishments are in operation, parking areas and pedestrian ways on the premises shall be lighted to an intensity of at least 0.6 foot candle. No such lighting shall be directed in a manner which illuminates adjoining residential premises and no source of incandescent or mercury vapor illumination shall be directly visible from any residential property, or from any street. No neon lights inside or outside structures shall be visible from any residential property, or from any street.
12. *Signs.* No signs intended to be read from off the premises shall be permitted in connection with convenience establishments except as generally permitted in the district for residential uses, and in addition one sign, not exceeding 10 square feet in area, mounted flat against the side of the building, for each face of the building exposed to a public street. Where more than one convenience establishment is located in the same building, signs in accordance with the above formula may be permitted for each. No such sign shall extend or be mounted above or beyond the wall of the building.
13. *Hours of operation.* Except for emergency activities at the offices of physicians and dentists, no convenience establishment shall be open for business between the hours of 10:00 p.m. and 7:00 a.m.
14. *Conduct of operations.* All sales, service, or display in connection with convenience establishments shall be within completely enclosed buildings, and there shall be no display, service, or storage outside such buildings. No public address systems or other devices for reproducing or amplifying voices or music shall be mounted outside such buildings or be audible beyond any line of the lot on which the building is situated.

Given controls of this kind, carefully tailored to meet local needs, it looks as though it might be possible to get the kind of trade and service facilities described back into convenient locations without disrupting the residential character of the neighborhood.

It might be mentioned in passing that the application of this kind of regulation in existing districts will frequently cure embarrassing nonconforming use, spot zoning, or use variance situations. Quite often, the corner grocery and related convenience facilities belong in locations where planners have not found a means to allow them. Boards of adjustment and legislative bodies have sometimes seen the justification for the use and been blind to the legal barriers, granting use variances or spot zonings over the outraged screams of planners. If the approach suggested above is polished and perfected, there may be a way to make everybody happy—and to promote public comfort, convenience, and general welfare.

Extensions of commercial development

Strip commercial development is older than zoning. In early form, as businesses clustered next to the sidewalk on downtown Main Street in small towns, or as rows of shops along the sidewalk in densely-settled residential areas in larger cities, pedestrian-oriented commercial strips made good sense. Everything was up the street or down the street or across the street within easy walking distance, and the street was no threat to pedestrians.

Came then the streetcar, the bus, the automobile, the explosion of the city into the countryside along radial arteries. The same forms evolved to serve concentrated pedestrians were adopted—not adapted—to serve a much larger population on wheels, scattered over a vastly greater area. The pedestrian-oriented pattern remained—built to the sidewalk or to where it would be if there was one—but the pedestrian was no longer there. Downtown Main Street was an area where people were pedestrians bent on conducting business. Outlying strip commercial districts were areas where travelers on their way someplace else had to be stopped to become customers. The pedestrian pattern didn't work, because everything was *not* just up the street, down the street, or across the street, within easy walking distance. The street was not to be crossed lightly, and everything was scattered from hell to breakfast.

And the pattern wasn't designed to meet the requirements of automobiles either. There wasn't enough parking at the curb, and the sidewalk-related building line made it difficult to put convenient parking anywhere else.

Somewhere along in there, the first planners came in. They inherited the sorry mess, the blighted commercial development, the decaying residences which had been trapped by commercial entrepreneurs, the vacant lands waiting hopefully to be converted to more of the same. They inherited also all the fixations as to vested rights to do it the way it had been done, to build to the sidewalk line, to get by without providing parking space, to scream at the passers-by with raucous signs.

The first planners, and those who have followed them, did what they could to limit further oozing of the worst of the garbage. This wasn't easy against pressure from those with "prime commercial property" on down the street, but they tried and are still trying. Planners got support for off-street parking and off-street loading requirements because all but a Neanderthal few saw that off-street parking and loading were essential to survival. Progress was made in a few places toward getting new buildings set back. In a very few cases, there was support for sign control when businessmen became aware that in competing for more and more signs the signs were becoming more expensive and less effective, and even irritating a growing number of customers.

Long after the planner first arrived, the planned shopping center came on the scene. The best centers are designed for the automotive age, provide ample off-street parking and loading, and are wise in the use of signs. The buildings set far back from the streets, and entrances and exits are so arranged as to facilitate access without creating undue friction with passing traffic.

This sets up the problem. In zoning, almost every city will have bowed to the inevitable and provided tremendous frontage in strip commercial zoning, recognizable in fact however euphemistic the name on the zoning map may be. It is imperative to contain the usual forms of strip commercial development, to do as much as can be done to keep it from exposing its unattractive backside to adjacent residential frontage, to try to limit signs, to require off-street parking in front of buildings, to provide for off-street loading, to encourage better new to replace worse old rather than to allow the mistakes of the past to multiply themselves and spread commercial blight.

As a general rule, this means drawing the zoning boundaries for strip commercial districts at the half-block depth to insure that the commercial property will back onto residential property in the rear. To go the full depth of the block would allow for deeper commercial development, but would not assure protection for residences and might mean pressures for jumping the street to the rear with commercial zoning.

In some instances, where it is proposed to install planned commercial developments in strip commercial zones (there is no prospect that they will ever take up anything like full strip commercial frontage) there may be a middle course. In the past, many ordinances have allowed parking in connection with commercial uses in adjacent residential districts under more or less rigidly controlled conditions. But this usually means that the parking is in the rear of the commercial buildings. Under careful controls, it may well be that the buildings themselves would be better located to the rear of the property, and would be less objectionable than the parking. Here's how an attempt was made in the form of a special exception provision:

X. *Extensions of Commercial Development.* In any district in which commercial use of property is permitted, the Board of Adjustment, upon favorable recommendation by the Planning Commission, may as a special exception permit the extension of such commercial use into a residential district if such extension is found to promote safety and improved traffic circulation on and adjoining the property and if the residential district can be appropriately protected from potentially adverse effects of such extension, provided:

1. *Minimum frontage, lot width.* The proposed development shall have minimum frontage of at least 150 feet on an arterial street in the district permitting commercial use, and the lot shall be at least 150 feet wide in all portions in such district.
2. *Limitations on extension.* No extension shall be permitted beyond the nearest street in the residential district, and no portion of the extension shall be wider than the width of the lot in the district permitting commercial use as measured at the district boundary.
3. *Limitations on access.* There shall be no direct vehicular access to any portion of the commercial development through the residential district, provided however that if an alley forms the boundary between the residential district and the district in which the commercial use is permitted, it may be used for such access.
4. *Height limitation.* No portion of any building in the commercial extension area shall exceed 15 feet in height within 25 feet, or 25 feet in height within 50 feet, of any lot line in the residential district except the lot line at the district boundary in which the commercial frontage is located. No portion of any building in the commercial extension area shall exceed the height limitations for the residential district into which the area is extended.
5. *Site planning; limitation on operations.* Site planning, design and location of structures and areas, and management of operations shall be such that orientation of commercial activities is toward

the frontage on the arterial street. There shall be no sales, service, storage, or display of goods or materials and no off-street loading operations, garbage or trash storage, or garbage or trash collection or disposal facilities visible in any portion of the commercial extension area from any portion of the residential district. No signs in the commercial extension area shall be visible from any portion of the residential district. There shall be no lighting of structures and premises in the commercial extension area which is inappropriate to the residential district.

6. *Yard requirements; buffering.* Yards and structural or vegetative buffering shall be provided to minimize the impact of the commercial extension on property in the residential district. The following minimum requirements may be increased where circumstances of a particular case make such increases necessary to achieve a stated public purpose, but shall not be diminished:
   a. *Front yard.* If the extension reaches any street in the residential district, a yard 25 feet in depth shall be provided adjacent to such street.
   b. *Side yards.* Where the extension adjoins side or rear lot lines in the residential district, side yards at least 15 feet in width shall be provided except where another commercial extension has been permitted adjacent to the proposed extension, in which case the provisions controlling spacing between buildings on adjacent properties in the district from which the extension is proposed shall govern relation between the commercial extensions.
   c. *Unusual lot patterns.* In the case of unusual lot patterns to which the above provisions are not clearly and directly applicable, yards serving the same functions, and having the same dimensions, shall be provided.
   d. *Yard landscaping, use.* All yards provided in the residential district in connection with commercial extensions, whether minimum yards or greater, shall be landscaped and maintained in a manner appropriate to the residential surroundings. No portion of any such required yard shall be used for off-street parking.
   e. *Screening; buffering.* Parking areas, and such other areas as are deemed likely to have adverse effects on surrounding property in the residential district, shall be appropriately screened by a masonry wall or solid fence not less than five nor more than seven feet in height. Such wall or fence shall be maintained in sound condition and good appearance, shall have no openings or gates permitting vehicular entrance or

egress to or from the residential district, and shall bear no signs visible from within the residential district. If approved by the Planning Commission, dense vegetative buffering may be substituted for all or a portion of such fence or wall, provided that such buffering shall not be unsightly at any season, nor create a fire hazard at any season, and that in all seasons it shall be equivalent in its screening effects to the fence or wall.

The Board of Adjustment may not grant special exceptions in this class of cases except upon favorable recommendation by the Planning Commission, and where Planning Commission recommendation is conditional, the Board shall not reduce the conditions, but the Board may add conditions in granting approval.

Townhouses

The townhouse is a new old form which may and probably should have an increasing role in the residential scheme of things. As a single-family dwelling which conserves land and public facilities it has much to recommend it.

Some say that the townhouse is merely row housing, and for them that's all it is. It can be row housing. It can be something which is partly row housing. Or it can be something which is not row housing, a grouping in irregular clusters, in the form of a cross, in swastika forms, and so on. But if we are to take advantage of the possibilities of the townhouse and want to make sure that it will be something besides row housing, the difference must be made clear in definitions and regulations. Here are draft provisions from the proposed Anchorage ordinance:

Y. *Townhouses*. For the purposes of this chapter, townhouses are single-family dwelling units constructed in a series or group including more than three units with some common walls. As such, they are a special type of single-family dwelling, to be excluded from certain regulations relating to single-family dwellings generally in this chapter, but subject to the requirements for single-family dwellings generally with respect to permitted principal and accessory uses and structures, prohibited uses and structures, height, number of off-street parking spaces, and signs.

Regulations as contained in this section shall be applied to townhouses permitted outright in any district, or in connection with special exceptions which include townhouses. No zoning permit shall be issued for townhouses, and the Board of Adjustment shall not issue a special exception involving townhouses, except upon a favorable or conditionally favorable report from the Planning Commission. Where conditions are attached by the Planning Commission, they shall be included as part of the zoning permit. If special exception is involved, the Board of Adjustment shall not grant such exception except with the conditions attached by the Planning Commission, but the Board may add conditions in granting approval.

1. *Site plan and design criteria, general.* It is the intent of this chapter that townhouses in areas where they are or may be permitted:
   a. May be appropriately intermingled with other types of housing;
   b. Shall not form long, unbroken lines of row housing; and
   c. Shall constitute groupings making efficient, economical, comfortable, and convenient use of land and open space and serving the public purposes of zoning by means alternative to conventional arrangements of yards and buildable areas.
2. *Site plan and design criteria, details.* In line with the general considerations above:
   a. Not more than six contiguous townhouses shall be built in a row with the same or approximately the same front line, and not more than 12 townhouses shall be contiguous.
   b. *Minimum width* for the portion of the lot on which the townhouse is to be constructed shall be 25 feet.[5]
   c. *Minimum lot area* shall be as required to meet other provisions of these regulations.
   d. *Separation requirements.* No portion of a townhouse or accessory structure in or related to one group of contiguous townhouses shall be closer than 20 feet to any portion of a townhouse or accessory structure related to another group, or to any building outside the townhouse area.
   e. *Yards.* No front, side, or rear yard as such is required in connection with any townhouse, but each townhouse shall have on its own lot one yard containing not less than 1,000 square feet,[6] reasonably secluded from view from streets or from neighboring property. Such yard shall not be used for off-street parking or for any accessory building.

5. Normally, minimum lot width for a townhouse should be lower than this.
6. This is an extraordinarily high requirement.

f. *Grouped parking facilities.* Insofar as practicable, off-street parking facilities shall be grouped in bays, either adjacent to streets or in the interior of blocks. No off-street parking space shall be more than 100 feet by the most direct pedestrian route, from a door of the dwelling unit it is intended to serve. Practicable methods of snow removal shall be assured by developers in connection with common parking facilities, and all such facilities shall be improved to city standards for off-street parking areas.

On minor streets, but not on collector or major streets, use of the right-of-way may be permitted for maneuvering incidental to parking where this will facilitate snow removal. On collector and arterial streets, common parking facilities for three or more automobiles shall provide space outside the public right-of-way for maneuvering incidental to parking.

The ordinance contains a general provision prohibiting impediments to visibility at street intersections. With townhouse developments in which there is no required front yard, it becomes necessary to protect visibility at the intersection of driveways with public streets:

---

g. *Visibility at access points for automobiles.* In addition to the general provisions of Section XXX concerning visibility across portions of corner lots at street intersections, the following requirements apply to all private drives and entrances to or exists from common parking areas. At the intersection of any private drive or entrance or exit for a common parking area with a public street, no fence, wall, hedge, or other planting or structure forming a material impediment to visibility between a height of two and a half feet and eight feet shall be erected, planted, placed, or maintained, and no vehicle so impeding visibility shall be parked within triangular areas defined by lines connecting points as follows:

Beginning at the point where the midline of the private drive or entrance or exit for a common parking area intersects the public right-of-way, thence to a point 35 feet along the right-of-way line in the direction of approaching traffic, thence to a point 25 feet toward the interior of the property along the previously described midline, and thence to point of beginning. No such visibility triangle need be maintained on the side of the drive, entrance, or exit away from approaching traffic on the same side of the street.

Profession: professional office defined

As a passing detail, the terms "profession" and "professional office" frequently give trouble in connection with home occupations because groups other than those intended try to get under the tent. Here's one way to handle it—by defining profession, by indicating professionals to be included, and by indicating specifically activities *not* to be included:

Profession; professional office. For purposes of this chapter, the term *profession* is limited in its application to physicians and surgeons, lawyers, members of the clergy, architects, and engineers, or other persons holding advanced degrees from accredited institutions of higher learning in the field in which they practice. The term is not here intended to include insurance agents, insurance adjusters, realtors, real estate salesmen, or persons engaged in trade or sales. In permitting *professional offices* as home occupations, and only as accessory uses, in certain districts, it is intended that such offices shall be subject to limitations placed on home occupations generally, but that only offices occupied by persons engaged in professions, as herein defined, shall be permitted.

Public lands and institutions

Public lands and institutions are usually allowed more or less incidentally in districts intended primarily for residential, commercial, or industrial uses. This works reasonably well, particularly if areas involved are small. But if land areas are large, it is sometimes desirable to establish a separate district classification.

Provisions on district designation and intent are as follows:

PLI Public Lands and Institutions. These districts are intended to include major public lands and major public and quasi-public institutional uses, including existing land reserves for future public and institutional use.

Permitted principal uses and structures, as listed in the schedule of district regulations, run like this.

---

1. Public parks, parkways, land reserves, and related facilities.

2. Public golf courses, playgrounds, playfields, and the like.
3. Public zoos, arboretums, museums, historic and cultural exhibits, and the like.
4. Public water conservation and flood control installations.
5. Public and quasi-public institutions, including schools, colleges, and universities, hospitals, children's homes, convalescent homes, homes for the aged, correctional institutions, rehabilitation centers, and the like.
6. Public housing and related facilities.
7. Public cemeteries.
8. Public sewerage and water supply installations.
9. Utilities installations.

If mapped PLI districts are reasonably large, and properly located, one reason for setting them apart from other districts becomes apparent from the uses listed. Normally, when it is time to locate hospitals, cemeteries, children's homes, correctional institutions, rehabilitation centers, and zoos, to take a few examples, groups appear to express enthusiasm for placing them somewhere away from their neighborhoods. The PLI device at least identifies lands on which these things are likely to be located and makes it a matter of record that they may be located there.

Placing public housing among permitted uses means that such developments would be freed from lot-by-lot zoning requirements which might apply if public housing were built in a conventional residential district.

In general, as will appear from regulations which follow, limitations on uses in this district are simple and general, and detailed restrictions are avoided. There are two reasons for this. In the first place, public agencies are involved, and it is hoped (possibly without adequate justification) that the quality of planning and development will be such that detailed restrictions won't be needed. As a second consideration, "higher" levels of government will be involved in much of the development, and in such cases zoning regulations adopted by a city would not be binding in any event.

Permitted accessory uses and structures. Uses and structures which are necessary or desirable adjuncts to permitted uses and structures, where such uses and structures are under the management or control of the public or quasi-public agency responsible for the permitted principal use or structure.

Prohibited uses and structures. Any use or structure not of a character indicated under permitted principal and accessory uses and structures, and any use or structure not under the management or control of a public or quasi-public agency.

There are no minimum lot requirements in this district, but yard requirements make it apparent that lots must be fairly sizable. At least there is to be ample clearance from streets and from adjoining residential districts.

Minimum yard requirements. A yard 25 feet in depth (if at the front or rear of the lot) and 25 feet in width (if at the side of the lot) shall be provided adjacent to any public street in this district. Where a lot in this district abuts or adjoins a lot in any residential district without an intervening street or alley, a yard corresponding to the yard required in the residential district shall be provided in the portion of the lot adjacent to the residential district boundary.

There is no limitation as to *lot coverage by buildings,* or as to *height of buildings,* except that a regulation applicable to all districts reads: " . . . no structure or portion of any structure hereafter erected shall necessitate increase in the established glide angle rules on approaches to airport runways, nor raising elevation of established turning circles."

Minimum off-street parking and loading requirements approach the ultimate in simplicity:

Sufficient off-street parking and off-street loading shall be provided so that no public street used for through traffic shall be used for either parking or loading.

(The ultimate *will* have been reached when laws are passed flatly prohibiting the use of public streets for off-street parking or loading except for minor streets in residential neighborhoods. At the time of this millennium, it will be found that traffic carrying capacity has increased substantially, and perhaps that streets need not be quite so wide. The millennium is not immediately at hand.)

Limitations on signs are also very simple:

No signs intended to be read from off the premises shall be permitted except identification, informational, or directional signs erected by public and quasi-public bodies in connection with permitted principal or accessory uses or for other public purposes.

General residential development districts

The second district classification which may be of general interest is called by a rather clumsy title, but its purpose is made clear by provisions on district designation and intent:

RG-D, General Residential Development. These districts consist of substantial areas (a) remaining undeveloped or sparsely developed because of terrain, soil, drainage problems, danger of flooding, or other physical limitation, (b) in uses likely to be temporary in nature which should be replaced by uses more appropriate to the location, or (c) sufficiently expansive and so related to adjacent lands as to permit use of new developmental concepts without adverse effects on nearby conventional development. Portions of these areas which can be developed safely are intended for the most part for general residential use and for related governmental, educational, religious, and other uses. In addition, subject to careful limitation, planned shopping centers may be permitted as special exceptions, as well as temporary transitional uses with restrictions as to duration and requirements as to condition at termination of such temporary use.

Permitted principal uses and structures:

1. Single-family dwellings, including townhouses subject to the requirements of Section 23-7S, two-family dwellings, multiple-family dwellings (including high-rise apartments subject to the provisions of Section 23-7I), and mobile homes in parks developed in accordance with Section 23-7G.
2. All uses permitted in PLI districts, provided that principal access to uses 1-3 and 5-6 thereunder shall be directly from arterial or collector streets.
3. Churches, provided that principal access shall be directly from arterial or collector streets.
4. Day nurseries and kindergartens.
5. Conventional full-scale private golf courses, but not separate reduced-scale golf courses, driving ranges, or putting greens.
6. Hotels and motels adjacent to arterial or collector streets only, and with principal access from such streets, provided however that no structure or parking in connection with such uses shall be more than 250 feet from such streets, that all parking areas not otherwise screened from residential lot lines shall be surrounded at such lot lines by a masonry wall not less than six feet in height, and that lighting shall be so controlled that no source of incandescent or mercury vapor illumination shall be directly visible at or beyond any lot line or from any public street.

7. Private clubs and lodges adjacent to arterial or collector streets only, and with principal access from such streets, provided however that no structure or parking in connection with such use shall be more than 150 feet from such streets, and that other restrictions shall be as for hotels and motels, above.

(References to Section 23 here and in what follows are to detailed material grouped under the head of "Supplementary Regulations.")

It will be noted that agricultural structures and uses have not been included in the group above. In most jurisdictions, this category probably should be included, considering the nature of the district.

Permitted accessory uses and structures. Uses and structures customarily accessory and clearly incidental to permitted or permissible uses and structures, including home occupations, with limitations as indicated in the definition thereof. Customary overnight parking of trucks, other than pickup or panel trucks not exceeding one ton capacity, or buses over 20 feet in length, or tractors, graders, or other heavy equipment shall not be considered a permitted accessory use except as required in connection with agricultural operations or uses permitted as special exceptions in the district, and in such instances parking shall be at least 150 feet from any public street.

In the special exception provisions for the RG-D district, those of RS, single-family, districts are included by reference. To give the full picture, the RS section is reproduced here. Again, references to portions of Section 23 are to supplementary regulations, some of which have been or will be discussed further.

Special exceptions permissible by Board of Adjustment in RS districts:

1. Group housing developments, subject to the requirements of Section 23-7F.

2. Utility substations, provided that location, lot area, screening, protection against "attractive nuisance" characteristics, access, and parking (if needed) shall be as required by the Board of Adjustment.

3. Temporary structures and operations in connection with, and on the site of, building or land developments, including grading, paving, installation of utilities, erection of field offices, structures for storage of building materials or equipment, parking or outdoor storage of trucks and other heavy equipment being used on the project, and the like, provided that no such permit shall be for a period of more than one

year, renewable by the Board for periods of not more than one year. In connection with such operations, one sign, not exceeding 50 square feet in area, may be erected not closer than 20 feet to any public street, nor closer than 10 feet to any side or rear property line on adjoining property.

4. Commercial extension, subject to the requirements of Section 23-7L.

5. Basement apartments, provided that there shall be no external evidence of the existence of such apartments, and that additional off-street parking space (other than the two spaces required for the single-family dwelling) shall be provided. Conditions attached to special exceptions in this class shall assure that concentrations of parking spaces for three or more cars shall not present an appearance inappropriate in the neighborhood.

Special exceptions permissible by Board of Adjustment in RG districts: as for RS and in addition:

1. Private and quasi-public playgrounds, playfields, and children's camps, subject to the requirements of Section 23-70.

2. Travel trailer parks and campgrounds, subject to the requirements of Section 23-7H.

3. Commercial open recreational uses, subject to the requirements of Section 23-7P.

4. Convenience establishments as for RG, subject to the requirements of Section 23-7M.

5. Exploitation of natural resources (commercial or industrial operations involving removal for sale, processing or use of timber, native vegetation, peat, muck, topsoil, fill, sand, gravel, rock, or any mineral) subject to the requirements of Section 23-7Q.

6. Planned shopping centers, subject to the requirements of Section 23-7R.

Where time limits are not otherwise established in these regulations, the Board of Adjustment may establish time limits for which special exceptions are to run in connection with classes of cases where uses are considered to be of an interim nature. Such time limitations, if established, shall give due regard to the nature and location of the interim use, the nature of improvements required, and the possibility of re-use of improvements in connection with uses generally permitted in the district, and provision for limitation shall include indication as to whether, and for how long, the special exception may be renewed on expiration.

Interim use with controlled termination. Sometimes permitting an interim use with controlled termination is in both public and private interest. In the case of exploitation of natural resources, discussed above, this was handled on a fixed basis. The last provision above gives the board of adjustment general authority to set time limits on uses which should be temporary in nature. The same principle might be used much more widely than at present with respect to permits not requiring board of adjustment action.

In areas like the RG-D district being discussed, such control of both kind and timing of use should be particularly helpful. Pressure comes on for an amendment, variance, or exception which will give the owner "relief" from a situation in which land in an area not ready for solid development is producing little or no return. If the "relief" is refused, the owner may suffer more than is honestly necessary while he waits for the area to mature. He may just sit and complain, or he may be forced into premature development of a kind which is permitted under the regulations but later turns out to be unwise for him and for the public.

On the other hand, unconditional governmental surrender to demands for "relief" may saddle the area with permanent handicaps to healthy growth which should come later. A use permitted to "help out" before the land was ready to urbanize becomes a vested right blocking sound urbanization.

Allowing interim uses with controlled termination provides a compromise solution with considerable merit.

Prohibited uses and structures as listed on the schedule of district regulations are handled by reference to limitations previously listed in other districts. In essence, they come out as follows for RG-D districts:

Any use or structure not of a character indicated under permitted principal and accessory uses and structures or permitted as a special exception; storage or use of mobile homes outside mobile home parks; storage in connection with trade, service, or manufacturing activities outside the district; storage or long-term parking of commercial or industrial vehicles or equipment except as otherwise specified; and any use or characteristic of use which fails to meet performance standards for the LM (Light Manufacturing) district as set forth in Section 23-7J.

Certainly there is nothing startling about these prohibitions. The reference to industrial performance standards might be noted as of some general utility. If such standards for light manufacturing districts are carefully drafted, it may be well to make them do double duty, rather than to leave the section on prohibited uses and structures decorated with futile language which courts have held void for vagueness: "or any use which is objectionable because of noise, smoke, odor, dust, gas, fumes, glare, vibration, radiation . . . ," etc., etc. Of course, the best move would be to develop specific standards for areas of this kind, but if this can't be done, standards applied in light manufacturing districts to assure that each use will be a good neighbor to others and to surrounding nonmanufacturing districts may serve as a substitute.

Minimum lot requirements, area and width, are specified for the district for the uses permitted, but since each city should make its own determinations in these matters, and since the tabulation is relatively complex, it is omitted here.

Minimum yard requirements (depth of front and rear yards, width of side yards). Here a design strait-jacket usually found in zoning ordinances is removed, or at least eased. In reading what follows, bear in mind the nature of the district and the fact that this is an area in which single-family conventional dwellings, townhouses, two-family dwellings, and multiple-family dwellings in a variety of forms including high-rise are permitted to mix. Remember also that yard requirements for certain types of uses have been specified in supplementary regulations—townhouses, group housing developments, high-rise apartments, convenience establishments, planned shopping centers, etc.

Single-family, two-family, and multiple-family dwellings other than as regulated in Supplementary Regulations; *day nurseries and kindergartens:*

Front yards: none required.

Side and rear yards: 5-foot minimum, provided that no side or rear yard adjacent to a lot which may be built upon shall be less than one-fourth of the average height of the adjacent portion of the building.

All other permitted or permissible uses and structures, other than as regulated in Supplementary Regulations:

Front yards: 20 feet.

Side and rear yards: 30 feet adjacent to lots developed or available for development for residential uses, 10 feet adjacent to streets other than at the front, 10 feet adjacent to nonresidential uses, public parks, or other permanent open space.

General regulations, all structures and uses

In addition to regulations above for front, side, and rear yards in this district, the following requirements shall apply generally. At the intersection of any private driveway, private street, or entrance or exit for any off-street parking area with a public street, no building or other structure, and no planting, shall be placed or maintained that will materially impede visibility between the heights of two and a half feet and eight feet, and no vehicle so impeding visibility shall be parked, within triangular areas enclosed by lines connecting points described as follows: beginning where the midline of the private drive, street, or entrance or exit for any off-street parking area intersects the public right-of-way, thence to a point 35 feet along the right-of-way line in the direction of approaching traffic, thence to a point 25 feet toward the interior of the property along the previously described midline, and thence to point of beginning. Such visibility triangles shall be so located that no construction permissible on adjacent property could interfere with the visibility required.

To this point, there have been two departures, one major and one minor, from common practice on yards in residential districts. The major departure is elimination of the front yard requirement (in a district where elimination of the front yard requirement is not a foregone conclusion because it is already built up without front yards).

Eliminating the requirement for front yards doesn't prevent those who wish from having front yards. But it doesn't make everyone provide a front yard because some people want one. The one sure public advantage in front yards is to give visibility for traffic. This has been taken care of by the general regulation concerning visibility triangles. With this out of the way, why should the public require that so much of the limited open space available around a dwelling should be located so that it is virtually nonfunctional? The same space would be vastly more useful away from the street, in a back yard or a court surrounded by parts of the house. There are solid advantages, public and private, in moving the house forward on the lot and reorganizing its interior so that the kitchen and the garage are near the street, with living and sleeping quarters away from it.

In new areas, it should be permissible—not mandatory, merely permissible—for those who want to sacrifice the dubious advantages of the front yard to do so. In all fairness, those who live in houses built the wrong way should refrain from rioting at the prospect that others may not have to do likewise.

The minor variation is in making side- and rear-yard minimums identical. Most ordinances require minimal side yards and substantial back yards. We are still requiring deep rear yards and permitting accessory buildings to be located in them. If five-foot yards are adequate for separation of buildings at the side, why aren't they sufficient for separation of buildings at the rear?

Again, there is nothing to keep anyone who wants a large rear yard from having one, but what about the man who wants an L-shaped house or one built in the form of a U around a court? Is there compelling public reason why he shouldn't have it?

Building spacing through deed restrictions

Comes now what may be one of the most promising features of the proposed ordinance. It has been generally agreed that where zoning is on a lot-by-lot basis, side- and rear-yard requirements are primarily for the purpose of separating buildings on adjacent lots. Even where side- and rear-yard requirements are at a minimum of five feet, as in the ordinance under discussion, there are times when it would be to the advantage of property owners to be able to use these required yards for construction, shifting buildings to one edge of a lot to leave more space on the other. If the public interest demands separation between buildings on adjacent lots, the public should be satisfied if the buildings are separated. There is nothing sacred about the yard requirements as such. The following provision from the proposed ordinance appears immediately after the material quoted above:

Special Provisions on Building Separation

As an alternative to side- and rear-yard requirements above, if owners of adjoining or abutting property shall agree (and shall make such agreement in the form of deed restrictions, with enforcement running to the city) to an arrangement of buildings on their respective lots which accomplishes the same or greater separation between such buildings as would have been accomplished by the yard requirements above stipulated, and shall construct such buildings in accordance with such agreement, the purpose of this chapter with respect to side and rear yards shall be considered to have been accomplished, and such side and rear yards, as related to such buildings and properties, shall not be required.

If zoning administrators want to raise a howl about the complexities of such an arrangement, let them. It should be possible to develop reasonably simple deed-restriction forms to handle such cases, and to keep maps and records in such shape that when applications come in for new construction on the lots involved, the administrator is alerted.

Zoning should give full protection to the public interest, but having done so, it should also give maximum leeway to private action. The deed restriction device, with enforcement running to the city, may have useful applications in a wide variety of situations. It is a means by which a great many zoning objectives, now approached rigidly and crudely, could be attained flexibly and with a considerable degree of sophistication. There is, of course, the problem that to a very considerable extent we still haven't decided exactly what our zoning objectives are.

Maximum lot coverage by all buildings

Maximum lot coverage limitations are usually very crude controls indeed. Their relation to the purposes of zoning is not always clear, and they are often poorly related to yard requirements in the same ordinance. It is not unknown for drafters of zoning to require yards which take up two-thirds of the required minimum lot, and then to allow 40 per cent lot coverage by buildings. This is inconsistent so far as minimum lots are concerned (and most lots tend to be minimum lots) and places an unnecessary and meaningless limitation on larger lots.

Taking a 60-by-100-foot lot as an example, under zoning which is all too common a 25-foot front yard, two five-foot side yards and a 30-foot rear yard must be set aside. This amounts to 3,750 square feet, about 63 per cent of the total lot area, leaving about 2,250 square feet (37 per cent) within which buildings may be erected. (To simplify matters, we ignore the fact that many ordinances permit construction of accessory buildings in required rear yards, so that they aren't really yards at all.) Buildings must be located in a rectangle of 45 by 50 feet set crossways in another rectangle 60 by 100 feet. Given this kind of zoning, the addition of lot coverage limitations seems superfluous.

In the RG-D district, maximum lot coverage by buildings is proposed at 40 per cent. Circumstances here (and in other cases where yard requirements are reduced to minimums required for separation of buildings on adjacent lots, and no buildings are permitted in required yards) are quite different from those in zoning which is entirely too usual.

Taking the 6,000-square-foot lot as an example again, with no front yard requirements as such, and with required side and rear yards at a five-foot minimum, only 1,250 square feet of the lot is in yards required for separation of buildings on adjacent properties. Add to this a maximum of about 300 feet for the required visibility triangle (usually part of the required triangle would be in a required yard) and only about 1,500 square feet of the lot (25 per cent) would be barred to building. This is quite a contrast to the 3,750 square feet (63 per cent) in the previous example. The "buildable area" would be a rectangle 50 by 95 feet (minus part or all of the visibility triangle at the access point for vehicles) oriented in the same direction as the 60-by-100-foot rectangle of the lot. Building separation and traffic safety have been provided for. What remains is determination of total open space somewhere on the lot.

Assuming that it is felt necessary to insure that no one can build upon 4,500 square feet of a 6,000-square-foot lot, some lot coverage limitation is indicated. The 40 per cent figure would mean that a total of 2,400 square feet could be built upon. Of the 3,600 square feet remaining open, around 1,500 square feet would be required side and rear yards and the visibility triangle, and 2,100 square feet might be anywhere on the lot—as a front yard, rear yard, court, side yard, or any combination.

Certainly this is not an unreasonable arrangement. It accomplishes demonstrable public objectives, but allows flexibility in private action. About the same amount of the site is left open as with usual yard requirements, but it can be used far more intelligently than is possible under "normal" zoning.

In the discussion above, application of proposed regulations to dwellings on 60-by-100-foot lots has been analyzed rather exhaustively. It is probable that a substantial part of the RG-D district will in time be built up in conventional single-family dwellings, possibly on narrower lots than those indicated. But it is hoped that there will also be considerable development of townhouses, high-rise apartments, group housing, and other forms. For some of these, special regulations have been developed as discussed previously. Hence the provision under "Maximum Lot Coverage by All Buildings" as proposed for the RG-D district in the Anchorage ordinance reads as follows:

Maximum Lot Coverage by All Buildings: 40 per cent except as otherwise provided with respect to specified uses in Section 23-7, Supplementary Regulations.

As with many other aspects of zoning, the matter of required open space around residences needs a great deal of painful, logical thought. We have become victims of formulas fixed during one phase of residential evolution which threaten to delay and impede logical improvements without providing compensating public advantage. To some extent, in fact, zoning in many of its present forms works against both public and private interests, promoting sprawl, raising the cost of public improvements and services, increasing private costs, limiting intelligent design, and restricting the usefulness of such open space as is available by requiring it to be in the wrong places.

Planned shopping centers

Planned shopping centers,[7] as covered in the Anchorage ordinance, are permissible in the RG-D district as a special exception by the board of adjustment, but only upon favorable recommendation by the planning commission. This method of treatment conforms to traditional zoning procedures so far as issuance of special exceptions is concerned, but requires technical review by a body which is staffed with professional planners. If planning commission approval is conditional, the board must include the conditions, but may add others of its own, and may require posting of a performance bond to assure that stated conditions are met.

Definition. For purposes of this chapter, a planned shopping center has an area of not less than five acres, planned and developed as a unit, and provides a variety of goods and services in stores and offices conveniently arranged with respect to each other and to off-street parking facilities provided with safe access from and to appropriate public streets.

7. Although indicated as a special exception in this case, the requirements might be adapted for planned shopping center developments requiring rezoning.

Intent concerning character of development. It is the intent of this chapter that the character of planned shopping centers shall be appropriate to the surrounding neighborhood, and that conditions and safeguards shall be established to assure, insofar as possible, that the development will protect and enhance the value of surrounding property, in addition to achieving other public purposes.

Location. Planned shopping centers shall be permitted as special exceptions only if they have at least 400 feet of frontage on arterial streets and only:

(a) Adjacent to areas zoned to permit general business within the city (provided that such areas shall be considered adjacent if separated only by a street or alley) or

(b) Similarly adjacent to unzoned areas outside the city which are developed for general business purposes, or

(c) Separated from either, and from other planned shopping centers, by a distance of at least one-half mile, measured along principal routes of travel.

The limitations on location tie the shopping centers to arterial streets. They are allowable adjacent to areas already zoned for general business, where they might be expected to provide a logical transition from strip commercial development to noncommercial development, and thus end the pressure for creeping stripism. They are allowable adjacent to unzoned areas outside the city in which general commercial development has already taken place, an arrangement which permits some flexibility in the treatment of property opposite these unprotected areas without throwing the whole in-city section wide open to commercial or industrial development.

Item (c), in effect, limits both number and location of planned shopping centers which may be established in interior portions of the RG-D district. Here some planned centers may in time be desirable, but an unlimited number are not. In general commercial districts, it is not good form to limit competition by specifying number of establishments or distances between them. The RG-D district is not a general commercial district, but is primarily residential in character. Here there is justification for limiting number and location of planned centers, and for control on their design and characteristics.

Permitted principal uses and structures. The following principal uses and structures may be permitted in any approved planned shopping center:

(a) Department stores; supermarkets; drug stores; bakeries; meat markets; delicatessens; liquor stores subject to licensing provisions or other regulations of the city; hardware, paint, and wallpaper stores; camera shops; florist shops; gift shops; hobby shops; stationery stores; apparel stores; shoe stores; variety stores; jewelry stores; stores for sales of gardening supplies and equipment; radio and TV stores; music stores;

(b) Eating and drinking establishments;

(c) Barber shops; beauty shops; cleaning and laundry agencies without major processing on the premises and establishments with coin-operated equipment for laundry and dry cleaning; shoe repair shops; repair establishments for household articles and appliances, restricted to those brought in and picked up by customers, and specifically excluding those with internal combustion engines; cold storage lockers;

(d) Offices, studios, medical and dental clinics, banking facilities; provided, however, that all sales, service, storage, and display shall be within completely enclosed buildings, that no goods shall be produced except for sale at retail on the premises, and that no food or drinks shall be sold for consumption out of doors on the premises or in automobiles on the premises.

Permitted accessory uses and structures. The following accessory uses and structures may be permitted in any approved planned shopping center: Uses and structures which are customarily accessory and clearly incidental and subordinate to permitted principal uses and structures, as stated and restricted above, and which do not involve operations or structures not in keeping with the character of the planned shopping center, or likely (as located, constructed, operated, or maintained) to have an adverse effect on the character of areas surrounding the shopping center. It is specifically provided that garbage and trash, unless kept in principal buildings, shall be kept in containers in accessory structures, and that neither the containers nor loose garbage or trash shall be visible from residential areas, from portions of the premises customarily open to customer parking or customer pedestrian or automotive traffic, or from public ways.

Prohibited uses and structures. The following uses and structures are specifically prohibited in any approved planned shopping center:

(a) Signs not relating to identification of premises and occupants, and to products sold or services rendered on the premises;

(b) Filling stations and repair garages; repair or testing of internal combustion engines;

(c) Outdoor sales, service (other than delivery of goods purchased to the automobiles of customers), or display;

(d) The playing of music or making of announcements directly or through mechanical or electronic devices in a manner audible at any residential lot line; and

(e) In general, any use or structure not of a nature specifically permitted under "Permitted Principal Uses and Structures" and "Permitted Accessory Uses and Structures" above.

Minimum lot dimensions. Minimum width of the lot shall be 400 feet, minimum area, five acres. No such lot shall be divided by any public street. In addition to these minimum requirements, the lot shall be of such size, shape, and location as to enable development of well-organized commercial facilities with proper access, ingress and egress, off-street parking and loading space, and other requirements.

Access to site. Vehicular access shall be only from arterial or collector streets except where unusual circumstances make minor accessways from minor streets practicable without adverse effects on property along such minor streets. Pedestrian access may be permitted at any location on the site.

Minimum yard and landscaping requirements; maintenance of visibility at access points; relation of yards to turnout and merging lanes. Yards with a minimum depth of 25 feet shall be provided around the entire perimeter of the planned shopping center, and additional depth may be required where necessary to protect adjacent property in portions of the perimeter. No internal yards need be provided, but where buildings on the lot are separated, the distance between them shall be at least five feet.

Along minor public streets, and adjacent to any required residential front- or side-yard line, a yard 25 feet in least dimension shall be landscaped and maintained in a manner appropriate to a residential neighborhood. No such landscaped yard shall be used for off-street parking or loading, but such required yards may be used for walkways, and portions not within 25 feet of residential lots may be used for drives other than principal entrances or exits.

Along collector and arterial public streets, yards may be used for off-street parking, drives, and walkways, provided however that a yard 25 feet in least dimension shall be landscaped and maintained in a manner appropriate to a residential neighborhood where the lot adjoins any required residential front- or side-yard line, with uses limited as provided above.

No landscaping, fences, terraces, or other natural or artificial features adjacent to any street shall be of a nature impairing visibility from or of approaching vehicular traffic where such visibility is important to safety, nor shall such features in any way create potential hazards to pedestrians. In particular, at vehicular entrances and exits, no off-street parking, landscaping, or other material impediment to visibility between the heights of three feet and eight feet shall be permitted within triangular areas defined by lines connecting points described as follows: Beginning at a point where the midline of the entrance or exit intersects the public right-of-way, thence to a point 35 feet along the right-of-way in the direction of approaching traffic, thence to a point 25 feet toward the interior of the lot along the midline of the entrance or exit, and thence to point of beginning.

Along collector and arterial public streets, turn-out lanes and merging lanes may be required to be constructed on the lot, with length and width as appropriate to flow of traffic, and traffic-separation devices may be required at such entrances and exits and along such merging lanes. Whether required or provided voluntarily, such turn-out and merging lanes may be included as part of the required yard adjacent to the public collector or arterial street, except that no such lane, and no entrance or exit, shall run through any part of any required landscaped yard adjacent to a required residential front or side yard.

Maximum height of structures. No portion of any structure shall project through imaginary planes leaning inward from lot lines at an angle of 45 degrees, nor necessitate increase in established glide angles or raise elevations of established turning circles in relation to any airport.

Minimum off-street parking and loading requirements. For each 100 square feet of gross floor area in buildings, one off-street parking space shall be provided. Off-street loading facilities shall be provided which do not require the use of required off-street parking space during hours when establishments in the center are open for business. All off-street parking and loading space shall be so located, improved, illuminated, operated, and maintained as to provide safe and convenient circulation on the premises and from adjacent streets, and to minimize potential frictions with adjoining residential property.

Limitations on signs. No signs intended to be read from off the premises shall be permitted except:

(a) Necessary signs for the control and direction of traffic on the premises or entering or leaving the premises, which may be located as required for effective performance of intended function, and which shall bear no advertising matter.

(b) One general identification sign structure, bearing one sign if mounted approximately parallel to the right-of-way or two signs if mounted back to back or angled to be read from opposite directions, for each frontage of the tract on an arterial or collector street. Such signs shall not be erected in any portion of any required landscaped yard adjacent to such streets or to residential property, but may be erected in portions not required to be landscaped. If so erected, such signs shall not create material impediments to visibility likely to be hazardous to vehicles or pedestrians entering or leaving the property. If two signs are used in portions of yards in which permitted, the maximum area of each shall be 75 square feet; if one sign, the maximum area shall be 150 square feet. When erected behind the interior boundary of the required yard, the areas indicated above may be doubled.

(c) Signs on buildings within the center may be erected as follows: For each 10 lineal feet of building fronting on public parking areas, and for each 20 lineal feet of building not fronting on such areas, but adjacent to and visible from them, a maximum of one sign and 10 square feet of sign surface area shall be permitted, provided however, that no establishment shall be restricted to less than four signs, or less than 40 square feet of surface area. Such signs shall refer only to the name and nature of the business conducted in the building and to goods and services offered, shall be mounted flat against the wall or window of the building or on marquees or awnings, or shall project horizontally not more than three feet from the wall of the building if not mounted on a marquee or awning. Insofar as reasonably feasible, such signs shall be oriented away from surrounding residential areas.

Preceding material establishes intent and specifications to guide applicants, the planning commission and staff, and the board of adjustment. Next comes administrative material on content of the plan, processing, and conditions (including time limits) which may be attached. Applicants should be familiarized with this before they begin selecting sites or making detailed plans. As with most zoning, explanation ahead of application may avert many headaches for all concerned.

In many jurisdictions, the fourth paragraph below may be of special interest.

Proposed development plan and other material to accompany application. Applications for special exceptions in this class shall be accompanied by information concerning ownership of lands involved, proposals for financing development, and such other material as may be necessary to demonstrate that the proposal is a bona fide move for actual development, and not merely an attempt to secure the special exception for special advantage. This material shall indicate a time schedule for development if the special exception is granted.

In addition to these and other materials which may be required in the circumstances of the particular case, applicants shall prepare and submit development plans covering the entire tract proposed for the planned shopping center, indicating existing conditions and development for an additional area including at least 300 feet from the boundaries of the lot, or such greater distance as may be indicated by the circumstances of the case. The plan shall be drawn to a scale of 50 or 100 feet to the inch, and shall indicate topography at two-foot contour intervals, except that in relatively flat territory the contour interval may be required to be one foot. Existing streams, marshes, natural drainageways, flood plains, and other natural features shall be indicated as well as existing streets, easements, utility installations, lot lines, and structures, with indications as to use.

The plan shall show, with dimensions, a properly organized and conveniently related arrangement of buildings, off-street parking and loading facilities, internal automotive and pedestrian circulation, entrances and exits to public streets and pedestrian ways, service areas and facilities, drainage, utilities connections, landscaping, fencing and walls, exterior lighting on the premises, size, location, and orientation of signs, and relation to and safeguards for all property surrounding the lot.

If appropriate in view of location of the site, the plan shall also show the manner of improving and maintaining in open use portions of the tract subject to periodic inundation, and shall demonstrate that hazards or damage to other property will not be created by any channeling, cutting, filling, bulkheading, or other treatment of water flow from or past the site, by erosion from increased rate, volume, or reduction of flow, by deposition of debris or other flood borne materials from the site or as a result of its development, by excessive slopes remaining at the edges of cuts or fills, by damaging increases in the ground water level of surrounding property, or by other actions in developing the tract and its ancillary facilities. If potential hazard or damage might reasonably be expected from any of these causes, the plan shall show how it is to be averted.

If it is proposed to develop the planned shopping center in stages, the plan shall indicate the stages and the timing of development.

Approval of vehicular circulation plan, parking, and loading facilities. The portions of the plan relating to location and design of ingress and egress, traffic controls, arrangement of off-street parking and loading facilities, and internal circulation pattern shall be referred to the city traffic engineer for study, and no such special exception shall be granted without his written approval of plans as submitted, or, if his approval is conditional, the special exception shall include the conditions. Additional conditions and safeguards on such matters may be included by the Planning Commission or the Board of Adjustment.

General conditions which may be attached. In reviewing the proposed development plan, the Planning Commission and the Board of Adjustment may require rearrangement of the structures or uses as proposed to assure that the requirements set forth above are met, and may condition approval on specified changes in the proposal. Where conditions are attached, no special exception may be granted except upon written agreement by the applicant to conform to such conditions.

In particular, where the plan indicates potential adverse effects on neighboring property, the Planning Commission or the Board of Adjustment may require rearrangement of the plan, increased yard width, walls or fences, vegetative screening, or other arrangements or devices necessary to provide reasonable protection.

Conditions concerning time limits. Any special exception in this class shall contain time limits relating to stages of development. The first stage shall include development of a major portion of the proposed center, and construction on this portion shall be substantially initiated during the first building season after issuance of the special exception and may be required to be completed within the first building season. In any case, completion of the first stage shall be required by the end of the second building season after issuance. Timing for the initiation and completion of other stages, if any, shall be prescribed by the Board of Adjustment.

If the first stage is not substantially initiated during the first building season, the special exception shall expire and be cancelled, and the applicants informed thereof. If completion of the first stage, or initiation and completion of additional stages as defined in the special exception, are not according to the schedule set, the Board may cancel the special exception entirely and require demolition of buildings or use in a manner conforming to general district requirements, permit use as proposed of structures and premises completed and completion of work substantially under way and no other (provided that off-street parking and other requirements shall be completed as appropriate to development), or permit an extension of the terms of the special exception applying to the particular stage for not more than one building season.

Where the special exception is cancelled, or where the center is not completed sufficiently to offer a reasonably full range of facilities, it shall not be considered a planned shopping center for the purposes of limiting location and development of planned shopping centers, and another planned shopping center may be permitted by special exception in the general area, provided that such center might otherwise be permitted under the terms limiting location and development of planned shopping centers.

(As an explanatory note, the reference to "building seasons" here reflects climatic conditions in Anchorage. For the most part, construction is limited to five or six months per year.)

The conditions concerning time limits should assure that shoestring ventures and those primarily for land speculation are kept to a minimum. There remains of course the possibility that a development not carried to completion would remain as a piece of a planned shopping center, but there is provision for stern measures, including demolition of the buildings or requirement that they be used for purposes generally permitted in the district, and there is also the possibility of tempering justice with mercy by allowing their use for commercial purposes as originally intended, but without giving them a monopoly which would prevent the development of a full-scale shopping center in the same area if it is otherwise justified.

Commercial open recreational uses

Commercial open recreational uses have distinct advantages as interim operations in districts or parts of districts which are undeveloped or sparsely developed, and which are destined in time to be of a general residential nature, but they can be troublesome in such locations unless carefully regulated as to character and duration. In Anchorage, the RG-D district (general residential) has as yet very little development. Here are the provisions relating to commercial open recreational uses permissible as special exceptions by the board of adjustment.

Section 23-7, Supplementary District Regulations

P. *Commercial open recreational uses.* In any district in which commercial open recreational uses, such as miniature golf courses, "par-3" golf courses, putting greens, driving ranges, trampolines, archery ranges, riding stables, skiing, skating, or sledding facilities and the like, operated for profit, may be permitted as special exceptions. In addition to other considerations, the following guides and standards shall govern:

1. *Location and access.* The location shall be appropriate to existing development and to development known to be proposed, or likely to be proposed, within two years. Access to the site shall neither create nor be exposed to traffic hazards for vehicles or pedestrians.

2. *Size of site.* As minimums, the site shall have a width of 200 feet and an area of one acre, and additional area or width may be required to provide spatial or other buffering appropriate to the production of

nearby development, existing or proposed or likely to be proposed within two years. Additional width or area may also be required in order to provide adequate off-street parking and loading space, without use of street right-of-way for maneuvering, parking, or loading.

3. *Plan and development.* The plan and development shall provide safe and convenient parking, entrances and exits, and safe operating conditions, with appropriate separation from public roads and adjacent property as developed or as proposed, or likely to be proposed, for development within two years.

4. *Protection of public streets and adjacent property from potentially adverse influences.* As required by existing development, and development proposed, or likely to be proposed, within two years, the Board shall establish conditions controlling noise, lights, and other potentially adverse influences. Conditions may be established regarding hours of operation. No portion of any off-street parking shall be within 25 feet of any public street right-of-way. No stable shall be within 300 feet of any property boundary.

5. *Signs.* The only signs to be permitted in connection with special exceptions in this category shall be not to exceed two directional signs (other than those erected by a public agency) with size and location to be approved by the Board, and not to exceed one sign, six square feet or less in area, for each frontage of the facility on a public street or highway. All such signs shall be removed on termination of the special exception.

6. *Duration.* No such special exception shall be issued for a period of more than two years, and any such special exception may include provision for termination prior to the expiration of the period for causes specified therein, or for termination by reason for development, use, or operation contrary to the provisions thereof. After termination of the initial period, such special exceptions may be renewed annually or for lesser periods (unless changing conditions indicate that renewal would not be in the public interest) with amended conditions and safeguards if circumstances warrant such amendment.

Any buildings or other improvements constructed or used in connection with such special exception may be required to be removed on termination of the special exception, and the Board may require posting of a performance bond to assure such removal.

Public and quasi-public playgrounds, playfields, and children's camps, not operated for profit, are permissible in the RG-D district with similar limitations, and for the same reasons. Here again, an open recreational use may be excellent while the area is developing, objectionable after surrounding lands have been built up. A longer term is allowable.

Section 23-7, Supplementary District Regulations

O. *Private and quasi-public playgrounds, playfields, and children's camps, not operated for profit.* In any district in which private and quasi-public playgrounds, playfields, and children's camps and the like, not operated for profit, may be permitted as special exceptions by the Board of Adjustment, in addition to other considerations the following guides and standards shall govern.

1. *Location and access.* The location shall be appropriate to existing development and development likely to take place within the term of the special exception. Access to the site shall neither create nor be exposed to traffic hazards for vehicles or pedestrians.

2. *Size of site.* The site shall be of a size and shape appropriate for the purposes proposed and to provide spatial or other buffering as needed to protect nearby development from potentially adverse effects, and to protect those using the site from potentially adverse effects of surrounding areas. The site shall also be of a size and shape which will allow adequate off-street parking and loading without use of street right-of-way for maneuvering, parking, or loading.

3. *Plan and development.* The plan and development shall provide safe and convenient parking, entrance and exits, and safe play conditions, with appropriate separation from roads and other hazards.

4. *Protection of property from potentially adverse influences.* As required by existing development, and development likely to take place within the term of the special exception, the Board shall establish conditions controlling noise, lights, and other potentially adverse influences on the site and may establish hours of operation. In addition, the Board may establish requirements as necessary to protect those using the site from potentially adverse off-site effects.

5. *Signs.* The only signs to be permitted in connection with special exceptions in this category shall be not to exceed two directional signs (other than those erected by a public agency) with size and location to be approved by the Board, and not to exceed one sign, two square feet or less in area, at each principal roadway entrance to the facility. All such signs shall be removed on termination of the special exception.

6. *Duration.* No such special exception shall be issued for a period of more than five years, renewable annually thereafter (unless changing conditions indicate that renewal would not be in the public interest) with amended conditions and safeguards if circumstances warrant such amendment. Any such special exception may include provision for termination prior to the expiration of the period for causes specified

therein, or for development, use, or operation contrary to the provisions thereof.

Any buildings or other structures erected or used in connection with such special exception may be required to be removed on termination of the special exception, and the Board may require posting of a performance bond to assure such removal.

Residual lot areas

Residual lot areas[8] create administrative problems unless there are guides. A man has enough area for three dwelling units, and "almost" enough for a fourth. There should be some rule as to when "almost" is considered enough. Here's how it is handled in the Anchorage supplementary regulations:

Section 23-7, Supplementary District Regulations

N. *Residual lot area.* In districts permitting two-family or multiple-family dwellings, where area of property is such that a portion remains after full requirements have been met for other dwelling units on the same property, the following rules shall guide the administrative official in issuing zoning permits, and no relaxation of these rules shall be permitted by a variance. If otherwise permitted by the regulations of the district:

Two units shall be permitted on a lot containing area required for one unit and 90 per cent of the area for a second.

Three units shall be permitted on a lot containing area required for two units and 85 per cent of the area required for a third.

Four units shall be permitted on a lot containing area required for three units and 80 per cent of the area required for a fourth.

One additional unit shall be permitted on a lot containing area required for four or more units and 75 per cent of the area required for the additional unit.

---

8. Where a floor area ratio is used as a residential density control, there is no problem with residual lot areas.

Residential zoning: *maybe we can do better*

Zoning, now over 50 years old, isn't far ahead of where it started. Things which began at the same time or later have shown some signs of progress—radio, TV, the automobile, the airplane, and so on. But with zoning, and particularly residential zoning, provisions adopted yesterday are often indistinguishable from those written in the 1920s.

We have beginnings of breakthrough in planned unit and cluster development which help in building new neighborhoods or communities from scratch. But such provisions haven't been extended to the thousands of square miles of established housing which must slowly replace themselves. "Natural" renewal is forced into the same old mold, or doesn't happen, in which case the bulldozer takes over. We know enough to do better than that.

We have let ourselves be trapped by tradition, by administrative custom, in some cases even by such trivia as definitions. A planning commission recently debated at length as to where townhouses belonged. They agreed that in fact, townhouses were single-family dwellings, but concluded that they would have to go into multifamily districts because the definition said that a dwelling containing three or more units in the same structure is a multifamily dwelling. Nobody suggested changing the definition.

Hypnotized by traditional form, we have lost contact with the *purposes* of zoning. We spend more and more time spreading defective regulations across the face of urban America, less and less on thinking about what zoning is supposed to do, and whether its ends could be met more effectively by means with more intelligence about them, and less tradition.

[*At this point the author summarizes standard enabling legislation. Since he has done so elsewhere in this collection, the material here is omitted.—Ed.*]

Definitions

In residential zoning, the definition of "dwelling unit" is of key importance. In the definition proposed here, an attempt is made to dispose of a problem which may be troublesome, intrusion of motels into multifamily districts. In some cases, motels have put cooking facilities into each rental unit and claimed the right to the same location as multifamily dwellings. The minimum time limit proposed is long enough to discourage most motel operations, but short enough to permit continuation of the practice of collecting weekly rents in some areas.

It is prudent to omit reference to independent toilet and bath, even though the proportion of dwelling units without such facilities is diminishing. Otherwise there is a no-man's-land in legislative and administrative practice in cases of shared toilet and bath.

Dwelling unit: A room or rooms connected together, constituting a separate, independent housekeeping establishment for one family only, for owner occupancy or for rental, lease, or other occupancy on a weekly or longer basis, physically separated from any other rooms or dwelling units, and containing independent cooking and sleeping facilities.

Mention of the term "family" makes it necessary to add a definition of that word, since it is used in zoning in a specialized sense. Here it is possible to handle items on which the silence of many ordinances may lead to trouble. Even in the most restricted districts, a room or two may be rented. There appears to be no harm in this, but an upper limit should be set. To avoid gaps, this limit should reach to the lower end of the spectrum on rooming houses and boarding houses.

The definition should also be flexible enough to allow servants, who would be excluded under exclusive "blood and marriage" language, and to allow small combinations of unrelated persons to occupy a dwelling unit, but it should bar large aggregations such as fraternities, sororities, clubs, or institutional groups.

Family: One or more persons occupying a single dwelling unit, provided that unless all members are related by blood or marriage, no such family shall contain over five persons, but further provided that domestic servants employed on the premises may be housed on the premises without being counted as a family or families and not more than two rooms may be occupied by a total of four or less roomers, who may also board with the families, and that four or less boarders, including roomers, may be accommodated. (For five or more roomers or boarders, see *boarding house* and *rooming house.*) The term "family" shall not be construed to mean a fraternity, sorority, club, or institutional group.

At this point, it is appropriate to sort dwellings into types for regulatory purposes. In most jurisdictions, it will not be necessary to make as detailed an array as is attempted here; in some, other types may be added. If there is clear and substantial need for distinguishing a dwelling type in order to regulate for the stated purposes of zoning, make the distinction; if not, don't.

Elements which *may* be so related (but are not always or necessarily related and sometimes can be controlled without distinction as to dwelling types) include density, ownership of the lot, height, and "character of the district and its peculiar suitability for particular uses."

As a passing note, power given by enabling legislation to protect "character of the district" is not used as widely or as intelligently as it should be. Even since *Berman v. Parker* (a U.S. Supreme Court case finding it "within the power of the legislature to determine that a community should be beautiful as well as healthy"), aesthetics has not been on very firm ground, partly because there is no definition of what is aesthetic and what is not (a matter on which there will be argument as long as tastes differ). But many court cases may well have been lost because someone insisted on dragging aesthetics into the argument needlessly.

Where aesthetics becomes a central issue, a conservative judge may rule adversely because aesthetics is not listed as a purpose of zoning and is a vague and indefinite guide. In a particular case, he may find support for his opinion in the fact that a substantial number of qualified witnesses find that the proposal does not offend their aesthetic sensibilities.

On the other hand, the same judge might be persuaded to a favorable finding if "character of the district" is of central importance. This is one of the things zoning is specifically empowered to protect. Existing character can be established by visual impression and by other means. The question then becomes, "is this appropriate in this setting?" rather than "is this beautiful?" Most people (including members of the judiciary) would be inclined to rule with more assurance on the former question, and if such a ruling will suffice, it is sound strategy to avoid the hazards of aesthetic definition.

Sorting residential types

One-family dwellings come in broad array, and failure to recognize this fact may lead to complications. Many ordinances appear to assume that there is only one category, the single-family detached, and sooner or later create difficulties because there is no definition or regulation of other forms or because there is rude awakening when mobile homes are found to meet the definition for single-family detached dwellings. In what follows, a general definition covers all forms of one-family dwellings, and subcategories are distinguished to the extent necessary for most regulations.

Dwelling, one-family: A building containing only one dwelling unit. The term is general, including such specialized forms as one-family detached, one-family semi-detached and one-family attached (row houses, townhouses, patio and atrium houses and the like if containing only one family). For regulatory purposes, the term is not to be construed to include mobile homes, travel trailers, housing mounted on self-propelled or drawn vehicles, tents, or other forms of portable or temporary housing.

This definition provides a form to be used in regulations where all types of one-family dwellings are to be permitted in a district. If only certain types are to be allowed, the appropriate specific nomenclature should be used.

Dwelling, one-family detached: A one-family dwelling entirely separated from structures on adjacent lots.

It is probably best to avoid the temptation to define the detached dwelling as "entirely surrounded by yards," or more particularly "entirely surrounded by yards on the same lot." In some cases, it may be desirable to permit building to certain property lines if requirements for light, air, on-site open space, building spacing, and traffic visibility can be met. This is a case where it is particularly important to leave room for flexibility, and careless language in the definition may create restrictions which have no substantial relation to zoning purposes and force monotonous development to both public and private disadvantage.

The definition which follows is needed because of the exclusion of mobile homes from the general definition of detached one-family dwellings. Usually mobile homes are specially regulated, and failure to make the distinction in definitions can lead to trouble.

Dwelling, mobile home: A detached one-family dwelling with all of the following characteristics:

(a) Designed for long-term occupancy, and containing sleeping accommodations, a flush toilet, a tub or shower bath, and kitchen facilities, with plumbing and electrical connections provided for attachment to outside systems.

(b) Designed to be transported after fabrication on its own wheels, on detachable wheels, or on flatbed or other trailers.

(c) Arriving at the site where it is to be occupied as a dwelling complete, including major appliances and furniture, and ready for occupancy except for minor and incidental unpacking and assembly operations, location on foundation supports, connection to utilities, and the like.

At this point, definitions overlapping one- and two-family classes might well follow, covering semi-detached and attached dwellings. Such definitions should clarify the distinction between one- and two-family uses and multiple dwellings. If "building" is inadequately defined as merely a structure with a roof, and "multifamily dwellings" are defined as having three or more units in one building, townhouses become excluded from one- and two-family districts because the continuous structure includes three or more dwelling units. The definition of building should be detailed enough to eliminate this kind of absurdity.

Building: A structure with a roof, intended for the shelter or enclosure of persons or property. Where roofed structures are separated from each other by party walls having no openings for passage, each portion so separated shall be considered a separate building.

The next definitions limit maximum occupancy at two units per building, firmly separating these types from multifamily structures. If necessary, some district regulations can make further limitation to one unit per building. As a cumbersome alternative, separate definitions could be provided for one- and two-family semi-detached dwellings and one- and two-family attached dwellings.

Dwelling, semi-detached: A building containing not more than two dwelling units, attached at the side to not more than one other building containing not more than two dwelling units by a party wall without openings, with each building having a separate lot with dimensions meeting regulations for the district, or so located on land in the same ownership that individual lots meeting district requirements could be provided, in which case the dimensions of such land shall not be reduced below those required for provision of separate lots.

As to the final provision above, it does not seem likely that any of the stated purposes of zoning are defeated if land in one ownership is used for construction of semi-detached dwellings in one ownership and the ownership is later divided, provided that adequate lot size is maintained for the combination and for the split.

Dwelling, attached: A building containing not more than two dwelling units, attached at the side or sides in a series of three or more principal buildings each containing not more than two dwelling units. At points of attachment, such buildings shall be separated from each other by fire walls extending from footings through roofs without openings which would permit the spread of fire from one building to another. Such buildings shall each have a separate lot with dimensions meeting regulations for the district, or be so located on land in the same ownership that individual lots meeting district requirements could be provided, in which case dimensions of such land shall not be reduced below those required for provision of separate lots. The term attached dwelling is intended to apply to row houses, townhouses, patio or atrium houses, or any form however termed which conforms to this definition.

A fire wall is required here in place of the party wall prescribed for semi-detached dwellings because of the larger number of units exposed to risk from spread of fire. If the building code requires such fire walls, there is no need to repeat the requirement in the definition, and its elimination here would be an improvement if the matter is covered elsewhere.

It is probably unnecessary to have formal definitions of row house, townhouse, and patio or atrium house. All are typically attached dwellings, although the townhouse or patio house might conceivably appear in either semi-detached or even detached form. Either the row house or the townhouse might include two dwelling units. The patio house is almost necessarily limited to one.

"Row housing" is often associated with unhappy monotony, block after block of dwellings with the same interior and exterior plans, the same roof-lines, the same materials, the same entries, the same jokes about going home to the wrong house. The better townhouses wear their rows with a difference, but merely calling a row house a townhouse doesn't do more than throw a status symbol into the sales pitch. To assure relief from monotony, regulations often call for variations in building lines after a set number of units, and require different roof lines, entries, and exterior colors or materials on adjoining units. This is probably justified as preserving or improving the character of the district, and is certainly an aesthetic lift. It can hardly be grounded in any of the other stated purposes of zoning. At any rate, the best place to set such requirements is in district regulations, rather than in definitions.

Row houses and townhouses are usually more than one story high. They are usually extraverted, though not to the extent of detached dwellings. In the front, they have numerous windows for observing (and being observed from) the street, across minimal front yards. Their lots are small, with length about four times width. The rear yard is often at least partially screened by walls or plantings, giving partial privacy which may be invaded by overview from rear windows of adjoining units. From inside rooms on the second story, unless the occupant moves close to the window, the view at the rear is primarily of structures on abutting lots.

The patio, atrium, or garden court house is something else again. U.S. examples of this form are usually one story high. William K. Wittausch, of Stanford Research Institute, describes it as: "a brand new idea, some 3,000 years old. It is based on lot line to lot line building of a house on an urban plot with the family's living being done around a garden court. It is the oldest form of urban housing we have.

It is likened to the Roman atrium house as the Romans copied it from the ancient Greeks, and to the traditional Austrian 'Hofhaus.' It is duplicated in the Near East, the Far East, wherever families were first concentrated in group settlements."[1]

The patio house may be attached on two or even three sides, since all of its window orientation can be to the garden court. This makes possible great flexibility in arrangement, including four-deep units in conventional rectangular blocks, with outer rows facing the street, inner rows taking access from a midblock pedestrian way, with parking at block ends, the block interior, or other convenient locations.

The patio house is introverted. Even in the midst of intense urban activity, it meditates with "that inward eye which is the bliss of solitude" on the intimate garden space enfolded with its windows and shielded by walls from the outside world.

If regulations are based on performance, special definitions of these varieties of row housing will not be needed, since lot area and coverage limitations, height limits, on-site open space, and parking and other requirements adapted to any one of the forms will fairly well fit all of them.

In some cases, it may be desired to allow in certain predominantly one-family districts two-family dwellings which are indistinguishable in appearance from surrounding one-family residences. Such a combination could take a variety of interior forms, with one unit above the other, one unit beside the other, or with units dovetailed vertically or horizontally in many ways.

Finding a term to fit such residences isn't easy. They might be called camouflaged two-family dwellings, or the word "duplex" can be altered to fit if it hasn't been preempted for other local usage. By dictionary definition, a duplex is a two-family dwelling, whether divided vertically or horizontally. Starting with this:

Dwelling, duplex: A building containing two dwelling units, having a single front entrance and being otherwise indistinguishable from a one-family dwelling in exterior appearance.

As another possibility, the definition could be omitted entirely, with district regulations for areas involved allowing two-family dwellings with restrictions as indicated in the definition.

1. William K. Wittausch, "The Patio House, A Suburban House for Urban Living," *Urban Land Institute Technical Bulletin No. 45* (Washington, D.C.: Urban Land Institute, 1963).

Multifamily dwellings

For multifamily dwellings, the basic definition can be fairly simple. The one suggested here is embroidered with a phrase concerning length of occupancy to prevent motels from moving into apartment areas, and language making it clear that condominiums and cooperative apartments are to be considered multifamily dwellings, just in case anyone is in doubt.

Multifamily dwelling: A building containing three or more dwelling units. The term includes cooperative apartments, condominiums, and the like. For purposes of these regulations, regardless of how rental units are equipped, any multifamily dwelling in which units are available for rental periods of less than one week shall be considered a hotel.

From this, things run off in several directions. There is first the matter of types of apartments. Then there is a need for definition of residence hotels, apartment hotels, and rooming and boarding houses, where residents will live for substantial periods. And to tie up the loose ends, there should be a definition of places for accommodation of transients, hotels, and similar establishments.

As to forms of multifamily dwellings, definitions may not be necessary since regulations should establish character by requirements on number of units, height, lot area per family, parking, size, location and use of open space on the lot, and similar matters. What follows can be used in constructing definitions if they are felt to be needed, and in establishing regulations.

In some parts of the country, a building with three to five dwelling units is called a *flat*. It is usually a high-intensity form, with small lot area per family and minimal yards. It is normally detached, but just barely.

A *garden apartment* is customarily a two-story structure without an elevator, but may run to three on sloping terrain. If density goes above 25 average-size units per net acre, the word "garden" is a euphemism, and 20 is better. This yields lot area per unit of about 2,000 square feet. Even with this, regulations should prescribe landscaped open space, or the garden is likely to be largely paved.

Beyond the garden apartment, economics creates a gap in the multifamily series. *Intermediate* apartments (to call them something—

there doesn't seem to be a common-use term) are usually about six stories high. Very few multifamily dwellings are built in the three- to five-story range. Six-story apartments usually work out to about 75 units per net acre with open parking, with building coverage at about 25 per cent, and parking covering most of the rest of the lot. Where parking is in garages (which it rarely is), there is room for better landscaping. Direct controls on land coverage by buildings and paved areas should prescribe landscaping at least in the form of shielding adverse views, and should preferably set a minimum for landscaped area.

High-rise apartments represent another jump caused by economics. If height is to go beyond six stories, it doesn't go merely to seven. If definition of high-rise is necessary, it could hinge on a height of 65 feet or over.

Properly regulated, high-rise apartments have substantial public and private advantages. The high-rise can give densities of 100 units per acre and more, with very low ground coverage and excellent view for occupants. Cost of public services per dwelling unit is low, public revenue per dwelling unit is high. Because of the structural concentration, this form is particularly well adapted to hilly terrain where it is important to protect against erosion and where construction expense for less intensive use might be prohibitive.

High-rise should be so located that it does not stream intense traffic through minor streets in low-density neighborhoods. High portions of buildings belong well back from adjacent buildable areas, partly to allow light and free flow of air and partly to protect view. Direct controls on impediments to principal views will be necessary in some areas, and it may be desirable to adopt a form of regulation discouraging a saw-tooth horizon along tops of important ridges.

Land coverage should be held low, particularly in suburban areas. Parking controls should protect against the sea-of-cars appearance, and garage parking is highly desirable. Open-space controls should set a minimum proportion of lot area for landscaping, with performance-type standards as to location of green areas. Given such regulations, high-rise can provide a park-like environment for occupants and their neighbors. Without such regulations, high-rise can be a disaster. Certainly it is a form with great promise as population pressures and need to prevent urban sprawl make it imperative to develop for high densities with reasonable amenities.

Specialized forms

There are some leftovers. Rooming houses, tourist homes, boarding houses, and hotels should be defined, and the definitions must be matched so that numerical overlaps don't cause complications. "Family" was so delineated that not more than four roomers and/or boarders were included. Hence, rooming or boarding houses or tourist homes should take up at this point, and run upward to a limit which will keep them relatively small (so that they may be allowed in areas where larger establishments would be out of place) and then larger establishments must be identified for regulatory purposes.

Rooming house: An establishment where lodging is provided for compensation (a) on a weekly or longer basis, (b) other than in dwelling units, (c) for from 5 to 19 persons, and (d) without service of meals to roomers. [For lodgings with meals, see *boarding house.* For similar lodging for 20 or more persons, see *residence hotel.*]

There is nothing sacred about either the upper or the lower limit, but if either is changed, other related figures should also be changed.

Tourist home: An establishment where lodging is provided for compensation (a) for periods of less than one week, (b) other than in dwelling units, (c) for from 5 to 19 persons, and (d) with breakfast only served to guests, or with no meals served to guests. [For transient lodging for 20 or more persons, see *hotel.*]

Differences between tourist home and rooming house are that the former provides lodging for periods of less than one week and may serve breakfast.

Boarding house: An establishment where meals and/or lodging is provided for compensation (a) by prearrangement, but without limitation on time periods involved, (b) with lodging for compensation other than in dwelling units, and (c) for a total of 5 to 19 roomers and/or boarders. [For similar facilities for 20 or more persons, see *hotel.*]

Although the boarding house is of diminishing importance in the U.S. scene, it still serves a useful function in some areas of the country. As defined here, it differs from a rooming house in that short-term guests are accommodated, from a tourist home in that three meals a day may be served, and to persons who are not lodgers. But the meals are to be served only by prearrangement, so a boarding house is different from a restaurant.

Hotel: An establishment where lodging is provided for compensation (a) other than in dwelling units, and (b) for 20 or more persons. Unless otherwise specified by district regulations, hotels may serve meals to both occupants and others. For purposes of these regulations, the term hotel shall be construed to include motel, motor court, auto court, tourist court, motor lodge, and similar facilities if for 20 or more occupants. [For smaller numbers of persons to be accommodated, see *tourist home, boarding house, rooming house.* For hotels with occupancy limited to periods of one week or longer, see *residence hotel.*]

It is becoming more and more difficult to distinguish between hotels and motels, and on the whole the distinction in definition is not necessary. Off-street parking requirements for either should be the same in the same district, as should yard and area requirements, height limitations, and so on. Hence, it is generally futile to try to separate establishments by location of parking with relation to access to individual units.

It is better to leave the matter of permission and orientation of news stands, gift shops, and other accessory establishments to the "Accessory Structure and Uses" column or section of district regulations. The serving of meals is reasonably basic regardless of location by district, but if desired this too could be left to be spelled out in the accessory section of the district regulations. If all these things are in the definition, either hotels may be excluded from districts in which they might otherwise logically belong or the district regulations will have to go into considerable detail as to what accessory uses will be allowed under what circumstances in individual districts. Since the latter course will probably have to be followed anyway, there is no point in cluttering up the definition.

Hotel, residential: An establishment where lodging is provided for compensation (a) other than in dwelling units, (b) on a weekly or longer basis, and (c) for 20 or more persons. Unless otherwise specified by district regulations, residence hotels may serve meals for compensation only to occupants and their guests. [For smaller numbers of persons to be accommodated for periods of a week or longer, see *rooming house.*]

Most combinations of residential uses will work themselves out through general ordinance provisions stating that combined uses must each meet all district requirements, or through special provisions applying to the combination. One combined category, increasingly popular for retirement housing, may need special definition:

Apartment hotel: An establishment in which are offered for compensation for a total of 20 or more persons any combination of dwelling units and residence hotel accommodations. For purposes of these regulations, if any of such rental units are available for periods of less than one week, the establishment shall be considered a hotel.

Special provisions applying to combinations will be particularly important in commercial areas where dwelling units are permitted in connection with commercial establishments. Here regulations should protect both the commercial efficiency of the district and the occupants of dwellings. Ground floor frontage in commercial districts should not be allowed to be used for residential purposes, since such use both breaks the flow of commercial pedestrian traffic and exposes residents to intensive street activity. The rear of commercial lots may be acceptable for residential use in some cases, particularly by owners or employees of businesses.

More often, vertical zoning will be appropriate, with the first floor reserved for activities of a commercial nature and residential uses permitted only above the first story. For more intensive commercial districts, the height restriction can be moved up. For example, in central business districts, particularly those with good views from higher stories, multifamily residential uses might be permitted only above the fifth or sixth story, holding the lower floors for nonresidential activities.

Spot zoning: *policy for a planning commission*

The following policy report, or something along the same lines, might well be adopted by planning commissions to serve as a guide in making their own decisions, as a demonstration to the courts that their decisions are on a solid foundation, and as a notice to applicants for zoning amendments as to the official position of the commission on such matters. Carried one step further, basic elements of the policy might be included in the amendments section of the zoning ordinance. —F.H.B.

Now and in the future, the prime objective of the planning commission is to develop plans and major policy recommendations concerning the development of the city. Any activity which distracts from these objectives, or uses time which might otherwise be spent in achieving them, should be limited to the minimum consistent with effective performance of administrative functions which are a secondary obligation of the commission and its staff.

Proposals for minor zoning amendments fall within this secondary category. An inordinate number of these involve spot zoning, which has the following characteristics:

1. Individuals seek to have property rezoned for their own private purposes.

2. Usually the amount of land involved is small and limited to one or two ownerships.

3. The proposed rezoning would give privileges not generally extended to property similarly located in the area.

4. Applications usually show little or no evidence of, or interest in, consideration of the general welfare of the public, the effect on surrounding property, whether *all* uses permitted in the classification sought are appropriate in the location proposed, or conformity to a comprehensive plan or to comprehensive planning principles.

In reversing the granting of a spot zoning, a high court covered some of these same points. The action granting the zoning

> appeared to be an attempt to accommodate an individual property owner. Properly, the commission could be moved only by consideration of public welfare, appropriate use of the land, and conformation to an established comprehensive plan. . . . There was nothing to show that any of these objectives was advanced here.[1]

A competent legal analyst has said this:

> Concerning zoning amendments . . . there have been few judicial rules laid down which can be universally applied. Of these few unmistakable policy decisions, the most universal and the most forcefully expressed is the condemnation of "spot zoning." . . . The spot zoning cases do not pose too great a problem for the court because the situation which they present is not of the "conflict of interest" type. One landowner, far from being unduly oppressed by a zoning ordinance, has engineered the passage of an amendment which benefits him specifically, leaving the surrounding area subject to the same restrictions which had previously affected him. Here, of course, the equities are with the zoning authority and with surrounding property holders, who may well find that the amendment inconveniences them if it does not materially lower the value of their property. The question is therefore whether it is reasonable to allow one owner to profit at the expense of his neighbors, and it will normally need overwhelming proof of public need to sustain an affirmative answer to this question.[2]

1. *Vece v. Zoning and Planning Commission, Town of West Haven, Conn.*, 172 A.2d 619 (1961).

2. Beverley J. Pooley, *Planning and Zoning in the United States* (Ann Arbor, Mich.: University of Michigan, Legislative Research Center, 1961). See particularly the section, "Amendment of the Zoning Ordinance," and comments on spot zoning, pp. 74-75.

Whether or not spot zoning cases get to court, sound policy for the planning commission is to accept clear and unequivocal court guidance as to what is and what is not legal.

The following policy is, therefore, adopted by the planning commission. No proposed zoning amendment will receive favorable recommendation unless:

1. The proposal will place all property similarly situated in the area in the same category, or in appropriate complementary categories.

2. There is convincing demonstration that *all* uses permitted under the proposed district classification would be in the general public interest and not merely in the interest of an individual or small group.

3. There is convincing demonstration that *all* uses permitted under the proposed district classification would be appropriate in the area included in the proposed change. (When a new district designation is assigned, *any* use permitted in the district is allowable, so long as it meets district requirements, and not merely uses which applicants state they intend to make of the property involved.)

4. There is convincing demonstration that the character of the neighborhood will not be materially and adversely affected by any use permitted in the proposed change.

5. The proposed change is in accord with the comprehensive plan and sound planning principles.

This policy shall be called to the attention of persons applying for what appear to be spot zoning changes in order to alert them to the tests which will be applied, and to minimize time spent by the commission in consideration of applications which cannot meet these tests.

Historic and cultural conservation: *some zoning suggestions*

Strong public interest demands conservation of areas and buildings of substantial historic or cultural significance. Effective conservation is more than merely holding the line. It requires renovation of structures for a useful purpose and improvement of their settings.

Prompt and organized public and private action is essential if conservation is to reach full potential. In many areas, a dwindling and irreplaceable heritage nears the point of no return. Elsewhere all that remains is the yellowing pages of history, with physical evidence of the charm of the past wiped out by a too often unlovely present.

The zoning suggested here is constructive, stimulating conservation and restoration of both general areas and individual structures and premises by permitting an unusually wide range of appropriate uses. It promotes a kind of improved neighborhood character which should make the uses economically successful.

Language of the local ordinance stems from provisions of Virginia enabling legislation. In other states, if similar local powers are not granted, they should be.

Desirable provisions in enabling legislation

Code of Virginia, Title 15.1, Chapter 11, as amended through 1964, provides useful special tools:

15.1-430 (b) *Historic area* means an area containing buildings or places in which historic events occurred or having special public value because of notable architectural or other features relating to the cultural or artistic heritage of the community, of such significance as to warrant conservation and preservation.

At 15.1-446, *areas for conservation* are indicated as appropriate elements in the comprehensive plan. At 15.1-489, protection "against destruction of or encroachment upon historic areas" is stated as a zoning purpose. To control adverse environmental influences, 15.1-491 (a) permits "variations in . . . general regulations in any district . . . *to ease transition* from one district to another."

One other item is important. Virginia rules of construction make it clear that "a word importing the plural number only may extend and be applied to one person or thing." This becomes one key to protection of individual buildings or premises.

Statement of intent

In establishing any district regulations, it is well to start with a clear statement of intent. The one below is drafted with enabling legislation firmly in mind. (In this particular city, there is a fine arts committee staffed by the planning commission, which takes the place of the special historic and cultural buildings committee which would otherwise be needed.)

Section 190—HC: Historic and Cultural Conservation Districts

190.1 *Intent.* Within districts now existing or hereafter created, it is intended to permit creation of Historic and Cultural Conservation districts in general areas *or for individual structures and premises* officially designated as having historic or cultural significance. Regulations within such districts are intended to protect against destruction of or encroachment upon such areas, structures, and premises, to encourage uses which will lead to their continuance, conservation, and improvement in a manner appropriate to the preservation of the cultural and historic heritage of the city, to prevent creation of environmental influences adverse to such purposes, and to assure that new structures and uses within such districts will be in keeping with the character to be preserved and enhanced.

It is further the intent of these regulations that the Planning Commission shall seek the advice and assistance of the Fine Arts Committee and the participation of historical associations and other organizations or individuals qualified by interest, training, and experience in achieving the objectives set forth.

"For individual structures and premises," italicized above, will raise the hackles of conservative zoners and attorneys. This sounds very much like spot zoning. A strong case can be made that it is not.

Protection of individual structures and premises

Protection of individual historic buildings and premises by creation of small districts is clearly distinguishable from cases branded by the courts as spot zoning. Size alone does not determine. Opinions adverse to spot zoning usually note that the action was apparently taken to benefit an individual owner, that a primary motive was private profit, and that there was inadequate consideration of, or interest in, the general public welfare, a comprehensive plan, or sound planning principles.

The procedure described here requires application by a public body (not a private individual) for zoning of a kind involving strong public interest. The zoning is not merely in accord with a comprehensive plan. It may well be a key element in the success of the plan.

A building of substantial historical or cultural significance may stand alone, and often does. Great men were not born, nor treaties signed, in groups of conveniently contiguous structures, and distinguished architecture remaining from the past too often is a lonely island surrounded by mediocrity. Rarity argues for rather than against protection of this kind of public interest.

In a typical spot zoning case, a lot in a residential neighborhood, similar to those around it and usable for the same purposes, is singled out for special private privilege and zoned to permit the owner to erect a gas station. In contrast, the historic structure is sharply distinguished from those around it, and publicly recognized to be different. Protection is for the public welfare, not for private advantage.

Even without Virginia enabling language, there seems to be solid justification for such zoning. With it, the justification is even stronger. The state definition of "historic area" does not set minimum size. And although the words "buildings or places" are used, the rule that "a word importing the plural number only may extend and be applied to one person or thing" gives reassurance.

Anchoring the floating zone

In what follows, rules are set for establishing historic and cultural conservation districts. No district is established on the zoning map until certain preliminary action has been taken. A zoning map amendment and other related action by the legislative body is required as each district is established. The procedure stipulated for preparation of applications and reports in connection with HC zoning, and the findings required in connection with action by the local legislative body are such as to make a court upset unlikely.

190.2. Preparation of Applications and Recommendations for HC Zoning.

Applications for HC zoning shall be prepared by the Planning Commission with the advice and assistance of the Fine Arts Committee. Each application shall contain information and recommendations as indicated below concerning the areas, buildings, and premises proposed for such zoning:

190.2.1. Proposed district boundaries shall in general be drawn to include all appropriate properties reasonably near to each other within the area, to include both sides of streets, and to divide the proposed district from other districts at rear lot lines or at other points where such divisions will create minimum inter-district frictions. Internal boundaries may divide the district into subareas as appropriate for regulatory purposes.

190.2.2. Proposed boundaries for transitional areas. If the proposed HC district is visually related to surrounding areas in such a way as to require transitional regulations to control potentially adverse environmental influences, proposed boundaries for such transitional areas shall be shown. Transitional areas may be subdivided for regulatory purposes.

190.2.3. A report shall be submitted with the application, establishing and defining the historic and cultural features of the district and describing the structures and features of substantial public significance, present trends and conditions, and desirable public objectives for conservation, development, or redevelopment. Such report shall include, among other pertinent matters:

a. *An analysis of existing structures* by period of construction (if known), architectural style (if significant), condition, present use, assessed valuation, and other matters relating to planning or regulating future development, such as location on lots, location of yards and other open spaces, access to interior of the block, and off-street parking provided. In addition to general analysis, two specific and detailed classifications shall be established:

(1) *A classification of individual structures and premises of substantial public interest,* with maps, photographs, and other data indicating the public importance of preservation and particular features it is desired to preserve.

(2) *A classification of existing structures, premises, and uses likely to have an adverse effect* on the desired character of the district, including those near and visually related to the district, with maps, photographs, and other data indicating the reasons for such classification.

b. *An analysis of lands not occupied by structures,* including lands near and visually related to the district. For public lands, ownership, use, and location shall be indicated. For private lands, assessed valuation shall be added.

c. *Recommendations concerning detailed regulations* to be applied within the district and its transitional areas, to supplement or modify general regulations set forth herein, including permitted and prohibited principal and accessory uses and structures, minimum lot and yard requirements, maximum lot coverage by all buildings, maximum height of structures, off-street parking and loading requirements, control of signs and exterior illumination, control of exterior character of buildings and sites, and control of additions to or removal of existing buildings.

In the report, the Commission may indicate special regulations which would apply to subareas within the district or its transitional areas.

Such report may also include plans for public action in or adjoining the district and likely to affect its character or development.

Preservation of important historic and cultural areas is of prime concern. It is, therefore, proper that the planning commission and its related committee of specialists should be responsible for preparing applications for HC zoning and supporting reports.

The report required is a study in depth which will serve in supporting official designation of special historic and cultural status. It becomes in effect an element of the comprehensive plan for the district and its transitional areas. It contains analysis, appraisal of problems and potentials, and selection of public objectives. As one means to attainment of those objectives, it proposes detailed regulations tailored to meet special requirements of the district and transitional areas, supplementing or modifying those set forth generally in later provisions.

Regulation by subareas within the district or within its transitional areas allows refinement of usual across-the-board regulation which is needed and justified in HC areas and simplifies mechanical treatment. Regulations within subareas can thus be made more sensitive to existing situations.

For example, in one block face the front yard pattern may vary considerably from that elsewhere. If the difference is important in determining character, the commission would recommend detailed setback lines for that particular block face, leaving the rest of the district subject to general rules. Or existing development may indicate need for height or use regulations in one part of the district differing from those applying generally. The commission would then recommend suitable rules for that part of the district in its report.

So long as there is clear delineation of subareas and the regulations apply equally within them, the requirement for uniformity of application within district boundaries appears to have been met. To all intents and purposes, the subarea designated is in itself an individual district.

Structures and premises of substantial public interest should be formally identified and classified, with information organized for planning reference in the report. For planning purposes, it may be almost equally important to locate and classify structures, premises, and uses most likely to have an adverse effect on the character of the district as a guide to public and private remedial action. If location of trouble spots is known, two birds can be killed with one stone in the course of redevelopment. All other things being equal, sites should be selected for new development which replace the worst of the old.

Action by governing body

Before proceeding to detailed district regulations, proposed provisions deal with the way the planning commission's reports and recommendations receive legislative sanction in action by the governing body, and the effect of the shift from mere recommendations to ordinance language.

190.3. Action by City Council.

If City Council approves creation of an HC district, its action shall include a declaration that the district is in fact of historic and cultural significance requiring protection against destruction and encroachment, that the classifications of individual structures and premises of substantial public interest and of structures, premises, and uses likely to have an adverse effect shall be used as an administrative guide, and that all or stated recommendations of the Planning Commission supplementing or modifying general regulations set forth herein are adopted by reference, and are to be applied with the district, its transitional areas, and the subareas indicated for each (if any). If Council action involves changes from the recommendations of the Planning Commission, such changes shall be subject to review and report by the Planning Commission before final passage.

Council declaration that the district is in fact historic and cultural gives official backing to planning commission findings. Formal legislative endorsement of classifications of buildings and premises sets the stage for administrative actions to be detailed later. And formal adoption by reference of all or specified portions of the planning commission's recommended modifications conveys necessary legal standing without cluttering up the general ordinance with details of limited application.

Substantive matters

To this point, emphasis has been on procedures. Procedures without standards allow extensive airing of unsupported opinions, but give little guidance to those who regulate or those who are regulated.

On substantive details, regulations should be fitted to local circumstances, not copied blindly. Regulations for broad application in HC districts should provide as good a general fit as possible. As specific districts are set up, the general regulations can be tailored, but it is usually better to have something to start from than to start over in each case.

As a caution to overzealous regulators, historic areas often have several generations of accumulated handicaps. Regulation to promote conservation and rehabilitation should not defeat its own ends by making conservation and rehabilitation economically impossible.

Permitted uses

One way to promote remedial action is to expand the range of uses permitted. This doesn't mean throwing the door wide open, of course. It does mean a careful analysis of uses which might fit in historic areas without damage to their character, and in marginal cases the establishment of general or specific performance standards.

In the specific example being discussed here, most of the areas being considered for HC zoning contain notable old housing which should be saved. The C-1 category of the ordinance allows residential, office, and restricted commercial uses like those generally allowed in neighborhood commercial districts. There has been considerable conversion of large old single-family houses (which are often on very small lots) into multiple-family use, and a liberal sprinkling of antique shops, corner groceries, and the like. There is strong and defensive neighborhood feeling, and regulation proposed is to support, guide, and defend upgrading which has already begun. Here's the language proposed in this case.

190.4. Uses Permitted.

190.4.1. Within HC district boundaries, as for C-1 (except as provided herein with respect to signs) and in addition establishments for arts and crafts, including sales, teaching, practice, and production and repair of articles in the arts and crafts field, provided that production establishments shall be limited to those requiring special artistic skills or manual skills of a handicraft nature, and shall not include those for mass manufacture of identical or substantially identical articles or activities which because of operational characteristics would be inappropriate to the character of the district.

190.4.2. Within transitional areas, if the general district classification of such areas is residential or C-1, as for such classification (except as provided herein with respect to signs); otherwise, as for the area within HC district boundaries.

The range of uses should be sufficiently broad to encourage kinds of development likely to make preservation and improvement of HC areas economically attractive. The present character of areas likely to be proposed for HC zoning in this case makes it appropriate to include arts and crafts activities, and language along the lines indicated should exclude general manufacturing of pink plaster flamingos and the like under the head of arts and crafts.

Those transitional areas already in residential or C-1 zoning would be unaffected by transitional use regulations except as regards signs. Those in other zoning categories would have the range of permitted uses trimmed to correspond with those allowed in the HC district. Here reliance is on the provision of Virginia enabling legislation allowing "variations or exceptions to the general regulations in any district . . . to ease the transition from one district to another." Where similar language is not available, all is not lost. A completely separate district could be established in the transitional area.

Lot regulations

Here again local circumstance should guide. The example involved in these regulations has very small existing lots, many only 25 feet wide (and occupied by *detached* dwellings). Under these circumstances, the statement of intent is particularly important.

190.5. Lot Regulations in HC Districts.

190.5.1. Intent. To the extent that existing patterns of lotting contribute to the character of HC districts, it is the intent of these regulations to encourage continuation of such patterns. It is further intended to prevent future fragmentation of land ownership likely to have adverse effects on such character.

190.5.2. Changes in lot dimensions. Lots or portions of lots existing in HC districts may be combined, but no existing lot, or combination of lots, parcels, or portions thereof, in single ownership at the time of zoning to HC status, shall be reduced in width, depth, or area without the approval of the Planning Commission. The Commission may grant individual applications for such approval upon a finding that such reduction would not adversely affect the character of the district in general or of surrounding property, or may establish general rules regarding approval to apply within the district or any subarea established.

190.5.3. Minimum lot area per dwelling unit shall be as specified for C-1, provided however that one-family detached dwellings shall be permitted on lots containing 2,500 square feet and that C-1 requirements on minimum lot area and width for structures containing three or more dwelling units shall not apply, although lot area per dwelling unit shall be as for C-1.

Yard requirements

Here again, local conditions should determine. In the city for which these regulations are proposed, there are some areas in which HC zoning seems likely where front yard depth is predominantly 20 feet, others where lesser front yards, or none, have been provided. The narrow lots have led to side yards which are minimal indeed. In rear yards, accessory buildings have been built very close to lot lines. In recognition of this pattern, the regulations proposed allow continuation of small side and rear yards in connection with new construction or even the use of party walls.

A provision on maximum lot coverage is added to prevent overcrowding of lots by buildings. Without this, the relatively small yard requirements might lead to abuses, with buildings built to fill the entire area within inner yard lines. The combination of yard and land coverage regulations allows flexibility in building design and placement of courts.

190.6. Yards, Courts, and Building Spacing in HC Districts.

190.6.1. Front yards shall be a minimum of 20 feet in depth, provided however that if 25 per cent or more of the frontage in the block face contains buildings providing lesser front yards, front yard requirements for the block face shall be the average of yards 20 feet or less in depth. Through lots shall have a front yard on each street as provided herein.

190.6.2. Where the side of a lot adjoins a street, a yard at least five feet wide shall be provided.

190.6.3. Other yards, courts, and building spacing. Except where there are common or attached walls at lot lines, with no space between buildings on adjacent lots, a horizontal distance of at least three feet shall be maintained between the nearest wall of the building and the lot line. When space is left between buildings on the same lot, or between buildings and fences or walls, the minimum horizontal dimension of such space shall be three feet.

All structures shall be so located on lots as to provide safe and convenient access for servicing and fire protection and to any off-street parking areas on the lot. Vision clearance requirements at street intersections and at intersections of private driveways with streets shall be as for C-1.

190.7. Maximum Lot Coverage by all Buildings in HC Districts.

No new building shall be erected and no addition shall be made to any existing building in such a way that more than 55 per cent of the area of the lot is covered with buildings.

Height regulations

In the items immediately preceding, limitations are set within the district only. Existing regulations in transitional areas would not be affected. So far as height is concerned, it may well be appropriate to establish limits applying both to the district and to transitional areas. In the provision below, the height limit is appropriate to the local situation and does not apply to steeples, towers, and other items which are exempted elsewhere in the ordinance.

190.8. Height Regulation.

No building hereafter erected in an HC district or its transitional areas shall exceed a height of 35 feet.

Off-street parking and loading regulations

Off-street parking can be a major problem in renovation of historic districts. Often such areas are built up in a manner which doesn't allow easy location of parking space on the lot with the use, particularly where permission of more intensive use (needed to encourage redevelopment) means that several spaces must be found on a small lot, with access problems compounded by narrow side yards.

The ordinance for which this amendment is being proposed is strict about off-street parking. It must either be on the same lot with the use or on a lot *in the same ownership* within a limited distance of the use it is intended to serve.

The provisions suggested below establish guidelines for provision of off-lot parking.

190.9. Off-Street Parking and Loading Regulations.

For uses within the boundaries of HC districts, off-street parking and loading space shall be as required for C-1, provided however that the following regulations shall apply to location of such facilities.

190.9.1. Generally prohibited in required front yards. No required off-street parking or loading space shall be located in any required front yard.

190.9.2. Off-site parking, grouped or other. It is the intent of these regulations to permit off-site parking where required on-site parking is impracticable or would have adverse effects on appearance of the property or of the district. It is also intended to encourage provision of such off-site parking in grouped facilities in interior-block parking lots or courts or at other appropriate locations which will be convenient for users, reduce interference with pedestrian and vehicular traffic by minimizing curb cuts and sidewalk crossings, and make available for other purposes those areas of lots which would otherwise be required to provide driveways or parking space.

In its report to City Council, the Planning Commission may recommend specific or general locations for such off-site or grouped facilities, specific or general indications as to the portions of the district which might appropriately use such facilities to satisfy off-street parking requirements, and suggested regulations to assure that space in such facilities will not be alienated from the uses for which they are required. If such recommendations are approved by City Council, such off-site or grouped parking facilities may thereafter be permitted in the locations and manner specified.

One thing the planning commission would consider in recommending location of off-site facilities is the map showing structures and premises likely to have adverse effect on the district. If such locations can be used appropriately for parking, emphasis in the report may be helpful, particularly if backed by code enforcement or selective removal in a neighborhood conservation program. If removal is required, a reuse which is both relatively inexpensive and profitable has been suggested. Even if removal is not required, property owners may get the idea. In some cases, public action to provide needed off-street parking space may be desirable or essential.[1]

Control of signs and exterior lighting

Signs and exterior lighting are important elements in district character. About all zoning can do is to control new developments (except where amortization powers are used). Hence zoning must be supplemented by organized persuasion.

In what follows, a floor is placed under sign control by the C-1 reference, which eliminates billboards and provides other minimal limitations. Usually the planning commission will want to recommend more inclusive or restrictive regulations on signs and to add limitations on lighting, to apply both within the HC district and in transitional

1. See "Off-Street Parking," p. 216.

areas designated. As with other adaptations of the general HC provisions, upon approval by city council, these recommendations would become an effective part of the ordinance.

190.10. Signs, Exterior Illumination.

It is the intent of these regulations to control location, size, number, and character of signs intended to be seen from off the premises on which they are erected, and to control location and character of exterior lighting of signs, structures, and premises in HC districts and their transitional areas in order to protect, improve, and enhance the character of such districts.

In general, and as a minimum, the sign regulations of C-1 districts shall apply in HC districts. In its report to City Council, the Planning Commission may recommend additional general or specific sign regulations, and regulations to apply to exterior lighting, to accomplish the purposes indicated. If such regulations are approved by City Council, they shall apply within the district and its transitional areas.

Administration

Special provisions are needed within the general administrative framework to handle HC zoning. The central device here is the certificate of appropriateness, required before permits and certificates of occupancy may be issued. Extraordinary qualifications of the group set up to deal with historic structures (in this case the Fine Arts Committee) should be exploited in administration of HC zoning. The planning commission will rarely be equipped with the necessary expertise, but should exercise a coordinating function and retain primary responsibility.

Language suggested here may serve as material to be adapted to local circumstances.

190.11. Administration.

After establishment of an HC district, with regulations for the district and its transitional areas as provided in Section 190.3, administrative procedures shall be as generally provided in this chapter except as indicated below.

190.11.1. Duties of Fine Arts Committee relating to special administrative procedures in HC districts. The Fine Arts Committee shall assist the Planning Commission in administration of special provisions relating to HC districts and their transitional areas as follows;

190.11.2. Where exterior appearance of any structure is involved, the zoning administrator shall issue no permit for erection, alteration, or improvement and no certificate of occupancy unless and until a certificate of appropriateness has been issued. The Board of Zoning Appeals shall take no action in cases where certificates of appropriateness are involved until actions on such certificates are concluded. Where certificates of appropriateness are required:

a. *Applications* shall be referred by the zoning administrator to the Fine Arts Committee for review and action with regard to a certificate of appropriateness unless general certification has been established as provided in (d) below. Within 60 days of receipt of the application and all material required for review in the particular case, the Fine Arts Committee shall act. If the Committee fails to act within 60 days, or at any time when it appears to the Planning Commission, for adequate reasons stated, that the Committee will be unable to act within 60 days, the Commission shall proceed to act on the matter. Certification by the Committee shall be considered as certification by the Planning Commission unless the Commission by general rule or stipulation in the particular case requires formal Commission endorsement of such certification.

These provisions establish routing procedures, define the relationship between the commission and the committee, give the commission intervention and backup powers, and set time limits.

---

b. *Material to be submitted for review.* By general rule or by specific request in a particular case, the Fine Arts Committee may require submission of any or all of the following in connection with the application: architectural plans, site plans, landscaping plans, proposed signs with appropriate detail as to character, proposed exterior lighting arrangements, elevations of all portions of structures with important relationships to public view (with indications as to construction materials, design of doors and windows, colors, and the like), photographs or perspective drawings indicating visual relationships to adjoining structures and spaces, and such other exhibits and reports as are necessary for its determinations.

c. *Issuance of certificate of appropriateness.* After examination of the material submitted and field examination if necessary in the case, the Committee shall issue a certificate of appropriateness only if it finds that the proposal is in fact appropriate to the character, appearance, and efficient functioning of the district and meets requirements established by City Council. In conferences with applicants, the Committee may permit modification of original proposals by applicants if such modifications are formally acknowledged, clearly indicated, and recorded. Any action by applicants following issuance of a permit requiring a certificate of appropriateness shall be in accord with the application and material approved.

The Committee shall not authorize issuance of any permit if it finds that the action proposed would adversely affect the primary character of the district or the setting of structures and premises of substantial public interest. Where certification is denied, the Commission shall state its reasons for denial.

d. *General certification of appropriateness for specific classes of cases* may be issued by the Committee upon approval by the Planning Commission if it is found that particular materials, designs, architectural features or styles, or other characteristics are generally acceptable and appropriate within the district or its transitional areas, and that continued detailed consideration of individual applications involving only such matters would be superfluous. In such cases, if the zoning administrator finds on examining the application that all aspects which would otherwise require Committee review are covered by general certification, he may proceed without referral to the Committee, identifying the general certification in the record concerning the application.

As the review committee gains experience, it would be able to eliminate considerable work on its own part, and red tape for applicants, by preparing the kind of blanket certifications indicated in (d). As one example (and as a matter to be handled promptly unless the committee is to bog down in detail), it would be well to provide a manual on approved sign sizes, styles and methods of mounting, and on lighting of signs and premises.

Moving or demolition of important structures

Administrative procedures covering these matters may play a central role in preservation, first in alerting those charged with conservation that moving or demolition is contemplated, and second in allowing time for needed action. Neither of the provisions below gives regulatory agencies power to block eventual moving or demolition. This could hardly be done within the law except through voluntary purchase or in extreme cases through the exercise of eminent domain powers.

But the time allowed may be a vital factor in organizing necessary public or private action to prevent irreparable loss.

Note that on demolition, a report to the planning commission is mandatory.

190.11.3. Moving structures of substantial public interest. No permit shall be issued for moving all or any significant part of a structure designated as having substantial public interest without a certificate of appropriateness from the Fine Arts Committee. Procedures, limitations, and requirements concerning such specification shall be generally as for Section 190.11.2, provided however that the Committee shall have six months in which to act on such certification and that unless such certification is issued within six months, the moving permit shall be issued without a certificate of appropriateness.

190.11.4. Demolition of structures of substantial public interest. No permit shall be issued for demolition of all or any significant part of a structure having substantial public interest before approval of such demolition permit by the Fine Arts Committee or failing such approval, as specified below. Applications for such permits shall be referred to the Committee for review and report to the Planning Commission.

The Committee shall review the circumstances and the condition of the structure or part proposed for demolition and shall report to the Planning Commission concerning feasibility of preservation. If preservation is found physically and/or economically infeasible by the Committee and the Planning Commission concurs in the findings, issuance of the demolition permit shall proceed.

If preservation is found to be physically and economically feasible, the Committee and the Commission shall take or encourage the taking of whatever steps seem likely to lead to such preservation, either on the site on which the structure is located or another site to which it might appropriately be removed.

Within six months from date of referral of application for a demolition permit, unless the owner of the property agrees to an extension of the time period or unless means acceptable to the owner have been found to preserve the structure, the demolition permit shall be issued.

Performance standards: *evolution, administration, instrumentation, and the gambling instinct*

Ever since Dennis O'Harrow invented performance standards in Pittsburgh in 1951—well, maybe he didn't invent them, but we stayed awake long enough during his speech for the notion to penetrate—we have felt that the idea was splendid. It was the sort of thing three or four hundred assorted engineers, psychologists, medicos, and other specialists should get together and tackle over a thick budget.

At the time we were writing zoning ordinances prohibiting uses "objectionable because of emission of noise, odor, smoke, gas, particulate matter, vibration, . . . " and so on, throwing in additional wordage to cover things which might conceivably be objectionable because of emission of. Like a good deal of bad zoning, this stood up well for a time.

But in the case of *Phillips Petroleum Co. v. Marie E. Anderson et al.* in Florida and similar cases elsewhere, the courts got around to asking: "Objectionable to whom?" Fortunately, this was the wrong question, so it was easy to answer. Put the board of adjustment in the middle. As a quasi-judicial body assumed "to apply the discretion of experts to exceptional instances," as Bassett put it, the board should be able to make reasonably impartial decisions as to what is and is not "objectionable" in the sense of being injurious to public health, safety, welfare, and morals.

This article originally appeared in *Bair Facts,* published by Chandler-Davis Publishing Co., Trenton, N. J. (1960). Reprinted by permission.

This isn't a bad gambit in the absence of anything better. If the noise or whatever it is appears objectionable to the board of adjustment, the courts should give this fact a great deal more weight than if it appears objectionable only to a cantankerous neighbor. It would be well, however, to prepare a firmer foundation.

Some day a judge with a gnawing ulcer or a penetrating mind may look down from the bench and say: "Bassett or no Bassett, this court cannot see how a housewife, a retired minister, two realtors, and a merchant, operating as a board of adjustment, can make determinations of a technical nature as required in this case. The statement that the board will 'apply the discretion of experts,' however often repeated, will not create expertness in a board none of whose members have had training or experience qualifying them to judge the questions at issue.

"Nor does the ordinance which establishes the board provide either methods of making determinations or standards by which the determinations can be judged by the board, or by experts whom the board might employ, or by the courts. The word 'objectionable' is a weak and inadequate substitute for standards.

"This court therefore finds. . . . " And there you are.

When the right question is asked, "Objectionable by what standards?" it would be well to have some standards to fall back on.

Performance standards for small cities

The question, for smaller cities, is whether the benefits of such standards can be had without excessive costs for instrumentation and administration. Too much noise, particulate matter (including smoke and dust), vibration, and so on, is too much in a smaller city as well as in a major metropolis. But can the smaller city get the benefits of the standards without maintaining a stable of experts equipped with the latest measuring doodads?

We think so, and here's how.

First swipe suitable standards from a reliable source, making such corrections as common sense indicates and caution permits. Then provide for the manner in which they are to be applied and administered, thus:

Ordinance provisions and commentary

Section 10. Application of Performance Standards.

After the effective date of this ordinance:

10.1. Any use established or changed to, and any building, structure, or land developed, constructed or used for, any permitted principal use, or any use permissible as a special exception, or any accessory use, shall comply with all of the performance standards herein set forth for the district involved.

10.2. If any existing use or building or other structure is extended, enlarged, or reconstructed, the performance standards for the district involved shall apply with respect to such extended, enlarged, or reconstructed portion or portions of such use, building, or other structure.

10.3. Within periods as listed below, all presently existing uses of lands, buildings, or other structures shall comply with the performance standards herein set forth for the districts involved.

(Here there should be a table with district designations across the top and performance elements down the left side, and with times for correction of deficiencies in appropriate columns.)

Comment: The first two provisions simply set the stage for application of the standards to new or altered or extended uses and structures. Section 10.3 goes considerably beyond that.

Section 10.3 is a type of provision related in principle to amortization provisions appearing increasingly in ordinances written by people who know what they are doing. It has longer-established legal basis in laws relating to abatement of nuisances.

In effect, the table sets time limits for correction of nonconforming *characteristics* of use. As in other amortization tables, this one should be carefully tailored to fit the frictions created by the nonconformities in the districts involved, the problems of making corrections, the circumstances of the community, and the sophistication of the courts in the state.

Section 11. Administration and Enforcement of Performance Standards.

11.1. *Intent concerning determinations involved in administration and enforcement of performance standards.* Determinations necessary for administration and enforcement of performance standards set forth herein range from those which can be made with satisfactory accuracy by a reasonable person using normal senses and no mechanical equipment to those requiring great technical competence and complex equipment for precise measurement. It is the intent of this ordinance that:

11.1.1. Where determinations can be made by the administrative official or other city employees, using equipment normally available to the city or obtainable without extraordinary expense, such determinations shall be so made before notice of violation is issued.

11.1.2. Where technical complexity or extraordinary expense makes it unreasonable for the city to maintain the personnel or equipment necessary for making difficult or unusual determinations, procedures shall be available for causing corrections of apparent violations of performance standards, for protecting individuals from arbitrary, capricious, and unreasonable administration and enforcement of performance standard regulations, and for protecting the general public from unnecessary costs for administration and enforcement.

Comment: This sets the operation up so that the courts and others involved can see why you are doing what you are about to do—set standards in fields where the city could not conceivably maintain the personnel and equipment necessary to apply them with any high degree of accuracy. How this feat can be accomplished is suggested in the following provisions.

11.2. *Performance standards relating to emission of smoke, fire, and explosive hazards where flash point of flammable materials is known, humidity, heat, glare, and electromagnetic interference.* If the administrative official finds, after making determinations in the manner set forth in this ordinance [here it might be well to refer to the specific section and subsections covering standards, methods, and devices for measuring], that there is violation of performance standards relating to emission of smoke, fire, and explosive hazards where flash point of flammable materials is known, humidity, heat, glare, or electromagnetic influence, he shall take or cause to be taken lawful action to cause correction to within the limits set by such performance standards. Failure to obey lawful orders concerning such correction shall be punishable as provided in Section________, Violations and Penalties.

Comment: Section 11.2 covers items where measurement is relatively simple and instrumentation required (if any) is not expensive. Section 11.3, which follows, involves the toughies. It is Section 11.3 which provides the basis for eating your cake without having it on hand. When it comes time to eat, you buy the cake.

11.3. *Performance standards relating to measurement of particulate matter, vibration, noise, fire, and explosive hazards where flash point of flammable materials is not known, toxic or noxious matter, odorous matter, and radiation hazards.* If, in the considered judgment of the administrative official, there is probable violation of the performance standards as set forth in [here again the section and subsections reference] ________ concerning emission of particulate matter, vibration, noise, fire, and explosive hazards where flash point of flammable materials is not known, toxic or noxious matter, odorous matter, or radiation hazards the following procedures shall be followed:

11.3.1. The administrative official shall give written notice, by registered mail or other means insuring a signed receipt for such notice, to the person or persons responsible for the alleged violation. The notice shall describe the particulars of the alleged violation and the reasons why the administrative official believes there is a violation in fact, and shall require an answer or correction of the alleged violation to the satisfaction of the administrative official within a time limit set by the administrative official. The notice shall state, and it is hereby declared, that failure to reply or to correct the alleged violation to the satisfaction of the administrative official within the time limit set constitutes admission of violation of the terms of this ordinance.

The notice shall further state that upon request of those to whom it is directed, technical determinations as described in this ordinance will be made, and that if violations as alleged are found, costs of such determinations shall be charged against those responsible for the violation, in addition to such other penalties as may be appropriate, but that if it is determined that no violation exists, the cost of the determination will be paid by the city.

Comment: It is here that the gambling instinct is brought into play. Anyone who is charged with violation of the performance standards on the basis of preliminary observations and such rule of thumb measurements as the administrative official may be able to use can bet that the administrative official is wrong, and has recourse to scientific measures for settling the wager. If he loses, it costs him. If he wins, it costs the city.

It is reasonable to assume that a good many apparent violations will be corrected without recourse to expensive measurements, so the city gets the benefits of performance standards without excessive continuing costs.

Needless to say, the administrative official should familiarize himself with performances meeting or failing to meet established standards, so that his subjective judgment will be improved. There have been conferences and short courses on many of the items involved in the past, and there will be more in the future. As the need arises, the instruction will increase.

11.3.2. If there is no reply within the time limit set, but the alleged violation is corrected to the satisfaction of the administrative official, he shall note "violation corrected" on his copy of the notice, and shall retain it among his official records, taking such other action as may be warranted.

11.3.3. If there is no reply within the time limit set (thus establishing admission of violation as provided in 11.3.1) and the alleged violation is not corrected to the satisfaction of the administrative official within the time limit set he shall proceed to take or cause to be taken such action as is warranted by continuation of a violation after notice to cease.

11.3.4. If a reply is received within the time limit set indicating that the alleged violation will be corrected to the satisfaction of the administrative official, but requesting additional time, the administrative official may grant an extension if he deems it warranted in the circumstances of the case and if the extension will not, in his opinion, cause imminent peril to life, health, or property.

11.3.5. If reply is received within the time limit set requesting technical determination as provided in this ordinance, and if the alleged violations continue, the administrative official may call in properly qualified experts to make the determinations. If expert findings indicate violation of the performance standards, the costs of the determinations shall be assessed against the properties or persons responsible for the violation, in addition to such other penalties as may be appropriate under the terms of Section________, Violations and Penalties.

If no violation is found, the costs of the determinations shall be paid by the city without assessment against the properties or persons involved.

That makes a start at least. The technique is being used in a number of ordinances. We think it will work and we think it is legal. To the best of our knowledge, it has only been challenged once, in a city with a population of 6,000. The city won.

Zoning for industrial waterfronts

Port activities are vital to the economies of many of our cities. Land needed for continuation and needed expansion of port facilities should be preserved for performance of port-related functions only. Without such protection, uses which might equally well locate elsewhere may intrude in a way which impedes efficient operation and blocks or complicates future development.

In the city which is in the process of adopting the regulations described below, most of the area involved was zoned for general industry, with some in residential or commercial categories. Residential development is, of course, out of place in a heavy industrial environment, and may create objections to essential operations. Some commercial operations are desirable adjuncts to performance of the principal function. Others need not be located in the port complex, and would do equally well elsewhere. The same thing is true of industry—some kinds belong, and some do not. So specialized waterfront industrial district regulations are desirable to sort things out.

The regulations appearing here were drafted in rough form and polished after discussion with representatives of the railroads, the port authority, and other groups with a primary interest in promotion of efficient performance of port functions. As presented, local procedural and substantive language has been altered to facilitate more general applications, and section numbers have been provided for cases where a schedule of district regulation is not used.

To start things off, intent provisions give guidance which should be helpful in making administrative determinations, and in court tests.

Section 000. WF-1: Waterfront Industrial District.

These regulations are intended to set apart and protect areas considered vital to the performance of port functions, and to provide for their efficient operation, continuation, and expansion. To these ends, it is intended to permit in such districts the full range of facilities necessary for successful and efficient performance of their functions. In order to reserve such areas for port-related activities only, it is intended to exclude both uses which could equally well be located elsewhere and uses inappropriate in districts of this character.

Following through on this statement of intent, permitted principal uses and structures are subdivided into two groups, those generally permitted as obviously belonging, and those permitted only if port-related.

Section 000.1. Permitted principal uses and structures.

000.1.1. *Generally permitted.*

(a) Piers, wharfs, and docks.

(b) Terminals for freight or passengers arriving or departing by ship.

(c) Facilities for construction, maintenance, and repair of vessels.

(d) Ship supply establishments and facilities.

(e) Railroads, including stations, yards, and related facilities.

(f) Wholesale and retail establishments dealing primarily in bulk materials delivered by ship, or by ship and railroad in combination.

(g) Military installations other than residential.

(h) Fire stations, police stations, and other similar public or private establishments, provided that no such installations likely to have adverse effects on, or to be adversely affected by, normal operations within the district shall be located within the district.

000.1.2. *Permitted only if port-related.*

The following uses shall be permitted only if directly and principally related to port function and facilities. If the administrative official finds that there is reasonable doubt about such relationship, he shall refer the matter to the Planning Department for technical determination and the Planning Department shall consult with the Port Authority or such other agencies and individuals as seem appropriate concerning the matter. Where technical determinations have been requested, the administrative official shall issue no permit except upon favorable findings by the Planning Department.

(a) Warehousing and storage, including open storage and bulk storage of flammable materials.
(b) Manufacturing and processing, providing that any such operation requiring a special exception in an M-3 district shall require a special exception in the WF-I district, and that all performance standards of the M-3 district shall apply.
(c) Distribution centers; packaging and crating operations.
(d) Truck terminals.
(e) Offices.
(f) Heliports; air strips not exceeding 2,000 feet in length.
(g) Utilities installations; radio or television transmission and relay stations.

The second group of uses above involves an unusual feature justified by the purpose of the regulations. Inclusion or exclusion is not determined by use alone, but also by whether the use *requires* a port-oriented location.

Where there is doubt, the zoning administrator asks for a technical determination from the planning department. In some jurisdictions, it may be argued that what is involved here is either a special exception or an interpretation, and should be processed by the board of adjustment. We believe that there are adequate reasons for proceeding on a different basis. Under the language of the Standard Enabling Act, which appears in basic form in most state enabling legislation, the board of adjustment is given three powers. These are often described in general terms as interpretation, special exception, and variance.

Language of the act underlying the function broadly described as *interpretation* reads: "To hear and decide appeals where it is alleged there is error in any order, requirement, decision, or determination made by an administrative official in the enforcement of this act. . . ." The purpose of the technical determinations is to assure that the chances for error are reduced. If an applicant or objector wishes to appeal on grounds of error *after* the permit has been issued or refused, he may still do so, but the planning department action in connection with such technical determinations is not the kind of interpretation described in the enabling legislation.

Similarly, there is a defensible distinction between a technical determination as to whether an activity is or is not port-related and a special exception. The board of adjustment is empowered "to hear and decide special exceptions to the terms of the ordinance upon which such board is required to pass under such ordinance." Under ordinance language as proposed, the board is *not* required to pass on the question of port relationship.

Section 000.2. Permitted accessory uses and structures.

Uses and structures which are customarily accessory and clearly incidental and subordinate to permitted principal uses and structures, provided however that no residential facilities shall be permitted in this district except for watchmen or caretakers whose work requires residence on the premises or for employees who will be temporarily quartered on the premises.

The proviso here is important. Good industrial district regulations will usually exclude residential uses except for watchmen or caretakers. It is poor policy to permit general residential use in industrial districts, and even to allow "housing for employees," which is broad enough language to open the door to "company town" housing. But railroads are often required by union agreements to provide quarters and meals at away-from-home points where train crews will be stopping, and similar arrangements are sometimes made by marine companies, particularly where short-run ferry trips are involved. Such temporary quarters may appropriately be located in waterfront industrial complexes for the convenience of the personnel involved.

Section 000.3. Uses and structures permissible only as special exceptions.

After public notice and hearing, and subject to appropriate special conditions and safeguards as well as the general requirements on special exceptions and the detailed requirements for specific exceptions set forth in Section XXX, the Board of Adjustment may permit the following as special exceptions, but only if port-related. If the Board finds that there is reasonable doubt about such relationship, it shall refer the matter to the Planning Department for technical determination and the Planning Department shall proceed as indicated in Section 000.1.2. In such cases, the Board shall issue no special exception except upon a finding by the Planning Department that the proposed structure or use is port-related.

(a) Manufacturing or processing requiring a special exception in an M-3 Heavy Industrial District.

(b) Off-lot parking where allowable for satisfaction of off-street parking requirements.

(c) Commercial or other parking lots and parking garages, including those for long-term storage of automobiles.
(d) Hiring halls and other places of assembly for registration or assignment of employment.

Material here is reasonably self-explanatory, but a note might be made about facilities for long-term storage of automobiles. Around marine installations, and particularly around shipping points of the Navy, there is often need for long-term parking of cars of servicemen or crew members for extended periods while away from the port. In allowing such use, it would be well to establish renewable time limitations, so that this function does not preempt land which will be needed for expansion of more basic port activities.

Section 000.4. Transitional uses, structures, and regulations.

Where this district adjoins any residential district, and for a distance of 150 feet into the WF-I district from the common boundary, no *use* shall be permitted which fails to meet the performance standards requirements of the M-1 Light Industrial District.

Within the WF-I district, and adjoining the residential district boundary, yards 25 feet in depth shall be provided wherever the boundary follows lot lines. There shall be no parking or open storage within such yards, and if there is parking or open storage within the remainder of the 150-foot transitional area, it shall be shielded from view from first-story windows, existing or potential, in the residential district, using buffering or screening as provided in Section YYY, Fences, Walls, Buffering, and Screening. This requirement shall not apply if topography is such that a fence or wall 10 feet high would not provide such screening.

Height limit within the transitional area shall begin at 25 feet at the district boundary, or at the inner line of the 25-foot yard if one is required, and shall rise on a 45 degree angle inward over the remainder of the transitional area.

Signs other than those permitted in the residential district shall not be erected within any required 25-foot yard adjacent to a residential district, and no advertising sign shall be erected in the 150-foot transitional area in such a way as to be legible from within the adjoining residential district.

Lighting within the transitional area shall be so located, shielded, or screened that no direct source of illumination shall be visible from any residential window, existing or potential, within the residential district. Reflected light shall be so controlled and directed that it is not objectionable within the residential district.

Transitional regulations proposed here should do much to prevent friction between the WF-I district and adjoining residential areas. Performance standards to which reference is made should ease the transition by encouraging location of least obnoxious operations in the portion of the district adjacent to residential areas. Tract size in most industrial districts of this kind will usually be ample to permit provision of the 25-foot yard without practical difficulty. As stated, the regulation does not require yards if the district boundary is the center line of a railroad, street, body of water, or similar location which in itself provides a spatial barrier.

Screening of open storage or parking areas (and prohibition of open storage and parking in any required yard) should reduce visual impact. An escape clause covers situations where the residential area is uphill from the industrial section and screening of impractical height would be required to block undesirable view.

Height limits as stated are particularly important where there is no general height limit within the WF-I district (as is the case in the present example). The 25-foot limit at the boundary (or the inner line of the required yard) and the 45 degree plane over the transitional area should give reasonable protection.

Signs in required transitional yards are properly limited to the same kinds as permitted in adjoining residential districts, and in the entire transitional strip it seems reasonable to exclude advertising signs oriented toward the residential district. Some adjustment of language will be necessary in ordinances where "advertising signs" are not defined. A simple definition would be "signs promoting the sale or use of a product or service." The limitation should be made to apply to on-site or off-site signs.

It is also important to control lighting in the strip adjacent to the residential district. In the language proposed, the limitation applies to the entire 150-foot strip, and not merely to the required yard, and to both direct and indirect lighting which might be unwelcome in residential areas. One shortcoming of the language cited is the use of the word "objectionable" instead of reference to a standard. Although "objectionable" is used in many ordinances, it is a term so vague as to be subject to very broad interpretation indeed, and could (and has) led to trouble in court. It would be far better to handle this matter by making some measurements of reflected light with a moderately sensitive light meter and deciding on the basis of readings where the "objectionable" horizon begins.

Strip commercial zoning

Strip commercial zoning is now largely a device for containing and limiting the blighting effects of development along a single street frontage. Of doubtful merit at the start, it is now an obsolescent zoning device. Used carelessly, it multiplies rather than reduces commercial and industrial blight, lowers rather than raises property values in its general area, increases traffic congestion by marginal friction, and adds to governmental costs.

As used here, "strip commercial" describes only development along the frontages of a single street, and does not include areas of concentrated business development such as shopping centers and central business districts. In contrast to concentrated commercial areas, strip commercial developments require that a person seeking a reasonable range of goods and services must travel a maximum distance from the point of first to last purchase. In a shopping center or the CBD, all visits are usually within walking distance from a parking space. In strip commercial, except for convenience purchases from a single type of establishment, far more automotive or pedestrian travel is required.

Historic forms

Historically, strip commercial development has taken three principal forms, two originating before the automobile and one since.

Outward from prime commercial centers. At the crossroads where towns started, businesses related to current needs occupied the "hot spots" and formed solid patterns around the "busy corner." The most important and successful enterprises held the prime locations, and as needs changed there was private redevelopment in city centers, with strong competition for prime locations. Secondary businesses and those which were less successful strung out along close-in streets, depending on walk-in trade generated by the combined pulling power of the commercial center, and competing for locations close to it. The marginal businesses generally were forced to occupy locations farthest from the prime corner. Vacancies, turnover rate, and physical deterioration was and is typically highest at the outer edges of CBD-centered commercial strips.

Areas of intensive residential development. Another form of strip commercial development evolved in areas where there was high residential density, often along streetcar lines. Here, small convenience establishments catered successfully to walk-in trade from the neighborhood. Daily shopping was of greater importance in those times because of the limitations of the ice box and greater dependence on unprocessed and unpreserved fruits, meats, and vegetables.

With walk-in trade, the best locations were near streetcar stops, and the corner grocery was a prime commercial contributor to neighborhood convenience. Other establishments usually settled for less desirable locations, around the corner or toward the center of the main block frontage.

In both the forms discussed above, development was typically on shallow lots, and entrances were made directly from the sidewalk.

Strip commercial for the automobile. A third form of strip commercial, now also obsolescent, evolved in response to the automobile. Originally, shopping by automobile along major streets required curb parking, and its inadequacy or complete removal created major handicaps, particularly where lot sizes or building locations made it difficult to provide convenient off-street parking.

Later, with a push from zoning, off-street parking was recognized as a necessity; and commercial development took place in greater depth or on larger lots to provide it. This tended to spread business out more than did earlier forms, limiting its attractiveness to walk-in trade and making it necessary for shoppers to drive from one store to another.

Strip commercial zoning for the automobile has been tremendously expensive to the public. Traffic moving into or out of the parking area congests one and often two lanes of the traffic artery, and may cause even more hazard and conflict where left turns are being made from the parking lot. As a result, highways designed for rapid movement of traffic have speed limits gradually reduced, congestion mounts, and it becomes necessary to widen the street (cutting down on available off-street parking area) or to build a by-pass. If the by-pass runs through previously residential neighborhoods, desirability of residence drops and the pressure mounts for still more strip commercial zoning. If it is granted, the pattern of deterioration of property and traffic flow repeats itself, leading to demands for street widening again, or for a new by-pass. In some cities, it is possible to trace to unwise strip commercial zoning through two or even three by-pass cycles.

A major factor in the move toward limited-access highways in many cities is undoubtedly the failure to control strip commercial development on arterial streets. Limited-access highways may solve the problem of moving through traffic (at great cost) but limited-access highways don't help eliminate remaining difficulties. The strip commercial areas continue to exist, and worse, to expand by creating blight in adjoining residential neighborhoods. In more dramatic actions, when two such areas creep to within a few blocks of each other, pressure goes on for closing the gap—by filling it in with more strip commercial zoning. If the gap is occupied by residences, the residential neighborhood deteriorates first into a residential slum and then, in many instances, into a commercial slum.

New commercial forms

Neighborhood, community, and regional shopping centers are a relatively recent response to the need for facilities efficiently designed for the automotive age. Their development has been amazingly rapid. Indeed, there is some concern among experts that the supply may be outrunning the demand. The emergence of this efficient and convenient form has had and will continue to have disastrous competitive effects on areas where retailing facilities were not designed with the automobile in mind, or where it was assumed that multiple-stop shopping would continue and expand indefinitely.

Central business districts are making massive efforts to recover their lost markets and find a new balance in functions to perform. In the meantime, as their prime locations become less and less prime, their strip commercial appendages become poorer and poorer as locations for businesses.

In areas of intensive residential development left over from streetcar days, a few convenience establishments continue to do well, or at least to survive, but the pattern of living has changed in such a way as to reduce the number of establishments needed and the area required for such use. The mechanical refrigerator, a vast new array of processed foods, the automobile, and the supermarket have all cut down on need for commercial frontage in such neighborhoods.

In strip commercial areas designed as a first response to the automobile, there is extensive distress. A large part of the commercial and service activity, which it was believed would fill the extensive frontage over-optimistically zoned for such purposes, now is going to shopping centers. There is a limit to the number of filling stations, eating and drinking establishments, automobile sales lots, motels, furniture stores, medical clinics, and other enterprises which can survive and prosper outside the mutually supporting complex of the shopping center. Since the strip commercial area is undesirable as a prime location for most businesses, it is increasingly occupied by marginal enterprises with a high mortality rate. New marginal entrepreneurs usually have insufficient resources to tear down and rebuild, so they either occupy run-down residential or commercial buildings with a minimum of renovation and upkeep, or build within limited budgets on vacant land. The strip commercial district (or a large part of it) becomes a sort of skid row for decrepit commercial and service establishments.

Under present circumstances, with planned shopping centers, planned office centers, medical centers, and other groupings convenient for motorists, the outlook for most of the strip commercial area—if left strip commercial—is for more rapid deterioration than in the past. Where land ownership, existing structural development, and appropriate land-use patterns to the rear will allow it, some of the frontage may be absorbed for new shopping centers, office centers, or multifamily housing on substantial tracts. In many cases, however, it will often be found advantageous in terms of money and time to seek vacant parcels rather than to become involved in complicated assembly of small frontage properties in diverse ownership along major streets, purchase of property to the rear to gain needed depth, and demolition of existing structures.

Certainly there is little prospect that a substantial part of the frontage now zoned strip commercial can ever be used for constructive purposes without extensive and expansive public renewal action. Enlarging the problem will not solve it.

Remedial action

Short of wholesale renewal, there are some remedial measures which may prove helpful. Where strip commercial zoning can be rolled back, it should be, with zoning more nearly in accord with public needs substituted. Where it cannot be rolled back, the line should be held firmly. The fact that there is no easy general solution to a grave problem does not mean that it should be allowed to become worse. To make it easier to hold the line, and to minimize the kind of hardships which lead to pressures for relaxing it, transitional regulation at common boundaries of residential and commercial districts seems indicated.

Transitional zoning can take several forms. Since major impact is between lots with the same frontage immediately adjacent to residential-commercial boundaries and not separated by a street, there is greatest need for transitional regulations here. Other transitional remedies can be applied where the joining boundary is along property lines in side- and rear-yard areas.

Yards. A common problem is the substantial difference in front-yard regulations in adjoining residential and commercial districts allowing commercial buildings near the boundary to jut out past the building line set for the residential district. Even when the commercial structure is set back voluntarily, massed parking next to the residential front yard may have undesirable effects.

Here, a solution may be to require the first commercial lot, or the first 50 or 100 feet within the commercial district (with the figures set to relate to the general lotting pattern) to provide a front yard of the full depth or perhaps half the depth of yards required in the residential district. Regulations can provide that a given amount of such front yard nearest the district boundary shall be landscaped and not used for drives or parking, and might even call for a low fence or hedge at the common boundary. (Such a barrier should be low to protect traffic visibility.)

Where commercial and residential lots adjoin at side- or rear-yard areas, the commercial lots may be required to provide side and rear yards greater than generally called for in the commercial district, in order to give increased spatial separation of commercial buildings from common district boundaries. For added protection, walls or vegetative screening of a substantial minimum height (five or six feet) may be required on such common boundaries where commercial uses are established. This gives a physical barrier against undesirable views from within the residential district, shields against automobile headlights, and helps reduce noise.

Lighting. Although walls and hedges help to eliminate some of the light from commercial districts, there is still a problem with high lights often used to illuminate commercial premises. On this point, transitional regulations can require that such lighting shall be so shielded and directed as to protect residential property from direct or reflected glare.

Signs. The effect of signs is such that transitional regulations should probably be extended to cover a considerable distance into the commercial district. Here a workable requirement might be that no sign erected on the same side of the street within 150 to 200 feet (or some appropriate distance) should be so placed or oriented as to be legible from within the residential district.

Measures outlined above would help reduce some of the blighting effects of commercial development on adjacent residential property, and would thus relieve some of the pressure for extending strip commercial boundaries because adjoining residential property has become blighted (leading to further blight and further creep). Another promising field for transitional regulation involves uses.

Uses. Where lots have common frontage, transitional regulations of uses can work both ways from the boundary, cutting down on the commercial range permitted within a specified distance of the district line and increasing the residential range. Thus, if the commercial district generally permits filling stations, drive-in eating and drinking establishments or other uses particularly obnoxious to occupants of the residential district, these uses would be barred in the transitional zone.

On the residential side of the line, again for a specified distance, uses in the transitional area would be increased, with the character of added uses depending on the general nature of the residential district.

Either where there is common frontage involved or where the residential property lies to the rear, off-street parking in connection with commercial uses is sometimes acceptable as a transitional use. In such cases, there must of course be proper control of yards, landscaping, lights, access, hours of operation, walls or vegetative screening, and other details.

Board of adjustment rules of procedure

The law requires boards of adjustment to adopt rules of procedures. If more boards took pains in drafting such rules—and followed the rules after they were adopted—zoning would be in much better shape.

Here is a suggested draft of rules of procedure, with notes as to why certain things were done. Check them against the rules of your own board of adjustment.

Article I—General Governing Rules

The Board of Adjustment (hereinafter referred to as the Board) shall be governed by the provisions of Chapter _____, [State] Statutes, the zoning ordinance of the city, and the rules of procedures set forth herein,[1] as adopted by the Board and approved by the City Commission. No rule herein shall be changed or waived without the affirmative vote of four members of the Board and the concurrence of the City Commission.[2]

This article originally appeared in *Bair Facts,* published by Chandler-Davis Publishing Co., Trenton, N. J. (1960). Reprinted by permission.

1. State law determines what is legal so far as the zoning ordinance is concerned; the zoning ordinance and state law determine what is legal so far as the rules of procedure are concerned. The Board may not legally adopt rules or take actions outside the scope of authority granted in the zoning ordinance, and the authority granted in the zoning ordinance must be in accordance with state law.

2. Requirement for approval by City Commission and for concurrence of City Commission in change or waiver is good "public relations" with the City Commisson, gives elected officials an appropriate opportunity to set policies, and gives the Board a chance to familiarize the City Commission with its operating rules. On changes and waivers, the requirement for action by the City Commission is a useful hedge against hasty actions under pressure.

Article II—Officers, Committees

1. The Board shall elect a chairman and vice-chairman (who shall be acting chairman in the absence of the chairman) annually in the month of ________.[3] The chairman may not succeed himself.[4]

2. The chairman (or in his absence the vice-chairman) shall preside at all meetings and hearings of the Board and decide all points of order and procedure. The chairman shall appoint any committees which may be found necessary, including a committee for preliminary review of appeals.[5]

3. A secretary (who need not be a member of the Board) shall be designated by the Board.[6] The secretary shall conduct all correspondence of the Board; keep a minute book recording attendance, the vote of each member upon each question, or if absent or failing to vote, indicating such fact; and records of examinations and hearings and other official actions; and shall carry such other official duties as may be assigned by the Board.

Article III—Meetings

1. THE REGULAR MEETING of the Board shall be held the ______________[third Tuesday or whatever date is desirable] of the month at 7:30 p.m., unless there is no cause for holding such meeting. If there is to be a regular meeting, the secretary shall inform the members of the Board at least 24 hours in advance.[7]

2. SPECIAL MEETINGS may be called by the chairman provided that at least 24 hours notice of such meeting is given each member.

3. A QUORUM shall consist of three members for the transaction

3. The date will usually be fixed according to the date on which the Board was originally established.

4. This provision is not essential, but helps to prevent monopoly of the office. It can be varied to permit the chairman to succeed himself only once, or as may seem desirable, or it can be eliminated entirely.

5. The committee for preliminary review of appeals is a "new" idea which was taken from procedures on subdivision regulation. See Article V, Sections 3, 4, and 5 for functions of the committee, and appropriate footnotes on Article V for reasons for establishing it.

6. Since there may be considerable work involved in the duties of the secretary, and since qualifications for a good secretary may be considerably different from qualifications for a Board member, it is desirable to permit the use of a regular city employee (on a part-time or full-time basis) as secretary of the Board.

7. This form assumes that it will usually not be necessary to hold regular meetings. If it is assumed that regular meetings will usually be held, the form should be reversed—"if there is not to be a regular meeting," etc.

of all business except reversal of decisions of the administrative official[8] and decisions to allow variance and special exceptions, which shall require a quorum of four.[9]

4. REPRESENTATION, PERSONAL INTEREST. Neither the secretary nor any member of the Board shall appear for or represent any person in any matter pending before the Board. No member of the Board shall hear or vote upon an appeal in which he is directly or indirectly interested in a personal or financial way.[10]

5. CONDUCT OF MEETINGS. All meetings shall be open to the public. The chairman, or in his absence the vice-chairman, may administer oaths or compel the attendance of witnesses. The order of business at meetings shall be as follows: (a) roll call; (b) reading of minutes of previous meetings; (c) reports of committees; (d) unfinished business; (e) hearing of cases; (f) new business.

6). ADJOURNED MEETINGS. The Board may adjourn a regular meeting if all business cannot be disposed of on the day set, and no further public notice shall be necessary for such a meeting if the time and place of its resumption is stated at the time of adjournment and is not changed after adjournment.

Article IV—Vacancies

Failure to attend three consecutive meetings, or three of any seven consecutive meetings, shall be considered automatic resignation from the Board, and upon such resignation, resignation by other means, or other vacancies occurring in office, the chairman shall inform the City Commission as promptly as possible, so that the City Commission may appoint a replacement to fill out the unexpired term.[11]

Article V—Appeals and Applications: Notice of Hearings; Amendments of Appeals

1. Appeals to the Board may be taken by any person affected by any zoning decision of the administrative official within 30 days after the

8. If the administrative official is called the building inspector or some other title in the ordinance, the title in the ordinance should be used here and elsewhere.
9. You can raise the quorum to four for any meeting, but don't lower the quorum below four for the items indicated—usual state law requires four.
10. This provision should not be necessary. It is necessary.
11. The first part of this article provides an essential method for getting rid of dead wood. Given members who won't attend meetings and won't resign, the Board can be paralyzed unless there is an automatic resignation provision. The second part is a usual provision of enabling legislation.

decision involved.[12] The appeal shall be filed in triplicate with the administrative official on a form provided by the Board of Adjustment, and all pertinent information required thereon shall be furnished before the appeal is considered filed.[13]

2. Upon receipt of the completed form, and payment of an appeal fee of $25,[14] the administrative official shall forthwith transmit the original and both copies of the appeal form to the secretary of the Board, together with all papers constituting the record upon which the action appealed from was taken.

3. The secretary shall as promptly as possible inform the committee for preliminary review concerning the appeal, and the committee may either discuss the matter with the applicant if the applicant desires or proceed directly to order public notice and hearing.[15] If the appeal is withdrawn before public notice is given, $15 of the appeal fee shall be returned to the applicant.

If the applicant elects to withdraw the appeal at this or any other stage before final determination by the Board, this fact shall be noted on the original and both copies of the application, with the signature of the applicant attesting withdrawal. The original shall be retained by the secretary for the files of the Board, one copy shall be returned to the administrative official and one copy shall be returned to the applicant.

4. If the appeal is not withdrawn, the committee for preliminary

12. Statutory language usually states: "Such appeal shall be taken within a reasonable time, as provided by the rules of the Board, by filing with the officer from whom the appeal is taken and with the Board of Adjustment a notice of appeal specifying the grounds thereof." "Reasonable time" as selected here is 30 days. This figure might be raised somewhat. It should probably not be lowered. The requirement in these rules that the appeal should be filed with the administrative official is an indication that the Board considers this to be filing with the Board also.

13. If the Board can't make up its mind as to what it wants in the way of supporting information (so that it can prepare a form) it should study its functions until it can prepare a form. The appellant should not have to hire a lawyer to determine how an application should be prepared. The requirement that all pertinent information be provided before the appeal is considered filed protects the Board from attempts to "stake out a claim" by submitting incomplete appeals and dragging things out indefinitely.

14. This amount should vary according to local circumstances. It should be sufficient to offset costs of administration and public notice.

15. The committee for preliminary review can serve a very useful function, discussing the case informally with the applicant, helping him to get his information properly organized, explaining points which he may not understand, and exploring the case in more detail than might be possible at the public hearing. This prehearing conference will save a great deal of time at the public hearing, and may convince the applicant that he has no case—which also saves him money, since part of his fee is refunded if he withdraws his application.

review may request the applicant to provide such additional information, not furnished on the form, as may be needed to determine the particular case[16] (which information shall be provided by the applicant before decision is made by the Board) and shall instruct the secretary to proceed with public notice of a hearing on the case.

5. The public notice shall be published not less than five calendar days prior to the hearing in a newspaper of local circulation, and in addition notice shall be posted on the premises affected and shall be transmitted to the appellant and such other parties in interest as the committee for preliminary review shall determine.[17] The notice shall state the name of the appellant, the location of the property, the action requested, and the time and place of the hearing.

6. Amendment of an appeal by the applicant may be permitted at any time prior to or during the public hearing, provided that no such amendment shall be such as to make the case different from its description in the notice of public hearing. If amendment is requested by the applicant after public notice of the hearing has been given, and such amendment is at variance with the information set forth in the public notice, the applicant shall pay an additional fee of $10 to cover amended public notice. If the amended notice can be published five calendar days prior to the hearing originally scheduled, the hearing on the amended appeal may be held on that date, otherwise the chairman shall announce that the hearing originally scheduled on the case will be deferred to a future meeting, before which appropriate public notice will be given, and will state the reasons for the deferral.

Article VI—Hearing; Rehearing

1. An appeal shall be heard within 40 days from time of filing of the completed application with the administrative official unless the appeal is withdrawn. If amended, the amended appeal shall be heard within 40 days from filing of completed amendment.[18] Appeals will be heard in order of receipt of applications; amended appeals will have priority according to date of amendment.

2. At the public hearing, the applicant or any other party may appear on his own behalf or be represented by agent or by attorney.

16. During the preliminary review, it may become apparent that additional information is needed to guide the Board in an intelligent determination of the case.

17. This is another advantage of having a committee for preliminary review—"parties in interest" in a particular case can be determined with respect to the specific case.

18. The number of days should be tailored to local circumstances—40 days would include time for public notice and one or in some cases two regular meetings of the Board.

3. Order of the hearing shall be:
   a. Statement of case by chairman.
   b. Supporting argument by applicant or his agent or attorney.
   c. Supporting arguments by others at the hearing.
   d. Opposing arguments by persons at the hearing.
   e. Rebuttal by those supporting appeal (other than applicant).
   f. Rebuttal by those opposed to appeal.
   g. Final rebuttal by applicant.

Witnesses may be called and factual evidence and exhibits submitted.

The chairman may establish appropriate time limits for arguments, but such time limits shall be equal for both sides. The chairman may request representatives of each side to speak for the entire group or portions of the group, but shall not require such representation against the wishes of the group involved.

4. Application for rehearing may be made in the same manner as the original appeal. Application for rehearing may be denied by the Board if from the record it shall appear that there has been no substantial change in facts, evidence, or conditions. However, any matter not previously reviewed may be heard again on motion adopted by unanimous vote of all members at a meeting at which a quorum is present.[19]

Article VII—Decisions

Final decision on an appeal shall be made within 35 calendar days[20] of the last public hearing at which it was considered, and shall be in the form of a resolution. Any resolution reversing any other order, requirement, decision, or determination of the administrative official or deciding in favor of the applicant on any special exception or variance, shall require the concurring vote of four members of the Board.[21] Failure to pass such resolution shall constitute automatic denial of the appeal.

The resolution shall show the reasons for the determination made,

19. There should be relatively few rehearings if the Board conducts its affairs properly. Some applicants may make nuisances of themselves by requesting repeated rehearings unless there is a provision by which the Board may deny rehearings. The final sentence in this section is intended to cover situations in which the Board awakens belatedly to the fact that it may have committed a blunder, and wants to reconsider its action. There is considerable dynamite in this provision, and it should be used sparingly—hence the requirement for unanimous vote.

20. This time limit should cover the next regular meeting.

21. "Concurring vote of four members of the Board" requirement comes from usual statutory provisions and should not be changed except in conformity with the statutes.

and if in favor of the applicant shall set forth any conditions or safeguards required, or any time limitations prescribed.

Notation concerning the decision shall be made on the original and both copies of the application. The original of the application, together with a copy of the resolution, shall remain in the files of the Board. One copy of the application, together with a copy of the resolution, shall be returned to the administrative official. The remaining copy of the application, together with a copy of the resolution, shall be returned to the applicant.

These rules of procedure were adopted by the Board of Adjustment ______[date]______.

/s/ ____________________
Chairman

Approved by City Commission ______[date]______
Mayor [or other official]
____

Boards of adjustment: *prohibition of use variances*

Most state enabling legislation contains language like this:

> The *board of adjustment* shall have the following powers: . . . (3) To authorize upon appeal in specific cases such variance from the terms of any ordinance as will not be contrary to the public interest when owing to special conditions a literal enforcement of the provisions of such ordinance will result in unnecessary hardship and so that the spirit of such ordinance shall be observed and substantial justice done.

In another section, there will usually be this provision: "The board of adjustment shall adopt rules in accordance with the provisions of any ordinance adopted pursuant to this article."

And at the beginning of the legislation, there customarily appears language to the effect that the *legislative body* may pass zoning ordinances, setting forth the purposes of such action, and specifying that the legislative body "shall provide for the manner in which such regulations . . . shall be determined . . . and from time to time amended." Amendment is to be by the legislative body only. There is no indication that it may delegate power to amend the ordinance, and certainly it is not within the customary framework of municipal government to permit an appointed board to legislate.

There are clear limitations on the powers of the legislative body. It must establish districts having some real relation to zoning purposes and regulations "shall be uniform for each class or kind of building throughout each district." Courts have held repeatedly that "spot" zoning—the zoning of land (usually in small pieces) for the convenience of the owner and without reference to the general plan or pattern of development—is illegal.

Comes now an individual, and on grounds of alleged hardship requests the board of adjustment to issue a variance to permit, on his property alone, a *use* which is not allowable in the district in which it is located. There can be no question that the board has the power to relax strict application of the terms of the ordinance to the extent necessary to allow a property owner to use his property for one of the uses *permitted* by the ordinance in the district. But does it have the power to permit a use *prohibited* by ordinance in the district? In effect, this is clearly amending the ordinance. In most instances, the "amendment" is in a form which would be "spot zoning" (and therefore illegal) if the legislative body did it.

We feel strongly that the answer is "NO." We have never seen a case where it appeared that issuance of a true use variance was justified. If there are such cases, they must be extremely rare. On the other hand, there are thousands of cases where in the guise of variances, boards of adjustment have "amended" the zoning ordinance. To protect the public from this kind of tinkering, it is highly desirable to state in unmistakable terms in the ordinance that the board of adjustment shall not issue use variances.

Where boards have been accustomed to exercising the power to zone, there may be resistance to such a prohibition. In one medium-sized city, in a 10-year period the board issued 277 variances permitting commercial uses in residential districts. For a considerable portion of the period, the board frankly accepted applications for "rezoning" rather than for variances. An area equal to 18 per cent of the actual commercial development in the city had been "zoned" commercial by the board.

A proposed provision in a new zoning ordinance prohibited use variances. It met strong opposition from the board, the city attorney, and local real estate interests, who held that the board was being illegally stripped of its powers. The city attorney stated (not for publication) that issuance of use variances was convenient because it relieved the governing body of the necessity for considering a great many zoning amendments. The city attorney stated (as a matter of record) that the state supreme court had upheld a land-use variance. (The case cited, on closer investigation, turned out to be a variance permitting an addition to a Sunday school, *allowed* as a use in the district, which would occupy a larger portion of the lot than the ordinance allowed generally. When this was brought to the attention of the attorney, he said that there was some difference of opinion as to what constituted a use variance.)

Quite frequently, there are situations where zoning should be amended. Here the cure is amendment, rather than issue of a variance. Consider the following statement from Kratovil's *Real Estate Law.*[1]

> An example of a hardship case calling for a variance would be where a lot is so irregular in shape that if all the front, rear, and side-line restrictions were observed, no building at all could be built on the lot. Or a lot in a residential area may be located on a busy intersection, with stores on all the other corners. Probably no one would build a house on this lot. A variance should be granted to build a store. Or a corner of a residential area may be cut off from the rest of the block by railroad tracks and be surrounded by factories. A variance should be given to use the land for industrial purposes.

In the first case, a variance would be entirely appropriate. In the second and third, the appropriate remedy is amendment of the zoning map, rather than issuance of a variance. If the governing body refused to amend the ordinance in cases like those described, we think a very good case could be made in court that it was being arbitrary, capricious, and unreasonable. If there is solid reason for refusing amendment, there is also solid reason for refusing a variance.

This brings us to another point, the matter of appeals to the courts. Opponents to prohibition of use variances quite frequently assert that elimination of the practice will (a) deprive applicants of the right of appeal, or (b) lead to excessive litigation. As a matter of fact, prohibition of use variances facilitates appeal to the courts, and deprives only of the right to appeal to a body which has no business issuing the kind of variance sought. There is a strict judicial attitude about exhaustion of administrative remedies. If there is a chance that a board of adjustment might grant the relief sought, the applicant must go to the board before going to court. But if the ordinance prohibits a

1. Robert Kratovil, *Real Estate Law* (3rd ed.; Englewood Cliffs, N.J.: Prentice-Hall, Inc., 1958), p. 412. When we reviewed this book, we said the section on "Zoning and Building Ordinances" is better than most treatments by people writing about real estate law, but that this was not an unqualified endorsement. Statements like the one quoted indicate why our enthusiasm was restrained.

use variance, the appeal may be made direct to the court. No administrative remedy is provided.

Pointing this out to the usual opponents does not weaken their opposition. They do not want to go to court, because they are aware that under court procedures their chances of playing fast and loose with the zoning ordinance are greatly diminished. The bogey of excessive ligitation is quickly laid by a handful of properly prepared court cases.

We believe strongly in the right to appeal, but we believe with equal fervor in protection of the public interest. If there should be a case where action resulting in the equivalent of a use variance is justified, we feel that no injustice is done if the appeal is to the courts rather than to the board of adjustment. Judging by a depressing record of board of adjustment actions in this field, the public interest is likely to be far better protected, and private applications more equitably weighed, if such cases are prepared and presented in the judicial atmosphere of a courtroom, against a background of legal precedent, procedure, and principles. If justice is the objective, the courts are the place to seek it. Zoning has nothing to fear from such tests if the ordinance has been properly prepared and maintained. (If the ordinance has not been properly prepared and maintained, stimulus from the courts is richly merited.) The individual has nothing to fear from such tests *if he has a case*. It is fairly obvious from the record that major opposition to prohibition of use variances comes from people who are accustomed to getting their way without having a case.

Making use-variance prohibition stick

Where there is opposition to prohibition of use variances, and particularly where courts are inexperienced in the ways of zoning and tests seem likely, it is important to phrase the ordinance with great care. Attack may come on grounds that the governing body may not deprive the board of any powers granted by the state enabling legislation. The first answer to this appears to be that the enabling legislation *does not give the board the power to amend the zoning ordinance,* and that amendment in the guise of a use variance is still amendment.

The second answer is in the language of the enabling act quoted at the beginning of this article. If "the board of adjustment shall adopt rules in accordance with the provisions of any ordinance adopted pursuant to this article," it can hardly be said that the intent of the legislation is that the legislative body may not adopt ordinance provisions affecting the operation of the board.

There is a third answer, framed in the language of the grant of power to authorize variances, but providing rules as to the manner in which variances shall be granted or denied. Below appears a section from a recent ordinance giving rules on variances generally (derived from prevailing court interpretations and opinions) and, at the end, settling the matter of use variances.

Section 320. *Powers and Duties of Board of Adjustment:* The Board of Adjustment shall have the following powers and duties. . . .

320.03. *Variances: Conditions Governing Applications: Procedures:* To authorize upon appeal in specific cases such variance from the terms of this ordinance as will not be contrary to the public interest where, owing to special conditions, a literal enforcement of the provisions of this ordinance would result in unnecessary hardship. A variance from the terms of this ordinance shall not be granted by the Board of Adjustment unless and until:

a. A written application is submitted demonstrating:
   1. That special conditions and circumstances exist which are peculiar to the land, structure, or building involved and which are not applicable to other lands, structures, or buildings in the same district;
   2. That literal interpretation of the provisions of this ordinance would deprive the applicant of rights commonly enjoyed by other properties in the same district under the terms of this ordinance;
   3. That the special conditions and circumstances do not result from the actions of the applicant, and
   4. That granting the variance requested will not confer on the applicant any special privilege that is denied by this ordinance to owners of other lands, structures, or buildings in the same district.

   No conforming use of neighboring lands, structures, or buildings in the same district, and no permitted use of lands, structures, or buildings in other districts shall be considered grounds for issuance of a variance.
b. Notice of public hearing shall be given as provided in Section ______ above;
c. The hearing shall be held. Any person may appear in person, or by agent, or by attorney;

d. The Board of Adjustment shall make findings that the requirements of Section 320.03(a) have been met by the applicant for a variance;
e. The Board of Adjustment shall further make a finding that the reasons set forth in the application justify the granting of the variance, and that the variance is the minimum variance that will make possible the reasonable use of the land, building, or structure;
f. The Board of Adjustment shall further make a finding that the granting of the variance will be in harmony with the general purpose and intent of this ordinance, and will not be injurious to the neighborhood, or otherwise detrimental to the public welfare.

In granting any variance, the Board of Adjustment may prescribe appropriate conditions and safeguards in conformity with this ordinance. Violation of such conditions and safeguards, when made part of the terms under which the variance is granted, shall be deemed a violation of this ordinance and punishable under Section_______, Penalties.

(Up to this point, it is almost inconceivable that the board could find reason for granting a *use* variance. "To make assurance doubly sure," the following paragraph nails things down.)

With respect to *uses* of land, buildings, and other structures, this ordinance is declared to be a definition of the public interest by City Council, and the spirit of this ordinance will not be observed by any variance which permits a use not generally or by special exception permitted in the district involved, or any use expressly or by implication prohibited, by the terms of this ordinance in said district. Therefore, under no circumstances shall the Board of Adjustment grant a variance to permit a use not generally or by special exception permitted in the district involved, or any use expressly or by implication prohibited, by the terms of this ordinance in said district.

Whatever a court might decide as to whether a board of adjustment might conceivably amend the ordinance in the guise of a use variance, there would be few courts willing to deny the right of the governing body to define the public interest. If the governing body defines public interest as indicated above, and declares that the "spirit of the ordinance" would not be observed by a use variance, it would take a singularly obtuse board of adjustment to issue such a variance and claim that it was in the public interest and observed the "spirit of the ordinance." It would also take an unusual court to uphold a board of adjustment which did so.

Nonconforming uses and use variances

One loose end remains. The ordinance quoted above states that no nonconforming use of neighboring lands or buildings in the same district shall be grounds for issuance of a variance. This provision should be inserted with care if there are extensive nonconforming uses. Two courses are open in such cases. The nonconforming uses, if they form quite a patch on the zoning map, may be included in a district of their own which makes them conforming. Or special exception provisions can be added which spell out what can be done adjacent to such uses, and including how surrounding property is to be safeguarded.

To permit nonconforming uses to be used as grounds for more of the same obviously allows spread of something which the zoning ordinance should try to eliminate, or at least contain. Given a nonconforming filling station in a residential neighborhood, if filling stations are to be permitted on each adjacent lot because nobody wants to build a house next to a filling station, the lots next adjacent also become eligible for filling stations. Thus nonconformity, declared out of place in the district, is allowed to spread, although the purpose of zoning is supposed to be to contain and, in time, to eliminate it. It would be far better practice to provide special exceptions which allow step-down buffering uses on the adjacent lots under carefully specified controlled conditions. This meets the issue squarely, and makes it unnecessary for the owners of adjoining lots to demonstrate hardship.

To summarize, there seems to be nothing in standard zoning enabling legislation which would prevent prohibition of use variances in the zoning ordinance. If the matter is properly handled, no court is likely to rule that the board of adjustment has been "deprived of its powers" by such provisions.

Courts have held that the board is not a law making body:

> The statute . . . cedes it no legislative authority. Hence *it has no power to amend the ordinance under which it functions. . . .*
>
> In exercising its discretion, the board of adjustment is not left free to make any determination whatever that appeals to its sense

> of justice. *It must abide by and comply with the standards prescribed by the local ordinance and zoning statutes.* [*Lee v. Board of Adjustment,* 226 NC 107]
>
> To attempt to give any small group of individuals such as a zoning commission or appeal board the power to determine in the exercise of its unrestricted authority what *uses* might be made of the properties in a community would not only be contrary to sound social policy but clearly unconstitutional. [*Devaney v. Board of Zoning Appeals,* 132 Conn. 537, 45 A.2d 828-9]

Prohibition of use variances would eliminate a major weakness in zoning machinery. If the zoning ordinance is well-drawn and carefully maintained in current shape, and if provision is made so that most real hardships (there shouldn't be many) involving land use are handled through well-drafted special exception provisions, the rare instances remaining might best be handled directly by the courts.

Boards of adjustment and how they got that way

We recently ran across another board of adjustment being richly generous with other people's zoning. It happens from time to time. This one was rezoning (via use variances) for commerce along a residential street because the city commission had made a mistake, the board chairman said. It turned out that over the past few years, the board had straightened out several miles of errors of this kind.

We like most of the people we have met on boards of adjustment. We even liked this man—he didn't know what he was doing or what he was supposed to be doing, but he had a wonderful spirit about it, and the members of his board were right in there pitching with him, strewing commerce up and down the streets, distributing zoning largesse to distressed widows and orphans, and being generally helpful. He dwelt at some length on the good he and his board had been able to do through the years they had worked together.

The town is now past zoning remedy. Gas stations festoon the most unlikely corners with their gay flags and friendly, beckoning signs. They snuggle against staid old residences rejuvenating, under their influence, with plastic fronts, beauty parlors, TV repair shops, undertaking establishments (and multitudinous "For Rent" notices). Billboards gladden the eye wherever there was a happy combination of location, destitution, and an enterprising operator. Everywhere there is a comfortable informality bordering (at least) on disorder.

How did it come about that we have lay boards performing duties of such complexity? Obviously the job involves legal and administrative operations requiring specialized training and experience. Equally obviously, most boards of adjustment don't have it. How did we get ourselves in this shape?

Bassett revisited

Back in 1936, Edward M. Bassett wrote a book called *Zoning—the Laws, Administration, and Court Decisions During the First Twenty Years.* In it he had much to say about the board of adjustment, or board of appeals.

Much of what he had to say is still applicable: "Local legislators should not be appointed." "The board of appeals is not a legislative body." "A member of a board of appeals should not have an interest in a proposed variance."

But there is a jarring note. Bassett refers repeatedly to the board as "presumed to be composed of experts," and "an expert administrative body." "Courts . . . declare that the function of the board is to exercise the discretion of experts." "The court hesitates to substitute its opinion for the conclusion of experts."

It may be that in Bassett's time, most boards of adjustment *were* composed of experts, or it may be merely that he wished they were. Current observation convinces us that it is not so now.

Many boards of adjustment are experts largely at punching holes in zoning, handing out special favors to special interest groups or individuals, and generally playing politics with zoning. Others are not experts at all, merely good-natured and ill-informed, trying to help everybody without realizing what they are doing to zoning or the public interest, and establishing broad precedents for even more liberal mistakes in the future.

Consider the New York City board of appeals, on which Bassett based many of his observations, and it becomes clear why he referred to its members as experts. It also becomes clear why many present boards of adjustment fall short of the mark.

Bassett's board of appeals

According to the charter of New York City as it existed in 1920, the board of appeals was part of an overall Board of Standards and

Appeals. The latter body was made up of the fire commissioner, the superintendent of buildings, the fire chief, and six other members to be appointed by the mayor.

There was no carte blanche on the qualifications of the appointed members. One was required to have at least 10 years experience as an architect, one to have not less than 10 years experience as a structural engineer, one to have not less than 10 years experience as a builder. The chairman was required to have not less than 15 years experience as an architect or structural engineer, and was to devote his full time to his duties as chairman: "He shall not engage in any other occupation, profession, or employment."

The board of appeals, as a subdivision of the larger body, was made up of the appointed members of the Board of Standards and Appeals (including the chairman of the general board as chairman of the board of appeals) plus the fire chief. The seven members thus included at least five with very strong technical qualifications: chairman—architect or structural engineer; architect member; structural engineer member; builder member; fire chief member; unspecified member; unspecified member.

For further assurance that the board's decisions would be sound and impartial, no member could pass on any question in which he or any corporation in which he was a stockholder or security holder had an interest.

How boards of adjustment descended

From this common ancestor, boards of adjustment with similar powers and duties sprang up across the country. It was probably a pretentious choice of paternity. Of the 48 *states,* 44 had a smaller population than New York City at the time, and it may be that in playing follow-the-leader Mudville, Warners Corners, and Winnepesaukee would have done well to give up when it came to the board of adjustment section, and seek a solution more in keeping with their own circumstances.

Mudville, Warners Corners, and Winnepesaukee did not give up. Since they could not climb the fence, they knocked a few boards out of it and went through. This impaired the utility of the fence, but the game went on.

Unable to meet New York scale qualifications for board membership, most cities simply eliminated qualifications and made the whole thing ultra-democratic. Anybody could join. This resulted in selection of board members without technical background to act as an "expert administrative body."

Some cities were more snobbish. They insisted on qualifications, but since they couldn't (and in many cases didn't want to) find personnel with the skills indicated in New York, they substituted others which assured availability at least. By custom and even by provisions in the zoning ordinance the members were chosen to represent special-interest groups—realtors, land developers, speculative builders, the apartment house owners association, and the like.

If these people were not equipped or inclined to handle zoning as impartial experts, they certainly knew what they wanted zoning to do and what they wanted to do to zoning. They took the bull by the horns, and if no horns were available, they supplied them.

The best of good intentions does not make a man an expert upon appointment to a board, and long association with his peers in uncertainty is unlikely to improve his performance. It is hard enough to get competent and impartial operation from well-intentioned and disinterested but poorly informed appointees. The case is worse when wolves are selected to guard the public sheep.

So it is that the decisions of boards of adjustment have often reflected lack of experience, lack of knowledge, or worse. Errors tend to multiply themselves. The board which gets off on the wrong foot and grants variances and special exceptions without legal justification finds itself very busy dealing with applications to repeat and enlarge the error.

Possible solutions to the problem

There are a number of solutions possible, and under varying circumstances all of them might be tried.

The most obvious step is careful selection of members of the board. It may not be possible to find people with strong technical qualifications to serve, but at least board members should be intelligent, not in a position to profit from board actions, and willing to learn.

It is particularly important that the board should be given maximum guidance as to its powers and the manner in which they should be exercised. Mere repetition of the language of the enabling act concerning appeals from alleged errors of the administrative official, appeals for variances, and decisions concerning special exceptions is not enough.

For a beginning on the kind of language which might be used, and comments on why it should be used, see *Text of a Model Zoning Ordinance* (Bair and Bartley, ASPO, 3rd ed., 1966), Section 9, "The Board of Adjustment; Powers and Duties," pages 51-60.

Certainly the board should be informed in the ordinance as to what must be demonstrated before a variance or special exception may properly be granted, and as to what courts have found to be legal and illegal. Part of this direction should come from the ordinance itself, part from other types of education.

There is no state in the nation where a board of adjustment cannot get educational assistance—from publications, from universities, from state agencies, from federal agencies, from statewide associations. The most valuable members—those who serve from a sense of civic responsibility without hope of gaining power, prestige, or profit—deserve all the help they can get. Those who are on the board to get what they can out of it for themselves and their friends need to have it impressed on them that there is a limit to what they can get away with inside the law. (Unfortunately, there is still plenty they can get away with legally, but there are *some* limits, and they should be liberally encouraged to stay within them.)

As another step in improving the performance of boards of adjustment, the assistance of the courts would be salutary. More administrative officials should take boards to court when they get out of line. As an officer of the city, presumably engaged in protecting the public interest, the building inspector or zoning administrator should have no hesitation about exercising the right given by the enabling legislation when the right needs to be exercised: "Any person . . . or any officer, department, board, or bureau of the municipality, may present to a court of record a petition, duly verified, setting forth that such decision" of the board of adjustment "is illegal, in whole or in part, specifying the grounds of the illegality."

Who is likely to be in a better position to know than the administrative official, or in a better position to act? Should a public official turn away from his duty because it is disagreeable, and wait for errors to be corrected by individuals who do not generally have the knowledge and quite often do not have the means to go to court?

There is yet another alternative, and unless the record of boards of adjustment improves, we may find ourselves driven to it. This involves doing away with boards of adjustment entirely, and providing an appeals procedure through a trained zoning examiner, backed, of course, by the courts, or possibly even the step of direct appeal to the courts. Special exceptions might well be handled by the planning commission, which is in a far better position than the board of adjustment to deal with them.

Index